MANAGEMENT IN THE THIRD WAVE

MANAGEMENT IN THE THIRD WAVE

H. Alan Raymond

Scott, Foresman and Company
Glenview, Illinois   London

Library of Congress Cataloging in Publication Data
Raymond, H. Alan.
   Management in the third wave.
   Bibliography: p.
   Includes index.
   1. Management.   2. Social history—1945—
I. Title.   II. Title: Third wave.
HD31.R39   1986   658   85-2333
ISBN 0-673-18035-2

1 2 3 4 5 6-RRC-90 89 88 87 86 85

ACKNOWLEDGMENTS

- Figure 1-7, "Four-sector aggregation of the United States work force 1860–1980," from *Study of the Information Society*, courtesy of Dr. Marc Porat.

- Figure 3-1, "Evolution of people's moods, needs, and motivations that follow a second wave corporate evolution." Based on material from William S. Royce and Arnold Mitchell, *Report No. 635, Stakeholders Values and Corporate Success.* © 1980 by Business Intelligence Program, SRI International, Reprinted by permission.

- ROLM Corporation philosophy, courtesy of ROLM Corporation.

- Hewlett-Packard corporate objectives, courtesy of Hewlett-Packard Company.

- *San Francisco Chronicle* article, March 7, 1984, reprinted with permission from The Associated Press.

- Excerpt from "Blowin' in the Wind," by Bob Dylan. © 1962 Warner Bros. Inc. All Rights Reserved. Used by Permission.

- Excerpt from "Union Sundown," by Bob Dylan. Copyright © by Special Rider Music. All rights reserved. International copyright secured. Reprinted by permission.

- Steven C. Brandt, *Entreprenuring*, © 1982 by Stephen C. Brandt, Addison-Wesley, Reading, Massachusetts. (The 10 Commandments). Reprinted with permission.

To all individuals who strive constantly
for excellence, creativity, and freedom,
wherever they may be

ACKNOWLEDGMENTS

I should like to make a special note of thanks to Gene Richeson, one of the founders of the Rolm Corporation, who read each chapter of the draft of this manuscript as it came off the word processor, offering his advice and guidance. Also special thanks to Alvin and Heidi Toffler, whose work and assistance were inspirational and invaluable, and to Steve Brandt, whose pioneering work on entrepreneurship has clarified this function as a primary engine of the economy. A special acknowledgment goes to Tom Peters, whose ideas, concepts, and antics served as a source of important stimulation.

Thanks go out also to members of the Stanford University faculty, and to Jeffry Pfeffer, who explained the dynamics of corporate bureaucratic politics. Dick Scott's lectures on government bureaucracy were never anything but provocative. Jim March's lively and haphazard seminars and his Friday afternoon popcorn and wine sessions were always enjoyable. I remember Hal Levitt looking out mistily into the foreground while he wiped the blackboard with the back of his sweater and stated that "Jesus Christ was the Teacher with a capital T." William Miller's common sense ideas on industrial policy were a refreshing contrast to the questionable discussions on the topic we have all had to endure. I will also remember the guided tour of his beautiful roses. Another special note to Dean Eugene Webb, who answered various critiques of the Business School with a quote from an unlikely authority: "Let a thousand flowers bloom."

Thanks, too, to the people of Silicon Valley, San Francisco, whose annual Black and White Ball puts any *Die Fledermaus* fantasy to shame, and to the people of California, where the third wave is being generated. They are current evidence of Tom Peter's dictum that it is "more fun having fun than not!" They work hard proving it daily.

Thanks to Stafford Beer and Frank George, who inspired my initial interest in systems and management, and Seymour Melman, with whom I had intense discussions on industrial-corporate organization. Norman Mintz was a source of guidance and stability to me during a time of instability and turmoil in the country and at Columbia University. I will always remember and respect my friends in the Canadian government: Erik Nielsen, whose dedication and integrity are notable, and Peter Meyboom, whose victories over creeping and massive bureaucracy are admirable. Thanks also to the Ford Motor Company, where I first encountered the mechanisms of the second wave.

I am grateful to Glenn Bacon of IBM, who reviewed the first draft of the manuscript; to Martha Gross of Tandem, who was a source of inspiration as well as of helpful suggestions; to Glenn Bacon of IBM and Richard Pascale and Jerry Porras of Stanford, who offered encouragement and advice; to Terry Schaeffer of Hewlett-Packard; to David Rosner, formerly of Fairchild and now a consultant for Intel; to Stacy Black of Pacific Gas and Electric; to Harry Sello, also formerly of Fairchild and currently an international consultant on technology; to Themis Michos, a Silicon Valley corporate lawyer, and to Ken Sletten, of Rudolf and Sletten, one of the largest Silicon Valley construction firms, who gave me invaluable information concerning the operations and problems of third wave corporations in transition. Finally, but not least, I thank my editors, Dick Staron, Sybil Sosin, and Roger Holloway, whose belief in the project and hard work enabled this work to reach you.

The investigation took place over several years, at the Ford Motor Company, the Columbia University Department of Industrial and Management Engineering and Department of Economics, the London School of Economics, the Brunel University Department of Cybernetics, the McGill University Anthropology of Development Program, the Carleton University School of International Affairs and Department of Economics, the Federal Government of Canada, where I headed the Secretariat for Futures Studies and served as Executive Assistant to a cabinet minister, and Stanford University's Graduate School of Business and Department of Sociology, Silicon Valley, and the University of California. The findings were first presented at a number of lectures at the Stanford University Graduate School of Business and at the American Management Association conference held in Los Angeles in 1983.

H. Alan Raymond, Ph.D.

CONTENTS

WHAT IS EXCELLENCE?

WHY DOES IT MATTER

There is a feeling now, that was not there before, and is not just on the surface of things, but penetrates all the way through; We've won it. It's going to get better now. You can sort of tell these things.

Robert M. Pirsig
Zen and the Art of Motorcycle Maintenance, 1974

INTRODUCTION

Management in the Third Wave investigates how the new parameters of a third wave civilization affect American business and government. These new parameters are rapidly increasing international competition, costs, population, and technology, and they have engulfed the United States much as an all-encompassing wave can engulf a sailing vessel.

To a large extent the fault for this turmoil is our own blindness. American management, society, and government have grown rigid, complacent, narcissistic, and "old." For the most part management has followed the precepts set down during the Industrial Revolution, breaking tasks down to their lowest level so that anyone with minimum intelligence could perform them. Henry Ford's methods were a prime example of this approach. He considered himself the "manager," while his "executives" merely administered the formulas and systems he developed. There was essentially no practice of management, only administration of the original plant and formulas created by the original entrepreneurs.

Industrial society is much like an ocean wave itself. Having reached its potential and being faced with increasing mass but decreasing momentum, it becomes unstable and crashes in turmoil; a new wave breaks below its surface, destabilizing it further.

In *Future Shock* and, more recently, *The Third Wave*, Alvin Toffler wrote comprehensively and systematically about the transition from an industrial to an information-driven society. Terming the agricultural revolution of about 10,000 years ago the "first wave" of change and the Industrial Revolution the "second wave," Toffler closely analyzed today's technosocial revolution and argued that it constitutes the "third wave" of historical change.

Various other books dealing with today's technological and economic transition have appeared, but these generally fail to adequately link new management theories with the critical nature of the transition the nation and the world are undergoing. Following Toffler's wave model, *Management in the Third Wave* provides a conceptual framework for, as well as presenting research results on, the current and future challenges of management.

Signs of the transition to the new society are seen in news stories of steel and automobile plant closings, of high-technology espionage, and of Chrysler's "turnaround" and the man behind it, Lee Iacocca, to whom many harried European industrialists now claim to "light a candle" each night. They might also note Chrysler's new slogan, "It's over, over there." Eventually corporations must discover that the only way to survive is to become increasingly flexible and precise, to work harder, to throw the old formulas out, and to become increasingly efficient. Someone recently referred to this as the "MASH" model, after the popular television series—everything is in turmoil; crisis invariably follows upon crisis; the resources, supplies, and human capital are never enough; each action is critical and must be precise; even when you are exhausted spiritually and physically, you must rally yourself and your fellows again and again; you must be dedicated even when you find the only thing you can be dedicated to is a rest; everyone has a precise but deceivingly informal part to play; management must really manage and not merely administer; everyone is needed; there is much or no meaning; there never seems to be an end in sight; and as a last resort you turn to spiritual guidance, be it from your fellows or from religion. In the old IBM vernacular, it is more important now than ever before to think, communicate, and act faster and better.

The third wave is much more than an increasing reliance on information and "high" technology. It is new forms of relating among people and between people and nature, new meanings, new forms of organization, new forms of management, a new society, and a new economy. The third wave has its roots, quite logically, in the first and second waves. The first wave of civilization was the agricultural wave. Agriculture technology allowed humans to form stable, stationary communities and gave them leisure time in which to develop arts and sciences. What we call civilization began to emerge. Medieval organization and hierarchy were the logical culmination of the ideas and technology of the first wave. Eventually, however, the medievalistic first wave was shaken and broken down, allowing the ideas, organizations, and technologies of the next wave to dominate.

This breakdown began with the Crusades, which forced European medievalism to confront an advanced, "alien" civilization, shattering many of its old beliefs and confounding much of its technology. As most of the power of feudalistic medievalism was engaged in the Middle East, the chains were necessarily loosened at home, resulting in increased freedom to create (although significant, such freedoms would be considered marginal today). The Magna Carta, which released the aristocracy from virtual bondage to the king, was one outcome of this new freedom. Increasing trade with the East resulted in increasing wealth for the merchant "class," upon whom the aristocracy became progressively more dependent financially. This new wealth, coupled with innovations imported from China, India, and the Middle East, paved the way for a large expansion in population, which in turn required new modes of organization, new ideas, new "markets," and new technologies.

During this era, later called the "Renaissance," "scouts," traders, and technological scavengers such as Marco Polo were sent to the East. One of these scouts suggested that the process might be sped up if a shorter route to the East could be found by going west. His name was Christopher Columbus. As significant as his discovery of the "new" world was the discovery and transportation to Europe of the gold of the conquered natives. This new wealth touched off massive inflation and led to the reorganization of European civilization, resulting in increased political and financial freedom for all classes. The king was no longer omnipotent; the "consciousness" of the first wave was shattered. This Renaissance, a time of turmoil, was thus a period of transition from the first wave to the second wave.

With a strong market for manufacture and trade, the situation was ripe for the development of industrial technology (machines) and industrial organizations (designed to behave like machines). The second wave thus began with an effort to move freedom into a "political" context and away from a "work" context. This process also created a new class of people, industrial workers, whose increasing wealth and numbers eventually led to growing demands for more freedom. These demands resulted in increasingly pluralistic democracies and later in socialistic or "communistic" forms of government.

In the "new" world the events followed a different course. European powers failed in their attempt to impose upon this "virgin" land old forms of organization and hierarchies; the demands and opportunities of a rich frontier would not allow it. Instead, new ideas of freedom, relationships, and organizations grew in the new land. The inhabitants, recently free of the old world, were determined to "make the world anew" in line with "God's natural plan." According to the philosophy of the time, this meant the freedom for each man to fulfill his potential as he saw fit, without injury to his fellows—the inalienable right to "life, liberty, and the pursuit of happiness." However, the industrial second wave soon crept upon the new land and here too began to move the pursuit of freedom into a political context and away from a work context; many of the ethics of the feudalistic first wave were thus maintained.

Free enterprise gradually gave way to corporate enterprise, and surprisingly similar feudal "baronies" were created in an industrial context. The failures and excesses of second wave organization resulted in "leftist," or "communistic," agitation and the formation of unions by workers protesting limitations on their freedom. Large bureaucracies were developed to suppress such inclinations and "organize" work. In the East these bureaucracies were called "state institutions"; in the West they were called "corporations." The means of enterprise were almost the exclusive purview of these organizations during the second wave.

World Wars I and II, and the technologies that grew out of them, shattered most of the concepts, organizations, and hierarchies of the second wave while transferring large amounts of wealth to the new world from the old. The stage was thus set for the third wave. These wars forced the "decolonization" of the world, the spread of suffrage in democracies, the spread of technology, and the overthrow of many feudalistic, bureaucratic power structures. Ironically, it is Japan, devastated at the end of World War II, that has become a leader of the third wave. In the short space of a century this nation has passed through to the third wave from the first, its speed perhaps due to the retention of much of its previous feudal discipline, unaffected by any prolonged "renaissance" of ideas about freedom.

We are now at the very edge of the third wave. The period around 1970 was a marked point of transition: youth was in revolt against the old order all around the world, the world monetary system had been overturned, new inventions such as the microchip appeared, and the fuel of the second wave— *cheap* raw materials and energy—was turned off.

The shocks come now, at a rapid clip: utilities are declaring bankruptcy, massive layoffs—a "leaning and meaning" of corporations—are taking place daily, the incidence of industrial violence by fellow workers against malingerers in Japan is increasing, German workers are so afraid of layoffs that they hesitate to call in sick even if they are, American workers have taken significant pay cuts, French workers riot against a "socialist" government, and Polish workers "strike" a "communist" government. The incidence of executive stress and "burnout" has reportedly more than doubled in all industrial countries, basic industries are on a decline, everyone is desperately trying to gain an edge in computer and related technology, and pleas for government help everywhere have risen to a loud chorus.

Where, if anywhere, is this all headed? What and where the third wave will bring us depend very much upon the clarity of our perceptions and actions during the current transition.

1

THE TRANSITION

THE THIRD WAVE

> A new civilization is emerging in our lives, and blind men everywhere are trying to suppress it. This new civilization brings with it new family styles; changed ways of working, loving, and living; a new economy; new political conflicts; and beyond all this a new consciousness as well.
>
> Alvin Toffler
> *The Third Wave*, 1980

DECLINE OF THE SECOND WAVE

My introduction to the second wave came while I was a young man working as an industrial engineer at an automobile assembly plant in Chicago during the late sixties. I soon found out that the only people really interested in efficiency-effectiveness or even in the integrity with which functions should be performed were a few industrial engineers at the plant.

The waste of material and people was enormous, and morale and spirit were distinctly lacking. Sometimes, out of malice or just from being numbed by the system, workers would not put on the correct number of bolts or nuts if they were not being closely watched. This type of negligence would result in costly "downtime" (repair time). Supervisors could often be found on coffee breaks or "out back" gossiping and smoking. A large white-collar staff existed to serve the plant manager whose function, I soon discovered, was largely to explain problems to Detroit, not to solve them. People seemed to be at the plant only to earn a living, to survive. Few if any believed or understood that there was any intrinsic purpose to their work.

Often I found myself commiserating with a friend who had just started in a similar position with a steel company. During our first discussion, he commented, "Jeez, if we are looked upon as the most efficient country in the world, I'd hate to even think what our competition is like!" Well, without question, we no longer are the most efficient, and we do think quite often about what the competition is like.

Some spirited engineers at the plant tried to interest management in robotics (unimates) by showing the possible cost savings. Management's answer basically implied that robotics seemed to be a lot of trouble, and since costs could be passed onto the public anyway, why bother? The Japanese later adopted and adapted these very same American robots to the manufacture of their automobiles. The episode that most graphically explained what seemed then a perplexing puzzle to me was the following, which I watched on the evening news one night.[1]

Leonard Woodcock, then president of the United Auto Workers, was asked if he felt the demands of his union to be excessive. With the pained expression of a man having to explain the clearly obvious for the tenth consecutive time, he replied that "they" had a formula into which such things were routinely fed in order to arrive at the price of an automobile. "They" were General Motors, the industry leader. What the union wanted could not be considered excessive if its demands could be passed onto the market. The market, which was controlled by the industry's giants, had to bear all such costs. Current reasoning said that such costs were not excessive if they could be passed on to the public, and they were. Gardner Means referred to this phenomenon as "administered pricing," not market pricing.[2]

In recent events, however, we have seen little evidence of excessive union demands or any demands at all. The picture is blurred in that the unions, at least marginally, have become part of "they" by placing a representative on the boards of directors (for example, at Chrysler), by buying factories and subsidiaries, and by partially identifying with ownership.

Organizations have been described as undergoing various kinds of

"You will never catch up with the new technology."

Drawing by Weber; © 1983 The New Yorker Magazine, Inc.

schizophrenic and anorexic behavior. Some corporations appear to have pursued an approach of continuous cuts of employees, plants, operations, and equipment until the firms cease to exist. This mistakenly has been referred to as the "leaner and meaner approach."

Executive turnover has increased several-fold since 1970, giving rise to such "new" phenomena as "golden parachutes." Work-related stress, nervous breakdowns, and executive burnout have resulted in an avalanche of claims against insurance companies. At the same time new business formations have soared, while the bankruptcy rate has mounted. Evidence of confusion and turmoil has become apparent at every turn.

WHO, WHAT AND WHERE ARE WE NOW?

What has changed? What has become of the second wave and formula management? What was it? Are we scrambling to find a new formula, perhaps, as the dimensions of the transition become clear? Is it X, Y, or Z? Is it a new "mean and lean" look? Is it a search for the Holy Grail? Is it a new industrial policy? Who are "they"? Who and where are we?

We are in the midst of transition from an industrial-mechanical society to an electronic information one. Alvin Toffler has called this the transition from a second wave to a third wave civilization, the first one having been an agricultural and nature-dependent civilization. Corporations and individuals who wish to prosper and remain viable are attempting this difficult and perplexing transition and transformation. It is not enough to realize, as second wave technology and industry shift overseas to countries entering the second wave from the first, that in order for us to maintain a competitive edge and comfortable lifestyle, we must shift to the new technologies and processes of the third wave. Our entire method of management and ways of behaving and thinking must also shift along with the new emphasis and pressures.

Countries newly adapted to second wave technology have comparative and accelerating cost advantages that will create mounting pressure for businesses and individuals in the United States. These pressures will continue to force changes in our thinking. Basic manufacturing and raw materials development will continue to shift overseas along with many second wave jobs and values. General Motors and U.S. Steel, for example, are considering arrangements to import much of their basic materials, slab steel, and parts, for final assembly and finishing here. Both companies are also adopting new methods of management. Kodak and Exxon are trying to shift into third wave technologies and markets, but are experiencing difficulties as they attempt to maintain most of their previous management styles and organizational structures.

How do we break into this new mind set and way of management? How is it different from our past, and how will it affect our future? These are the questions being asked. We will attempt to shed some light on the possible answers in the following pages.

THE THREE WAVES OF CIVILIZATION AND TECHNOLOGY

First wave dominance came to an end in the United States around 1870 following the Civil War, which represented, among other conflicts, an intense struggle between the remnants of the agricultural first wave and the rising mechanical-industrial wave. The valor of a cavalry charge was not enough against the overwhelming mechanical-industrial resources made available by the new technology. President Lincoln reportedly said (to one of his generals who complained of Grant's drunkenness and possible battle losses because of it) that he did not care as long as Grant won the last battle. Lincoln's reported attitude was an example of thinking that contrasted the industrial second wave North with the first wave, feudal South.

Begun in conflict, the second wave also faded during a struggle. Second wave dominance began to decline around 1970, during a conflict that may become recognized as the "second" civil war—a war that was fought on the information-electronics front, not in the mud and jungles of Southeast Asia.

As one of the many quasi participants in that initial conflict, having been at Woodstock and on the scene of the Columbia University "disturbances," I was struck by the spontaneous and seemingly organic nature of that "movement," which had no discernible leaders but seemed to flow as one. It was like a Rocky Mountain lake before freeze up. When you toss a pebble into the lake at this time, a sheet of ice spreads across the surface. This action or reaction instigates a change that seems inevitable.

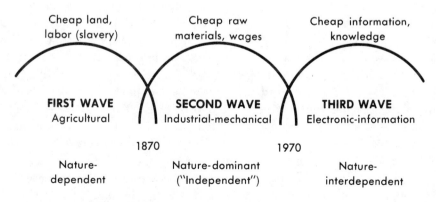

EXHIBIT 1-1   Technology-driven waves of civilization.

The Nature-Dependent First Wave

The first wave was primarily fueled by cheap land that was universally available. The ethic that could be best used to describe this wave was that of free enterprise. Competition was considered positive because most families were self-sufficient farmers who did not depend upon the market for survival. Education took place principally in the home, on the farm, and on the job. Society was unitary (small independent units), decentralized, and collaborative. Neighbors lent willing hands and resources to each other. Owners and workers were indistinguishable, usually being one and the same where slavery did not exist. Information about what was going on was generally available to all. The unitary first wave society declined with the disappearance of cheap land and cheap labor (slavery), and the beginning of second wave technology, spearheaded by the railroad.

The Nature-"Dominant" Second Wave

The second wave was fueled by cheap natural resources that could be exploited only by major capital investments in their production and manufacture. The industrial world, relatively simple, centralized, and linear, could be manipulated by formula. Formula management created a new economy based upon mechanical thinking, "independent" from nature.

Proprietorship, the sense of owning a stake in the enterprise, became separated from work while enterprises became separated into workers and owners. Most workers adopted the "I just work here" approach. Using formula management techniques, owners factored this attitude into the equation and made no attempts to change it. This situation resulted in enormous waste and inefficiencies, but it was effective for owners as long as raw materials remained cheap. Alexis de Tocqueville, when sailing down the Ohio River in the late eighteenth century, remarked upon the difference between the slave state of Kentucky and the free state of Ohio.[3] On the Ohio side were handsome homes, neat fields, industrious activity, entrepreneurs, and rich harvests; but on the Kentucky side, he saw only indolence. Not only were slaves working with half a heart, but their masters refused to work or come near the fields in fear that work would demean their status. Yet, although conditions in Kentucky were wasteful, they were effective for the owners as long as land and labor were cheap.

For survival, families found themselves dependent upon an organization and its success in the market. Competition was considered dangerous both by workers and by owners or their surrogates, the managers. Whenever possible, competition was modified or eliminated by establishing market control or by government regulation.

Market control arose when one or a small number of companies established control over a particular market for a product or series of products, preventing the entry of new entrepreneurs into that market. The Standard Oil Company was expert at eliminating the competition, using such methods as massive advertising campaigns, predatory pricing (pricing so low for a period of time that a competitor would be forced into bankruptcy), and other less savory methods. Society moved from an era of independent free enterprise to one of corporate enterprise. As long as entry into the market depended upon control of the corporations that controlled the market, competition had to center upon efforts to control these corporations.

Thus, the era of bureaucratic politics began. Information about what was going on was limited in quantity and quality to each level of the hierarchy. This was sometimes referred to as "mushroom management," that is, keeping people in various "shades" of darkness, and occasionally throwing some manure on them.

The obverse became a kind of "conspicuous consumption" of information, an indication of power and status: "I know something you don't know!" As the bureaucratic structure proliferated and entrenched itself in organizations,

"I'm afraid everything is in short supply, Excellency, except stooges."

Drawing by Donald Reilly; © 1983 The New Yorker Magazine, Inc.

corporations behaved less and less like natural systems and therefore became less and less compatible with natural human inclinations. An educational system had to develop to fashion individuals who could function within such structures. Too often, however, even after extensive "education," many could not survive in this socioeconomic system, and many so-called social problems developed.

Formula management:
The driving force of the second wave

Market control allowed formula management, the management or administrative form of the second wave, to reign. Formula management, as its name implies, relied upon the manipulation of certain specific and limited factors for corporations to achieve a steady stream of income. This was possible only in a relatively static business environment that thrived on low competition. Formula management is a relatively simplistic, primitive, and easy form of management that requires little thinking when a marginally competitive market will allow its existence. Formula management followed six general rules:

1.   Get as much market control as possible and keep it. For example, AT&T was a virtual monopoly and held complete market control until recently.

2.   Maximize cash flow and revenues, not profits. For example, General Motors, the industry leader, was number one even though the company could not legally establish a monopoly. Being number one often had little to do with having the best per-unit profit picture; it was having the most sales or cash flows. Theoretically, number one could "crush" potential competition. This type of market control is termed an oligopoly and often existed only at the sufferance of federal antitrust statutes.

3.   Minimize fixed costs principally by depreciating plant and equipment costs to zero as quickly as possible and by keeping them at zero. This often led to retention of obsolete equipment in spite of such government measures as fast write-offs. For example, Ford's outdated accounting system mentality made the introduction of new, advanced, and effective equipment difficult if not impossible. Management had to alter its thinking before Ford's transformation could be achieved.

4.   Maximize flexible costs principally by building up as much *slack* (unnecessary staff, equipment, or inventory) as possible of high sales, while still satisfying minimum profit expectations. Expend this slack during periods of depressed sales to maintain a steady level of income. Companies such as U.S. Steel usually did this by adding large amounts of staff and inventories, with funds which partially would have gone into taxes. The addition of redundant staff also served incidentally to absorb

potential entrepreneurs who might have disrupted the system much as the ancient Chinese mandarinate did.

> The personal goals of managers (personal income, size of staff, esteem, power) will often lead to a "bargained" budget, whereby managers intentionally create slack as a protective device. Slack can be defined in a cost context as the difference between the minimum necessary costs and the actual costs of the firm. (Slack may be called padding in some organizations.) This seeking of slack permeates all budgeting in every conceivable sort of organization. Little has been done to counteract it.
>
> Charles T. Horngren
> *Cost Accounting: A Managerial Emphasis*

5. Integrate horizontally and vertically to maintain a tight control over supply as well as over the market. Integration of suppliers sometimes took the form of intimidation rather than of outright purchase. For example, Standard Oil's aggressive tactics to control petroleum supply and market led to federal prosecution and breakup of the trust.
6. Promote primarily on the basis of personal loyalty; establish a firm internal power base and controlled hierarchy. For example, Chrysler Corporation used this method and other second wave tactics that led it into "the valley of death" before Lee Iacocca's takeover.

Formula management became the driving force of second wave society. The educational system was fashioned to provide the socialized and obedient workers required by second wave organizations. Government evolved to serve and oppose formula management; corporations evolved to allow its practice.

Rise of industrial corporatism

Corporate evolution during the second wave generally followed the process described below, developing along an economic cycle that was generated by the birth, dominance, and death of a new composite technology.

Gunslinger-pioneer When a new technology creates a market, the field is wide open. There exist many more or less equal competitors, as in the initial stages of the automobile industry. Competition takes the form closest to classic free enterprise. A new company growing out of a new technology is flexible and fast, with minimal formalization of structure. The organization

13

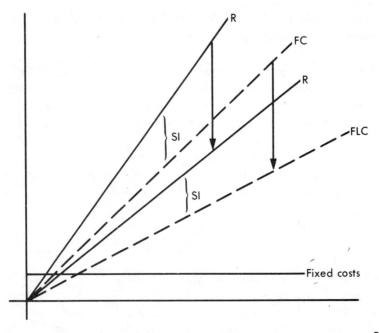

R = Revenues
FLC = Flexible
SI = Satisfying
income

EXHIBIT 1-2   With formula management, second wave companies manipulate flexible costs (slack) to maintain a satisfying income, afforded by market control.

operates in an environment in which opportunities or problems, and the "windows" for their solution, move in swift succession across the horizon. The response must be rapid and accurate. Individuals must be creative and innovative and must act quickly to make independent decisions. The organization must also be able to align itself quickly to provide resources to back individual decisions, and it must seek a defined objective. Definition between workers and owners is not at all clear, if any definition exists at all. Chance and uncertainty play a major role in the ultimate survival of such a firm. As risk is high, reward usually is also. Although hitting a target is dependent upon chance, the more information and computing power a firm has, the more accurately and precisely it can move. It is therefore highly information dependent. Investments mainly go to product development and testing, so the company can penetrate a market and create consumers. Markets are fleeting, precise, and specialized. Many of the newer high-technology firms, such as Victor, APPLE, Osborne, Compaq, and Grid, are or were in this phase. Some will and some have progressed to the next phase; some will not. The gunslinger-pioneer organizational form is reminiscent of the early phases of the railroad industry when about 6,000 rail companies sprang up at the beginning of the second wave. Only 36 of any significance remained in 1970.

Entrepreneurial The entrepreneurial corporate form arises after the firm has produced a salable product that establishes its presence in the market. The company remains as flexible as it was in the gunslinger-pioneer form, but it moves less rapidly because it becomes more selective about targets. It becomes, therefore, even more dependent on information. A degree of formalization appears since there is some dichotomy between owners and workers because the organization is required to interact with the environment in more formal ways. A corporate "culture" begins to become apparent, the essential ethic being a "team" spirit that is collaborative, not hierarchical. More effort and investments go into product engineering and quality control as the firm attempts to gain control over specific market segments, thereby reducing the element of chance in its viability. The business environment remains eclectic, dynamic, and uncertain. Rewards and corporate advancement continue to be based upon results. The corporate action is dynamic and organic; therefore, the management style must also be organic. APPLE is a good example of a current entrepreneurial corporation.

Corporate This corporate organizational form develops after the firm has gained some significant market control by establishing itself in particular niches of the market. Survival becomes a remote question, and corporate attention turns to maximizing its cash flow, consolidating its gains, and embarking upon an occasional new venture. The organizational structure becomes increasingly formalized. As hierarchies develop, political action becomes directed internally rather than externally. As a consequence of the ensuing political struggle, cliques develop to control the firm. The cliques contest to gain the "commanding heights"; the organization, to determine its values—its corporate culture, its objectives, and who or which group may use its resources. The shareholders are essentially capital *rentiers* to be satisfied with an expected "rent." Rewards or advancement increasingly becomes based upon personal loyalty, rather than upon results, because of the political behavior of the organization. Entrepreneurship, creativity, and initiative become questionable attributes when they are observed to disturb the political balance and regular flow of business, which are dominated by the firm's already established base.

15

Decision making becomes increasingly regularized and standardized. The corporation makes conscious efforts to coexist with the reduced field of competitors rather than to compete with them. Investments begin to flow primarily to marketing and advertising, so the firm can consolidate and extend market control. Formula management becomes the management style. Exxon and General Motors are good examples of the corporate organizational form.

Bureaucratic The bureaucratic corporate form develops after the corporation has gained a large amount of market control and after the competitive field is reduced to only a relative few. The contest for corporate control has largely subsided, and its values and objectives are more or less defined. Advancement is slow and based upon seniority, personal loyalty, and loyalty to the corporate form of culture (corporate socialism). Few if any new ventures are attempted; and entrepreneurship, creativity, and initiative are discouraged, since such characteristics would disturb the equilibrium that the firm is committed to maintaining. Decision making emanates from the center as the organizational form basically becomes functional and mechanical. Individuals subvert their personalities to become "organizational" people. In order to extend the life of the technology and the product, the organization increases investments in marketing and advertising while new technologies generally are ignored. Formula management becomes firmly established. Most utility and insurance companies are good current examples of bureaucratic organizations. During the second wave, some companies were aware of the dangers of the bureaucratic form.

> When General Motors in the twenties began to expand rapidly, it was laid down by the top executives that it should not in its own best interest keep its market quota low enough to make impossible the existence of strong competitors, not for philanthropic or political reasons (antitrust legislation aside), but simply from the point of view of the corporation's efficiency and profitability. It is clear that there is a certain tension between corporate interest in the existence of strong and vigorous competition and the way success is measured in terms of a steady tightening of the corporation's hold on the market. In other words, there may be a point where a business may succeed too well for its own good.

> Peter Drucker
> *The Concept of the Corporation, 1945*

Chaotic   When a new technology breaks into the market, the technology breaks the dominance of the incumbent oligopoly. The incumbent firms soon find themselves in chaos because the mechanisms of formula management will not compensate for their decreased sales, which is not a temporary economic phenomenon. "Reorganizations" take place, consultants and new management are brought in, government help is sought, negotiations take place with creditors, and turmoil reigns. Turmoil continues until these firms modify their corporate culture to a more competitive form, merge with other companies, or declare bankruptcy. The more competitive form may resemble a firm's former gunslinger-pioneer or entrepreneurial form. If a firm emerges in a more competitive and viable form, its chaotic phase evolves into a creative and competitive structure (e.g., look at the experiences of the Chrysler and Timex corporations). If the company cannot pull itself out of chaos, as with Studebaker or what currently might be happening to International Harvester, the experience may be very negative and/or terminal.

THE NATURE-"INTERDEPENDENT" THIRD WAVE

The determinants of the third wave—increasingly intense, open competition, constantly changing and improving technology, and expensive resources—may not allow this kind of corporate evolution to continue, however, and may force most firms to remain in the more competitive end of the process. Furthermore, corporations already evolving into corporate or bureaucratic forms may find it necessary to adapt back to a more competitive form in order to survive and prosper. This poses a major challenge to most corporate resources and wills. Many corporate leaders will have to embark upon new paths of thought and a new mind set.

The third wave is founded upon and fueled by cheap, widely accessible

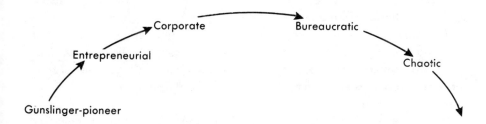

EXHIBIT 1-3   Organizational forms of second wave corporations evolved along the economic cycle that was induced by the rise and fall of a new technology. This was most prevalent during the second wave.

17

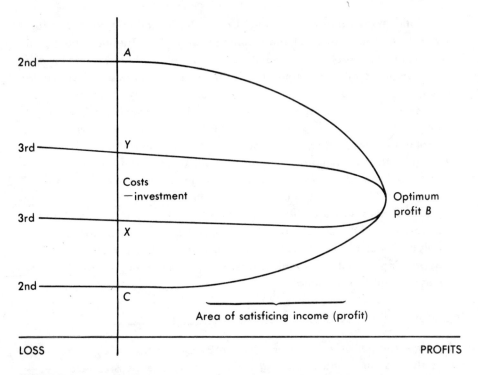

EXHIBIT 1-4   In an effort to maximize cash flow and slack (flexible costs), the second wave firm did not target the optimum maximum profit, but it did target some point close to a satisfactory (shareholder's) profit (see *ABC*). The third wave firm must target the optimum maximum profit/cost (*XBY*) because the curve under which profit is possible has tightened due to increased competition and resource costs. The corporation would lose its position if it deviated from the curve. Efficiency and effectiveness, not slack, are then what ensure corporate survival. The smaller target requires more accurate delivery. This concept is discussed in *Market Structure and Economic Performance* by F. M. Scherer (New York: Rand McNally, 1970).

information and computing power, which have made the means of market entry (entrepreneurship) and the means of competition almost universally available. Cheap information and computing power also have allowed the approximate cost of effective resources (the actual resources applied in achieving objectives not counting slack or waste) to remain constant or decline. While costs continue to rise, increasing efficiency and effective use due to declining information and computing costs allow the end user to actually get more for the money.

Competition can no longer be considered dangerous because individual survival, at least in the physical sense, is guaranteed by the state. The third wave creates a three-dimensional world in which the action is dynamic and continuous, the possibilities are seemingly endless, and the successes go to the quick and accurate. Business management must be organic and dynamic because the speed at which events change has increased rapidly, so possible options have multiplied correspondingly.

Information becomes increasingly critical with the increasing speed at which events change. Companies could afford to restrict information as a method of control during the second wave; but the restriction of information in the rapidly changing third wave becomes debilitating to corporations. Not only has information about what is going on become available again, as it was in the first wave, but its flow and circulation are more actively encouraged in third wave corporations. Competition is moving back to an era of free enterprise from an era of corporate enterprise. The third wave is nature interdependent, organic, and decentralized.

Entrepreneurial-corporate

While the entrepreneurial-corporate form may be most appropriate with dynamic change and rapidly moving targets, it may be inappropriate after a corporation has achieved significant success and after the market establishes

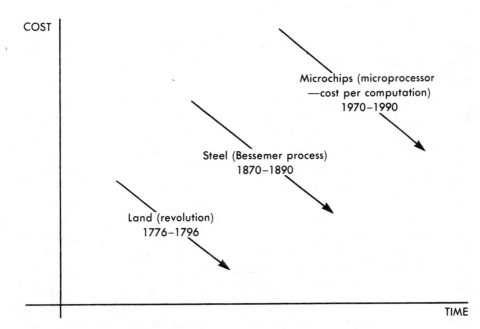

EXHIBIT 1-5   Declines of basic material (fuel) costs in the second and third waves. The cost of steel fell rapidly with the advent of the second wave. Computing costs fell rapidly with the soming of the third wave.

19

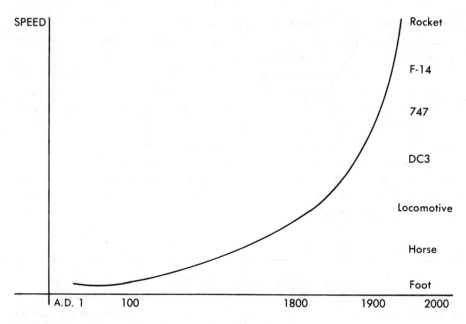

EXHIBIT 1-6   The speed at which technology and events change has increased rapidly in the third wave. Note the direct geometric rise.

more stability. As markets become established, successful businesses become more oriented toward mass marketing and mass production than toward specialized and quick one-hit stings. The entrepreneurial firm runs upon a fuel of high-quality, entrepreneurial people, but the educational establishment and society are still largely training minds for second wave organizations. At present, the number of people needed for entrepreneurial firms is deficient, because the best leave to form their own firms and because the educational process is lacking. This deficiency makes recruitment of the right kind of people difficult and creates a need for a hybrid entrepreneurial-corporate organizational form.

When a firm establishes a significant share in a large but changing market, it can adopt an entrepreneurial-corporate form of operation. The market changes rapidly because electronic information technology dominates. The entrepreneurial-corporate organization remains flexible and dynamic by utilizing a high-powered, high-quality core that ranges over the more formalized and mechanical corporate extensions. This core prods, directs, and galvanizes the corporation. Its management remains organic and utilizes an effective corporate culture and ideology, which encompass a sense of proprietorship, partnership, and team spirit.

Principles, values, and objectives are the primary guideposts, not rules, status, and fear. Entrepreneurial-corporate people are usually too occupied and excited to bother with bureaucratic politics. Action within the corporation remains interactive, dynamic, innovative, creative, but *focused*. Management is organic, free wheeling, decentralized, decisive, entrepreneurial, but *planned*. Casio is an excellent example. It has refrained as much as possible from entering into manufacturing. By concentrating upon engineering and marketing, Casio finds out what customers want or might want and gets that product to them as soon as possible. Through this process, Casio has managed to shorten product life cycles considerably and hit maximum profits while keeping its competitors continually off balance. To run this organic system, the company has placed a premium upon hiring organic, dynamic, and precise people.

Society and the educational system will increasingly shift their emphasis to produce enterprising, information and computer literate people who will meet the demands and challenges of the third wave and of an increasing number of entrepreneurial-corporate organizations. By having people with this kind of education, firms eventually will become more entrepreneurial and organic and less bureaucratic. This will occur once the basic building blocks become available to everyone.

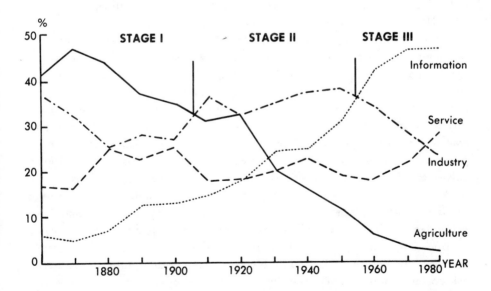

EXHIBIT 1-7   Four-sector aggregation of the United States work force 1860–1980 (using median estimates of information workers). The shifts in occupations are generated by the third wave. **Source:** *Study of the Information Society* by Marc Porats.

21

Organic management and the third wave

During the first wave, people depended upon nature and to a large degree ran their lives by the seasons; the interaction was organic. During the second wave, society felt it could manage and direct nature. Formula management came into being. Society has found during the third wave that nature cannot ultimately be managed, but must be interacted with. People are inter-dependent with, not dependent upon, nature, and therefore management must be organic. To a degree, organic management is a contradictory term, but it is valid. We can no longer try to manage nature, we must live in compatibility with it. Management must take place under natural or "organic" law, and natural systems of organization must take the place of mechanical structures.

Organic management is the management style of the third wave, the style of an information-oriented, efficient, and effective society. Organic manage-ment relies upon the design of flexible and responsive organizations. It allows the development of a corporate culture that, while providing the framework for decision making on a decentralized basis, does not hinder creativity, entrepreneurship, and innovation. Organic management guides an organism, not a machine. In this mode, the chief executive officer (CEO) develops a corporate culture by "plugging" in the right people or by "geneti-cally splicing the right genes," in order for corporate evolution to move in the right direction. The CEO becomes the catalyst of the creation, but not its pilot. He or she is in a sense the ultimate artist of the corporation.

Increasing efficiency and effectiveness are the key to coping with and breaking into the third wave. Increased quality is necessary because corpora-tions can no longer rely upon overwhelming resources, consequent slack, and waste to achieve their purpose. Efficiency no longer means turning out more products per hour; it means delivering functional use. A product is no longer a box or something physical, it is more a service. What will it do? How fast and well will it do it? How reliable is it? Borg-Warner, for example, no longer produces a standard hardware valve when an order comes in but designs a valve according to the required utility of its customer's customer. Things have to work the first time and keep on working, because to maintain excess reserves is too expensive and is getting more so. As physical resources become more expensive, the human capital required to create a product becomes relatively cheaper and more necessary. For instance, while you may be able to afford only one machine with which to do a certain job instead of four, that machine will do four times as much four times as well and break down four times less frequently. Even though the machine may cost three times as much, its actual applied effective utility is greater than that of the previous four machines, and its operating costs are much less. Because increased human capital is infused

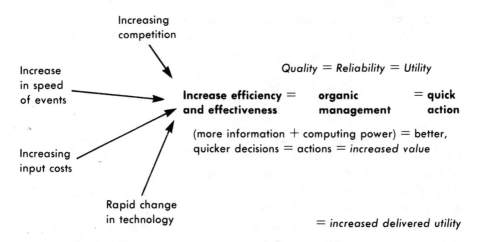

Increasing
competition

Increase
in speed
of events

Increasing
input costs

Rapid change
in technology

Quality = Reliability = Utility

Increase efficiency =   **organic**   **= quick**
and effectiveness   **management**   **action**

(more information + computing power) = better,
quicker decisions = actions = *increased value*

= *increased delivered utility*

EXHIBIT 1-8   Organic management is the most efficient, effective, and rapid form by which
corporations can meet third wave technological challenges.

into the design, engineering, quality control, and testing of a product, the
product will be more efficient and will last longer.

Corporations cannot create efficient and effective products simply by
adopting new technologies or by launching into new markets. They must
completely reorient their thinking, management style, and evolutionary
structure in order to eventually become organic corporations. Then workers are
no longer "laborers," they become full participants.

> For a long time we thought of the hourly employees as coming to work with
> hands and forgetting they had a brain.
>
> R. P. Leifer, Director of Productivity
> Lockheed, California

ORGANIC RESTRUCTURING OF SOCIETY AND BUSINESS

Corporations are restructuring by involving all participants in the continued
restructuring of manufacturing, sales, quality control, and planning. Engineers
are given time in marketing and sales; salespeople spend time in design and
quality control; production workers get involved in manufacturing design and
planning; and many managers no longer hide behind a desk in a remote
building but actively work in every division.

23

Our costs were 60% materials and 10% labor, so we focused on getting our manufacturing workers to help us restructure manufacturing to chip away at that huge cost of material.

Robert Rawlings
Rawlings Sporting Goods

Tandem has given the bulk of responsibility for quality and volume control to production workers in its new plants. The company supplies them with sophisticated data through on-line terminals and with applicable education (through corporate training programs) to use this data to track production and quality. Second wave firms that have attempted the transition in technology without a concurrent transformation in organization have run into severe difficulties. Robots and computers are useless without the right people and the right organization.

Utility companies are classic examples of second wave bureaucracy, waste, and inefficiency. Because of raw material costs, oil shortages, and rising demands, they have been forced into the high technology of nuclear energy and related markets. Many have not been able to cope or to make effective transitions. Costs of many nuclear power projects, such as that of Cincinnati Gas & Electric, have doubled or tripled, forcing many utility companies into severe financial straits. The Washington state power system known as Whoops has, for example, posed serious problems for investors. The difficulties utility companies have had in managing the new situation, as dramatized by the Three Mile Island incident, underscore the fact that these second wave management systems have been unable to cope with new technology, new pressures, or new demands. Upon investigating the current management of Three Mile Island, the Nuclear Regulatory Commission, no purveyor of stringent management standards, reacted with disgust and stated: "The idea that the plant will in the future be operated by GPU (General Public Utilities) should be abandoned."[4]

As a part of the third wave management, unions are agreeing to steady paring of previously overstaffed operations; relaxation of rules in order for union members to be flexible and to do each other's work—white-collar staff can perform blue-collar work if necessary; wage and benefit cuts; increased performance criteria; and pay based upon profit sharing.

Hospitals, also long examples of second wave waste, inefficiency, and obsolescent management techniques, are faced with third wave demands and pressures from a less tolerant public and government. They are now beginning to scramble for efficiency and effectiveness by moving rapidly away from staffing by formula and from related featherbedding. For example, a hospital department such as radiology often requires a defined number of people even if that many staff is not really needed. The government has since decreed that hospital expenses beyond a certain amount, for such items as operating costs, supplies, and equipment, will be "eaten" by the hospital. If the hospital spends below the specified amount, it may keep the differential. Eli Ginsberg of Columbia University recently stated that, unless hospitals trim fat and shape up, they will become the "steel industry of the 1980s," and possibly the 1990s, too.

The Pentagon, also a long-term indulgent in second wave waste, inefficiency, and bureaucracy, is experiencing pressures from mounting deficits and political demands for change. To increase efficiency and effectiveness, according to a new Pentagon convert, the Pentagon must deliver more "bang for the buck"; this can be accomplished by doing away with "corporate pets," moving increasingly toward competitive bidding and away from "sole sourcing," and cutting staffing requirements (the new class of Ageis cruiser, for example, requires less than one-fourth the personnel of World War II cruisers). The Pentagon can continue operations without the $800 screwdriver and the $100 bolt.

Increasing deregulation has put severe pressures on all facets of the transportation industry. The number of competitors in both road and ground transport has almost doubled since deregulation was initiated. While increasing effectiveness, the rail industry has cut total employment from around 1 million in 1972 to about half that in the 1980s. And still other industries have been affected by the third wave. Increased automation has allowed many banks to streamline and cut slack while others have sought help through mergers. For the first time, the telecommunications industry is serious about trimming slack. The entertainment industry's apparent loss on the VCR court action is an example of change it is subject to, and so is the fact that the film most characteristic of the third wave, *Chariots of Fire,* is foreign. Organizations in all walks of life are finding themselves under increasingly severe pressures to make the transition into the third wave. If they cannot, they will wither, perish, or succumb to a takeover by others. (Not too surprising is the fact that although takeovers were not a major, or even respectable, business of investment bankers fifteen years ago, they are very much so today.)

We have lived through the age of big industry and the age of the giant corporation, but I believe this is the age of the entrepreneur, the age of the individual.

Ronald Reagan
St. Johns University
March 28, 1985

2

THE CORPORATE CHALLENGE

"HOW DO YOU MAKE AN ELEPHANT TAP DANCE?"

". . . I have no formula for winning a race. Everyone runs in her own way, or his own way. And where does the power come from to see the race through to its end? From within. . . .
. . . That is how you run a straight race."

Eric Liddell
CHARIOTS OF FIRE

THE CHALLENGE OF THE THIRD WAVE

There appear to be three approaches to transition: (1) to adapt and make the most of change; (2) to beat back the waves as much as legend states that King Canute did; or (3) to get the business declared a ward of the government, at least partially. The choice correspondingly appears clear, but to many companies it is at best blurred, even though the latter two choices are inevitably futile. Expensive resources, increasing competition, and rapidly improving and changing technology—the dynamics of the third wave growth—will not allow the continuation of second wave procedures. Governments, with their own political and budget limitations, will not be able to take on an endless stream of indigents. How various corporations are attempting to meet the challenge of the third wave is discussed in this chapter.

IBM: LEARNING TO TAP DANCE

IBM came as close as any company to perfecting formula management, but it faced an extended antitrust suit as a result. When confronted with reality,

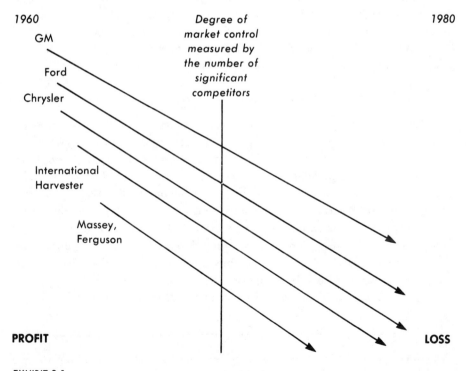

EXHIBIT 2-1

27

however, IBM was able to meet the challenge. It has begun a serious effort to make the company organic, to make the "elephant tap dance," as an IBM executive said.[1] One element of the program is IBM's creation of a highly competitive and entrepreneurial internal market. Within this market, independent business units (IBUs), or small unitary "firms," compete intensely for the design of the product. Product manufacturing is for the most part contracted out to other companies. The risks are major, as are the rewards, and a sense of proprietorship is restored. Limitations are placed upon the budgets and time of such IBUs. Creativity, entrepreneurship, and innovation are encouraged. The company is doing many things not only differently but radically so.

For the first time, IBM is contracting out manufacturing, software, and marketing. It has adopted an "open architecture" approach to its product engineering, which allows for the enhancement of its products with non-IBM products. Company products are appearing in department stores, such as Sears and Macy's, for the first time. The company is further massaging the future by setting up a system by which consumers will be able to maintain their products with some help from dealers. This is radically different from the previous policy of keeping the customer dependent upon IBM for maintenance. The company is reaching out and seizing every opportunity in a dynamic and changing environment. In adopting this flexible approach, IBM is becoming one of the core units in third wave society. Can the elephant dance fast enough? Wheel and deal in any direction quickly and accurately? Turn on a dime? The people at IBM have a strong belief that they can. Odds are IBM will.

APPLE

APPLE is the prototype third wave corporation. A highly flexible, high-powered, high-quality central core directs operations by contracting work out. The actual configuration of the corporation changes from day to day or even from minute to minute. APPLE's plant and equipment, while the best possible, are not excessive. Its inventory is kept to a minimum by the JIT (just in time) inventory system. Efficiency is maximized and slack and hierarchy minimized. Access to information and computing power is maximal and universally available. Without slack, problems are forced to the surface, confronted, and fixed. The message is clear: Be innovative, be creative, make proposals, or clear out. APPLE may have been the sting that made the elephant, IBM, move. APPLE, too, is succeeding in becoming a core unit in the third wave.

EXXON

Exxon, an old oil company, has been trying many different approaches, one of which was to enter the electronic information business directly by buying companies in that business. Exxon hoped that some of the dynamic, entrepreneurial capabilities of the new purchases would rub off on the parent. The result, however, was quite the reverse and quite disastrous. Since then the company has learned from its mistakes and is making the appropriate adjustments. Company people have realized the importance of shooting quickly, often, and accurately because of limitations on resources and time. It may cost as much or more to make one product as to make many; for example, wildcatters drill about ten times the number of wells as Exxon for the same cost. Exxon has begun serious efforts to trim slack with the slogan, "We are too fat!" It has also decided to go back to the oil industry.

U.S. STEEL

U.S. Steel, an old steel company, that is perhaps still archetypal of the second wave, has tried a similar approach to that used by Exxon. U.S. Steel has purchased an oil company, but it has also attempted to become a partial ward of the government. Neither approach will solve its basic problem of bureaucratic structure and mind set. Like many second wave corporations, it operated like a baseball franchise: the company hired and fired first basemen or pitchers and simultaneously tried to keep a strong "bench" in reserve. If things did not go well, it could always fire the manager. Since the market was assured, the franchise only had to deliver a minimum amount of excitement to the audience. There would, of course, always be next year. Now, there may not be another season because the franchise is on the line. Even if the company is in the league next year, it may not be playing by rules it can understand; it may not be equipped to play by those rules. This environment is forcing U.S. Steel to change. Its primary customers, the automobile companies, have put the steel industry on a competitive bid basis for the first time, forcing the company to adjust its procedures and structures. U.S. Steel is recognizing that it has entered an environment in which the rules are constantly changing and new players continually come and go, and where competition constantly increases.

THE JAPANESE TAP DANCE

The world of the late 1940s in Japan was one of scarce and expensive resources with intense and difficult competitive circumstances. This period in Japanese history is analogous to the third wave environment many corporations face today. The Japanese corporation developed from the "Zaibatsu" or big family corporation, which had its roots in the extended feudal family or clan. The participants in the corporation were in a very real sense members of the family. The successes and respect gained by the corporation were theirs, as were the failures and shame. They did not "just work there."[2] Commitment,

29

collaboration, hard work, and sacrifice were typical characteristics. This was the world and inheritance of Honda and other Japanese companies.

They were forced to become organic organizations naturally, and they still are. In competition with American firms, they quite consciously look for the formula being used by the Americans, in order to exploit its inflexibility. Japanese companies seize opportunities to move into a market when the competition's formula or strategy does not fit with current reality, i.e., things that the formula overlooks, has not foreseen, or cannot adjust to.

Honda

Honda's initial penetration into the American market followed such a pattern. Its first thrust into the larger motorcycle market failed because its products could not endure heavy American use. The company was quick to notice that its "super cub" might be appropriate for the light-use market, a market niche neglected by American firms. Honda learns quickly and adjusts quickly. Organic firms are good at exploiting the inflexibility of bureaucracies. Honda's management has kept the pot stirred and instilled an ethic of creativity and innovation in the organization by exhibiting its unorthodox, unpredictable, and sometimes bizarre behavior. The resultant corporation is an increasingly competitive and dynamic organism.

Xerox

"A good idea just doesn't fall into your lap, you have to go out and look for it." (Even if you have to go dancing!) For a long time, Xerox Corporation did not seem to consider its slogan as seriously as it seemed to rest on its laurels and presumed market control and share. Finally its competition exploded with new products and new technology, which precipitated a crisis. Over the past few years, Xerox has been scrambling to adjust and to become dynamic and organic.

Ford Motor Company

"Quality is job one!" A few years ago, the ideas of efficiency and quality were treated with mild amusement at Ford. They no longer are. Robots, previously considered with bored detachment, are now being instituted wherever possible. Inefficient plants, previously considered part of the immovable norm, are being closed, and slack is being sold off and laid off. The union has purchased factories and has become a partial proprietary partner with the company. A major effort is underway to remake the organization into a dynamic organism. Collaborative quality teams are now common. Interaction between all levels within the company is encouraged, in contrast to a previous formal, almost feudalistic communication structure. Management levels are being eliminated as much as possible. The company is moving directly into the electronic information business and toward other targets of opportunity.

Chrysler Corporation

"Chrysler has walked through the valley of death and will survive, but many other companies still have that walk to make," Lee Iacocca, Chrysler's chairman, recently said.[3] He was speaking with the authority of experience. Chrysler has made a determined effort to transform itself by cutting slack wherever possible. The effort between the union and management has been collaborative. A member of the union now sits on the board of directors. Members of Chrysler are experiencing a new team spirit and a sense of proprietorship. More effort has been made to increase quality and to target the needs of the consumer. The company has transformed itself from a staggering second wave dinosaur to one approaching the organic and adaptive third wave form. The people at Chrysler now believe in themselves and in the company. "The competition was good. We had to be better," is now their watchword.

Hewlett-Packard

From the start, Hewlett-Packard chose to be an organic third wave corporation. "We can do better," is the corporate battle cry. In entering the highly competitive electronic information market, Hewlett-Packard knew it had to be on the forefront of innovation, creativity, and quality. Management primarily has a "genetic" engineering role. Internal structures appear and disappear so often because the company is a flexible and interactive organism at times without any discernible structure. Team spirit and sense of proprietorship are extensively prevalent among its members. There appears to be a minimum number of management levels. Members act upon their ideas, and new products hit the market at a staggering rate. Hewlett-Packard is the professional gunslinger par excellence. Its equipment and people are the "best"; it can shoot rapidly and usually can hit its target in the center.

Timex

In the 1950s and 1960s, Timex was firmly established as the power in the inexpensive watch market and followed the precepts of formula management. This lasted until the new technology of the electronic watch, which Timex had chosen to ignore, blasted its foundations. The company experienced a chaotic stage where all "loose passengers were being tossed out of the troika," no doubt to the wolves. Plants were being closed. Government assistance and mergers were sought on an international basis. Assets were sold. While Timex still appears somewhat chaotic, the company has gone directly into the electronic information business with a line of new products, some of which have failed and some of which have succeeded.

BELL & HOWELL

Bell & Howell "has done nothing but cut and concentrate on businesses in which it has excellent franchises, good positions, and high profitability," an analyst remarked recently to the *New York Times*.[4] The company is no longer in the camera manufacturing or retailing business. It is moving directly into the electronic information market with mailing equipment, video cassettes, microfilm products, and technical education institutes. More and more companies will confront reality, trim and turn in a different direction as Bell & Howell has done. The company is also realigning its structure, staff, and systems to become more responsive, responsible, and dynamic.

GENERAL MOTORS

GM was and largely still is a "textbook" case of formula management. While its market control and dominance have been shaken significantly, GM continues to exercise control of the market to a large degree. It has nevertheless taken steps to unclog some of its arteries. Inefficient plants have been closed. Study teams have been sent over to Japan. The company is installing robots and other new technology at a fast clip. Suppliers, in many cases for the first time, have been put on a competitive bid basis. Levels of management are being cut. More money is being spent on product engineering and quality control. Quality of work life (QWL) has become a major cornerstone of the company. The not invented here (NIH) resistance factor is being whittled down. Some people are being promoted on the basis of results and not on clique loyalty. Some of the internecine warfare and politics have abated because the corporation has induced a semblance of collaboration since it has been under "siege." Its workers have taken over some operations and have a restored sense of proprietorship in the company; however, many may still "just work here." Nonetheless, the company is making impressive strides in transforming itself into an organic, "mean and lean" corporation that can wheel quickly in any direction. It is cutting slack wherever possible. "Inventory is evil!" a GM executive said. In relation to that, the company has instituted the JIT inventory system.[5] By using robots, GM is attempting to cut assembly time in half. The prod is the Japanese, who are perceived to have a cost and quality advantage of as much as 20% owing to superior productivity, craftsmanship, and efficiency.

General Motors is also trying an internal competitive approach in which competitive teams produce new product lines that ultimately will be judged by the market. In addition, the company is forging a joint venture with Toyota in California, Nova, which has been largely surrendered to Japanese manufacturers, primarily to learn "how to do it right" (Toyota's slogan). This is a radical departure from "what's good for General Motors is good for the country!" The company recognizes that its main purpose must be to serve the market, not the other way around, if it wishes to remain viable. It is also now embarked on a "Star Trek" (GM phrase) strategy to enter the information age.

AT&T

American Telephone and Telegraph was and largely still is the second wave formula management organization par excellence. Like IBM, the company faced an extended antitrust suit, but unlike IBM, AT&T lost. Its size was huge, its dominance of the market absolute. The public bought what AT&T deigned to sell; and its income was guaranteed. The recent consent decree shook AT&T from its comfortable position and split up the behemoth. While there has been much hype in regard to the split, including one constituent CEO playing the theme from *Chariots of Fire* on the first day of new business, possibly some time must transpire before these new baby elephants learn to tap dance.[6] To date, the personnel seem to be essentially the same and seem to behave much as they always have (with some added confusion). The set of products is essentially unchanged. While noticeable efforts are being made to reorient the corporate cultures and to make these companies dynamic and organic, the effects are not yet apparent. Bureaucracy still seems to be rampant, although thousands are being laid off. The company's competition remains insignificant, but AT&T has adopted a new slogan: "Not just a new image. A new beginning."

ITT

If AT&T was the formula management company par excellence in the second wave, International Telephone and Telegraph was the personification of the precision formula management company with Harold Geneen at the helm. He created a precise and evident formula for everything in every nook and cranny. Internecine strife and political plotting were constant and rampant, a result of individuals and groups seemingly being deliberately set against one another. With the company's efforts to grasp and maintain as much market control as possible wherever a market could be found, the pressure was intense. Formulas were analyzed and reanalyzed. If the rate of return on equity were measured, the company would have shown a fair standing, but soon after Geneen left, ITT began to crumble, which happens to any formula once a key ingredient is removed. It has since been in a depressed state, but is making some forward progress since axing poor products and companies and streamlining operations. Slack is being cut while new high-quality personnel are being added. Information and computer access are also being built up.

KODAK

For many years, Kodak successfully ignored new technology, such as Xerography and the instant camera, to stick with its formula. After much resistance, the corporation decided to go after Polaroid, but Kodak's action was largely a case of too little too late. The explosion of video technology, however, has finally spurred the elephant into action. In struggling to become trim and organic, Kodak has discovered that its bureaucratic style and structure are like the federal government's: It takes things on much more easily than it can get rid of them. Nevertheless, the company has taken a tough approach to cutting slack, postponing pay raises, laying off unnecessary employees, and encouraging early retirements. Innovative products, once passed over, are being reassessed.[7]

An intense "strategic," but largely not organic, approach to new technology is being developed. The company is launching into new areas of electronic-information technology, but too often individuals in new acquisitions have quit, complaining that Kodak's style is bureaucratic and that the company doesn't understand the high-speed–decision-competitive environment of "high tech." Kodak is beginning to step toward closing this "culture gap" by becoming more attuned to its environment and by learning to serve it, rather than the other way around. It has, for instance, established a new market intelligence group. Products to which the market is not responding well are scheduled to be cut. Although Kodak is trying to hire outstanding people, it is facing difficulty in doing so because of its geographic location and because of the inherent corporate culture. The company is trying to change its corporate culture, but the transition is difficult and arduous.

INTERNATIONAL HARVESTER

International Harvester is an old formula management company that tried to ignore its environment as much as possible; in consequence, when the turmoil of transition to the third wave hit the company's foundations, it began to crumble.

34

Because of its bureaucratic style, International Harvester had a large amount of slack and many inefficient, obsolete plants; in addition, vast numbers of people were promoted upon loyalty to form, the environment-market was ignored, and there were significant labor and quality problems caused by the neglect of the individual. Then, IH entered the chaotic stage of corporate evolution. Consultants were called in, reorganization took place, and management was turned over rapidly. The current management is ruthlessly cutting costs and slack in order to develop the cash flow necessary to stave off creditors and to survive. Even though the economy has picked up, International Harvester's comeback may be difficult because the economy is more efficient. Fewer inputs are needed to produce more, whether the inputs consist of raw materials or equipment. It may be that if a company is not in the business of increased efficiency and effectiveness, it is in the wrong business.[8]

International Harvester must ask: Are these products in this business? Does the market want these products? The company has created a basis from which a new method of operation is possible by closing seventeen plants and subsidiaries that did not perform, and by cutting slack and inventory. The cuts and closures are a step toward an organic and dynamic form, but the company is not concentrating on the problems of (1) immediate cash demands to ensure a longer term of survival, (2) new technology to change the actual products, (3) new management technology to change the method of operation, and (4) radical surgery of the farm equipment division, which was sold off to Tenneco. The question remains: Does the company have the panache to pull it off?

COMPAQ

COMPAQ is a new third wave corporation that took off like the proverbial bullet by nailing the blind spot or niche in the portable, IBM-compatible computer market. The company was built from the ground up with highly qualified people; with an automated, efficient, and effective plant; with emphasis on quality; and with streamlined marketing. Within a year of launching, COMPAQ is capable of producing over 10,000 quality units a month. The company has hit quickly, accurately, and very profitably.

SCHLUMBERGER

Schlumberger's CEO recently commented upon the corporation's philosophy in the *New Yorker*.

The company is an extension of personal values—humility, loyalty, preserving faith in an idea, serving people, being trusted, being open minded to different cultures, being ambitious and competitive and yet mindful of tradition.[9]

The key in a corporation or in government is motivating people and forging a consensus. People need to believe in something larger than themselves. We have the responsibility that religion used to have. A good company must not be just a slave to profits; it must strive to perform a service and to beat its competitors. In addition, it must measure itself a higher standard and seek perfection.

> [The ongoing creation of the corporation being an art form in itself] . . . Corporate success must be measured over a long span of time, which includes a high level of profits.[10]

People, research, and corporate culture are the competitive edge of the company. It has steadily increased its investments in R&D to a level where such investments are now over 5 percent of revenues. Plant and equipment are not allowed to become obsolete or to deteriorate. In 1982 alone, Schlumberger invested over $1 billion in a new plant and in equipment. The company is moving decisively into the frontier industries of the electronic information wave with computer assisted design–computer assisted manufacturing (CAD-CAM) and artifical intelligence (AI).

Schlumberger has had a very difficult time entering new fields. Its painful experience with the takeover of Fairchild is a prime example, but the company has learned from its mistakes and is trying hard to make the transition.

Schlumberger found its previous hierarchical style to be unsuitable, especially when applied to the third wave electronic information companies that is acquired, so the company is adapting its style. It had, and to some degree still has, problems with understanding the people and the industry at Fairchild ("They didn't wear suits all the time?!"), as opposed to the oil–wire line industry, in which they have had a virtual monopoly. Schlumberger is coming to grips with many of these major problems, especially with its need for increased autonomy, creative freedom, and decision-making speed. Although the company has gained new direction and wisdom, it is still learning.

OSBORNE

Osborne is an example of a company that could not make the evolutionary transition into the corporate organizational form. In 1982 Adam Osborne said: "He who lives on the cutting edge of technology will die on that edge."[11] It seems, however, that Osborne cut itself on the rapidly receding edge of computer technology in 1983. It could not make the transition from the entrepreneurial form to the entrepreneurial-corporate form. It could not create the necessary framework and controls for mass marketing and mass production. Osborne's operations were chaotic, and the company filed for reorganization under chapter 11 of the bankruptcy laws. Osborne is now making another attempt with newly designed products.

TEXAS INSTRUMENTS

Texas Instruments, a quick-hit gunslinger specialist in instruments, managed to develop a large, prosperous company before entering the mass production, mass marketing field. It too had difficulty making the transition from the entrepreneurial form to the entrepreneurial-corporate form. The company sought to adapt through matrix management, or committee management, but as with any committee, responsibility got lost in meetings. TI also could not develop the necessary framework and controls; consequently, it suffered a loss in excess of $150 million by attempting to mass market computers. Unlike Osborne, Texas Instruments could sustain its loss. The resultant chaos and stress aided the company in creating a competitive corporation. A spokesperson for the company said that Texas Instruments had lost "the formula," but "we had the tendency to substitute mechanics for thought!" [12] The company now recognizes that it exists in a dynamic, organic environment in which thought is more viable than formulas.

MCKESSON

McKesson, an old second wave firm, has made a determined effort to transform itself by cutting low-growth assets and by pushing into the electronic information business. It has put increased ingenuity, computing power, and information into inventory control and distribution. Over the past decade, the company has cut low-growth assets, obsolete plant and equipment, and slack in excess of $250 million, while investing over $650 million in high-growth efficiency and effectiveness. Delivering value to customers is McKesson's main focus in order for customers to have the most efficient and effective product when they need it.

ROLM

ROLM is the premier third wave corporation. The company is on the forefront of electronic information technology, having the latest in computer and telecommunication equipment. Its growth has been phenomenal over the past decade, and its pioneering of new organic management techniques has created "a great place to work." ROLM people are among the most outstanding that can be found, and so are their resultant products. ROLM was so outstanding that IBM bought it. More will be said about this company in subsequent chapters.

PACIFIC TELESIS

Pacific Telesis is one of the seven dwarfs that emerged from the AT&T breakup. The company has made a serious effort to trim slack and to forge into areas of high potential growth by cutting its number of employees by about 20%; by investing in such areas as fiberoptics, digital equipment, new consumer products, and electronic publishing; and by reducing its debt in order to maximize cash liquidity. Although many of the old second wave structures remain, Pacific Telesis has generated enough momentum to overcome many of its inherited handicaps from the monopoly or formula management era.

MCI

MCI is the company that got the AT&T elephant to move. It fought a David and Goliath battle through antitrust legislation until it won. The company felt that the AT&T monopoly garnered excessive profits from high rates for long distance services and saw an extremely profitable situation if it could compete with AT&T. MCI is the organic mammal that toppled the mechanical dinosaur. "We are on a roll. Don't go up against anybody on a roll!" says Bill McGowan, MCI's CEO.[13] In the company, it is said that MCI stands for "McGowan comes into cash" or sometimes just for "money coming in."[14] The inflow of cash has allowed MCI to pursue an unequaled expansion program, with telecommunication services reaching every telephone in the country. The corporation is now reaching out to other countries and will be extending other services, such as a new electronic mail service for computers. It is staffed by high-quality, dynamic people with the imagination and guts and determination to pursue a good idea.

CONTINENTAL AIRLINES

In attempting to become leaner and meaner in the new highly competitive deregulated airline industry, Continental Airlines chose a novel route. It declared bankruptcy under chapter 11, which allowed the company to rescind contracts and labor agreements. There are costs to this approach, but the airline obviously believed that they are worth it. Under the protection of bankruptcy laws, Continental cut costs, salaries, service contracts, and routes.

The airline concentrated all its abilities upon select routes and upon cutting fares to the bone.[15]

PEOPLE EXPRESS

People Express is a new airline that is making money. All its people are managers and direct shareholders; that is, they do whatever is necessary because they have a serious stake in the company's performance. The airline's equipment is the latest, and its direct costs to customers are the lowest. Its pilots, for instance, are paid less than half of what Continental's pilots make, yet the company has thousands of applications. Why? People want to participate in and create something for which they will receive a fair reward (through shares); they do not want to be just "employees." The company is an excellent example of a dynamic, organic third wave organization.

EASTERN AIRLINES

Eastern Airlines is known as a lean and mean organization, and in some cases it may be a bit too lean. Eastern has noted Continental's tactics and has demanded that its employees make some salary concessions or it, too, will declare bankruptcy. In addition to cutting staff and salaries, Eastern is phasing out old equipment and investing in the new generation of fuel-efficient aircraft. Its organizational structure seems to still need improvement despite the near-Herculean efforts of its CEO and the positive intentions of its staff. Its attempt to adopt new equipment and technology outstripped its corporate transformation, causing financial problems. Its CEO is using this as a lever to accelerate Eastern Airline's transformation.

FRONTIER AIRLINES

Frontier Airlines, caught up in the increasing competitive squeeze, adopted another novel approach. The company started another airline, Frontier Horizon, to which it is transferring much of its staff, equipment, and routes. Because the new airline does not have a union contract and unwanted service contracts, it is considered to be in a much better situation to offer competitive fares. It is also selling what is left of Frontier Airlines to its employees.

SOUTHERN PACIFIC–SANTA FE RAILROAD COMPANY

Southern Pacific and Santa Fe are two classic second wave railroad companies that have just "merged" in an effort to compete in the third wave. The merger has allowed the company to phase out unprofitable operations, equipment, and lines; to cut slack; and to concentrate on business with the most potential. The new rail company also is phasing out old second wave management and bringing in third wave management. The retiring chairman of Southern Pacific said upon leaving, "I'm the last of a dying breed of dinosaurs"; and the new CEO of Southern Pacific–Santa Fe said recently, "I'm going to have to crack some heads."[16]

MONDAVI WINES

Robert Mondavi is fond of saying that when he first started, the business was a family operation, with him, his father, and a guy in the cellar, and it still is. He often goes traveling to look for new grapes and processes and takes his family, including his employees with him. He has cultivated the expansion, success, and quality of his organization with aggressiveness and intensity. The Mondavi company sweats over every piece of equipment, every participant, and every bottle of wine to produce the best and to discover how to make it better. The company has become the leading seller of quality California wines.

FUJI FILM

Fuji Film, along with Polaroid, is the sting that made the Kodak elephant move. The company has followed a careful strategic plan of hitting competitive areas in which it has a better or even chance of winning over Kodak. Fuji has also followed the policy of investing in areas of comparative potential by capitalizing upon its experience in chemical, photo-optical, and coating technologies. The resultant growth of the company, which sent chills up its competitors' spines, has been close to 30 percent per annum. Fuji has concentrated on building a strategically oriented organic corporation that can quickly find and fill the niches its competition has missed.

JAMES RIVER MILLS

James River Mills was an archetypal, sleepy second wave operation with obsolete equipment, markets, management, and products. Then Halsey and Williams, two dynamic entrepreneurs, took over and turned the company toward being a third wave organization. They did it by changing the management, by investing in new equipment, by putting the company on a new structural basis, by cutting slack, and by targeting special niches that were missed by its competitors. These measures resulted in dynamic growth for the company, which leaped 100 places on the *Fortune* 500 list in one year.

JAGUAR

Jaguar was perhaps the most rigid bureaucratic company existing on government sufferance to be found. When John Egan took over the CEO's job, he found incredible sloth, ignorance, waste, inefficiency, lethargy, and almost nonexistent morale. His watchword to the employees could well have been, "Do you know what you are doing to each other, to the company?" The new conservative government would no longer suffer a losing proposition. The company would be forced into bankruptcy if some black ink were not found soon. Egan videotaped various company operations for its employees to examine exactly what they were doing. He commented as follows on the state of the company:

> In the machine shop, for instance, all the workers had left their benches, cleaned up, and were waiting in line at the time clock a full 15 minutes before quitting time. In the accounting department the film showed more than half the employees reading novels, others gathered in groups talking, and virtually no work being carried out. It was basic, either we changed or the firm closed. Most workers got the message.[17]

Employees were fired or laid off, and the workforce was also reduced by attrition; all of this was accomplished with union cooperation. Jaguar went from a work force of 10,500 in 1980 to one of 8,000 today while production has doubled and quality has taken a quantum leap. Suppliers were also brought into line: defective parts were returned at the suppliers' expense, and they had to pay for any parts that failed under warranty. They got the message because Jaguar communicated it. Things have improved so much that Jaguar is now among the top-rated quality cars.

KYOCERA

One of the fastest growing and most innovative firms anywhere is the Kyocera Corporation of Japan. Its motto is, "Respect the Divine and Respect People," which means, for the participants, an evolving search for self-realization and self-actualization. In Kyocera, self-actualization means the development of self through the development of the company. The following attitudes are stressed:

Faithfulness to the Kyocera philosophy

Dedication to Kyocera's objectives

Enthusiasm in pursuing those objectives

41

Spirit, animation, and courage

Management by consensus/cooperation; group solidarity in sentiment and belief

People are not hired at Kyocera, they are "adopted," and once adopted, they are expected to earn or prove their worthiness. Upper management considers the Kyocera participants as family on a twenty-four hour basis, as they do their own immediate families. Organization is developed around leaders or section heads; each section is a responsible and viable unit under the general observance of upper management. Kyocera's main objectives are to build a growing and viable company and to make a profit.

These are just some of the examples of efforts made at a successful transition and transformation.

SUMMARY

We are in transition to a new era where the power of formula management in terms of the hierarchy will have substantially diminished, where power is gradually evolving to, as *Business Week* describes it, a "new corporate elite," composed of entrepreneurs, owners, employees, community groups and information generators. The stubborness and fear of the old management class is, and has been, exploited very profitably by "corporate raiders" such as T. Boone Pickens, Saul Steinberg, the Bass Brothers, or Carl Ichan. There has been a lot of management writing recently that indicates you can make the transition by copying the Japanese and some blue chip American firms, and breathing cooperation and consensus in the company, with financial analysis as a poor afterthought. Financial controls will always be important and necessary in a successful enterprise. However, as these examples have shown, there is no one way that is right and many that are wrong. Indeed, some of the so-called blue chip, "excellent" firms such as Digital Equipment, Exxon, Texas Instruments, and Atari have had very serious problems recently. What we can best do here is to draw you into a comprehensive and investigative journey which we hope will stimulate you to thinking useful thoughts/concepts and developing strategies appropriate for you and your firm.

3

ORGANIC
MANAGEMENT

THE
TRANSFORMATION

I always voted at my party's call and never
thought of thinking for myself at all!
I thought so little they rewarded me by making
me the ruler of the Queen's Navee
Now landsman all whoever you may be, if you
want to rise to the top of the tree
Be careful to be guided by this golden rule
Stick close to your desks, and never go to sea!
And you all may be rulers of the Queen's Navee

W. S. Gilbert
HMS Pinafore, 1867

THE CURRENT MANAGEMENT MIND

A look of knowing concern passed over a man's visage as he said quite suddenly, "That is how we train our MBAs!"

This incident took place at a lecture I gave, at which I played the above Gilbert & Sullivan piece. The man was a professor at a leading business school. It is interesting to note that this bit of management commentary from *HMS Pinafore* was written during what could be considered as the bureaucratic stage of the British Empire. It is in strong contrast to the earlier entrepreneurs, men like Drake, Nelson, Raffles, Clive, and Raleigh, who did go to sea and took up opportunities on the front lines.

Are we experiencing a similar bureaucratic frame of mind?

Do business schools still teach bureaucratic formula management?

Why are there no business schools to speak of in Japan, the leading exponent of organic management?

The answers to the first two questions are yes, unfortunately, but some people are beginning to see the light. Tom Peters, Richard Pascale, Jerry Porras, and Michael Ray at Stanford University are pioneers in American organic management. In addressing the observed need of business schools to revamp, Raymond E. Miles, the new dean of the University of California Business School at Berkeley, recently stated these major objectives: "Our graduates will be more entrepreneurial. We'll also give more emphasis to international finance, economic policy, and information systems management."[1]

It is appropriate that Miles should address these areas for improvement because business schools have, for the most part, turned out second wave corporate bureaucrats who have become anachronisms if not liabilities. More entrepreneurs have arisen from other disciplines, such as engineering, although the odd entrepreneur has managed to pass through the business school regimen. Business schools have also been notoriously egocentric, chauvinistic, and not terribly concerned with international trade or governments. These attributes were appropriate for the second wave but not for the third.

Not only should business schools change, but their candidates must also change from security-oriented, chauvinistic people to social and international entrepreneurs. Business school selection procedures will have to change. It is absurd schlock to believe that people can become socially conscious, entrepreneurial, and internationally minded by taking a smattering of courses over a one- or two-year period if they do not value these characteristics already.

Business schools cannot magically transform people. To paraphrase Steve Jobs, businesses should look for great, creative, innovative people who are basically that way in the first place—"people who in the sixties would have been demonstrating, who now are playing in punk rock bands on the weekends."[2]

Business schools need to find people who are and would be growing and creating change wherever they are or may be. MBA candidates usually have been people who have done well in status quo activities; e.g., they have had work experience at GM or AT&T. They have also performed well on quantitative tests, such as the graduate management aptitude test (GMAT), but they are not people who have effected very much change.

In a third wave environment, corporations have to plug competitive, creative, innovative, and electric people into a living framework, and give them a share in the action and in the results. In this way a competitive edge is created and maintained, ensuring survival in the third wave.

> The competitive edge is created by innovating faster, better products and by executing operations better and faster, with better and faster people.
>
> Lewis Glucksman, CEO
> Lehman Brothers KL, 1984

It is tempting to conclude that since the Japanese and the Germans don't have business schools, we shouldn't either. However, that would be an erroneous assessment. Just as the Japanese corporation has its roots in the extended family or clan, Japanese management training takes place within the extended family in an interactive and organic way. The child's duty is to follow in the family traditions; the family's duty is to train and educate its children.

In the more unstructured, independent American family, this type of process is the exception rather than the rule. Training in organic management must take place in our educational system, in which two years of business school can be only the culmination. It takes much longer to train organic managers, primarily because they must learn to interact with and guide a complex, dynamic, and evolving organism.

> I wore clean collars and a brand new suit
> To pass examination at the Institute
> Pass examination did so well for me
> That I am now the ruler of the Queen's Navee!
>
> W. S. Gilbert
> HMS Pinafore, 1867

Loyalty to Form

Fortune magazine proclaimed that the best selling management texts by a wide margin have been John Molloy's *Dress for Success* books, which is indicative of the second wave society's value of form. Market control and the capability of creating large amounts of slack by second wave formula management allowed promotion based on loyalty to form, not results.

In the second wave corporation, a currently dominant group or person would dictate the "correct" form, which often led to the segregation of people from the promotion stream. For instance, at one major American corporation it used to be, and may still be, commonly acknowledged that a person had to be a company "type," i.e., "six feet two, eyes of blue," in order to be promoted into the executive ranks.

The determinants of the third wave, however, require results as a basis for survival and promotion. Many previously segregated groups and individuals, including women and adolescents, are returning to the mainstream of advancement and competition, and the percentage of women in the work force has risen dramatically since 1970.

J. Ferranti, the innovative CEO of Ferranti Electronics, was once asked what it took to become a CEO. He replied that if you were tall, well dressed, handsome, and well spoken (a description that did not fit him well), that would help a lot, "but if you look like me, it doesn't hurt to own the company."[3]

Loyalty to form, cliques, and people was the primary method of advancement throughout bureaucratic second wave organizations—i.e., never thinking for yourself at all and always voting at your party's call. In some organizations this was called the promotion of the "nonobvious choice." Less than capable persons were naturally more dependent on their patrons. In turn, placing those deemed to be capable into senior positions was considered dangerous to those not so capable who, as a measure of self-defense, often sought and succeeded in having more pliable individuals placed in executive positions.

Not surprisingly, the groups of people that dominated the large bureaucracies of the second wave were very good at loyalty and mediocrity, but not so good at thinking creatively or innovatively. Indeed, promotion of the nonobvious was a major factor in the decline of the British Empire. A recent study revealed that the criteria for promotion used by Japanese firms were almost twice as objective as those used by their American counterparts, because their criteria were based on results.

In this relation, Nolan Bushnell recently[4] complained it was not as much fun in Silicon Valley these days due to the "Harvardization" (MBA–bureaucratization) of the valley. He said form was beginning to replace substance as a value in the valley, a sure indication of creeping bureaucracy.

It's becoming like a frat rush these days to get venture capital; that is, you need your "face" men up front, and these are usually some high form, low substance, Harvard MBA type. Most Venture Capitalists, populated as they are, do not really understand entrepreneurship; they used to come around and complain that we did not have an organization chart, they did not know who was doing what, and why we didn't move to some more pleasant surroundings instead of a converted skating rink? Bureaucracy in local government is beginning to also really stifle entrepreneurship and creativity in the valley. If we lose Silicon Valley, the country will have lost a great treasure. Many companies today are getting into trouble because they were founded on easy venture capital money, because they had the right form, but when the flow of venture capital cash began to dry up they

"It's been moved and seconded that some of us will keep our mustaches, some of us will shave them off; some of us will wear gray flannel, some of us will wear brown flannel; some of us will wear rep ties, others foulards; some of us will wear horn-rimmed glasses, some steel-rimmed; et cetera."

Drawing by Opie; © 1983 The New Yorker Magazine, Inc.

had very little internally generated cash, very little substance, to fall back upon. The valley has to return to the mean and lean form of production and innovation, where you have engineers and management working hard wherever they are needed, even on the line. When we had a crisis the engineers had to work on the line, they soon found out where many of the poor designs were, how they impeded productivity, and after the crisis and the engineers went back to their jobs they issued over 100 engineering design changes. We had the link between all parts of the organization. It was a process, now we have separation and bureaucratization. If we keep going this way our competitive edge will be lost and all we will have in the valley is a bunch of boutique designers. In Hong Kong I've seen compacted factories the size of this room (an auditorium) that are non-stop and put out about the same amount of product as the entire Atari operation. That's the kind of competitive world market we live in. A lot of us, especially government are not awake to that fact. If we are going to continue to have fun and be profitable we have to return to a mean and lean strategy!

Echoing Nolan Bushnell's sentiments another successful entrepreneur complained, "We used to go out for a hamburger and beer, in our jeans, and discuss the next technological innovation. Now we go to the Lion and Compass [started and owned by Nolan Bushnell], in our Brioni suits, for 'Nouvelle cuisine' and Chardonnay (wine) and discuss the latest tax shelter condominium project in Maui or Tahoe. About the only one who wears jeans around here now is Steve Jobs and even he is switching to cords. What has happened around here?"

As if to confirm his point, the most popular new play in Silicon Valley last season was one called "YUP" or "Young Urban Professionals," concerning young chic MBA types who move into a "funky" neighborhood and "renovate" it with croissant and wine bars. While bureaucracy and all its trappings may have reared its ugly head, I believe the dynamic is far too strong to crush, but form and creeping bureaucratization remain real threats to be dealt with.

Bureaucracy was also a prime cause of the American Revolution—which was precipitated by a schism between the bureaucratic establishment in Britain and the power and entrepreneurial freedom of a new wave being established in America. British bureaucracy had as its prime objective the continuance of the "mercantile" system, i.e., maintaining the status quo, restricting American enterprise to farming and to the most basic industries. The stamp and tea acts are significant examples of British bureaucratic repression which attempted to retard talent, creativity, and progress.

ORGANIC THINKING

I am not an advocate for the frequent changes in laws and institutions but laws and institutions must go hand in hand with the progress of the human mind. As that becomes more developed, more enlightened, as new discoveries are made, new truths discovered, and manners and opinions change with the change of circumstances, institutions and laws must advance also to keep pace with the times. We might as well require a man to wear still the coat which fitted him when a boy, as civilized society to remain ever under the regimen of their barbarous ancestors.

Thomas Jefferson, 1775

Thomas Jefferson well understood organic management. His creations were not static mechanisms, but dynamic, living, and evolving. He also understood that it was unnatural to place those of lesser talent and "virtue" over those of more, just because those with less were closest to some particular form specified at the time. Jefferson perhaps could see the flow of history more easily from his vantage point, but it is unfortunate that second wave society could not have taken a firmer hold of his concepts. His essential message is simple and still relevant, however. Times and people change; therefore, organizations and whatever drives them must change in concert. Only the best will do. Those that do not change will disappear because loyalty to form is no longer enough to stay in the game.

What then is organic management? How is it performed? How can it be instituted? Steve Jobs, chairman of APPLE, was recently asked at a lecture whether he considered himself more of a business manager than a scientist. He replied with some irritation, "Neither. I consider myself an artist whose job is to plug in great people—people who in the sixties would have been demonstrating —who now are playing in punk rock bands on weekends. We have such great people. I look forward every day to going to work!"[5]

To create and be a catalyst of a living, evolving organism is the essence of organic management. An organization comprised of people is not a machine to be punched or manipulated according to a manual or formula. The organism is dynamic, interdependent, and interactive with its constituents, including its management and its environment. You interact with it; you don't "administer" it.

For a variety of reasons, Japanese companies have become known as the pioneers in the art of innovative corporate design by creating a unique blend of entrepreneurship and feudalistic bureaucracy from the ashes of defeat. Their organic corporations are challenging the world for economic supremacy.

ORGANIC MANAGEMENT AT HONDA

"It's important to make decisions on the spot, without asking for instructions from headquarters. That's what I did," Kiyoshi Kawashima, head of Honda, said.[6] He was referring to the difficulty headquarters often has with assessing information second hand, then making the appropriate decision before the opportunity disappears. Headquarters often comes to the wrong conclusion. But making decisions on the spot clearly did not hinder Kawashima's career.

The organic corporation reacts quickly and accurately. While decisions are made independently at Honda, they are made under the framework laid down by the corporate *warp*. The corporate warp, as explained by Honda management, are the management objectives and philosophy that remain in place and guide the web of corporate activity woven around it. Honda's chief goal, even when the company was a small, struggling, and almost bankrupt postwar enterprise, was to become a successful, profitable worldwide corporation.

All individuals in the Honda organization must continually develop their potential in order for the growing pool of human resource and talent to be utilized to the maximum extent. Honda built and maintains this pool for three reasons: (1) to close in on the market in the event of a natural, momentary decline of traditional mechanical firms; (2) to continually search for the "blind spots"; and (3) to exploit the gaps in the formulas of traditional second wave firms. The company considers free-market competition to be a long war in which its corporate participants must be nurtured so that they may persevere and ultimately triumph.

A graphic example of the efficacy of this procedure happened during and shortly after the recession of 1974–75. United States electronic firms laid off large numbers of people while their counterparts in Japan did not. The result: when recovery did take place, the Japanese were able to jump in with both feet while the Americans were still gearing up. Honda measures profit in terms of its long-range future, which is defined by the corporate warp. How does a company measure its gain in confidence, skill, creative ability, and efficiency on an annual ledger?

While a corporation must act like numerous gunslingers in search of an opening, it must have the ammunition to fire. Honda's answer was to create a separate organization for technological development. The "expert system" is composed of a number of experts who interact on an accepted basis with the rest of the company. The technology developed is both technical and

50

managerial; that is, while there are experts who develop hardware and software, there are also experts who develop new management and business techniques in terms of customer demand and corporate capability. Technology development follows the needs of the market (the customer) for which Honda developed the sales, engineering, and development (SED) system: What will sell (sales)? What can we design and build (engineering)? What can we produce and market (development)?

Most of these experts, who know that their function is to provide a continuing store of techniques, information, ideas, innovation, ingenuity, and creativity, are homegrown—raised and developed at Honda. During their careers, experts move in a three-dimensional space throughout the corporation to inspire action, solve problems, and act as catalysts for innovation or change. They appear when needed and then disappear, much as Gandalf, the wizard in J. R. R. Tolkien's *Lord of the Rings,* did whenever the small band of adventurers needed him. Gandalf seemed to move in some other dimension, but was always aware of where the "quest" was and what dangers or opportunities needed to be faced.

In this way, a valuable resource is maintained and built upon, instead of being sidetracked by the Brown effect, named after the first of the tribe that I encountered, in which competent experts are promoted into management as a reward. Too often these experts become incompetent managers, thus adding to growing and largely useless levels of middle management. The Japanese have not been immune to this effect themselves. There have been recent commentaries about the problem of "window tribes"—large numbers of middle managers who have no duties other than to stare blankly out of windows.

Honda recognized early on that the genius of innovation and creativity could not be nurtured in the traditional inflexible and inefficient corporate pyramid. The two founders of Honda have said that they would probably not have survived the pyramid system if they had been subject to it. In Honda's organic corporate form, responsibility and decision making are initiated at the individual level, wherever that may be for each particular person. Individuals are rewarded according to results. The rewards are not always monetary and may consist largely of increased respect, which is often valued more than cash in Japanese culture. If a participant in the company is told that he or she is doing his or her part and more for the team, the compliment may mean more to that participant than an Olympic medal means to an athlete.

Honda's management also thinks that individuals have more inspiration and can give more than the individuals think they have and can give. Similarly, the company thinks that it can get more out of a piece of equipment than is defined in a manual, more out of raw materials than is defined in the formula, and more out of the market than market research can delineate. To be creative, Honda believes that its participants must drive and press themselves and their peers; therefore, the company must have outstanding people to continue as an organic corporation. One of its hiring tenets is to go after people that "you might not like personally because he or she is not like you." In this way, a vibrant mix of different types of talented people maintains the synergy of the corporation. Inbreeding is actively discouraged.

Honda is also one of the pioneers of the JIT inventory system, which keeps inventory at a minimum by forcing problems to the surface and by maximizing cash liquidity. The just in time inventory system has also been applied to Honda's people, which eliminates slack, and to marketing, where product supply is deliberately limited to weed out problem distributors and refine retail channels.

In addition to being encouraged by the expert system, creativity is fostered by the use of a notebook. Each participant maintains a creativity notebook in which to write ideas about how every activity is performed and how it can be improved. Individuals rotate to handle different functions, which encourages flexibility and brings out undiscovered talents. Participants are encouraged to bring their ideas along with them to maximize a cross fertilization of ideas. To get the best out of its people, Honda realizes that they must have fun as well as be challenged. In addition to providing recreational facilities, the corporation sponsors a number of annual corporate events, such as a creativity contest in which all those who wish to compete are subsidized to develop some new and usually bizarre contraption. In this way, people's minds become an internal, interactive part of the firm. Commenting upon warnings about the quality of American labor in relation to their development of a plant in Columbus, Ohio, a senior Honda executive said, "The problem is not one of the quality of American labor but of the quality of American management."[7]

Honda has developed a dynamic and organic organism that offers much knowledge from which American firms can benefit. Chiefly, *know* and *care* about participants or members of the organization. Who are they? What are their potentials? How can they interact to create and grow? Members must be nurtured and developed because *they* make the organization work and give it a competitive edge. The importance of the "happy" worker and "happy" consumer; a concept virtually laughed at twenty years ago, has gained a new importance and new understanding in the organic corporation.

An Organic American Corporation: ROLM

ROLM is an example of an American organic corporation that pays the utmost attention to employee and customer well-being (even to the point of having on-site recreational facilities for its employees). ROLM, like Honda, is guided by a corporate warp that embodies a corporate philosophy of principles and objectives. All members know where they should head and how they should interact in getting there, which is the basic concept of ROLM's corporate warp. How does ROLM do it? The company, like all other organic companies, has as its primary initiative the recruitment, maintainance, and enhancement of superior and diverse people.

The four guiding principles and objectives of ROLM are:

* To make a profit
* To grow
* To offer quality products and customer support
* To create a great place to work

The company sees these principles as interdependent and interactive. One cannot exist without the others.

ROLM philosophy provides a bond for this highly decentralized company. We do our best to maintain an entrepreneurial spirit and to avoid bureaucracy through broad decentralization of responsibility and authority. This approach necessarily leads to differences in opinion. However, we believe this is the only environment that provides the individual freedom required for creative thinking and rapid response to the changing needs of the marketplace. We are convinced that a highly structured bureaucratic organization is much less effective than our organization. Certainly that form of organization would never attract the excellent people we have at ROLM. ROLM philosophy is the basis for most of our decision making. It indicates much of what we are doing at ROLM and where we are headed.

W. Kenneth Oshman, president
ROLM Corporation, 1983

The company explains its four objectives like this: Profit is necessary in order for ROLM to thoughtfully plan for the future and to avoid undue pressures from the competitive environment. A healthy profit picture allows increased risk and entrepreneurial action, as well as the development of company people. Profit is considered a necessary input for the operation of the firm, not primarily an output for the owners.

Growth is required for the company to remain viable, to become increasingly competitive, and to provide challenge to its people on a continuous basis.

Growth is defined not merely in terms of corporate revenues or assets but in terms of the growth of each individual. Growth is not the creation of an expanding empire or the desire to be number one, as it was defined in second wave corporations.

ROLM sees quality as a necessary principle to ensure the continued viability of the company. In order to maintain quality, ROLM has developed a mutual commitment between the company and its customers. The relationship is not seen as predatory and competitive, but as mutually rewarding and encouraging. In its relationship with customers, the company recognizes that it cannot offer quality if it does not have quality people or quality working conditions.

Creating a great place to work is essential in attracting the best and brightest people and in keeping them motivated. ROLM sees people, not formulas, as the key to the company's success. People create an entrepreneurial, dynamic organization.

The company identifies success with many attributes and encourages its members to follow certain precepts.

* Avoid bureaucracy; keep practices simple, but make sure they are communicated, understood, and effective.
* Freely communicate ideas and suggestions.
* Show initiative to assure you understand the performance expectations of your job.
* Avoid "finger pointing." When you see a stalemate, encourage discussion to get the problem solved.
* Discourage rumors by communicating facts upwards, downwards, and sideways throughout the company.
* Use written communications when it makes sense to do so. Recognize the value of face to face communication.
* Focus on substance; it is always more important than form.
* Take a large view of your job; do whatever it takes to make your tasks succeed whether or not it is part of your "job."
* Solve problems, don't make excuses or look for fault in others. Don't act "on the record" to prove someone wrong; help make it right. Focus on the important issues; let the inconsequential slip.
* Build teamwork inside and outside your work group; it avoids bureaucracy.
* Fix problems as we grow; don't stop growing to fix problems. Don't fix things that aren't broken.
* Set personally challenging and difficult goals that support departmental and corporate objectives.[8]

ROLM managers are encouraged to be hardworking catalysts and role models who can interact with all members. Managers are not just observers. Their job performance and success depend on the following principles:

* Level with people. Communicate your expectations—encourage honest response.
* Get decisions made as close to the action as possible; don't second guess them unless you have good reasons which you communicate. Let people plan and control as much as possible of their own work.
* Assure that people understand job performance expectations; then encourage their individual initiative to expand.
* Promote from within whenever feasible; seriously consider ROLM people if they want promotion.
* Identify and create an environment that motivates all ROLM people.
* Maintain equal opportunity and affirmative action practices that meet the spirit as well as the letter of the law. Assist individuals to compete and succeed, and reward them on the basis of merit.
* Recognize individual accomplishment in and out of your immediate work sphere. Praise in public; criticize in private. Don't point to third parties to rationalize your failures.
* Help ROLM people build their self image; treat them as individuals.
* Assure that people are paid fairly considering the labor market, internal equity, and individual worth to the company; then give merit increases only.
* Communicate praise to individuals in the group; buffer them from group criticism; make sure they are aware of any real shortcomings.
* Give salary and performance reviews on time.
* Use written practices, policies, and guidelines in designating routine tasks critical to the smooth functioning of the organization. If they don't reflect reality, rewrite them.
* Follow important projects and take continual corrective action, if necessary to keep them on track.
* Manage by walking around. Recognize potential problem areas before they become major.
* Encourage each individual to develop his/her skills for career advancement.
* Act as if the future of our business depends upon how the customer views your actions.
* Show concern for the customer's business.

* Know your authority and act to the limits (i.e., it's okay to make an aggressive mistake).[9]

For those employees who have customer contact, ROLM offers the following guidelines:

* Solve the Customer's problem, even if it's not ordinarily your job.
* Act as if you work for the Customer and your next raise or promotion depends upon how they evaluate your performance (it does).
* Take a personal interest in the success of the Customer's business.
* Act as if they are the only account you're working on.
* Be the Customer's advocate inside ROLM. If you have to raise hell to get their problem solved—do it.
* The first step in getting loyalty from customers is to show your loyalty to them.
* Follow-up. Follow-up. Follow-up. If you have any doubt that a Customer is satisfied, follow up, talk to them, and find out what it will take to get them satisfied.
* Never, never, never, short change a Customer. Always find out if there is anything else you can do.
* Be proactive, not reactive, to Customers' issues.[10]

These points also apply to all members of the company, whether they have close customer contact or not, because every member has indirect contact with society and does project the ROLM image.

The philosophy, the warp, creates its own particular "karma" or truth in the ROLM organization by generating the motivating dynamic for growth and success. Constant feedback and reinforcement affect these principles, objectives, and attributes of success. Management is committed to a continuing dialogue on these and related issues in order for the corporate warp to be evolutionary rather than static. A premium is placed on the clarity of communication and honesty in relationships, on initiative and creativity, and on obtaining results and longer term views. Bureaucracy and general corporate aging are seen as a dreaded disease.

The corporate philosophy is also the subject of several annual informal conferences given in Monterey, California, or in similar locations. All involved in these conferences get down to basics—what has been the record? How can the warp be improved and better implemented?

In an approach similar to that of Japanese corporations, ROLM wants to meld a team or family spirit into the organization. Such measures as superior benefits and lavish, on-site recreational facilities that include a large swimming pool, saunas, hot tubs, tennis courts, and whirlpools, are used to enhance this spirit. Regular social activities, such as beer busts at which participants can socially and organically link, are also part of the schedule. Corporate participants are encouraged to like and care for each other, as each is considered to be the company. Being a ROLM person has very definite connotations.

Just before the advent of the third wave, ROLM was created by young entrepreneurs who correctly thought that their creativity was being stifled in second wave corporations. They thought that they could create a much better type of corporation, which would encourage and enhance creativity and initiative. ROLM is the result, an example of a dynamic American entrepreneurial-corporate company par excellence. It is typical of the new organic companies that are emerging to maintain an American competitive edge.

THE THIRD WAVE ENTREPRENEURS AND THE NEW FREEDOM

To most of these new-style, organic entrepreneurs, their creations are the triumph of a principle, the vindication of an important idea. Making large sums of money is no more important than winning, producing quality products, developing an organization in which its participants are happy, and proving that they were right.

> I've often been interviewed by journalists about how to make a lot of money in the high technology field, and they are quite surprised when I tell them we were pursuing something we enjoyed and thought worthwhile, and the large sums of money we made were just incidental.
>
> > Gene Richeson, founder
> > ROLM Corporation

This ideal is indicative of the new organic consciousness of third wave entrepreneurs. This value and mind transformation also affects the resident executives of old second wave companies as they undergo transformation. Similar ideals drove people to create "a new world" with the American Revolution; such ideals also drove men like Lincoln to liberate the slaves. Gene Richeson, whose creativity at ROLM helped create the American organic corporation, is now working for world peace.

57

> I saw myself as a slave owner, ripping off the work of other people, and I knew I had to do something to change working conditions.
>
> As quoted by Michael Maccoby
> *The Gamesman*, 1977

Maccoby also discusses how a similar feeling affected another executive who gave all the stock in the company that he owned to the employees and dedicated himself to creating a viable, democratic, organic corporation established on the principle of "maximizing the humanness of every employee." The broth of humanity, is by definition, created primarily from people as well as from philosophy. Great, creative people are needed even though every person is different. How is the best mixture of people created, developed, and evolved? This is a major question facing most third wave executives.

In his book *The Gamesman*, Maccoby discusses four types of people: the craftsman, the company man, the jungle fighter, and the gamesman.

The craftsman is a first wave type who cares most about the product.

The company man is the prototype second wave industrial executive who cares most about security, loyalty, and the status quo.

The gamesman is the third wave type who cares about the product, the organization (the people), and the triumph of the ethic (the idea and the principle).

The jungle fighter spans all three waves. Many entrepreneurs are like this. This type cares most about doing things, creating something new, breaking old molds, and having the power to implement ideas. The jungle fighter, who loves the struggle and intrigue as objects in themselves, can be found clawing through organizations in all three waves.

PERSONAL CHARACTERISTICS IN THE DESIGN OF THIRD WAVE ORGANIZATIONS

These categories are useful in assessing how the organic corporation should be designed and evolve, how the right mix might be arrived at, but it should be borne in mind that most people are various combinations of these categories, and more. Assuming that your goal is to build an entrepreneurial-corporate company, you would want mostly the gamesman type, but in some positions the company man, craftsman, or jungle fighter may be appropriate. Such combinations of diverse people provide the yeast that causes the organism growth in a long-term, desired direction. To a large extent, the organic mix is self-designed and rolls with the flow.

The short-term and frequently shortsighted positions win out with disturbing regularity because American business is top heavy with the ever-expanding numbers of business school graduates who are trained advocates of the short-term profit. It is not entirely coincidence that the same years [that] have seen industry increasingly, almost exclusively, run by financially oriented business school graduates have also seen the worst productivity performance since the Depression.

> Michael P. Schulhof, vice president
> Sony of America, 1982

For their corporations and themselves to be successful, management is increasingly aware that they must design the corporation for longer term viability and profit and that this design must not be based upon financial numbers but upon people and related strategy. The long-term nature of the corporate warp of Kyocera, which prohibited the lay off of people or the disposal of equipment during the downturn in the semiconductor industry in the early seventies, allowed the company to seize most of the market for semiconductor housings when the market rebounded. Financial analysis would have dictated the dispersal of equipment and people, instead of the absorption of temporary loss. The temporary loss was simply a cost of longer term profit.

In designing a corporation, the objective is to avoid the typical second wave scenario by which a corporation proceeds from the pioneer-gunslinger corporate form to the bureaucratic, then eventually to the chaotic. The objective should be to design an adaptive, evolutionary corporation that will evolve to the entrepreneurial-corporate form. This is done primarily by plugging in the right people and by creating the right strategic warp, which is only the first step. People's moods, needs, and motivations change as the corporation evolves, so the warp and interactions modify accordingly.

Moods, emotions, and spirit are important factors in the design of the entrepreneurial-corporate organization. Most second wave corporations have been designed to be cold, analytical, and dry, while the adjectives most often used to describe organic third wave corporations have been "human," "warm," and "fluid." As the corporation evolves, these human factors have to be "tuned" to avoid corporate decline, bureaucratization, and chaos. There are many ways in which this tuning can be done.

> One of the best, if not the best, "tuners" was Jesus Christ. He told stories and parables and demonstrated his courage, his compassion, his willingness to sacrifice for others and to lead by following.

> Dynamic Silicon Valley firm executive

59

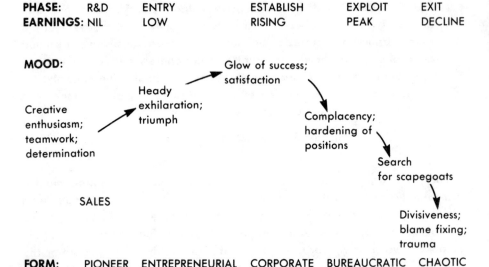

PHASE:	R&D	ENTRY		ESTABLISH	EXPLOIT	EXIT
EARNINGS:	NIL	LOW		RISING	PEAK	DECLINE

MOOD:

Glow of success;
satisfaction

Heady
exhilaration;
triumph

Creative
enthusiasm;
teamwork;
determination

Complacency;
hardening of
positions

Search
for scapegoats

SALES

Divisiveness;
blame fixing;
trauma

FORM:	PIONEER	ENTREPRENEURIAL	CORPORATE	BUREAUCRATIC	CHAOTIC
TIME:					

EXHIBIT 3-1   Evolution of people's moods, needs, and motivations that follow a second wave corporate evolution. **Source:** Adapted from William S. Royce and Arnold Mitchell, Report No. 635, *Stakeholder Values and Corporate Success.* Copyright 1980 by Business Intelligence Program, SRI International.

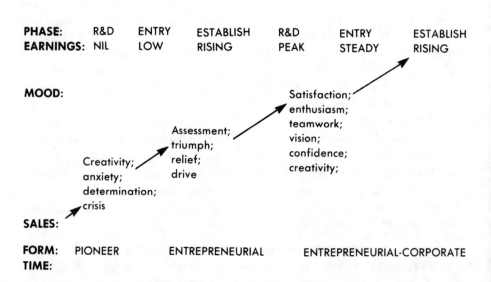

PHASE:	R&D	ENTRY	ESTABLISH	R&D	ENTRY	ESTABLISH
EARNINGS:	NIL	LOW	RISING	PEAK	STEADY	RISING

MOOD:

Satisfaction;
enthusiasm;
teamwork;
vision;
confidence;
creativity;

Assessment;
triumph;
relief;
drive

Creativity;
anxiety;
determination;
crisis

SALES:

FORM:	PIONEER	ENTREPRENEURIAL	ENTREPRENEURIAL-CORPORATE
TIME:			

EXHIBIT 3-2   Evolution of people's moods, needs, and motivations that follow a third wave corporate evolution.

One of the most dramatic stories I can remember which illustrates this point is the one about Alexander the Great when he was marching with his weary army across the Persian desert on his return from India. As water ran out, he was offered the last cup. He lifted the cup high above his head and poured it into the sand. With that gesture, it seemed as though the whole army drank as one, and marched on with a renewed and heightened spirit. In another story, upon setting out to conquer the East, Alexander distributed all his property to his men (the first profit sharing?) and was asked, "What have you left for yourself?" He replied, "My hopes." He and his men went on to a wave of conquests that were limited in the end only by his death. Alexander was also careful to give his men a larger purpose than the simple gain of gold and profit, that purpose being to unite all people in peace and brotherhood. To carry out this end, he had all his men and himself marry women from the East.

Napoleon was another outstanding example of a motivator of men, one who understood that it is easier to lead men by their hearts than by their minds. He said that if only the medals would hold out he would one day rule the world. The larger purpose to which Napoleon committed his men was to bring *liberté, egalité,* and *fraternité* (freedom, equality, and brotherhood) to all. The revolution he led became a European revolution. At times the number of men of non-French origin in his army vastly outnumbered his French soldiers. These motivating sentiments were in part developed from the ideology put forward by Thomas Jefferson as the purpose for the American Revolution.

On a more simple everyday level, there are excellent examples of fine tuning. In *The Creative Organization,* David Olgilvy, of Olgilvy and Mather, discusses how the head chef at the Majestic, where he worked when he lived in Paris, could tell by the patter in the kitchen what needed to be tuned and how. The head chef once walked over to Olgilvy, who was making a soufflé, and told everybody quietly, "That is how to do it." Olgilvy's commitment and productivity increased significantly from that moment on. The art of creating the most excellent cuisine possible was the larger purpose to which the head chef had committed his troop. Olgilvy also describes how emotionally bereft people feel upon leaving a well-functioning organization.

A plant manager at one of GM's new "self-managed" plants was asked to account for the increased productivity of the plant. He replied that it was due to the ability of the self-managed work groups to self-design and self-tune themselves within the new corporate environment.

The organic third wave corporation is a dynamic flux of interacting emotions, principles, objectives, moods, spirit, motivations, drives, and concepts. The organic manager continually gains insights into how these various forces in flux interact and understands how to stimulate, "genetically" engineer, and splice together a viable, living, evolutionary organization.

CREATING AN ORGANIC CORPORATION

How then is such an organic corporation created? How does it come into being? How is such synergy achieved?

To answer these questions, let us look at the DNA, the genetic code, for one of the best examples of such a corporation—Hewlett-Packard.

The achievements of an organization are the results of the combined efforts of each individual in the organization working toward common objectives. These objectives should be realistic, should be clearly understood by everyone in the organization, and should reflect the organization's basic character and personality.

The objectives are:

* *Profit:* To achieve sufficient profit to finance our company growth and to provide the resources we need to achieve our other corporate objectives.
* *Customers:* To provide products and services of the highest quality and the greatest possible value to our customers, thereby gaining and holding their respect and loyalty.
* *Fields of interest:* To build on our strength in the company's traditional fields of interest, and to enter new fields only when it is consistent with the basic purpose of our business and when we can assure ourselves of making a needed and profitable contribution to the field.
* *Growth:* To let our growth be limited only by our profits and our ability to develop and produce innovative products that satisfy real customer needs.
* *Our people:* To help HP people share in the company's success, which they make possible; to provide job security based on their performance; to insure them a safe and pleasant work environment; to recognize their individual achievements; and to help them gain a sense of satisfaction and accomplishment from their work.
* *Management:* To foster initiative and creativity by allowing the individual great freedom of action in attaining well-defined objectives.
* *Citizenship:* To honor our obligations to society by being an economic, intellectual, and social asset to each nation and to each community in which we operate.

If the organization is to fulfill its objectives, it should strive to meet certain other fundamental requirements:

First, there should be highly capable, innovative people throughout the organization. Moreover, these people should have the opportunity—through continuing programs of training and education—to upgrade their skills and capabilities. This is especially important in a technical business where the rate of progress is rapid. Techniques that are good today will be outdated in the future, and people should always be looking for new and better ways to do their work.

Second, the organization should have objectives and leadership which generate enthusiasm at all levels. People in important management positions should not only be enthusiastic themselves, they should be selected for their ability to engender enthusiasm among their associates. There can be no place, especially among the people charged with management responsibility, for half-hearted interest or half-hearted effort.

Third, the organization should conduct its affairs with uncompromising honesty and integrity. People at every level should be expected to adhere to the highest standards of business ethics, and to understand that anything less is totally unacceptable. As a practical matter, ethical conduct cannot be assured by written policies or codes; it must be an integral part of the organization, a deeply ingrained tradition that is passed from one generation of employees to another.

Fourth, even though an organization is made up of people fully meeting the first three requisite requirements, all levels should work in unison toward common objectives, recognizing that it is only through effective effort that the ultimate in efficiency and achievement can be obtained.

It has been our policy at Hewlett-Packard not to have a tight military-type organization, but rather to have overall objectives which are clearly stated and agreed upon, and to give people the freedom to work toward those goals they determine best for their own areas of responsibility.

Our Hewlett-Packard objectives were initially published in 1957. Since then they have been modified from time to time, reflecting the changing nature of our business and social environment.[11]

KEY TO SUCCESSFUL ORGANIC MANAGEMENT

The key words in Hewlett-Packard's "DNA," or in any corporation's DNA, are *communication, commitment, integrity, creativity,* and *initiative.*[12] The synergy of interacting parts cannot be realized without constant communication of objectives: Where are you and the company going? Commitment is the motivating force that gives form to the organism. Integrity gives structural strength to the interactive form. Creativity and initiative generate the evolution of the organism, which allows it to adapt to changing requirements. If the parts were individual knits in a cloth, integrity would be its bonded strength, the corporate philosophy the weaver's warp or guide, commitment the quality of the material, and creativity and initiative the spirit and mind of the weaver in whom the parts are integral.

The organism becomes like the rugby team in which each player knows what role to play in any circumstance. The players know (1) where the team is going; (2) the longer term objective—to win the game and the league championship; (3) the short-term objective—to score; and (4) when the ball is in the air, who is to be there to receive it and exactly what that person will do with it. All the team members have confidence in themselves and their teammates. If a player tosses the ball without looking, or even without thinking, his instincts and those of his colleagues will be effective and efficient in catching it. This is the team as a corporate organism.

I had once thought it a joke that the British Empire was created on the playing fields of Eton. It is not. Communication can be clear and efficient only upon well-traveled ground.

> They are what might be called "dual" or "poly" organizations, capable of assuming two or more distinct structural shapes as conditions warrant— rather like some plastic of the future that will change shape when heat or cold is applied but spring back into a basic form when the temperature is in its normal range.

> Alvin Toffler
> *The Third Wave,* 1980

This kind of organic polymorphism will avoid the problem of the schizophrenic organization. One of the primary causes of the schizophrenic organization has been the second wave hierarchy in which "intelligent" people, many with MBAs or more advanced degrees, were fed into the upper layers to make decisions and to create solutions. Those presumed to be not so intelligent were fed into the lower strata. The people fed into the upper strata were trained to and were expected to *have* solutions or explanations, not to *seek out* and develop solutions. The lower level people were not expected to have solutions. Consequently, the organization often developed a split personality. The people who actually did the work, knew many of the solutions, and had new ideas were not consulted; but when the people at the upper layers did develop solutions, those solutions often did not quite fit the reality. This often led to schism and conflict. To allow ideas and solutions to emanate from the lower levels would devalue a company's investment in education, would unbalance the organization, and would undermine authority. If the higher echelon had to go to the lower levels for ideas and solutions, how could they justify being paid more?

People previously trained in business academics usually developed very linear, mechanical views of progress, profit, and management. A deviation from this view often left them uneasy, and feeling that they had somehow been devalued. They were not trained to think but to plug numbers or people into formulas, to administrate set systems. This attitude fostered schizophrenia in the organization, as did a number of other inconsistencies. The only solution for such a company is to develop an organic organization in which people share responsibility, profits, and authority. Management will still be needed to make this sort of organization happen. Management needs to be a catalyst, a creative force (which may be why most managers in Japan come from some creative background, such as engineering, and not generally from a business or law training), a role model, and a guide to released energy.

THE ORGANISM'S INTERNAL DYNAMICS

It takes two to Tandem

Tandem Corporation slogan
California, 1977

ORGANIC ACTION

Some months ago, I was standing on the deck of a popular restaurant near Ocean City, Maryland, watching the seemingly erratic behavior of a school of small fish. The school moved randomly in one direction, then moved suddenly in another, with no apparent purpose. Yet, upon closer examination, the fish seemed to be pursuing various insects or small water creatures that would intersect the course of the school at random points. A fish would immediately notice this "target of opportunity" and go after it. The whole school would quickly realign itself behind this fish and pursue the new direction with precision and speed, until another fish noticed another opportunity, which would replace the one already exploited. The new opportunity seemed to be communicated instantly to all the other members of the school, and the group decided as one to pursue the new objective. That school, made up of many different individual fish, acted as an organic whole. Each and every objective was not achieved, but it is interesting how quickly the school would realize that it was pursuing a poor objective and would find a substitute.

The organic third wave corporation follows such a model. It may, however, have to be more plastic; that is, the corporation may have to be able to mold itself instantly into several high-powered groups pursuing several but related objectives, as well as be able to align itself into a precise and swift organic whole. In a 1969 *Forbes* article, Henry Singleton coincidentally compared Teledyne's companies to a school of fish. A friend of mine pointed out what Singleton had failed to say—all of Teledyne's companies were inside his net, and that net was the corporate warp he had designed.

FORMULA RIGIDITY

In the second wave corporation, there was usually only one direction dictated by the formula. The firm required that individuals carry out the formula, and if they didn't, there were always others (slack) who would. Implementation did not require initiative or creativity, which in many circumstances would have resulted only in the subversion of both the formula and its related objective— obedience and loyalty above all.

To encourage such characteristics, second wave corporations tried to instill the belief that if you (as the employee) obeyed the rules, the organization would take care of you. If you didn't, there was always somebody capable who was willing to take your place. Just as the second wave society encouraged the production of standardized and similar products, it insisted on standardized and similar employees. You were an expendable input into the formula, not a part of the company, even though you were dependent upon the company and the formula for a monetary income, very often for your economic survival. To foster this dependence, the company would "urge" and often even intimidate you into marriage, children, and an income-debilitating mortgage.

At best, employees of the second wave corporation resented this dependence and the accompanying imposition of their personalities. A "they" and "us" syndrome developed, demarked usually as management versus workers. The work environment was one of continuous threat, real or implied, and the ultimate and quite reasonable reaction was: "Why should I do any more than the minimum for these bastards!"

Unfortunate or fortunate as this attitude was, management surprisingly expected and factored it into the formula. One second wave manager had inscribed in Latin on a brass plaque upon his wall, "Let them hate so long as they obey." Another was quoted as saying that employees should "not only eat it, but they should eat it with a smile and ask for seconds!" This attitude, however, is changing as managers become educated and sensitized, as indicated by the following quote from a Ford manager[1] on restoring a sense of proprietorship.

> If you expect a worker to fail and you put half a dozen inspectors down the line to catch his mistakes, he'll probably meet your expectations. If, however, you give him a say in how his job is done, if you incorporate his suggestions into the manufacturing process, and if you tell him he's responsible for assuring that the product he helped design works every time, he will make far fewer mistakes.
>
> Louis E. Lataif, general manager
> Ford Division

As early as 1945, Peter Drucker observed many of these problems, and management was clearly aware of them; but change did not come about because our values and economics did not demand change. The pressures of the third wave had not yet been applied, and society had not yet experienced the value shifts of the wave.

> There is little chance for anybody below the executive level to find satisfaction in a job whose relation is very obscure. For the great majority of automobile workers, the only meaning of the job is in the pay check, not in anything connected with the work or product. Work appears as something unnatural, a disagreeable, meaningless, and stultifying condition of getting the pay check devoid of dignity as well as importance. No wonder that this puts a premium on slovenly work, on slow downs, and on other tricks to get the same pay check with less work. No wonder that results in the unhappy discontented worker—because a pay check is not enough to base one's self-respect on. The best way to sum up is by quoting a craftsman of the old school [typical of the independent entrepreneur] whom I met years ago. He had just decided to leave a well-paid job in the automobile industry. When I asked him why he was unhappy in Detroit, he said "The whole place is on relief; even if they have jobs, they still behave and act as if they were unemployed."
>
> Peter Drucker
> The Concept of the Corporation, 1945

Another precept of second wave management was the old "divide and conquer" routine in which employees were continually set against one another. All were encouraged to form rival groups. Although this did provide some useful competitive drive, the internecine strife was destructive and often led to the decline of the corporation. A member's existence in the corporation meant nothing other than survival and defeat of the enemy. In the final analysis, the formula was all that mattered, as was true in the case of Geneen and ITT. A common joke at the time had it that Geneen insisted on pointing out to his subordinates that he and God had the same first initial!

CORPORATION MEMBERS—THE CELLS OF THE ORGANISM

The third wave corporation cannot afford to operate with slack. People are no longer expendable in the third wave corporation because each and every one is a unique store of precisely applicable expertise (human capital), or else they would not be there. Along with respect for the unique contributive capability of the individual, a more collaborative work ethic has returned to the work place. Group decision making is required because once the decision is made, everyone's cooperation is necessary for successful implementation. No one can be replaced effectively. The corporation's capital, therefore, becomes invested primarily in its constituent people and not in its plant and equipment. Its people have been given a share of the "action"—stock or shares in the company—plus other forms of variable, indirect income, such as recreation facilities. A sense of proprietorship is restored, and the failure or success of the corporation belongs to its people in a real sense. As it is theirs and as a major part of their lives are entwined in it, the corporation becomes, in the organic sense, a central focus for people's beliefs and puts meaning into their lives.

The corporate culture can no longer simply assert a number of rules, it also must provide meaning. In a New Yorker article (June 1983), Schlumberger's CEO said that meaning in terms of the corporate culture was beginning to replace religion. Flexibility and personal satisfaction—putting out as much as one can because one's friends and partners, not "those bastards," are depending on you—have become important, so there is less effort to create a monetary dependence upon the company via accelerated marriage plans, children, and mortgages. Individuals are freer to seek such objectives at their own natural pace. In a recent APPLE advertisement, a cleverly hidden note from one individual to another suggested that they get together and share their lives because they shared so much in the beliefs of the "Samurai Ichiban Corporation," seemingly a code name for APPLE. Marriage has become a part of belief and not of formula in a corporate sense.

Peter Drucker, in *Concept of the Corporation,* was one of the first to comment upon the relationship of work to emotion. During World War II, the army had offered to bring a bomber to a plant to show the workers the ultimate result and function of a number of small but necessary parts that they were making. The plant manager refused initially but later relented.

> It seemed to him not only a waste of time that would have been better on production, but also without interest to the workers. To his amazement, this visit created the most intense excitement among the workers and resulted in an almost unbelievable increase in morale and productive efficiency. . . . It was from the maintenance crew that the workers first learned what the parts were which they had been producing for two years, where they were used in the bomber, and how important they were. It had never occurred to management to inform the workers of such elementary facts; nor had it ever occurred to management that knowledge of these facts might have any effect on worker morale and productivity. The manager himself concluded from this experience that it is his most important reconversion job to establish a relationship between the workers and their peacetime product as close and as satisfying as that established by the bomber visit.

The participant in the organic corporation has ceased to be an "employee" and instead had become a partner, a consumer, a producer, a recreative partner, and a contributor in a long-run adventure. He or she is no longer a commodity to be factored into the formula; what the participant does must provide usable information. Since that information is a product of what the participant does, he or she consumes a large measure of what is created. In that sense, the information does not disappear once it is consumed; it is passed on as a corporate product.

Decentralization of the entrepreneur

The participant in the corporation may not necessarily be a long-term member of the corporation. Recent surveys have shown that as many as 35 percent of those who work for corporations could work at home. These people and the corporation may eventually realize a better and more profitable margin for all if employees worked at home as individual entrepreneurs or corporate contractees. These entrepreneurs would receive higher monetary incomes from the corporation as well as be able to contract out their services to other corporations. Home-based entrepreneurs would also serve the corporation's need to be flexible and to act with a minimum number of people. It is much

70

harder and takes longer to get a consensus when there are too many people involved.

Communication, as well as communication of direction, is key in the well-run corporation, so that all participants may work in synchronization with a maximum of synergy. As Jim Treybig, the CEO of Tandem, has said:

> In a start-up company of 30 people, passing the philosophy by "word of mouth" is easy, and with 1,500 employees it is still possible. But when the company grows from 1,500 to 11,500, it becomes a much more difficult task to share the philosophy in this manner.[2]

Self-management

In order for people to give all that they have, they must pull in the direction to which they have a natural tendency. They must pull in "tandem" and they must pull as specified by the corporate culture if the maximum synergy and directional power are to be obtained.

Tandem considers it essential that each participant know in which direction the company is going and, in relation to that, in which direction the participant is going. In this way, people can "self-manage" their function. However, self-management requires above-average or "outstanding" people. Not quite outstanding people may have to be peer managed or supervised by a manager. Unfortunately, management supervision necessitates an extra corporate layer, increasing costs and lowering efficiency and effectiveness.

Outstanding people are the foundation upon which Tandem and any other organic corporation are based. Direction and strategy, financial resources, and a definition of the environment flow from people. A structural flaw in the foundation and in its relationships clearly will cause a firm to crumble. If profits are not distributed equitably to participants, the best will leave, corporate strategy and direction will suffer, and profits will fall. In turn, the firm's diminished financial status will lessen its capability to hire outstanding people. When members of a corporation have developed organic and dynamic patterns of interrelating, feedback and initiation of new action and new feedback will flow automatically.

Self-management and team spirit can be utilized effectively only when all participants in a firm perceive a significant challenge, a significant opportunity (reward), and competition. As corporations get larger and obtain more stability and market control, they lose the ability to challenge and motivate their participants in direct proportion to their size. Instead of looking for opportunities through the growth and expansion of the corporation, participants begin to look for opportunities internally (bureaucratic politics), to look

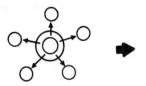

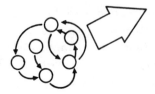

Centrally
directed firm:
momentum is lost in
conflict resolution
and directional enforcement

Self-managed (team)
organic firm:
momentum is
synergized and
maximized

EXHIBIT 4-1   In a self-managed organic firm in which members work as a team, effort
and momentum are synergized and maximized.

elsewhere (another corporation), or to look to their own ventures. A firm can maintain an organic and entrepreneurial critical mass only by keeping units competitively small and challenged. Although it is important to keep the drive alive, many of the corporate functions, such as, shipping and receiving may work effectively with less than the maximum amount of creativity and innovation. These functions are the "channels" of innovation; to be effective they must be efficient. To be efficient they must have all the "bugs" worked out, on a continuous basis. They are what make creativity and innovation real. Opponents of the Roman legions said, "Their drills were bloodless battles and their battles bloody drills!"[3]

In order to get the jump on the competition, a firm must respond with lightening speed and precision. A member of a championship rugby team, which consistently devastated its opponents, said that the team's success was due to many hours of practice and drill. Then, when they played the competition, each member _knew_ in almost every circumstance what every other member was likely to do and where each would be without having to think or even look. The reaction and initiation time of the team was significantly less than any competitor as a result. In relationship to the practice and reaction concept, the Japanese apply the JIT (Just In Time) process to their channels as well as to their inventories. The effective team reminds me of the school of fish whose action and interaction appear instinctive and instantaneous.

The clever combatant looks to the effect of combined energy and does not require too much from individuals. He takes individual talent into account and uses each man according to his capabilities. He does not demand perfection from the untalented. When he utilizes combined energy, his fighting men become, as it were . . . the momentum of a round stone rolled down a mountain thousands of feet in height.

Sun Tzu
The Art of War

THE CORPORATION AS A LIVING ORGANISM

The organic corporation is a living organism that, according to its nature, is disposed to be eternal. The corporation has seen many forms since its inception, among which has been its short-term use as an instrument of extraction. The extraction has been from nature and from society for immediate personal gain. Immediate personal gain was an effective motive for first wave society. Adam Smith said that the overall best interests of first wave society resulted from each individual entrepreneur seeking his or her own best interest, but Smith could not foresee the long-term consequences of second wave technology, and the social, environmental, and institutional characteristics of corporations.

The corporation, however, was created as a perpetual institution to serve the needs of society, chief among which were the people who composed the corporation. Chief Justice John Marshall commented upon the characteristics of the corporation in 1816. "Among the most important are immortality . . . and individuality, properties by which a perpetual succession of men, in succession, with these qualities and these capacities, that corporations were invented and are In use."[4] Marshall saw corporations not only as purveyors of particular products or services—"these capacities"—but also as purveyors of certain ethics—"these qualities"—without which the corporation implicitly could not maintain its capacities.

IBM's DYNAMICS

The IBM corporation is one of the most outstanding examples of the internal and socially oriented corporation that embodies a defined ethic. Thomas Watson, Sr., considered the company an eternal extension of himself, his values, and his family. Even today, many years after his death, his myth, his ethics, and his style are still alive and considered to be the driving force behind the company by most participants in IBM. One of his biographers has said: "The metamorphosis was complete. Watson was IBM."[5]

In its early stages under Watson, IBM was one of the first basic prototypes of the organic corporation. Watson learned his lessons well at NCR, an early primitive version of the organic corporation under the extraordinary leadership of Jimmy Patterson. Patterson created what is referred to as a "paternalistic," although ruthless and bloodthirsty corporation. When asked about his motives for being what was then considered extraordinarily paternalistic, he said: "It pays. Hungry people, people with bad diets or in poor health are not good producers."[6] He built facilities that would be considered unnecessarily extravagant even today in many regions. The facilities not only contained pools, glass walls, good lighting, dining and changing areas, flowers, vines, private lockers and showers, but employees were entitled to free hot meals, medical care, and family counseling. In return, participants were expected to give their full loyalty, enthusiasm, and commitment to the company's ethics, prosperity, and corporate "soul." In short, for salvation, employees had to become converts to the corporate religion. Among the activities participants performed in obedience and conformity was attendance at inspirational "sermons" that would serve to "uplift their souls." Every participant (including Watson himself) was trained in how to act, dress, play, and exercise, in where to live, and sometimes in whom to marry. The company also engaged in the most ruthless of business tactics in order to "knock out" its competitors, which ultimately resulted in the prosecution and conviction of Patterson, Watson, and other associates for the restraint of trade.

Watson refined and improved the lessons he had learned at NCR after he was fired by Patterson and was forced to start his own business. One of his major improvements was the elimination of "bossism." No one was to function as the traditional "boss" who only made decisions by saying yes or no. Watson's company leaders had to work harder than anyone else to get the job done, and they had to give maximum assistance to other members. The NCR system of awards, medals, conventions, and general positive reinforcement was expanded. Even corporate songs were made part of corporate life eventually. Watson's primary improvement was to generate dual drives in the organization. He realized that IBM could not evolve and survive if the company followed one defined template. Not only must all participants *believe* in IBM, they must also *think* to generate creativity and innovation.

> We are one great big family. . . . If you look upon me as the head of the family, I want you to come to me as often as you feel that I can do anything for you. Feel free to come and open your hearts and make your requests, just the same as one would in going to the head of a family.
>
> Thomas Watson, Sr.
> IBM

Watson recognized, rewarded, and promoted capable managers. Incompetent managers were demoted to positions in which they could be more useful or they were fired, instead of being promoted to some, often ficticious, senior post. The layers of useless and costly management thus were avoided. The company progressed in part also by pursuing some of the more aggressive NCR practices, so it too came under federal antitrust and restraint of trade prosecution. In spite of Watson's favorite admonition, "Never feel satisfied," IBM fell prey to complacency and became a partially bureaucratic organization. Bureaucratic politics became so common that an executive's main occupation was described as "playing office." The old IBM paternalism was considered a thing of the past and was replaced by regimentation and Machiavellianism. The most frightening vision IBM executives maintained at the time was one of rampant free enterprise, both within the company and without. Many of the advanced corporate executives did and still do consider this kind of corporate aging to be dangerous to the long-term health of the company.

In the last few years, IBM has begun to deal with its bureaucratic problems by, first, attempting the redesign of the corporation as an entrepreneurial-corporate organization and, second, exploring the new business opportunities that opened up when the government dropped its antitrust prosecution. For logical and aesthetic reasons, Tom Watson, Jr., was bothered by the regimentation, conformity, lack of assertiveness, and avoidance of risk that had begun to characterize the company. He complained that if he were to come in one morning wearing a pink shirt, everyone would come in the next morning wearing the same thing—however, the consensus was that the chances of Mr. Watson ever wearing a pink shirt were next to zero!

Watson gave orders to recruit "wild ducks," people who did not conform and were not afraid to think deviant thoughts. (A common skeptical response in the company about this was that "even wild ducks have to fly in formation.") Even so, such activities as the singing of somewhat mindless company songs were phased out, and massive amounts of money were pumped into research and development. Entrepreneurialism, risk-taking, and innovative thinking are once again becoming valued ethics at IBM.

In pursuit of its new image, IBM tells the following story about Henry Ford and his Fellows program, although some people who knew Henry Ford find the story doubtful.

> The story goes that Henry Ford hired an efficiency expert to evaluate his company. After a few weeks, the expert made his final report. It was highly favorable except for one thing. "It's that man down the hall," said the expert. "Every time I go by his office he's just sitting there with his feet on his desk. He's wasting your money." "That man," replied Mr. Ford, "once had an idea that saved us millions of dollars. At that time I believe his feet were planted right where they are now." At IBM, we have 46

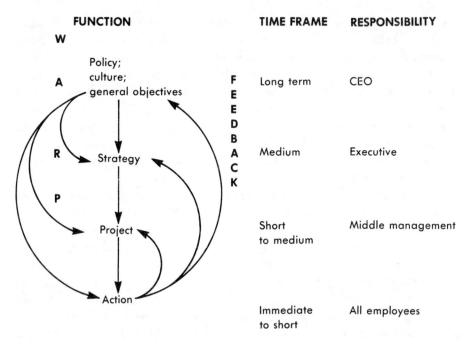

FUNCTION	TIME FRAME	RESPONSIBILITY

W

A Policy; culture; general objectives — Long term — CEO

FEEDBACK

R Strategy — Medium — Executive

P Project — Short to medium — Middle management

Action — Immediate to short — All employees

EXHIBIT 4-2 Time frame in which all members of an organic firm carry out their responsibilities, which are dictated by the corporate warp.

people like that, and we don't worry about where they put their feet either. . . . We may not always know what they're doing, much less how they do it. But we do know this: The best way to inspire an IBM Fellow is to get out of the way.[7]

Tom Watson, Jr., and his colleagues gradually shifted the corporate behemoth toward a more entrepreneurial mode. Whether the elephant has learned to tap dance yet still meets with some disagreement, but no one can disagree that IBM is trying.

The company also has become a significant social institution, supporting universities, initially Columbia, government research, charities, and communities throughout the world. People at IBM understand that precise, constructive efforts even outside of the immediate corporate sphere can be crucial to the corporation's long-term positive evolution.

Profit is not limited to this year's bottom line. The company has pioneered its dynamics on a social level as well as on a business one. New forms of management, such as IBUs, have been developed along with efforts to increase minority entrepreneurship because IBM recognizes that it is an open, not a closed, system.

5

THE ORGANISM'S EXTERNAL DYNAMICS

Think!

IBM

CORPORATIONS AND THEIR ENVIRONMENT

The second wave corporation evolved to manage and control the market, the environment. The third wave corporation must, however evolve and be designed to interact with the environment, to support the required mutual interdependence. The market or environment of the third wave cannot be controlled. The number of dynamic organizations or systems with which the corporation must interact effectively has greatly increased, so that in order for the third wave corporation to survive and prosper, it needs to be designed to interact with and react effectively to other dynamic systems that compose its environment. The correct design maximizes mutual profit and synergy between a corporation and a system.

Some systems interacting with the corporation are tangible, such as other corporations and governments; but others, such as the economic system, the social value system, the community, and the international system of politics, are less so. Although interactions involving these systems and the corporation did take place during the second wave as a matter of course, they have multiplied in number and form during the third wave.

Inflation, interest rates, and consumer confidence are among the economic factors that have changed erratically and rapidly during the third wave, making the reciprocal actions and influences that corporations and the community have upon each other critical.

MOTIVATION, DEMOTIVATION, AND DECLINE

The CEO of Schlumberger recently spoke of the only two things that might, in the long run, threaten the company. The first was thermonuclear war, over which the company has no control. The second and also "deadly" factor is demotivation, which Schlumberger can control to a certain extent.

> In less than thirty years, although America has the same natural resources, has the best educational system in the world, has the most innovative technical creativity, I think it is a fact that many Americans became demotivated. You can notice it whether you ride in a taxi in New York, whether you shop in a department store in Houston, whether you try to cash a check in a bank in Boston, whether you travel on most U.S. airlines. Workers and employees have lost the motivation that moved America forward after the war. During the same period, an exactly opposite trend took place in Japan. . . . America fell asleep. Is Schlumberger going to fall asleep too?

> P. Riboud, CEO
> Schlumberger, 1983

Whether Mr. Riboud is right or not, his concerns do highlight the very important interaction between the corporate culture and the national culture, local culture, or current mood.

For example, a local church group held "brainstorming" sessions in which ideas on what they wanted now and in the future were written up on "flip charts." They were as follows:

Now:

More ecumenical events, such as a special thanksgiving service

A well-*organized* church and school

Evening bible study group

Weekly *prayer* group

RESPONSIBLE

COMMUNICATIVE

SYSTEM

Traditionalists and Modernists working together amicably toward a parish with unity under God

More trees

Happiness in work and worship

Monthly Saturday church cleanup and pot luck dinner

By 1985:

Monthly socials

Evenings for music in the library (Big bands & Beethoven)

Functions by lay ministers

Becoming a center of value for the community

Regular evensong

Guest speakers with different points of view

Musical training for nonmusical people

More landscaping

Establish a companion foreign parish

Help to the local needy—financial and other

By 1988:

- Increase the number of memberships of young families with children by 50 percent
- Reach goal of new church building fund that includes development of a music and culture center
- Complete landscaping
- Hold regular music socials
- Retain and increase flexibility and respect for other points of view
- Foster children and teen groups
- Develop the existing ministry in ancient, traditionalist, and contemporary doctrine

- Increase education of parishioners
- Double the list of parishioners
- Purchase a new organ
- Enrich church programs
- Install stained glass
- Increase awareness and involvement of its members in social issues

This small church group is evidently much more aware of itself than many large corporations. It realizes how it wants to function; where it is going; what is its place in the environment and community; and what are and should be its important values and activities.

The origin of the "sleeping sickness" seems to lie in large corporations. People working in large companies still care and are motivated, but the channels for their creativity and motivation have become hardened and obsolete. A recent *Fortune* magazine article[1] indicated that many people are bored by the tedium in large corporate bureaucracies. Out of ennui, participants actually fall asleep sometimes, and the sleepers are not just the junior officers. Such mind "blitzing" is not only harmful to the individual, it also damages a corporation's ability to think, plan, and execute collectively.

THE CORPORATION'S PLACE

In many instances, the large corporation has forgotten that it is as much a community group as the small church is. The corporation is composed of community members and is responsible to its participants, to its community, and to society. People in the community have come together to pursue a set of values and a mission that gives purpose and meaning to their lives. The corporation is not a singular entity divorced from society, but an organic assembly of many interacting members operating under a set of shared values and objectives. As such, the corporation exists in its people, in their homes, families, and town halls. To remain viable and meaningful, the corporation must play an important part in the community and in society. Spread over many homes and families, the corporation does not exist only in a factory or an office building; the totality that is the corporation embodies its interaction within society as well as within itself.

Someone once said that the largest, most effective organization in the world is the Catholic church, which is involved in numerous activities but has the least amount of management layers. The Church does not function under the guidance of direct management but under the corporate warp or philosophy of Catholic theology. By its very nature, the organization is adaptive and organic, interacting and integrating with its environment in a natural, flexible, and systematic manner. Perhaps the primary reason for the Catholic Church's successful development is its active cultivation of its market, primarily to benefit the Church itself. By definition, all members of the organizational structure actively believe in the Church's purpose and in their own mission as a consequence.

Similarly, Toyota hopes that everyone who purchases one of its products or who works in the company will become a member of the Toyota "family" and a believer in its products. The company is not so much seeking the short-run profits or market share that can be obtained by price cuts, but longer term adherents.

THE NEEDS OF THE CONSUMER

The typical second wave relationship between customer and producer was that the consumer bought what the producer chose to sell, and was "educated" to like it through advertising. Often a confrontational type of relationship resulted. Consumer and producer negotiated to see who could get the best immediate "deal," which usually benefitted the producer. This type of relationship alienated both parties and engendered a negative atmosphere in business. Consumer advocates, such as Ralph Nader, arose to challenge and expose the formula managers, e.g., General Motors.

Toyota seeks to avoid this type of confrontational relationship based upon the short-term gain, as many other Japanese companies do. Instead, Toyota searches for a point at which the needs of the consumer and of the company can best be met in order for both to get the best long-term deal. When the consumer's and the producer's needs are met, mutual trust and confidence develop between both. The Japanese see this as building an increasingly large business "net," or network, because the consumer is a business associate with whom the company again hopes to do business. The company considers the consumer who buys its product as someone who has voted for it and who believes in it. Have you ever met a politician who is not sincerely gratified when you mention you voted for him? To a company like Toyota, the consumer is, therefore, someone to be respected and treated with benevolence; hence the corporate emphasis is on quality and service.

Whether second wave approaches to the consumer are possible any longer is questionable because the consumer has better access to information and has many more choices. Imagine you have something you need done, but you need a special type of product to do it. Product A does 60 percent of the job, B does 70 percent, and C, 90 percent. They all cost the same, but clearly product C has greater *delivered* utility. The consumer can no longer be "educated" to buy a product; instead the product must reliably do the job. The consumer is now a part of the corporation.

As the third wave progresses and as competition and costs mount, each company must constantly accelerate its delivery of efficiency and effectiveness, the product's delivered utility. Each product, as its infused information intensity increases, becomes more of a specialized and reliable service. Each service becomes more individualized and tailored. No longer can the company say, as Henry Ford once said, "They can have any color as long as its black!" or as one of the robber barons once said, "The public be damned!" The public is now part of the company. If the company does not more precisely meet consumers' needs and whims, there is another one behind it that will or will try. The public no longer has to buy what the seller deigns to sell. The market is no longer a one-way street for any corporation. To meet the needs of the consumer more exactly, a tighter and more intense feedback loop has developed between consumers and their customers (corporations). *The essence of competition in the third wave is being first with the knowledge of what the consumer wants and/or needs.* Since a company is made up of people, each person in the company develops his or her own constituency, a segment of consumers to whom he or she is particularly responsive. The person thereby, to an extent, becomes a lobby for interests vital to the segment and the company. These representatives advance in the company, to a large measure, based on how keenly they perceive the requirements of "their" consumers, and how well the company capitalizes upon these perceptions.

INTEGRATING SUPPLIERS

Suppliers during the second wave were usually much smaller than the companies that controlled the market for their resultant consumer products. Because the consumer took what the company produced, the company also took what the suppliers produced with few questions asked. Suppliers, therefore, often were successful in developing a strong relationship with large companies. This state of affairs has changed, however, since increasing pressures from the environment have impacted upon these companies. The pressures are forced onto company suppliers in turn. Some corporations that have had particular suppliers on allocation now choose regarding price but with respect to quality also. For example, General Motors now considers U.S. Steel, formerly its steel supplier, on a competitive bid basis with other steel manufacturers.

Companies that receive defective parts are shipping these parts back to the supplier at the supplier's expense. Parts that fail under warranty are charged to the supplier (e.g., Jaguar). Company engineers and technicians are unexpectedly going through supplier's plants to inspect raw materials and manufacturing techniques. Probably at one time, suppliers thought such people to be myths. The pressures seem relentless as companies constantly demand

82

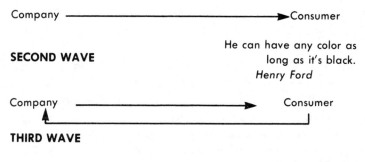

SECOND WAVE

He can have any color as
long as it's black.
Henry Ford

THIRD WAVE

EXHIBIT 5-1   Bonds increasingly tightened between the consumer and
the company in third wave feedback loops, as opposed to second wave loops
in which the company had control and had no need to receive consumer
feedback.

that their suppliers do better. The pressures give rise to many loud complaints
and concurrent anguish. The market is no longer easy and comfortable for
companies and/or their suppliers.

THE CORPORATION'S SELF-IMAGE

Ronald Reagan recently commented upon the relationship between images
and reality: "Perceptions are reality."[2] In that consumers often buy products
because of aesthetics and/or to fulfill some psychic need; nevertheless, they
seek to fill real needs, however intangible such needs may be. Why does a certain brand of toilet tissue cost significantly more than another that is almost
identical? Is it because a company like Procter & Gamble has the marketing and
advertising behind that brand. Why does a company buy a more expensive
computer that can do less than a cheaper one? Is it because the IBM computer
has an aesthetic quality that attracts the company's CEO or because the CEO
wants customers to identify him or her with IBM? Perceptions are reality, and a
company's image translates into actions. If spirits soar at a company because its
members feel more efficient with an IBM computer than with another kind, then
the company will be more efficient. If a consumer believes that he or she will be
happier with a Procter & Gamble product, that consumer will be. Images are
reality. Each employee in a company should take every opportunity to extend
and improve the company's image.

A company's self-image deserves constant attention because this image
defines its actions and will lead the company in a specified direction. The
company is also energy, energy going in a direction. Echoing Steve Jobs'

thoughts, APPLE's new president John Sculley talked about the energy of the company and the kind of people that gave it that energy:

> People who are achievement oriented, who like to get involved with things, who like to do things themselves and who are willing to make the investment in terms of time and money to get into personal computing and really get excited about it. If these people weren't doing personal computing, they'd be learning how to climb mountains. They're just high-energy people who really like to keep active. The kind of people that, if they're in business, you probably find in the office on Saturday mornings working on projects. You probably find them to be creative people who are interested in ideas, and people who really want to be on the frontier, on the leading edge of what's going on in the world.[3]

The corporation is a vehicle for energy and for adventure. An interactive energy and motivating force for adventure charges the business environment and makes all companies move with celerity. That is why APPLE placed a full page ad welcoming IBM to the personal computer market, to which APPLE adds "seriously." Companies are on a mutual, interactive course of high adventure whether they realize this course or not.

THE CORPORATION AS A SYSTEM OF BELIEF

Whether consciously or unconsciously, companies also are vehicles of national values and objectives. Many companies are becoming more sensitive to such values and objectives and to their international role in perpetuating and propagating them. Less and less do they see America's business as only business. Many high-technology firms will not do business with or in countries that conflict with their values. Steve Jobs will state, on every appropriate occasion, APPLE's part in this country's historical role and in helping to perpetuate American ideals.

The corporation is essentially an open system that emits values, images, products, waste, profits, utility, efficiency or inefficiency, effectiveness or ineffectiveness, and people as outputs into the environment. It absorbs similar things as inputs in return. A company's outputs and inputs enter into and return from an environment that is dynamic and organic in nature because it is composed of other active systems. The process of interaction is not mechanical but organic, therefore, it is not clearly definable and must be managed upon its form or parameters and not upon its structures. It is essentially a system of beliefs.

The reality of the open system is why corporate narcissism, a corporation being primarily concerned with its own internal structure, is so dangerous. The bureaucratic form is the most susceptible to this disease, usually because the corporation operating within this form believes that it has achieved indeterminate control over its markets or its environment. If the corporation becomes narcissistic, it will be less sensitive to reality. Its output products will gradually lose their value while the company will receive less input from the environment. If the corporation receives less and less from the environment, it becomes internally and externally unstable, requiring reorganization or subsidy. If it achieves enough of either, the corporation will again stabilize; if not it will gradually disintegrate.

In order to remain an open system, the corporation's objective should be to maintain an entrepreneurial-corporate organizational form. This form allows the corporation to organically adapt to the environment on an ongoing basis. By operating under this form, the corporation can attain a consensus of constant evolution and adaptation. With the corporate and bureaucratic organizational forms, this consensus does not exist. The bureaucratic company tries to ignore change, which results in its ultimate collapse. With the corporate form of operation, the corporation grudgingly concurs that change must come about because the company is really "up against it." The change is reactionary rather than anticipatory, such as occurred with most corporations in the auto industry. In the corporate form, people who try to initiate change, adaptation, and evolution without understanding the clear and evident critical danger may put themselves at risk. A corporation functioning under the entrepreneurial organizational form tries to be far ahead of change, whereas one using the gunslinger-pioneer form tries to make change. A corporation operating under the entrepreneurial-corporate form attempts to be slightly ahead of change.

Bureaucratic organizations are tilting at windmills and, though occasionally hitting one, are usually committing professional suicide, whatever the realities may be. When under serious threat, a bureaucracy will often seek to make sacrifices or create scapegoats rather than to change or adapt. The essence of a bureaucracy is the hierarchical power structure, which is threatened by any change. Its sacrifices, if available, are most often those who advocate change because change is the enemy. For example, a department that was trying to initiate change in one corporation was destroyed as a sacrifice. If no sacrifices or scapegoats are internally available, a corporation can bring in one, even at a senior level, or rent one, such as a consultant. Sacrificial offerings usually give the impression of serious change without anything really taking place. They often serve to prolong the status quo before stockholders, voters, and directors finally discover the fraud.

The increasing pressures to change often also increase the pressures on a bureaucracy to find sacrifices. In such companies, even change initiated from the top stands a poor chance of actually being implemented. Change initiated from lower levels is usually futile and suicidal. Chrysler, however, initiated change from the top with everyone "onside" and did succeed. Change may have to be precipitated by a crisis, whether it be real or manufactured.

Negative change occurs, for example, when large second wave organizations think that they can buy their way into the third wave by purchasing progressive companies in the electronic information field. More often than not, the result has been disastrous, as with Exxon, Schlumberger (initially), and Kodak. These companies tried to impose their hierarchical style upon the corporations they acquired. Second wave hierarchies were designed with interchangeable parts and people, like assembly lines, therefore, it did not matter who occupied the positions as long as those people could function on a second or even third rate level. In the third wave, however, it does matter who occupies what position because people *are* the corporation. First rate people will not generally work for third or second rate people, especially in a bureaucratic hierarchy, so they leave *and cannot be replaced.*

A second wave organization, requiring much analysis, many committees, and political gamesmanship, cannot function in a fast third wave environment in which decisions are required *right now.* The company cannot wait for political maneuverings. Many large corporations fell into traps of their own making, insisting that they, as the parent, knew better. After people leave and after taking significant losses, the company ends up as a shell. Such large corporations must understand that they cannot buy their way into the wave, nor do they necessarily know how to manage in the third wave. If they did, they would not try to buy in. Many corporations that have followed this path have shown little respect for what they have bought. Every corporation must realize that viability must start with its own transformation. If the corporate culture does not provide meaning and action, the company is going to lose good people who will find a corporation that has them or who will create their own. A company must have a competitive corporate culture if it is to survive and coexist with the environment and all other systems of society. This usually calls for a determined transformation and openness to new ideas.

6

AMERICAN ORGANIC MANAGEMENT

THE IDEOLOGICAL COUNTEROFFENSIVE

America has a pioneering spirit, a spirit of innovation we have to beat.

Japanese embassy attaché
1939

THE ESSENTIAL AMERICAN ETHIC

This Japanese opinion may seem somewhat surprising to many who experienced American second wave management, which was still the rage before World War II. What this Japanese attaché[1] was sensing was the undercurrent of innovation and creativity that flowed through American society and culture despite formula management. Even today, the Japanese are quick to concede America's strong lead in pioneering technologies.

Contrary to current popular belief, Japanese corporations were and many still are extremely bureaucratic and mechanical, although individual units within them are quite dynamic. Japan's national defeat in World War II made it quite clear that change and adaptation had to come about, and thus American ideology was grafted onto the Japanese tree. The ideology of entrepreneurial competition, of treating participants in the enterprise with dignity and respect, of seizing opportunities, of freedom to innovate, of collaboration, of technical quality, and of progress were not original Japanese ideas, as many currently seem to think. It was the synergy between Japanese tradition and heritage and American ideology that allowed Japan to take the economic offensive.

If anything these ideas were American, placed and given momentum during the formative stages of the American nation, but somehow these ideas became muddled and confused in America during the second wave. Corporate enterprise, formula management, and the resultant bureaucracy subverted

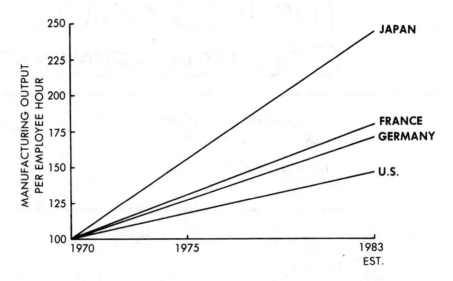

<u>EXHIBIT 6-1</u>   Productivity growth trends; manufacturing output per employee hour.

the momentum of free enterprise. When the third wave hit and increased entrepreneurialism and innovation, many American corporations and individuals found themselves unprepared and uncompetitive. In a sense, the Japanese have been beating us at a game we invented, a game upon which they have improved and added their own unique twists. The Japanese have incorporated an evolving internal corporate culture of innovation, collaboration, and entrepreneurialism. It is this evolutionary corporate ideology and related strategy that has given many Japanese corporations their advantage, drive, and momentum. Analysis is not necessarily part of the ideology, as MITI discovered after it hired two Ph.D. economists and then got rid of them relatively quickly. The corporate battleground is becoming much less one of formulas and abilities to apply large amounts of capital, and more one of ideologies, ideas, strategies, and information. These new determinants of the third wave are what create and destroy capital.

Many Japanese executives willingly trace the origins of their ideas for national collaborative planning and corporate management to Alexander Hamilton, to the Allied Commander General MacArthur, and to the desperate conditions after World War II that forced maximum cooperation.

American ideology started from an incredible base and developed free enterprise and freedom until the large corporation became dominant in American society with the advent of the second wave. Instead of being something in which the average person could take an active role, ideology became regulated to professional "politicians" and the realm of politics. Ideology did not enter the realm of the corporation. Formulas were of importance to the corporation, not ideology. The ideas that "We hold these truths to be self-evident [reality]: that all men are created equal [equal opportunity], that they are endowed . . . with Rights, . . . Life, Liberty, and the pursuit of Happiness [self-actualization]" compose free enterprise and were regulated outside the corporate realm.[2] While these powerful ideologies were considered worthy ideals by our founding "corporate" fathers, they were not considered by them to be in line with or applicable to the corporate "reality." Town meetings became a part of past history, as ideologic democracy gave way to "pragmatism".

The particular Japanese genius and circumstance allowed them to infuse dynamic ideology as the predominant force in their corporations. Such ideology (seen as one of the primary causes for the success of the American armed forces) could be applied with tremendously powerful results. Now some leading Japanese business leaders openly discuss how it is Japan's turn to reach and help America because of the debt that the Japanese incurred by learning so much from the Americans.

REVITALIZING AMERICAN IDEOLOGY

One of the reasons for Japan's progress in the business world has been its relatively small investment in its military, which has in part resulted from a provision put into the Japanese Constitution prohibiting the development of a war capacity, put there at American insistence. Another example of American influence is the good labor relations in Germany, including the participation of labor in key management decisions, which was instituted by Americans to encourage democracy.

Americans may or may not need this "help." A new generation of revitalized and ideology-driven American third wave companies has given strong new impetus to the American economy. Many, still however, refuse to confront reality or to act upon it for reasons that are part illusionary.

Two recent quotes from executives of a leading American corporation are:[3]

Now that we've got our act together, let's go out and kick ass!

We will devastate them.

Did they both miss the point? Can they understand that long-term success does not come from short-term aggression but from spirit, the spirit of thought and application which is permanent?

IMPORTANCE OF TALENT, VIRTUE, AND IDENTITY

There is a natural aristocracy among men . . . the grounds of these are virtue and talent. That form of government is best that provides for the pure selection of these natural aristoi into the offices of government [power].

Thomas Jefferson
1813

Results (virtue and talent), demonstrated both in the bottom line and in building the company, have become in most competitive corporations the preeminent criteria for rewards. A viable organic corporation dealing with a dynamic third wave environment must have a constant stream of results in addition to the ideas and motivating ideologies that provide the momentum for results. Promotion must be based on results or potential results, because although monetary rewards are important, maximum results cannot be obtained by such incentives alone. The participant in the corporation needs to believe in some larger purpose, meaning, or adventure—an individual must be able to realize an identity through the corporation.

James McDonnell, founder and CEO of McDonnell-Douglas, gave corporate briefings over the public address system on a regular basis. These briefings were often filled with high tension and emotion, especially during the company's key participation in the Apollo program, which landed a man on the moon. Perhaps the high point of these briefings was when MacDonnel gave a moving, moment-by-moment account of the mission's launch. To quote a senior executive, "There was not a dry eye in the place."[4]

Although it may be difficult for many CEOs to approach such a moment of high drama, whatever the corporation is engaged in is and should be made to be clearly understood as important. This understanding of corporate importance, of corporate adventure, and of the individual's importance in being a part of the action-adventure gives that extra drive to the corporation and identity to the individual.

> If an individual or people [or corporation] ceases to believe in itself, its ideals, others with firmer aims and beliefs will climb into the saddle. When a nation no longer desires place, power, position, influence, has no wish that its ways of thought should prevail, no desire to impress its seal upon future events, how can you suppose it will continue to stand in this hurly-burly world? Power in the world, the prizes of the world, must go to those who value them and think them worth the effort to secure. Civilizations arise and continue to exist—and all history is witness to the truth—when conditions are hard, only when they are continually threatened, only when they are determined to maintain and defend their rule. They decline and fall when the external pressure is removed, or the inner spirit decays.
>
> W. MacNeil Dixon, 1957
> Gifford Lectures
> St. Andrews University

THE AMERICAN COUNTEROFFENSIVE

American business needs to take an increased ideological counteroffensive. The American store of bankable ideology is massive, but it has not been used or built upon with much vigor in business since the time of Abraham Lincoln and the end of the first wave. The ethic has descended from the almost spiritual determination of the founding fathers "to make the world anew" to Calvin Coolidge's comment that "America's business is business" (business then being formulas). Ideology, ideas, information are what move the third wave, not formulas.

Some young Japanese executives who were recently queried for possible explanations concerning their country's success in relationship to American backwardness answered that American businesspeople do not really understand the necessity of cutting costs and slack and of improving competitiveness. Americans do not understand the context of the third wave. Further, American workers do not understand their part in the competitive race. Neither American executives nor workers understand the conceptual framework in which they operate.

Many people thought that it was innovative and generally a good idea when Ed Carlsen showed such interest in getting to know his new company, United Airlines, by walking around. What they did not realize was what was taking place on a subliminal level. He indicated by his dress, by his manner, and by his questions and expressions what was important and in what direction the corporation should now be taking, which indicated what fit at United and what did not. Like McDonnell, Carlsen was defining (1) meaning/ideology on a "real time" basis, (2) what was important, and (3) where the company was going and why. This is a positive definition. An example of negative definition was that of Harold Geneen of ITT. Geneen clearly demonstrated what was important (formulas, facts) but did not infuse the needed ethic or allow enough freedom for an intrinsic synergy to develop. As a result, ITT developed some serious problems after Geneen left, and to some extent, the company still suffers from the experience.

It's all blown to hell but the ethic is still there!

Tracy Kidder ("Tom West")
The Soul of a New Machine, 1983

Tom West is the fictional hero of a real-life development, the creation of a high-speed Data General computer, discussed in Tracy Kidder's novel, *The Soul of a New Machine.* He made the above comment after the project team was broken up after the successful completion of its mission. The corporate ethic or DNA code was the important aspect because it dictated the future evolutionary path of the corporation, no matter who became its participants. The evolutionary ethic defined how projects should be approached.

Creating corporate drive

A successful and popular method of creating a corporate ethic is to weave a legend or myth. The CEO of a rapidly growing Silicon Valley corporation said that his success in creating legends or corporate myths was due to his ability to foster the right internal *corporate* self-image and his knowledge of how to catch the right wave—a crisis or opportunity. One such legend is Edwin Lands going without food or sleep for two weeks while he developed his classic film to compete with the Kodak products. Corporate slogans, pictures, and songs are other methods by which ethics are encouraged. A corporation might even shift its operations to an area in which the local ethic is considered beneficial and may be infused into the firm. Some studies have shown that part of the success of corporations, like Maytag, is due to their geographical location where the local ethic is more productive.

A chief executive officer's keen sensitivity toward the internal and external dynamics of a corporate culture or ethic is essential to the development of a successful corporation. In a real sense, the CEO is a genetic designer or engineer. A genetic corporate design can be developed in many ways, including: (1) generation of the necessary ethics; (2) genetic splicing of people with the desired corporate genes; (3) setting of specific challenges that inspire a desired evolution; (4) engineering a careful merger or joint venture; (5) altering the operational field of the corporation; or (6) hiring a consultant to redesign, reorient, and reeducate the organism. Certain corporate genetic DNA has proved popular, such as that from Procter & Gamble, IBM, the Stanford Graduate School of Business, or the Harvard Business School, each of which represents a specific corporate design. Initially such people were sought because they possessed some formulas that would be useful. Increasingly they are being sought because they represent a specific and useful set of ethics that corporations can infuse into their corporate cultures.

Splicing corporate DNA

Alumax, with revenues over $1 billion annually, is a joint corporate venture between Mitsui of Japan and Amax of the United States. In many ways, it personifies the classical third wave corporation, even though the company is not in the high-technology or electronic information business. Alumax deals with the heavy and basic industry of aluminum production. It has a small dynamic core of less than 100 participants, including secretaries and clerks. Most operations are contracted out, and much of the corporate assets are in liquid form (e.g., short term deposits, cash), which allows the company to deal quickly in any new direction. Its earnings from such assets (interest) were particularly significant when interest rates shot through the ceiling, while other companies with large investments in plants, equipment, staff, and inventories suffered under the burden of high interest rates. Alumax is a successful blend of United States and Japanese corporate DNA.

Although an ideological counteroffensive is required by the United States, there is no reason why some of the better Japanese ideas cannot be usefully grafted to the American tree. After all, this tactic was used by the Japanese when they started their offensive. American corporations can develop increased dynamism from the cross-fertilization of such ideas and ideologies, creating a "hybrid" vigor of synergistic evolution.

The careful blending of the corporate culture with the local culture, domestically or internationally, can provide this type of hybrid synergy. MacDonald's is a prominent success in blending its approach with the local culture while maintaining the basic integrity of the business. In Paris MacDonald's serves wine while in London Ronald MacDonald is regarded as English. There is a distinct French flavor in the Parisian operation of serving wine just as there is a distinct English way of serving hamburgers in the London operation. The basics, service, remain the same in both operations. From this mode of operation the corporation develops multiple evolutionary processes that can feed one another. Almost all the innovations MacDonald's has instituted have come from divergent franchises, not from the corporate head-quarters. It is this synergy of evolution, the grabbing of dynamic and constructive genes from as many divergent sources as possible, that gives extra drive and punch to many outstanding corporations. This synergistic process of evolving prevents corporations from becoming inbred and unable to cope with the reality of the environment. A dynamic, organic corporation is built upon the acquisition of outstanding corporate genes composed of outstanding people.

OUTSTANDING PEOPLE

Successful third wave organizations are built around outstanding people. Corporate growth follows the natural course generated by the interests and capabilities of such people.

The people are the corporation!

Soichiro Honda, CEO

It's hard to find Eagles, but you must!

H. Ross Perot
Texas high-tech CEO

It is these people that will be the company!

James Treybig
Silicon Valley CEO

Organic organizations are built around people. People cannot, as they often were during the mechanical second wave era, be built around the organization, especially not around some static concept of an organizational flow chart. People must be given the freedom and resources to grow, to create, to innovate, and to activate in order for the corporation to realize their and its full potential. The corporate culture must also catalyze these people into an aggressive, interactive seething, living, growing network–organism.

It is a little like composing music: a note comes, it bounces off another note, then another, they then hit together and don't quite mesh and they try again and something clicks and then something else clicks and then another and another, and then a rhythm becomes clear, and the pace picks up and then you have a critical mass, as ideas bounce off and feed on one another—energy—and you have a corporation. It reminds me a bit of the piece "Duelin' Banjos" where two expert banjos bounce notes off one another until a great composition materializes, and takes off. Asked why he hired so many musicians, Steve Jobs replied, "When you want to understand something that has never been understood before, what you have to do is construct a conceptual scaffolding. And if you're trying to design a computer you will literally immerse yourself in the thousands of details necessary; all of a sudden, as the scaffolding gets set up high enough, it will all become clearer and clearer and that's when the breakthrough starts. It is a rhythmic experience, or it is an experience where everything's related to everything else and it's all intertwined. And it's such a fragile delicate experience that it's very much like music. But you could never describe it to anyone." The congregation, energy, and motivation of outstanding people are a lot like this as they bounce off each other's energy and ideas creating a driving critical mass.

This is, however, the ideal and depends a great deal upon the corporation's ability to hire a continuous and growing stream of outstanding people. As discussed in Chapter 3, our educational system and social channels are geared toward producing people for second wave organizations; the products of the establishment as such are generally standardized and average. A dynamic organization may successfully follow the precepts of American organic management, but fall victim to its own success in the process. The company may become inundated with orders, establishing a large market very quickly. The pressures to grow and produce at a rapid rate may force the company to hire average or even subaverage personnel, under the rationalization that these participants can be "made" extraordinary under the benign influence of the corporation in due time (the priority is to maintain growth and fill orders). Many such average people have usually found it difficult to function within an organic corporation.

> I was hired as a software engineer six months ago. I've only met my boss once in all that time, and all they seem to want from me is business proposals, not software design. I've never made proposals before, and anyway, where's my damn job description!
>
> > Employee at a rapidly growing
> > Silicon Valley corporation

Although the wave of the future is clear, we are still in a transitional stage. There may not be enough competent entrepreneurial firms or people to contract out work yet. IBM has once again faced this problem in its own classical way. Although many firms to which it contracts out now are not quite up to IBM standards, the company nevertheless uses these contractees as much as possible, because it knows that without such experience and help this external capability will not be developed. As a consequence, IBM has decided to take on the "temporary" burden of some temporary disillusionment in the market with its products such as the PC Jr.

IBM also recognizes that, although its people can be brought along, the majority (even at IBM) cannot ever become truly outstanding, that is, able to function organically and dynamically, with little or no guidance.

IBM also recognizes that its capability to satisfy many parts of its established market can be fulfilled with ordinary people because production and service is a question of routine in a stabilized market. However as such markets become increasingly affected by the determinants of the third wave, the need for outstanding people increases. As external capabilities increase, many of IBM's operations will be contracted out, and most of those that remain internally will become more organic and dynamic.

Many rapidly growing electronic information firms have run full tilt into this problem. Hewlett-Packard has recognized its encounter with this problem and is reorganizing around a corporate form. After a period of intense growth, many companies seem to have progressed directly from the entrepreneurial stage to the chaotic stage because the pool of outstanding people dries up. Many of their own outstanding people are either hired by other firms or leave to start their own companies. These rapidly growing firms, therefore, are forced to hire less than outstanding people who become the company. These members require guidance, formalization, job descriptions, and management; in other words, they require a corporate form.

A TEMPORARY TRANSITIONAL CORPORATE FORM

A corporate form to meet less than the ideal is not a dangerous organizational form if handled with care. This form is partially organic and partially bureaucratic. Only the bureaucratic and chaotic forms are truly dangerous to a corporation's viability. After growth and success are experienced, these companies are under the impression that the gunslinger-pioneer organizational form of the entrepreneurial form is what works. They are right given an infinite supply of outstanding people; but the supply is not infinite nor is the need for outstanding people crucial as the company becomes established, identifies its niches, and grows into "mass" marketing. An organizational form must be created temporarily, until a corporation's transition into the third wave becomes complete and until the social-educational system and the external capability catch up with the need.

What is this transitional, interim corporate stage? Control Data, IBM, Atari, APPLE, Texas Instruments, and Osborne have found interesting answers to that question. Their transitional forms bear some resemblance to the earlier second wave corporate form, but they are nevertheless innovations in the corporate form, and can be loosely classed around the entrepreneurial-corporate form.

Control Data

Control Data encourages many of its more entrepreneurially minded participants to develop their creative impulses by supporting them; by working out a business plan with them; by working out the financing and often taking an equitable stake in the new company, which means that Control Data becomes either a supplier or a customer. In this way, Control Data naturally grows in entrepreneurial dynamism and external capability.

IBM

IBM has chosen to create an internalized corporate free market in which the more dynamic and entrepreneurially minded participants can group together in IBUs. These independent business units fiercely compete with each other for extraordinary rewards, if they win. If they lose, many leave. If individuals who join IBUs lose in the competition in the internal market, they may return to the regular corporate stream.

Atari

Atari is perhaps a classic example of a company that succumbed to myopic vision induced by extraordinary growth. It grew and progressed quickly, from the entrepreneurial to the chaotic corporate phase. After a period of turmoil, bloodletting, and teeth gnashing, Atari has recognized that it must progress into the entrepreneurial-corporate form of management. The company now understands that it is a mass marketer and not a quick-hitting gunslinger. Atari must define and consolidate its position in the market. While the chaos induced by its initial period of development poses a great deal of problems, Atari has made it easier for its participants to accept a new corporate form and whatever reorganization comes with it. Much of the reorganization consists of contracting work, mainly manufacturing, to Asian firms and leaving the main body primarily as a design and marketing operation.

APPLE

APPLE has recognized that it must continue progress into the entrepreneurial-corporate organizational form. The company hired a CEO well versed in the corporate form and in mass marketing from Pepsi. APPLE, however, was not in a chaotic state as was Atari. A large amount of its conflict is creative and is being generated between the established entrepreneurial form and the new corporate dictates. APPLE has also decided to make its entire operation an interrelated organic process from manufacturing to sales. The probable deliberate results will be an increasingly dynamic entrepreneurial-corporate firm that maintains rapid innovation while serving mass markets.

Texas Instruments

After a series of staggering losses, Texas Instruments is beginning to realize that it is not in the quick-hit entrepreneurial game anymore, nor is it in some matrix-committee-managed never never land. The company must adapt an entrepreneurial-corporate form better suited to mass marketing. Because the number of outstanding people who could was lacking, Texas Instruments resorted to management by committee. Committees produce the proverbial camel, not the desired thoroughbred. Under the matrix-committee system, committees became responsible and not people. When a committee of fictional entity becomes responsible for anything, the results are also fictional. To increase its flexibility and resources, Texas Instruments is increasingly aware that it must develop externalized capable participants to whom it can contract out work.

Osborne

After a period of rapid growth, Osborne also ran into the extraordinary people barrier. Ordinary people can cope adequately with a stable and slow-growth situation, but it takes extraordinary people to deal with fast change and rapid growth. Ordinary people will create chaos in this environment. Osborne clearly entered this chaotic stage. It has taken a similar yet different approach to solving the problem than did Texas Instruments, by severely cutting its already lean staff. Redefinition at Osborne seems to have taken the form of cutting and reorganization under chapter 11 of the bankruptcy laws. Osborne's strategy may be similar to the classic opossum's trick—wait for the other fellow to move first, but be ready to move yourself quickly in order to find the missed niches, a viable method of survival.

SPEARHEAD OF THE COUNTEROFFENSIVE

It was said of Alfred Sloan that one of his proudest achievements was the creation of a system, General Motors, in which almost anyone with ordinary intelligence and drive could run. This axiom is becoming less true as the noose of the third wave tightens. Corporations now must clearly move toward the entrepreneurial-corporate form of management. The entrepreneurial-corporate form perhaps performs best for current business needs because it has the channels and the muscles to serve the mass markets, while it can effectively utilize the organic dynamism of American ideology. To create and drive this form, managers are going to have to manage, think, and act instead of administer. The percentage of managers with college degrees has approximately doubled since the advent of the third wave, which indicates the increasing importance of this type of human capital.

The organic entrepreneurial-corporate form of management, the lean, mean, and quick mode, is the spearhead of the third wave, the ideal American counteroffensive. Everywhere you look now, corporations are shaping up and trimming down. Goodrich, for example, has claimed to have attained a 40 percent decrease in waste and dramatic increases in quality since 1974. John Young, CEO of Hewlett-Packard, has said what American business is discovering: Increases in quality cost less, not more, in terms of final unit cost.

Many of the dinosaurs finally realize that expensive down or repair time could be avoided, as well as many of the warranty costs and sale losses.

FAST REACTION AND ACTION

The entrepreneurial-corporate organizational form is necessary until the external entrepreneurial capability develops to fill the needs of an increasingly demanding public. Entrepreneurship, innovation, and creativity in a corporation are useless without the systems, the muscle, and the channels with which to generate action and ideas. An entrepreneurial-corporate firm acts in a dynamic organic way, like a school of fish. Participants in the firm sense an opportunity within the warp of corporate objectives. Other units of the organism quickly line up to back the decision resulting from the opportunity taken. Corporate systems need quick responses and backup resources to make ideas work and to make the corporation work. Such systems come into play simply when the company is small and entrepreneurial because it is easy to know what fellow participants are doing, what they need and are capable of, and in what direction they are going. In order to maintain momentum and interactive synergy when the corporation grows, however, systems must be designed into its growth to back up decisions. The corporation then can quickly align itself to deal with opportunities or problems.

Corporate systems provide the framework within which networks constantly change to meet challenges. Corporate policy, ethic, culture, and ideology should generate the necessary systems and their natural evolution. These systems may include random friendships throughout the corporation as well as more formal meetings and computer networks, so that any member can know what and who is interested and available to work on any particular challenge. Such systems might be called networks, connections, or the corporation's external capability.

IBM and APPLE have chosen to maximize their external capability by allowing networks to spread and grow through an "open architecture" approach, i.e., by allowing any of their external systems to become peripheral suppliers to the market. Many companies are also adopting a tough but benign approach to their suppliers, such as making suppliers pay for traceable repair time and warranty costs, yet simultaneously, they are lending people and facilities to assist suppliers in improving productivity and quality. Northrop, for example, has lent employee teams to suppliers at no cost to improve quality and to cut the rate of rejections by a third. In a related context, one of AT&T's best campaigns stressed the need "to keep in touch" even though immediate business may have been concluded. When it came time again to do business, the interaction might be generated from the maintenance of the connection.

In this way, the organism can immediately swing its capability behind any issue, adding "real time" accounting, inventory, and cash flow systems to interpersonal networks. The more a corporation knows about itself and its environment, the more capability it will be able to utilize on a current basis, cutting down on useless and costly slack.

CORPORATE "BIONICS"

Information is the "blood" of the organism. The more quickly the quantity and quality of information can flow along efficient systems, the more quickly these systems can assess, analyze, and decide upon the information given. Decisions are then acted upon by manufacturing systems, sales and marketing systems, and support systems that must be designed to be increasingly flexible, synergistic, liberating, and nonrestrictive. These systems are the muscles and sinews of the organism. They must be kept in shape to avoid flab and slack; they must be challenged, exercised, examined, and improved on a constant basis, in order for the creativity and innovation of a corporation to have purpose. This is again what IBM and APPLE do on a consistent basis. This is what they must do to keep ahead of the competition.

A chief executive officer must have information on where the corporation is, where it is going, and how to design it in an evolutionary way to get the corporation to where it wants to be. One of the most exciting developments of the third wave is bioengineering, in which living, evolving people are developed—instead of dead mechanical things that do not evolve—by splicing together the information gathered from each targeted individual.

THE SPIRIT OF THE COUNTEROFFENSIVE

> The beauty of our nation is that we're alive and well, and that means we're always changing. You can see it in the food we eat—in the blocks around here there's Mexican, there's everything.
>
> Robert Riddell, director USO
> New York, 1983

Riddell's statement hits the guts of the issue. We have a wide variety of resources, human and physical, upon which to draw, possibly more than any other nation has. That is why times of crises cause a nation to knit together into an interactive organism. The knitting together of America is now accelerating as the first significant challenge to its economic and technological leadership

101

emerges. Coming together in the national interest and concern for productivity and technological progress can be seen in American schools, factory "quality circles," executive boardrooms, laboratories, and homes.

Government and industry are seriously discussing a national "industrial policy" for the first time. Both generally agree that the directive type of industrial policy will not work because it is not in line with our national character. A policy that will work is one that encourages, supports, and maximizes the resources already at hand—America's variety and pioneering spirit. For example, the cost of patents and their marketing could be declarable against other income up to a certain amount. The cost of education should be considered a capital loss that can be declared against future income. A special type of research and development corporation should be instituted. Some policies, like these, could be drafted into a national industrial policy that would not interfere with directive planning but would knit the country closer together, generating increased synergy. American business and government can triumph over this challenge by encouraging the entrepreneurial-pioneering drives and the interactive variety of its people.

As a priority in terms of this challenge, the institution of a truly inexpensive, interactive national telecommunications "grid," or nervous system, should be pursued with all possible deliberation. This grid will allow the transfer and targeting of resources and human capital to wherever they are most useful. The generation and evolution of ideas and knowledge will be increasingly enhanced with the use of such a grid. The acceleration of technological change and productivity will be greatly increased. In a number of areas, this rate of acceleration has been slowing relative to our competitors.

Japan's progress also can be attributed to their interactive telecommunications grid, which is currently more efficient-effective and is moving at a faster rate than this country's. It is not enough to rest our hopes on divestiture to increase the progress of the national grid, because our ethic and mind set have not really changed fast enough concerning divestment and split. Competition from non-AT&T sources is still relatively insignificant and will stay that way for the foreseeable future because technology is not spread and instituted fast enough in the system. The consumer is not being educated fast enough. A determined effort should be made to accelerate the progress and decrease the cost of the national telecommunications grid. It is along this grid that ideas and ideologies flow. This grid is the nervous system of the counteroffensive.

This new ethic, this ideological counteroffensive, which was largely begun in Silicon Valley is having a very strong and pervasive effect throughout the country. The Japanese are concerned about this "new" phenomena in America. A Japanese official recently complained that one of his primary duties seemed to be chauffeuring visiting Japanese brass around Silicon Valley, which seems in its own way to be even more popular than Disneyland! A recent Japanese study group voiced both its admiration and concern about the management in Silicon Valley, commenting that the energy and creativity in the valley caused people to "work too hard," principally because there was "too much competition in Silicon Valley."[5]

7

ENTREPRENEURSHIP, FREEDOM, AND THE NEW LIFESTYLE

Entrepreneuring is a spirited way of life.

Steven C. Brandt, Ph.D.
Entrepreneuring, 1980

The only true law is that which leads to freedom.

Richard Bach
Jonathan Livingston Seagull

HUMAN VERSUS MACHINE

What may be the essential ethic of the third wave is spirit, drive, and the ability and capacity to live and experience life to the fullest. With its propensity to categorize, formularize, and create hierarchies, second wave business dampened and in many cases crushed the human spirit by turning it into something similar to a machine. A person did things because they were expected, because the formula called for them; and so the individual became partially mechanical. Jobs during the second wave were standardized so almost anybody could perform them; individuals like parts were interchangeable. It did not matter much if one part broke down, the company replaced it with one of the many spares. Employees could come and go without affecting the organization very much.

> Let [a person] spend too much of his life at the mechanics of practicality and either he must become something less than a man or his very mechanical efficiency will become impaired by the frustrations stored up in his irrational human personality. An ulcer . . . is an unkissed imagination taking its revenge for having been jilted.
>
> John Ciardi
> *An Ulcer, Gentlemen, Is an Unwritten Poem*

When I began my first job, in the late 1960s, as an industrial engineer at an automobile assembly plant in Chicago, I found it quite perplexing and discouraging that the assembly workers, especially if they were older, would respond only with grunts when questioned. Whether this was because they had been numbed by their "work" or because they feared anyone in a "white" shirt (symbolizing the hierarchy), it was really quite sad. It became increasingly so as I watched, and in some cases timed, these men who worked like machines for the better part of their waking lives. Yet these men were not machines and they rebelled by slowing the pace of the line, by slipping away from the job, by not coming in, by "trashing" company equipment, and by doing only half the job so that downtime repair mounted. Much less was produced in terms of quality and quantity than could have been. The plant was dirty, drab, and dreary; and management was equally depressing as they usually chose to give up, perhaps because it was easier to lay the blame on a "labor" problem, as they commiserated with one another over lunch in their well-appointed and subsidized executive dining room. The engineers had a "decent" dining room, cafeteria-style, but when you went down to the workers' dining facilities, the atmosphere got worse and was definitely substandard.

Two Chrysler assembly workers put a 13-hour stranglehold on the company's huge Jefferson Avenue plant Tuesday, idling some 5,000 employees. The two men scaled over a 10-foot-high wire crib and pushed the control button, cutting off the electricity. . . . Workers gave them a wire cable which they used to secure the crib. More workers gave them heavy chains and locks to further secure their positions. When the men finally came out at 7:11 P.M. . . . they were given a hero's ride out of the plant.

Detroit Free Press,
25–26 July 1973

The installation of FM music in all luncheon facilities at the plant where I worked was initially viewed with great perplexion. After a minor battle with the establishment, I managed to make the installations permanent. Most third wave firms now have unitary, common facilities for all participants.

PEOPLE VERSUS FORMULAS

Upon taking over the reigns of Dana, Rene McPherson was reported to have burned all the formulas he could find in front of middle managers. He replaced them with one page of corporate warp or philosophy in which there were no different types of people, i.e., workers, engineers, management, but only productive people and entrepreneurial people.

We must solve our economic problems by outthinking them, not over-powering them.

Senator Gary Hart, 1982

Creation was unitary during the first wave as the farmer sowed and tended his crops through completion and the craftsman who began a project finished it. During the second wave, creation, sometimes referred to as "labor," was fragmented, divided, and formularized. People literally became partial machines. Creation during the third wave is moving back toward the unitary process in which functions that should be performed by machines, e.g., robots, increasingly are. People are becoming entrepreneurs again, involved with the entire creative process from the beginning to the end. The means of initiating and completing the creative process—information and computing power, design—and the means for activation—contractees and telecommunications—are once again becoming generally available.

In the interim stage before the rest of the world enters the third wave, mechanical functions that cannot be immediately automated for various reasons are being contracted out to corporations of other nations that are in or entering into the second wave. As mechanical functions become increasingly less valuable and entrepreneurial functions more so, the already apparent pressure to develop entrepreneurs within and without corporate structures will mount. The third wave, a liberating wave unlike the constrictive second, will generate a force of creativity and enterprise that will initially stagger the imagination. Already leading third wave gurus, like Nolan Bushnell of Silicon Valley, are projecting growth rates in excess of 20 percent in the late 1980s.

> It is the all around businessman—the entrepreneur—who has the best chance of reaching the top . . . a landscape rich in opportunity, richer by far than even those that unfolded during the golden eras of the Industrial Revolution.
>
> John Paul Getty
> "How to Be a Successful Businessman"

Indicative of rising rates of growth are the increasingly large amounts of cash being channeled into research and development by governments, corporations, individuals, and universities.

Third wave growth initially may seem to be similar to the beginning of second wave growth in which business opportunities were there for the taking. Many new firms rushed about with new technology, and eventually a few came to dominate each market; but the two waves are at best only superficially similar. The second wave was based upon definable resources, which ultimately had a limit, but information (computing power) is not definable, nor are there any limits, at least for the moment. Even at the beginning of the second wave when raw materials were extremely bountiful, they could still be controlled or "cornered": i.e., their consequent limitation was apparent.

CORPORATE ENTREPRENEURIALISM

Individuals are literally faced with a new world in which they can, for a change, define and make their own futures, instead of having them made by formulas. Organizations and corporations that take advantage of and contribute to this new flexibility will be the ones to survive and prosper. There are, however, limits to the extent that a corporation may be able to generate and stimulate entrepreneurial force internally. In relation to the increasing corporate need for flexibility and quick response, corporations will encourage individuals, either within or without the corporate structure, to form ventures or joint ventures with which the corporation may usefully interact.

As corporations adapt to the new corporate style of contracting out, the need for new, flexible entrepreneurial firms is increasing geometrically and will continue to increase dramatically. Corporations are already bemoaning the shortage of good firms to which they can contract out work.

RESPONSIBILITY AND RISKY ADVENTURE

For those who want to try the life of ultimate freedom and responsibility, Professor Steven C. Brandt of the Graduate School of Business at Stanford University prescribes the following "ten commandments" for entrepreneurs in his book *Entrepreneuring:*

1. Limit the number of primary participants to people who can conciously agree upon and contribute directly to that which the enterprise is to accomplish, for whom, and by when. In other words, do not begin with slack either in personnel, in resources, or in time.
2. Define the business of the enterprise in terms of what is to be bought, precisely by whom, and why. Know your market.
3. Concentrate all available resources on accomplishing two or three specific operational objectives within a given time period. Have and keep a concrete vision.
4. Prepare and work from a written plan that delineates who in the total organization is to do what by when. Have a plan.
5. Employ key people with proven records of success at doing what needs to be done in a manner consistent with the desired value system of the enterprise. Develop a corporate culture with people and values.
6. Reward individual performance that exceeds agreed upon standards. Maintain a sense of proprietorship.
7. Expand methodically from a profitable base toward a balanced business. Be meticulous and realistic in developing the business.
8. Project, monitor, and conserve cash and credit capability. Know the current money state of the business: Cash = Liquidity = Survival.
9. Maintain a detached point of view. Do not get emotionally attached; treat it as a business and not your lover.
10. Anticipate incessant change by periodically testing adopted plans for their consistency with the realities of the world marketplace. Observe and correct.[1]

Another important point to remember is to maintain and increase corporate credibility internally and externally. Often, a relatively easy way to develop credibility for a fledgling company is to obtain a government contract. For credibility to be maintained, however, the company must deliver because nowhere is a failure more widely broadcast than in Washington. As one of their primary responsibilities, the Small Business Administration of the United States federal government and similar agencies of other governments are obligated to assist entrepreneurs in obtaining such contracts.

At no period in the past or in the foreseeable future will the time be better for entrepreneurs to try their skills than in the present. The forces of the third wave have created enormous survival pressures for entrepreneurship in every sector of business. Nowhere is this more noticeable than in the trend-setting state of California where the rate of new business ventures and the amount of available venture capital has more than quadrupled in the last few years.

The combination of high technology, ingenuity, necessity, capital, new markets, and new high-energy entrepreneurs are providing the momentum that is moving America ever faster into the third wave. Perhaps the most indicative trend is that governments everywhere, as they see their traditional tax bases stagnate, are actually becoming eager to help the entrepreneur by realigning tax systems and offering grants and information at an unprecedented rate. The cutting edge of this momentum is electronic computing technology, which has progressed at a rapid clip. Its effective use has been hindered by lag in the development of information technology, known as software. Every advance in hardware opens up geometric possibilities and needs for software. Software contains the specific application of specific information that will provide the greatest competitive edge for entrepreneurs. Software will be made with increasing efficiency and effectiveness, opening up vast new frontiers and opportunities for entrepreneurs. IBM is projecting that by the mid-1990s as much as 40% of its revenue will come from software.

THE NEW CORPORATE ENTREPRENEURIALISM

While the pressures on all corporations and individuals to become more innovative and entrepreneurial have increased geometrically during the third wave, the pressures on middle management in all corporate forms are and will be particularly intense. These middle managers are the activators or the engines who make things happen. A prototype of the new middle manager is Tom West in *The Soul of a New Machine*. If CEOs are essentially a form of the corporate warp-constitution, middle managers are the corporate entrepreneurs or politicians (in a positive role) who play under the warp's umbrella. They use the principles and objectives of the warp to build projects and direct teams toward achievements, commitments, and excitement. They mobilize people and resources. They are important corporate entrepreneurs of the new wave.

To do their jobs they must, as all politicians must, develop a following above and below them. They must become skilled users of the corporate principles and objectives and, to do so in the longer run, they must develop an absolute trust in the integrity of those principles. To develop projects and constituents, middle managers must constantly sell themselves and their propositions based upon the third wave principles of intensive quality, efficiency, amusement, adventure, effectiveness, and longer term value, not upon simple financial analysis. Middle managers also are "mentors" of both the project and its team; therefore, they must seek resources and protect the group from jealousies and insecurities, as Tom West did by "soft peddling" the project and the team. Who could be afraid of a bunch of kids and a project considered a "kludge"?

Corporations also like to tie an individual's "behind" to a project by forcing him or her to go outside normal channels and rules, but not outside the warp. There is risk involved in undertaking the project, since it cannot then be easily dropped in midstream. Commitment to the project is thereby forced, as Tom West and his team's was. Such a process also creates maximum team cohesiveness. The team will sink or swim together (or "hang together or hang separately").

In the entrepreneurial organizational form, middle managers' role is to do whatever seems right at the moment. In the pioneer-gunslinger form, it is shoot first and ask questions later. In the bureaucratic form, they largely must prevent change and maintain the status quo. The role of middle managers in the entrepreneurial-corporate organizational form is quick, appropriate action and change.

The primary function of the middle manager in the third wave is to focus and maximize the interactive energy of the corporation in positive and synergistic directions. That is why the raw energy or material is important to him or her. That is why corporations need people who have high energy and would naturally climb mountains wherever they are. Middle managers should be people who are natural entrepreneurs because they need to be and because they enjoy it.

GOVERNMENT ENTREPRENEURIALISM

I once said, not entirely in jest, that we should be glad that we don't get all the government we pay for! While there is some truth to that comment, it largely misses the point. Government is a service and should be performed with maximum efficiency and effectiveness like any other service. Would you be pleased with a poor postal service or a poor energy policy? If you pay for good service, you should get it. This is why entrepreneurialism in government has a purpose. In governments, as in corporations, many things can be done better.

Above all, DO something!

Tom Peters and Robert Waterman
In Search of Excellence

Government entrepreneurs have to behave similarly to corporate entrepreneurs. They have to become entrepreneurial politicians, build a growing constituency and following, and create missions and commitments. Second wave government bureaucrats often sought the safety of inaction through committees or other devices. When forced to act, they usually relied upon formulas and programs as solutions to problems, not upon thinking. They also learned that the larger a problem got, the bigger the program that could be applied and consequently the larger the "empire." It followed that the solution to any problem meant the devolution of any program and its people.

Third wave government entrepreneurs have to realize that problems are more often solved or neutralized by interactive policies and by transmitted values than by new or existing programs. Unfortunately government bureaucracy still measures success largely by budgets, programs, and empires. The increasing budget contingencies of the third wave, however, will squeeze such negative values and accelerate the shift to new and more positive criteria. In relation to increasing budgets, governments are realizing that money and programs thrown at a problem will not necessarily resolve it. In some cases, these measures prolong the problem.

An example of this was the ill-fated Canadian Energy Program sold by an aggressive second wave government bureaucrat. What seemed logical in equations and charts at one particular point in time simply could not remain so in a dynamic environment. Programs and budgets once initiated remain relatively inflexible. Some pundits in Canada are now referring to the energy program as Canada's greatest peacetime disaster. Similar things can be said of many of the Johnson administration's Great Society programs. Adjustments of problems through policies on taxes or education are now being recognized as much more flexible and effective.

THE LIFEBLOOD OF ENTREPRENEURIALISM

Entrepreneurship in both government and business corporations must develop interpersonal trust and knowledge and maximize access to current information. These factors build interpersonal networks, which are the basis of any entrepreneurial action. The more information and networks an entrepreneur has access to, the more efficient and effective he or she will be. A friend in business recently drew this equation for me:

111

$$E = MI^2$$

He equated E with entrepreneurship—the energy or ability to work and create order; M with money; and I with information. Although we generally rely upon formulas disproportionally to their actual value, this one merits attention and thought.

We derive information from two sources: (1) formal, e.g., databases, libraries, archives; and (2) informal, through interpersonal networks. Informal information and the bases for entrepreneurial action are the main reasons why many third wave companies have put such an emphasis upon such activities as "beer busts" and parties where such organic networks are created. As trust and interpersonal knowledge develop over time, this network grows, creating more channels for entrepreneurial action. Layoffs and similar corporate disruptions serve to damage or destroy such growing networks, which are the corporation's growing nerve system in effect. The propagating of networks is perhaps one of the prime reasons why the Japanese try not to undertake such disruptive action. The corporation's capabilities to deal effectively with opportunities and problems are these living and growing networks.

These networks have always been important highways of commerce, but in the new wave they will be the primary channels of entrepreneurial action. The bottom line for many is that there will be no other jobs than those they create, because of the increased efficiency and effectiveness of the new era.

Jefferson gave the following advice to a would-be political entrepreneur in France that still applies to all entrepreneurs: "Ferret people out of their hovels, as I have done, look into their kettles . . . loll on their beds. . . . You [shall] then be able to apply your knowledge to the softening of their beds or the throwing of a morsel of meat into their kettle of vegetables."[2]

8

INTERNATIONAL COMPETITION

When it costs too much to build it at home
You just build it cheaper someplace else.

Bob Dylan, 1984

GROWING INTERNATIONAL COMPETITION

Rapidly increasing world competition is the new reality that all American businesses are beginning to recognize; it is a world of growing interdependencies and fast business. Growing dependencies and increasing national powers have forced the international corporation to consider corporate profits, national development, and international partnership as a way to progress and survive.

The Global 2000 report, commissioned by the Carter administration, projects a geometric rise in the world's population from just over 5 billion currently to over 10 billion by the year 2030, with most of the increase occurring in Eurasia. Further, according to this report, the world's gross national product (GNP) will grow from $6 trillion to around $15 trillion (based on the 1975 United States dollar). The vast bulk of GNP growth will be generated outside of North America.[1] Competition at today's levels will seem insignificant.

If you think you've seen competition, you ain't seen anything yet!

IBM executive, 1984

The hope has been that through "high tech" America will win the export battle giving those in "low tech" some latitude in making the necessary transition and bearing its consequent costs. However, the trade results of 1983–84 show that America has slipped into a serious "high tech" trade deficit. A recent productivity report to the White House developed the following reasons for this slippage, (1) too little spent on civilian R&D; (2) it does little good to design advanced products if they can be manufactured more cheaply overseas; (3) the high cost of American capital; (4) antitrust obstacles; (5) adversary relationships between management and labor; (6) a government out of touch with world trade realities (*Business Week* March 11, 1985).

Internationalization, competition, and the amount and speed at which money is deployed has accelerated, but the rate at which such factors change will increase by the 1990s to a point where our forward progress now will be seen as immobile. The amount of America's total production sold internationally has risen from under 5 percent a few decades ago to close to 20 percent currently. Many businesses have found that they are dependent upon foreign trade for profits and possibly for survival, and many more will.

International debt and liquidity have swelled to enormous proportions. Although doomsayers often point out that the bankruptcy of any one country in debt would cause the collapse of the international monetary system, it is unlikely to happen. The international community has too much to lose to allow this to happen (a similar situation exists in terms of the use of nuclear arms). Some banks will lose some interest payments, and some countries will be forced to devalue their currencies further. This is all that will happen and in fact is happening. The most important aspect, however, is the large growth in the world's money supply and its liquidity because one country's debt is another's deposit or investment. As banks operate on a ratio basis with central monetary authorities, this supply is constantly being accelerated. Electronic information technology has also been a major factor in accelerating the supply and deployment of money. For instance, money used to back loans in North America is sent electronically to Asia and then to Europe for other purposes when the sun sets, arriving back in time for the sunrise. International banking is even more difficult to follow since funds skip back and forth through several continents in the same day. The result has been vast sums of money constantly being advantageously deployed and redeployed as fast as a speeding electron.

The productive employment of these fast moving and growing pools of capital is critical to the economic questions of the day. Without adequate employment of such funds, they are sheltered in real estate, gold, silver, and other hard goods, which drives up the prices of these commodities and the rate of inflation. How capital is utilized has created another primary reason for corporations to accelerate in entrepreneurship, creativity, innovation, and thinking.

Velocity of business

Such speeds of transaction will inevitably create more pressures for more of the same as business successes create more deposits and investments, requiring an ever increasing rate of business velocity. Business velocity may roughly be equated to the number of significant productive business transactions completed per unit of time. If there exists a speed barrier to business velocity, we do not as yet have the faintest conception of what it is. Because there appears to be no current danger of any such barrier to limit business velocity, the challenge is to create an ever expanding base for the acceleration of business velocity and for the deployment of ever increasing amounts of capital to stabilize inflation. An electronic database, consisting of patents and manufacturing processes, governed by the United Nations or some other international agency, may be one way to create an ever expanding foundation for business.

INTERNATIONAL FINANCIAL SYSTEM

The current international financial system is clearly inefficient and ineffective in most developing countries, leading to the ineffective use of loan funds. Such loans have been used for subsistence measures, not for new productive efforts, because ineffective political and economic systems have not met the social needs of the populace. More often than not, these ineffective systems have served to suppress the rise of local entrepreneurs and the development of effective indigenous financial systems. A method and process need to be devised to develop effective local financial systems and to fund valid local entrepreneurs. Maurice Mann, vice-chairman of A. G. Becker Paribas, Inc., said that a good first step would be to develop an international secondary mortgage market for mortgages in emerging countries. This secondary market would encourage thrift and savings, thereby aiding in the establishment of local funds for capital loans as well as for mortgages. Business training centers in certain strategic locations, staffed by retired executives or executives on leave from third wave countries, may be another possibility in aiding the inefficient political and economic systems of developing nations.

The pressure of food requirements

Another key projection of the Global 2000 report is that while world food consumption will rapidly climb, food production will rise only in North America and Australia.[2] Trade competition in manufacturing, therefore, will become increasingly more important to those countries that rely increasingly upon imports to feed themselves. Correspondingly, trade competitiveness in manufactures may lose some importance in those countries enjoying increased revenues from food exports.

Each Japanese school child is constantly drilled in the importance of work and cooperation because these two factors allow Japan to earn enough to feed itself, through the export of manufactures. This is one reason that has been postulated concerning the successful rise of Japanese corporations. Countries in such circumstances will become increasingly severe competitors because they must to survive. Japan is now number one in world trade. The consequences of business and economic failure for food-importing countries are severe now and will continue to be as their populations expand, usually at a rate faster than in North America.

The increasing need to import more food, along with other factors to be discussed, may force many communist bloc countries into the world market to a larger and more substantial degree. It may also force many nations to create or modify native corporations as instruments of national policy and needs. The competitive arena, therefore, will increasingly feel the force of the state behind the corporation.

Raw materials pressures

Raw materials demanded by a rapidly increasing number of people and competitive corporations will continue to escalate in cost. After the current lull, the cost of energy will spiral upward. Fuel for energy will continue to be the enforcer, the main pressure behind the movement into the third wave. Because the efficient use of energy is being forced upon the world, growth rates of energy used may be driven down from 5 percent to 3 percent to 2 percent and even farther. Increasing raw material costs will persist in pressurizing corporations to increase efficiency and effectiveness, to become leaner and meaner, to be creative, and to react faster on all fronts. In turn, consumers will be similarly pressed, causing demands for availability, delivery, quality, and

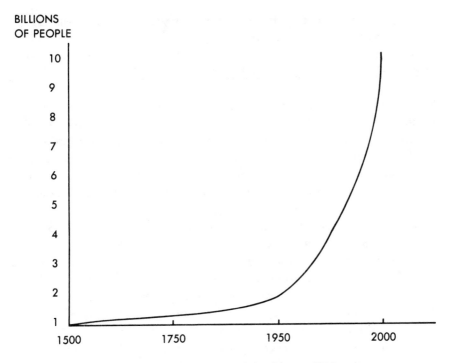

BILLIONS
OF PEOPLE

<u>EXHIBIT 8-1</u>   Projected world population growth by the year 2000.

durability, efficiency-effectiveness, and style. Style will become increasingly important as people become more educated, affluent, and competitive.

INTERNATIONAL SYNERGY

The third wave environment is changing at a fast pace; therefore, American corporations must interact organically with their environments. Gone are the days a formula could be dictated in the inimitable John Wayne manner. Now we have to understand the other side. International as well as domestic competition must become mutually synergistic in order for all sides to be winners and continuing partners in a world economy. Speed of communication and travel have created the McLuhanesque "global" village in which we have to learn how to live with those with whom we have done business. We cannot simply move on to the next deal, the next village, the next valley, or the next frontier. We have to live with business associates, whether they be consumers, suppliers, foreign governments, or competitors. Some corporations will not understand this but they eventually must. Many corporations will consciously

117

have to evolve and develop this new mind set. Many countries will have to develop a new international consciousness.

INVESTMENT IN THE INTERNATIONAL MARKETPLACE

While having dinner with a friend who was part of a developing country's influential group, I questioned him as to why, since the country was receiving large amounts of funds from the export of vast amounts of raw materials and significant amounts of "foreign aid," the country had not progressed further in establishing prosperous businesses that could employ more of the people and thereby alleviate some of the pervasive poverty. He replied with a wry, amused smile: "Why should we as long as we can live off our raw materials and the Americans?" When he spoke of "we," he meant his particular group. By Americans he meant the American corporations that were investing large sums in raw material extraction. Americans working in these corporations were, by a matter of necessity, more closely linked with his group than with the general populace. He also meant the large sums of United States "aid" which were often siphoned indirectly for the use of himself and his friends. From his narrow perspective and in the short term, he was, of course, right.

One senior Western official recently implied that Switzerland was the largest ultimate recipient of foreign aid. This has long been a situation exploited by the opposition. Inappropriate private use of capital will change, if for no other reason, because the world is becoming an increasingly integrated marketplace.

We can speed the change and trip the opposition if we develop measures to assist local entrepreneurs and not invest capital and effort in nonproductive elements of a society. Such an approach is not entirely altruistic as a strong link can be made to security issues and to the need of many corporations to find more cost-effective and reliable third parties to whom they can contract work. Eventually a truly international marketplace will come into being with the advent of world television networks made possible by the Direct Broadcast Satellite, making possible the direct access of large numbers of developing peoples to the international marketplace, bypassing many obstacles to trade, and in turn increasing international competition.

Many long-term projections forecast the shortage of critical minerals. The gradual depletion of any mineral will not bring any industry to a sudden halt. Corporations will invest money into developing substitutes, as happened when the supplies of rubber, nitrates, and camphor diminished. Shortages in the quantity of oil are pushing many corporations into development of alternative energy resources and into conservation. Although some substitute products will cost less, the majority will cost more, creating greater pressures on corporations to tighten operations.

HUMAN CAPITAL AND SOCIAL INFRASTRUCTURE

Many problems of both developing and developed countries may be assisted by the increased fluidity of international labor, of which the European "guest" worker system is a prototype. In North America a de facto guest worker system exists in which as many as 20 million people have come from Mexico to the United States and Canada. It may be far better to develop an official program in tandem with a North American Common Market of some form. Such a step might also provide a useful "hothouse" for the North American economy, as well as acting as a force for economic and political stabilization.

Another step toward international labor stabilization would be a planned and focused program to develop many second wave industries then gradually to replace them with third wave businesses in emerging countries that want them. Though some individuals, like Servan-Schreiber, believe that developing countries can make the leap into the third wave bypassing the second, the vast majority cannot because they must first develop a key process of the third wave—they must create large amounts of human capital. If Hong Kong, Singapore, and Taiwan are countries at least partially progressing into the third wave it is because significant educational establishments were already in place many years ago and because many indigenous movers and shakers attended graduate and undergraduate universities in North America and Europe. A social infrastructure must be developed before the economic system can evolve. Watersheds for the development of such infrastructures in Europe and Japan were the Renaissance and the Meiji restoration.

In many developing countries today, some second and third wave economic structures are being imposed upon first wave or nonexistent social infrastructures. Such blind development has created much turmoil and suffering because many social systems have not developed along with the economic and technological expansion. Some societies, for example, are still oriented toward producing a large number of offspring, with the assumption that only a few will survive native diseases; but modern medicine has increased survival rates and decreased death rates, causing overpopulation, erosion, and starvation. Such developing countries have been precariously balanced upon new technology. When shifts in inputs occur, such as the change in oil prices, the results have often been tragic. Developing nations do not have the necessary social infrastructures which allowed countries in Europe and Japan to bounce back from economic devastation. These developing countries must pursue a

119

determined effort to develop social infrastructures in tandem with economic development.

It is in the progressive, developing areas, such as Hong Kong and Singapore, that many of the products of the third wave are being assembled. Companies caught in the pressures of third wave competition—*automate, immigrate,* or *evaporate*—have chosen to immigrate to the developing world. To be competitive, companies in this squeeze must know on a current basis where a product can be manufactured at the lowest cost and at the best quality. Corporations can achieve a growing international capability only by employing and educating the right people. In relations more people from offshore will need to be integrated into corporate structures. The competitive edge is people, and the corporation that has the international edge will also have the domestic edge. One of Ronald Reagan's great strengths is that he knows that the nation's economy, and therefore security, is inextricably linked to the nation's morale and spiritual strength. Similarly, a corporation's economic strength is linked inextricably to its morale and spiritual strength. Economic and consequently business strength are based on the precision of fulfillments of contractual agreements. Each item or service sold, whether it be between an employee and a corporation, or between a corporation and a customer or supplier, is an implicit or explicit contract between two parties. How well the contract is carried out, how well you keep your word, is dependent upon the precision and care of its execution. On the part of the customer, his or her implicit contract is to buy the product or service again if the contract is carried out by the corporation as expected. Often, the customer is not really very explicit about what he or she expects from a contract, until usually he or she has a conscious or unconscious feeling of dissatisfaction. The successful corporation will define and refine continuously the terms of the contract. The reason many people patronize MacDonalds is that they know that a contract for a hamburger or whatever will be filled with reasonable precision each time they visit. Similarly at Disneyland they know they will be able to spend some time in a clean, friendly environment that works everytime they visit and renew that contract. Without a will to see these contracts through with precision, none of these corporations would last very long. Both Disney and MacDonalds have had the vision to hire young people who can believe in the spirit of the particular morality that is critical to the firms' success, before they become cynical or jaded. The stronger a corporation's morality and spirit is, the faster and better contracts will be carried out, and the faster and better the contractual linkages will be. J. Paul Getty once fired a man for taking small amounts of petty cash because, even though he was worth what he took and more, he was violating an implicit contract with the corporation, which some employees sometimes feel justified in doing; but as in any contract problem that may be insoluable through negotiation, the only remedy is dissolution of the contract, resignation. The corporation, in order to avoid such occurrences, must get close to the employee to know what he or she expects out of the contract.

That is really the message of Tom Peters, about being closer to the customer, or the employee. This is essentially the reason too for Japan's success. People external to Japan have often complained about how long it takes for the Japanese to make a decision. They don't understand that each member of the team is agreeing eventually to a very solemn contract, and God help whoever does not carry out his or her contract to the letter; socially and economically he or she would suffer severely. That is why when the Japanese take on a project or sell a product or treat their employees as they do, they put more into it than would seem to be absolutely necessary. They want to be sure that the contract is carried out, and actually feel a sense of disgrace if the customer does not carry out his or her contract by renewing or repurchase, or if an employee fails or leaves.

Many developing countries' primary problem is not economic development but moral and spiritual development, without which contracts cannot be carried out, and without which economic growth cannot occur. Socialism for all its antithesis for free enterprise is really in developing countries laying the foundation for free enterprise by organizing the country. China is an excellent example, a country demoralized and degraded by countless rapacious rulers of an internal or external origin has been turned around by the socialists into a country of both strong morality and spirit. Socialism in Eastern Europe is merely a defensive manifestation of Russia which over the centuries had suffered so much at the hands of invaders, and will in time relax as Russia becomes more economically and politically organic and secure. Organic free enterprise is a natural state that all countries will eventually come to.

The world's governments will play more direct roles in international business in the future, and North American governments will be forced to respond in kind. Embassies will have to play more of a commercial and assistance role (as their old diplomatic roles wane because of advancing telecommunications) in projecting local markets, developing new contacts, smoothing commercial red tape, assessing opportunities, and arranging financing. The international commercial facet of government may become one of the most important roles of government in the years ahead. This international collaborative role with business is necessary not only for commercial reasons but also for ideological and security reasons.

THE COMING ORGANIC-IZATION OF THE SOCIALIST NATIONS

The revolutions of Russia and China were not revolutions against capitalism but against feudalism. They were rebellions of the second wave against the order of the first wave. These countries did not experience the revolutions of the Renaissance or the Meiji restoration, and needed to set about developing an infrastructure for the second wave. Marxist ideology, with its capability for simplification and adaption to feudalistic problems, proved more useful in these revolutions than democratic processes of revolution which require a more educated and concentrated mass of citizens. The socialization of Eastern Europe was an accident of war and not of a process. Later socialist revolutions were primarily against later day forms of feudalism.

Socialism performed a role similar to corporate capitalism in developing second wave industry and technology. Socialist hierarchies existed upon the administration of rules and formulas by large bureaucracies, as corporate hierarchies did. People became cogs in great socialist machines, much as they had become in large corporate machines. Both systems essentially mobilized large amounts of capital and sought to exploit cheap resources and dominate nature.

It was easy initially to motivate people by telling them that their survival was at stake and that they were the vanguard of new socialist ideals; but since survival has become an abstraction and socialist ideals do not mean much to those who have known no other system, ideological capital is running out. Socialist economies and societies are beginning to slow and loosen. Alcoholism and hooliganism are reported to have risen sharply, indicating that Marxist ideology is not natural or in line with human inclinations just as bureaucracies in the West are not.

Bureaucratic structures and processes cannot cope effectively with the third wave, whether they be socialist or capitalist. They will have to give way to more democratic structures. Poor industrial espionage will never be an adequate substitute for creativity and innovation, whether it is conducted by a corporation or a state. Consequently, the Western lead in third wave technology will continue to grow. Socialist countries will have to organic-ize to loosen up, much as many old-line companies have had to, and as more entrepreneurially oriented China is already doing. Socialism has, in a sense, prepared the social infrastructure for the third wave, much as corporate enterprise prepared the way for the third wave in the West.

It has been said that the socialization of Russia and China was the best thing that ever happened to Western capitalism. As I once said in jest: "What if they had chosen the capitalist route like Japan did? We would be facing now the equivalent of fourteen Japans? We are reeling under the assault of only one!" This may be an exaggeration perhaps, but when these countries organize third wave systems, we may be facing intensive competition.

The bottom line is that the transition must proceed as quickly as possible because only by moving to the faster, more efficient, entrepreneurially driven economy can North America retain its economic, political, and social position in the world.

Henry L. Hillman, one of the largest single-venture capitalists investing heavily in new high-tech ventures, taking, as *Business Week* (Jan. 21, 1985, p. 74) describes it, "his family fortune [estimated to be in excess of $1 billion] on the same journey America is on—from the fading world of smokestack industry to a shiny new era of high technology," describes the situation as follows:

> There is more change taking place now than at any other time in my business career, . . . [but only a few business leaders] have a full understanding of the threat we face from growing international competition. . . . I find myself almost wanting to shake people and say "Don't you realize what is happening?"

9

THE ROLE OF GOVERNMENT IN THE THIRD WAVE

... a wise and frugal government which shall restrain men from injuring one another, which shall leave them otherwise free to regulate their own pursuits of industry. ...

Thomas Jefferson

[The government that is the best is the government that governs least.]

CREATING THE CLIMATE

In spite of the current myth that Japan's success has been due to the directional management given by government, the most successful firms in Japan, in the United States, and in many other countries have often succeeded in spite of government, not because of it. For instance, in the 1950s the Japanese government's Ministry of International Trade and Industry (MITI) wanted to combine all Japanese auto production into two or three producers, which the companies steadfastly refused to do. These companies, including Honda, which the government tried to keep out of the industry altogether, went on to exceed all competition.

Government, however, does have a definite place in economic development, and it should. The first computer and the first commercially viable passenger jet aircraft could not have been developed without government assistance, direct or indirect. There is no way for individual companies to pioneer the space effort that has produced the satellite telecommunications system, for one thing. Government clearly has a role in science and technology development from which active, entrepreneurial companies may be nurtured. As opposed to myths about it, MITI's primary role is to support and encourage business, not to direct it.

Entrepreneurial companies do best in a rich, free-flowing environment of opportunities, new technology, and minimal structure. Government's task is to provide the best possible entrepreneurial environment, with due regard for consumers, so as to provide, in a national context, the freest most dynamic, viable, flexible, possible economy. In an economic and political system based upon free enterprise, the ability to participate fully in that society by being able to use the business tools of that free enterprising society can be considered as a basic right of participation in third wave society. During the second wave, reading and writing were the tools of functional labor by which a corporation participated in society.

> The corporation as a representative institution of American society must hold out the promise of adequately fulfilling the aspirations and beliefs of the American people. A conflict between the requirements of corporate life and the basic beliefs and promises of American society would ultimately destroy the allegiance to our form of government and society. Hence, we must analyze whether the corporation is satisfying these basic demands: the promise that opportunities be equal and rewards commensurate to abilities and efforts; the promise that each member of society, however humble, be a citizen with the status, function, and dignity of a member of society and with a chance of individual fulfillment in his

125

social life; finally, the promise that big and small, rich and poor, powerful and weak be partners in a joint enterprise rather than opponents benefiting from each other's loss.

Peter Drucker
Concept of the Corporation

If the bulk of second wave formula managers had understood what Peter Drucker has said, perhaps the conflict of the late sixties and early seventies could have been modified. As they adjust to the third wave, corporations are not only showing an increasing understanding of their social role, but they also are realizing how this understanding can increase their viability and profitability. The Japanese corporation has demonstrated this. The imposed government role in preserving corporations' dreams and rights is changing, consequently, from one of intervention to one of encouragement.

GOVERNMENT IN TRANSITION

Many of government's previous functions, such as medical care, education, a fair share in profits, recreation, patriotism, community service, and support for the arts, have been and will continue to be taken over by corporations. Government's role then is to support and encourage this trend, so that the best possible transition of these functions may be made. As corporations enter the third wave, they seem to be entering a new "adult" phase in which they can no longer act as selfish, spoiled, or vicious children who require supervision. As adults, they become more aware of their social responsibilities and roles and therefore require less supervision.

Just as the development of the organic corporation will strip away many layers of costly, obsolete middle management, this development will also strip away many layers of costly, obsolete government bureaucracy, and entire government agencies in some cases. Second wave slack will eventually fall away.

Michael A. Ledeen, senior Fellow at Georgetown University and advisor to the Secretary of State, wrote in *The Wall Street Journal* the following under the heading "Better Foreign Policy with Half the Bureaucrats."

I can guarantee that both the State Department and the Pentagon are probably twice their necessary size. That means that the business of the nation can be conducted by roughly half of the people who are now employed in these two buildings and the rest are basically taking up space and creating problems. Since they have to do something, they generate paper, organize meetings, insist on their prerogatives in the "policy process"—thereby compelling other people to generate more paper and hold still more meetings—leak, sabotage policy, and generally make mischief. In addition, they draw salaries and fringe benefits, consume overhead and eventually are paid substantial pensions. As things stand now, hardly any of them can be fired.

Deregulation, a significant trend during the seventies, has picked up steam and will continue to do so in the United States. No country in an increasingly competitive world can afford to protect and subsidize one industry over another. Deregulation, however, does not mean a diminishing role for government but a shift from an adversary and supervisory role to one of cooperation and teamwork with business. New and more demands will be placed upon government to replace the obsolete roles that have drifted away. The determinants of the third wave are also changing our government: (1) rapidly increasing unit costs are increasing deficits; (2) other governments are taking an increasingly direct role in international competition; and (3) economic phenomena are becoming increasingly difficult to modify according to formula.

Federal, state, and local governments must also learn to do more and to be different with less. They must become increasingly efficient, effective, dynamic, and organic, especially in their interactions with business. Governments are under rising pressures from their consumers, their citizens, to provide better, more specialized services at lower costs. High-powered, media-supported lobby groups and measures like proposition 13 have put the squeeze on government. One way of answering these challenges has been for the federal government to shift more of its role to the local level and to the private sector through such measures as decentralization and deregulation. Such measures have cut many layers of management and bureaucracy, as well as having saved money. Taxpayers have been outraged at examples of government waste, such as the $10,000 pin (renamed a wrench) bought by the Air Force. As the apparent and hidden powers of federal bureaucracy grew and pro-liferated, many state and local governments felt forced to emulate this trend. Because of this situation, a positive feedback system developed: Businesses grew by "taking in each others' wash." The paring and decentralization of the federal bureaucracy has shifted much work onto the shoulders of many disguisedly unemployed state and local governments. As this trend proceeds and as demands increase and change, governments will find it more difficult to apply formula management techniques, and to use, tolerate, or build slack. Under political and budgetary pressures, the paring will continue and cannot be sidetracked by agency-sponsored evaluations of budgets and programs.

127

President Reagan recently commented upon employment cuts by the federal government: "The government is actually doing things more efficiently than it was doing before. We're still providing the needed services with fewer people. The savings to the taxpayers is nearly a billion and a half a year in salaries alone."[1]

President Reagan has gone on to describe how the greatest obstacle to increased effectiveness and efficiency is poor management. The Grace Commission found that the greatest impediment to better management is the government information system. In effect, this system produces more noise than information. The main culprit is the government's computer systems and networks, which are either a mess, or outdated, or nonexistent.

A policy of more precise *information* is necessary. During the second wave, the ethic of throwing money and formulas at any and all problems spawned a vast external but hidden bureaucracy of consultants and grant, research, and contract administrators. In those days, government contracts were given on a cost-plus basis by which a "fair" profit was made on a percentage of cost. The cost-plus system provided an inbuilt incentive to increase not decrease costs; and because the end of a program or contract meant the unemployment of many such administrators, there was an inbuilt incentive to delay and prolong projects and programs. Now contractors are increasingly being forced to absorb many unforeseen and excess costs, instead of being able to renegotiate or increase their profits. A growing number of government contractors, especially defense contractors, have had to take a lean and mean approach because the government's external bureaucracy is being trimmed. Government has also found it necessary to go after perceived fraud seriously, as in the case of General Dynamics. General Dynamics purportedly underbid a contract deliberately, knowing it could "renegotiate" to obtain a higher price.

GOVERNMENT COSTS

The paring of government expenditures to increase efficiency and effectiveness is no longer a question of choice but of necessity. A deficit of the size projected not only indicates a society's inability to pay for what it wants (and impending chaos), but it also measures the relative inefficiency and ineffectiveness of bigger and more expensive equipment and programs. Automobile companies promoted this second wave ideology of bigger and more expensive in their efforts to fight foreign competition. Our auto industry tried to sell the public on the concept that the American automobile was the best buy because it was the cheapest by the pound. Everyone should have been driving army surplus tanks if the public had bought that line.

In 1981 a *Scientific American* article described how an Egyptian missile destroyed an Israeli destroyer costing many times as much. The ship that delivered the missile stood far out of range of the destroyer. The effective delivered utility of the Israeli destroyer was essentially zero. Increased precision, information, speed, and technology demolished a massive bulk costing many times as much. In comparison, the United States federal government is also finding out that effective local programs cost much less than broad expensive federal programs in many instances. Motivation requires work at both federal and local levels.

> If you're going to play together as a team, you've got to care for one another. . . . Each player has to be thinking about the next guy and saying to himself: "If I don't block that man, Paul is going to get his legs broken. I have to do my job well in order that he can do his." The difference between mediocrity and greatness is the feeling these guys have for each other. Most people call it team spirit. When the players are embued with that special feeling, you know you've got yourself a winning team. . . . It's the same thing, whether you're running a ball club or a corporation. After all, does one man build a car all by himself?[2]
>
> Vince Lombardi, coach
> Green Bay Packers

REALIGNMENT OF GOVERNMENT IDEOLOGY AND INSTITUTIONS

Government administrators will have to be (1) increasingly well educated; (2) of higher human capital; (3) more national and international in scope and collaboration; (4) business and consumer oriented, as business and consumers become increasingly integrated; and (5) more flexible and versatile. While government administrators' quality and willingness to assist must be improved, American traditions will not support the establishment of an elite bureaucracy, as is established in Japan, France, and many other nations. The redesign will ultimately be American.

> I think that in the next ten to twenty years, all institutions are going to have to alter radically the way they organize work and manage their workers. The successful institutions are going to be those that design their administrative systems to fit the full dimension of man—a dimension much

larger than anything we know today. Government institutions, especially HEW have a particularly pressing obligation to lead the way.

Elsa Porter, assistant secretary of administration, 1978

Although the founding fathers were well aware of the necessity of evolutionary change, those that came after them, especially those that came after 1870 and the advent of the second wave, were not so astute. The assessment, improvement, and realignment of institutions and ideologies has progressed little. We have become used to looking backward for inspiration, not forward. The Japanese, on the other hand, are constantly assessing their institutions and ideologies and are looking outward and forward for new ideas to add to and improve their base. Within the last 100 years, they also have undertaken two all-encompassing reassessments and realignments of both ideologies and institutions; the first one was taken under the Meiji restoration and the second after World War II. If we do not want to run out of ideological capital, we must change our procedures and improve our institutions, many of which are in trouble. We must develop a capability to build ideological capital and to design and redesign institutions.

GOVERNMENT BUREAUCRACIES

By definition, government bureaucracies are the ultimate monopoly, and they have absolute market control. It may be said that change comes to some degree with each administration, but members of the bureaucracy have a tendency to form a self-protective, insular, and perpetuating society. Previous to the Reagan administration, the expansion of government employees and agencies had been explosive, and to some quite frightening. Since 1970 the size of both the internal and external bureaucracy had more than tripled. The number of lawyers in Washington quadrupled, not only indicating the growth of the external bureaucracy but also its growing power and the shift of the bulk of policy development from Congress. In the nineteenth century, a member of the Canadian government made the following comment about this propensity of a bureaucracy.

He [the executive] may flutter and struggle in the net, as some well meaning [executives] have done, but he must resign himself to his fate, and like a snared bird be content with the narrow limits assigned to him by his keepers. I have known one sneered at, bullied, and almost shut out of society, while his obstinate resistance to the system created a suspicion that he might not become its victim, but I never knew one who, even with the full support of the representative branch backed by the full confidence of his sovereign, . . . was able to contend with the small knot of functionaries who form the councils, fill the offices, and wield the power of government. The plain reason is because while he is amenable to his sovereign, and the members of the Assembly are controlled by their constituents, these men are not responsible at all [to an electorate], and can always protect and sustain each other whether assailed by the representatives of the sovereign or the representatives of the people.[3]

In a state of pure monopoly and absolute market control, the organization becomes more concerned with its own internal structure than with shifts in the external environment because it controls the external environment. Not having to concern itself with the external environment, the organization becomes enmeshed in internal politics and strife and suffers in consequence from hardening of the arteries. Bureaucracies have been notoriously uninnovative, uncreative, and slow to respond. An executive or CEO must find ways to motivate and activate the bureaucracy if the synergy of the nation is to be realized. The Japanese bureaucracy has inherited the respect and traditions of the Samurai warrior class which had the service of the people and the emperor as a prime principle, their own personal lives being of no importance. This attitude generates a national service consciousness of self-sacrifice in the Japanese bureaucracy. For various reasons, this self-sacrificing attitude does not exist in most Western bureaucracies. In the American bureaucracy, the essential ethic of moral selflessness and interactive collaboration must be improved substantially. The consequence of an entrenched and immovable bureaucracy is eventually chaos and ruin, as it is in the corporate world.

GOVERNMENT MOTIVATION

If you want to leave something behind besides your official portraits . . . develop a theme. Take a stand at the start. . . . Reach into and motivate the bureaucracy.

> Mark Green, director
> Congress Watch, 1979

A heroine who has struggled with this problem is Elsa Porter, assistant secretary for administration under President Carter. Her programs were for the most part also kept on by the Reagan administration. She realized early that organizations, even in government, were people, not machines, who should not be operated according to a manual or formula. She recognized what it entails for the federal government to enter the third wave. Individuals working in government need challenge, motivation, care, respect, intellectual creativity, meaning, purpose, and human interaction just as people within corporations do. In the often intense political atmosphere of Washington, people naturally want to develop protective mechanisms, such as working to rule, clique memberships, counteroffensives, and basic mistrust of the system and others within it. These mechanisms, however, only engender more of the same and create a state of near catatonia and freeze up in some government organizations, with the participants feeling that whatever direction they may take will be considered the wrong one—a pattern that gives rise to frustration, anger, and depressions.

New government

If America is to adapt successfully to the third wave and compete successfully in the international sphere, this situation cannot continue. American business needs a collaborative government, no matter how much some old diehards yell about the cooperation. Elsa Porter understood this and set out to transform mechanical hierarchical organizations into organic and dynamic ones. Government organizations are at the forefront of the third wave, generating, controlling, and dispensing information. They must also take on a new collaborative role in the third wave, as deregulation picks up steam. One of Porter's first initiatives was to dispense third wave literature, such as Alvin Toffler's *Third Wave*, for reading and study.

While Ms. Porter pushed the development of a more dynamic ethic, she devoted considerable effort and time to modifying and harmonizing organizational systems through which human interactions could grow. She has given numerous lectures about the changes that are underway in an effort to broaden the too-often myopic vision of members in many of these organizations. By understanding the relationship between mind and body, as many third wave Silicon Valley firms have, she encouraged the development of on-site exercise programs. Exercise and fitness assist thinking, interaction, and psychological stability.

Porter understood that the organization represents energy, which must be generated and given direction and synergy. She believed that such human energy must be channeled where it can do the most good for all. Human energy must be focused against the "evil" forces of malevolent and arbitrary action. The key ingredient for an organization is good people, especially at the middle management level. Middle management is key in translating the energy of an organization into a dynamic and organic form. For this energy to be translated and to grow, it must be reinforced by success, with whatever measures are appropriate. It is the spirit and experience of success that builds organizational force and energy. Porter fervently believed in this spirit and in people's need to believe in the worth of a cause in order to expend their best efforts.

The moral and spiritual force

People are agglomerations of all that is human—emotions, insecurities, inadequacies, courage, hopes. To get the organization moving with the maximum positive momentum, Porter realized that she had to interact with all these traits of humanity. To her it was paramount that a new ethic be developed and incorporated and that bureaucrats understand what an important mission they have to perform and what the broader scope of their mission is. She understood the importance of a new evolutionary corporate warp under which the various participants might collaborate and unite. Ms. Porter also understood that she was the steel that gives form, structure, and strength to the warp much as the steel framework does for a skyscraper. At the same time, she understood that the warp gave her strength, legitimacy, and authority. This warp was her moral power. She knew that she had to be the foundation point around which the organism evolved and that the organism must evolve if it is to transform itself to cope with the third wave.

The moral law causes the people to be in complete accord with their ruler, so that they will follow him regardless of their lives, undismayed by danger.

Sun Tzu
The Art of War

Comprehending that a major transition and transformation was underway, Ms. Porter took time off in 1970 to search for a new approach. She looked for answers at Harvard but found that the university was more hidebound and mechanically structured in its thinking than many agencies in Washington. "I learned they had no answers at Harvard, [at the Business School and the John F. Kennedy School of Government] and that some of the experts refused to talk with each other. I realized that the management controls needed in government were different from those that work in business and that to humanize the federal bureaucracy meant starting on new ground."[4] It was said that many of her programs were successful, but not noticeable because the generated changes seemed to have come about as a result of natural evolutionary processes.

133

THE ORGANIC CONCEPT

When the founding fathers set up our nation the country was governed more by principles and policies than by laws and programs. The process and evolution of political thought was common to most conversations. With the coming of the industrial second wave and large masses of immigration from countries that did not share in the English tradition of evolutionary politics, government began to adopt a structured mechanical form. America was treated as a giant wealth-creating machine that had only to be programmed and regulated to provide the maximum, or at least satisfactory, results. This country ceased to be primarily a qualitative place to live because the main emphasis of quality no longer rested upon spiritual values. In short, second wave society forgot the line of thinking implicit in the founding fathers' work—that the nation was an evolutionary organism made up of independent, free people. It chose instead to create steel mills, factories, and an increasingly powerful central government.

THE REGENERATION

A noticeable shift back to the earlier form of government is taking place in the third wave. Deregulation has created new opportunities for independent business. Political issues have begun to revolve around issues, such as the environment and the quality of life, that are not necessarily related to business growth and wealth. The government has begun to shift from programs to policies and from regulation to values as methods of governing. More power and revenues are being allocated to local authorities in order to get capability as close as possible to where it is needed. A centralized government can no longer cope effectively, if it ever could, with the rapidly changing complexity of the third wave. Political thought and processes have once again become a part of most conversations. The third wave has in essence engendered a new nation.

The nature of the transition from a government of regulation and programs to a decentralized government of values and policies requires that the values, ethic, and corporate warp of the working level of government be recharged and interconnected. The change in values must occur externally as well as internally, or else the necessary spirit and motive force needed for national competitive transformation will be inadequate.

Quantifying everything is another aspect of government that will have to change. Government during the second wave, like corporations, utilized formulas and tried to govern by numbers. Bureaucrats tried to quantify everything, their main numerical indicator being the GNP. It is no longer a viable approach. To illustrate, many pundits have said that America has suffered a substantial decline in the growth rate of the GNP since the advent of the third wave in 1970; therefore, the national well-being is in decline. The gross national product was a measure of effectiveness during the second wave because the achievement of objectives was related to the amount of resources that could be thrown at them. During the third wave, however, effectiveness is more a result of the information applied to an objective. Generally, the more information that is applied, the fewer resources, and related waste, are required. It is therefore possible to obtain increasing effectiveness using fewer resources. Since it is not yet possible to get accurate monetary valuations of all applied information, the value of information cannot be reflected accurately in the GNP.

If it were possible to measure the intensity of information applied, that information intensity most probably would show a significant and rapid increase on a per capita and national basis since 1970 and the advent of the third wave. It has been pointed out that with the advent of the second wave, in the couple of decades following 1870, the wholesale price index declined by more than 100 percent, because of the cheap resources made available by second wave technology. This decline indicated an improvement in national well-being. If it were possible to accurately measure the cost of information consumed, there would no doubt be a dramatic drop in the cost of information since 1970. Information intensity would now be a much better indicator of effectiveness and national well-being.

Consequently, government is beginning to shift its emphasis from managing and generating numbers to managing, producing, and disseminating information, hence its shift from programs and budgets to policies and values. Government is increasingly under pressure to become mean and lean, efficient and effective. One administrator who understood the consequences of the pressures of the third wave said that he could see increasing public pressures for increased efficiency and effectiveness because of budgetary constraints and such continued initiatives as proposition 13, followed possibly by "proposition 14. We have to look carefully out three to five years, see what we are going to have to be doing, and see what our competition will have to be doing, and do it better at less cost," he added.[5] He might have also added—"if the agency and myself are to survive."

INFORMATION DEPLOYMENT

America has among the best available channels to deploy resources, people, and money; but our capability to do so is poor because we do not know when to best utilize these resources, people, and monies. Government can at least partially fill this gap in our capability to use what is available to us by producing continual information and assessment of (1) internal and external markets, (2) job opportunities, and (3) long-run projections and scenarios in forms that can be readily used. Much information is and has been produced, but it is not readily accessible nor can it be easily researched. Government should convert to electronic databases for public access. These databases should also have the most advanced software available, allowing automatic search and logical inferences. The more information that can be used for the deployment of resources, people, and money, the more efficient and effective they will be. (Incidentally, the government will collect more taxes in the process, partially because turnover will be accelerated, allowing the system to quickly pay for itself.) This service is perhaps closer to the crucial role performed by MITI, which does not entail any sort of "directive" industrial planning. Accelerated and more accurate organic deployment will result in substantial increases in competitive capability.

VALUES AND POLICIES IN GOVERNING

Although the Carter administration well understood the worth of values and policies in governing, it did not execute its understanding well. The Reagan administration, perhaps from Mr. Reagan's experience in projecting values and role models, knows how to execute government by values and policies. It matters what is said, how it is said and presented, and how it is visualized and remembered. Perhaps the prime lesson taught by the Reagan administration is that images (visual or mental) are actions, and as such, they do much to accomplish objectives and build confidence. Ronald Reagan would never be photographed dropping out of a 10-kilometer run.

Government needs to clarify its role and the role it will be playing in the future. What are the rules of the game, and in which direction will government evolve, if it is to evolve? The methodology to clarify and stabilize an evolutionary economy in the past was a somewhat haphazard use of fiscal and monetary policy, with a good dose of Keynesian economics buttressed by defense expenditures. It was thought that government's domestic role could be separate from its international role, i.e., that you could have "guns and butter," but the Viet Nam conflict changed that concept. From that episode, government has realized that it can play a far stronger role on the international scene by ensuring an increasingly powerful economy, that economic information and growth are the first line of national security.

Synergy in growth

Defense and related space expenditures have played a haphazard role in generating growth. Such expenditures and monetary and fiscal policies should follow some form of longer term framework related to social and economic/

business needs. A first step could be some form of synergistic, integrative, and commercial framework for government expenditures on research and development over a longer time schedule. Such a framework could take the form of an interactive electronic research network (e.g., the ARPANET-PARC network discussed later). Such a network could gradually shift the centralization of research from a few centers to an interactive, synergistic national grid that would allow many smaller scale outfits to bid on research and development contracts. Software development, perhaps the essential focus of research, would be greatly enhanced by such a network.

The interactively directed expenditure on a national research and development net would be far more effective in stabilizing and energizing the economy than the haphazard measures now in place. This network would not aid in national planning, which on a directive basis cannot work; it would merely supply some integrative-interactive thought to ongoing expenditures, thereby maximizing their positive effect and minimizing waste and negative effects.

Industrial policy

Government's new role is similar to the new role of business management, which is less directive and regulatory and more facilitative and collaborative. In this new role, a new consciousness has to permeate government. Industrial policy should mean just that and should not relate to government planning in the least. Industrial policy should collaborate with and evolve around government planning, not be incorporated within the plan.

Government, also like management, must do its utmost to encourage entrepreneurship. One of the best ways to do so is through the tax structure. Dividends from new, arms-length start-ups should not be taxed for ten years, and capital gains from such start-ups should not be taxed for five years. The costs of patenting and marketing a new idea should be deductible against other income. Savings and investments in productive instead of fixed assets should be encouraged and not punished. For example, interest from savings in Japan is largely free of taxation, while investment in housing is only minimally tax deductible. In the United States, tax deductibility for housing started out as an incentive for people to own their own homes, but has now become a major impediment to the objective because the ability to deduct interest paid on mortgages has driven the cost of housing out of most people's reach and into the realm of speculation. Housing is more valued now as a tax shelter than as a people shelter.

Government also has a responsibility to control and minimize its own spending so that it does not borrow money needed by the private sector. Data Resources International of Cambridge, Massachusetts, has estimated that private-sector industry will require $3 trillion of investment over the next ten years to make the transition into third wave. The role of government should be, as Jefferson said, to create a viable environment for people to pursue their natural propensity for industry and creativity. Government should get out of their way and not to try to do it for them.

> The merchants will manage commerce the better, the more they are left free to manage for themselves.

> Thomas Jefferson, 1800
> (Excerpt from advertisement, American Association of Railroads, March 1985, *SF Chronicle.)*

The revolution against bureaucracy is not restricted. In Peking students of Peking University recently held an antibureaucracy costume party. Among the more imaginative costumes was one worn by a student who came wrapped in red tape and another with the Chinese characters "no" and "maybe" stamped on various parts of his body, including his forehead. The following *San Francisco Chronicle,* March 7, 1984, article is an all too clear illustration of how organizations in the bureaucratic stage lose touch with reality and become more concerned with their own internal structures. They are an evident danger to themselves and society. A man named Boff pleaded with the Dallas Fire Department to send an ambulance for his stricken stepmother. Boff sued the department for $300,000 in damages because of its response to the situation.

Nurse:	And what is the problem there?
Boff:	I don't know, if I knew I wouldn't be . . .
Nurse:	Sir would you answer my questions, please? What is the problem?
Boff:	She is having trouble breathing.
Nurse:	How old is this person?
Boff:	She is 60 years old.
Nurse:	Where is she now?
Boff:	She is in the bedroom right now.
Nurse:	Can I speak with her please?
Boff:	No, you can't. She seems like she's incoherent.
Nurse:	Why is she incoherent?
Boff:	How the hell do I know?
Nurse:	Sir, don't curse me.
Boff:	Well I don't care. You stupid . . . questions you're asking.

	Give me someone who knows what they're doing. Why don't you send an ambulance out here?
Nurse:	Sir we only come out on life-threatening emergencies.
Boff:	Well this is a life-threatening emergency.
Nurse:	Hold on, sir. I'll let you speak with my super . . . uh, officer.
Supervisor:	Hello?
Boff:	What do I have to do to get an ambulance to this house?
Supervisor:	You have to answer the nurse's questions.
Boff:	All right. What are they before she dies, will you you please tell me what the hell you want?
Supervisor:	Well I'll tell you what, if you curse one more time I'm gonna hang up this phone.
Boff:	Well I'll tell you what, if this were your mother in there and can't breathe what would you do?
Supervisor:	You answer the nurse's questions and we'll get you some help.
Boff:	She is having difficulty breathing . . . she cannot talk.
Supervisor:	OK, she's back on the air. Don't you cuss her again.
Nurse:	OK, sir, I need to talk to her still.
Boff:	You can't. She is incoherent.
Nurse:	Let me talk to her, sir.
Boff:	[to his roommate] Please tell her she's incoherent and cannot talk [to the nurse]. She cannot talk at all.
Nurse:	Why?
Boff:	Well, how am I supposed to know?
Nurse:	Well give her the phone.
Boff:	[to his roommate] Give her the phone in there. Give her the phone. I know she can't talk but they want to talk to her. . . . But she can't talk [to the nurse]. . . . Forget it. I'll call the main hospital around here, all right?
Nurse:	OK, Bye-bye.

Boff called the nearby Mesquite Hospital but was told it could not send an ambulance to his house in Dallas, the television station reported. With Mrs. Boff's condition worsening, Boff's roommate, Dennis Fleming, placed a second call to the emergency number.

Nurse:	Are you the same man I was talking to earlier?
Fleming:	No, that was my roommate.
Nurse:	Uh, huh. Why can't I talk to the lady?

Fleming:	She cannot talk.
Nurse:	Why?
Fleming:	She's in . . . she's just out of it. In fact, he's going in there now. He thinks she's dead.
Nurse:	What do you mean by "out of it"?
Fleming:	She is incoherent.
Boff:	[back on the line] She is dead now. Thank you, ma'am! Would you please send an ambulance? Would you please send an ambulance here?

10

STRATEGY AND ORGANIC ACTION

The highest form of generalship is to balk the enemy's plans.

Sun Tzu
The Art of War

ORGANIC STRATEGY

There is a story about how the famous but somewhat bureaucratic Procter & Gamble got "skunked." A new spray cleanser called Formula 409 had become quite successful in a market that Procter & Gamble considered its prerogative. The company developed a new product called Cinch and decided to test market it in Denver. The Formula 409 people got wind of this and pulled their product from the Denver area. Procter & Gamble was pleased with the test market results and decided to market Cinch nationally. The Formula 409 people had expected this to happen and had prepared to launch a special campaign in each region just before the introduction of Cinch. In addition, a six-month supply of Formula 409 was given away with each purchase, saturating the market for a minimum of half a year. When Cinch became available for consumer purchase, Procter & Gamble did not know what killed the market and its effort. Not only was Cinch a failure, this strategic move indefinitely forestalled Procter & Gamble from making another effort in the same market. The Formula 409 people, in balking the Procter & Gamble plan, followed Sun Tzu's advice and General MacArthur's strategy of hitting them where they ain't.

The third wave corporation recognizes that it operates in a dynamic environment composed of other living systems that offer excellent or poor options. Without the necessary quality and quantity of information, the corporation can sometimes be deceived by the interaction. It follows that the better the information possessed by a corporation, and the poorer the information possessed by its competitors, the fewer obstacles and resistance will impede the corporation. The corporation will follow an easier path to its objective. Convincing interacting firms of the inconsequence of one's actions and avoiding interaction are ways of obtaining the "cooperation" of competitors.

Courses of possible action for the corporation can now be modeled instantaneously via computers and sophisticated software, so they may be considered quickly and acted upon. Japanese firms constantly assess not only the strategic position of a competitor but also where the competition might be in the future, and where they themselves are and where they will be in relation to the competition. Consequently, they have a good idea of where the competitive advantages and disadvantages might lie. If a competitor gains an advantage in his or her present course of action, even though he or she presents no threat at the moment, it may be best to sidetrack or balk the competition.

Nolan Bushnell often tells with a wry smile the story of how he always kept a hologram on his desk when he was starting Atari. He would use the hologram to convince the spies of mechanical arcade game makers that video games were just a passing fad because holographic games were the wave of the future. He deterred them from the market; he balked the competition. He knew that it would take a massive computer, larger than any in existence, to play holographic games. Bushnell did, however, sell Atari to Warner. The video game industry has declined, and Atari has taken it on the chin because video games were a fad to a large degree, but not because of any threat from holographic technology.

THE PRIMARY STRATEGIC CHALLENGE

Information is the primary strategic challenge faced by corporations. Mechanical firms will not be able to cope with ever-increasing requirements for better information and quick action in an environment of intense information and noise. It is becoming relatively easier for organic corporations to determine the course of action of mechanical corporations and to seize upon their weak points.

Because the organic corporation is not centrally directed, strategic thinking must be built into the corporate warp or culture. The difference between the professional gunslinger and the amateur who is quick on the draw is strategic thinking. Corporate members must learn to think and act in unison. United thought and action is an ongoing process that requires constant review and adjustment through feedback from all concerned.

In this way, the corporation can progress from a random hit-or-miss type of operation, from the gunslinger-pioneer organizational form to the entrepreneurial-corporate form in which the probabilities of creative success are increased. While Hewlett-Packard is a leading exponent of the entrepreneurial form, the company readily admits that one of its primary concerns is how to maintain the momentum and spirit of responsible and strategic entrepreneurialism. How can Hewlett-Packard maintain a way of thinking and evolving to keep the company dynamic, prosperous, and in the forefront of technology?

We need to keep the entrepreneurial spirit alive in the corporation.

John Young, CEO
Hewlett-Packard

To maintain a viable organic form, the corporation must constantly be assessed and designed by all involved in order for it to become a strategic evolutionary organism. Entrepreneurial action is the result of strategic thinking and of a particular consciousness, rather than of an analysis and formula.

STRATEGIC THINKING

Strategic success cannot be reduced to a formula, nor can anyone become a strategic thinker by reading a book. Nevertheless, there are habits of mind and modes of thinking that can be acquired through practice to help you free the creative power of your subconscious and improve your odds of coming up with winning concepts. . . . Creativity, mental productivity, and the power of strategic insight know no national boundaries.

Kenichi Ohmae
The Mind of the Strategist, 1982

That creative strategy is the result of unorthodox thinking is implicit in Dr. Ohmae's statement. A group experience and certain habits of the mind, such as looking for the nonobvious and related possibilities, enhance creative strategy. Strategic thinking and action is the result of a process of interaction and evolution that produces a particular mind set among its players. The participants are players because this is very much a game with serious consequences.

STIMULATING INNOVATIVE THOUGHT

To induce innovative thinking, to stimulate it, to grease its wheels, managers in the organic corporation have acted in bizarre ways, gone into fits of temper, created crises, and used many imaginative ways of rewarding and encouraging this process. One manager had a special hot line installed in his office. He instructed everyone to call him on the line with any innovative idea no matter how small it was. The manager then would write a commendation and would give a suitable reward to the person who succeeded in creating an innovation. Considered especially important and given a special award were any innovations that contributed to a strategic competitive edge. Such tactics stimulated all players to think strategically because it soon became clear who was playing, who was winning, and who was thinking.

Strategic organic action flows naturally from motivated, aware, and creative people who must be given the necessary strategic base to achieve their and their company's potential. Intrinsic to this strategic base is:

- Careful placement of a product in a growing market (being at the right place at the right time)
- Creation and development of a positive customer and industry image
- Technological edge
- Increasing experience in sales and service of products
- Increasing knowledge of the competition
- Strategic placement of an evolving technology within specific niches
- Increasing knowledge of customer needs and financial requirements
- An increasing general knowledge base
- Evolutionary, efficient, and effective systems for independent action and control
- Financial improvement to increase profits
- Constant recruitment of outstanding people
- Challenge, opportunity, meaning, adventure, excitement, and profit for all

Upon such a base, the corporation builds a dynamic fermentation process that creates the necessary juices for strategic action. From this fermenting process

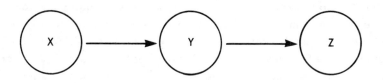

PARAMETERS

EXHIBIT 10-1   Corporations move toward their objectives in a series of states (a permutation). A permutation must move within its parameters (deviation usually causes degeneration). Second wave parameters were relatively wide and stable, so organizations did not have to adapt or change very much to get from X to Z. Second wave organizations were relatively insensitive to their external and internal environments, and feedback was not an important factor.

comes the development of the strategic mind. The strategic mind becomes used to the necessary habits of strategic thought in the process.

Primary questions that must be considered are: Where is the strategic and interactive comparative advantage? And what can be done to achieve this advantage in an evolutionary way?

Through an interactive process, the corporation becomes an organism, like the school of fish or the championship rugby team described in chapter 3. The targets of opportunity are assessed on the spot, the appropriate decision and action are taken, and the whole school of individuals flows behind each action as an organism.

NUMBERS AND ANALYSIS

Numbers and analysis are useful in their proper context, but too often corporate bureaucrats have axes to grind, knives to insert, empires to build, and CEOs to manage. They are simply looking for a place to hide, or they may find numbers and copious analysis very useful. The honest use or misuse of numbers and analysis can be misleading. In developing strategy and action, the corporation must relate the value of numbers and analysis to the speed of environmental change and to the speed at which such numbers can be churned into useful information upon which members can act. The slower the rate of change in the environment, the more useful and relevant the analysis because an analysis always describes a previous set of relationships or their extension

145

and not the current reality, no matter how fast the analysis can be produced. The slower the rate of change, the closer the analysis comes to describing current reality and to producing information. In a fast changing environment, any lag between information and action becomes increasingly critical because information in such an environment deteriorates to noise quickly. In the final scenes of the movie *Star Wars*, spiritual Ben advises Luke to drop the computer controls, the numbers, and to rely upon "the force," his mind, to make the decision and to act.

The ultimate computer is the human mind.

John F. Kennedy

"May the force be with you."

Ronald Reagan

STRATEGIC SHARING

When you capture spoils from the enemy, they must be used as rewards so that all your men have desire to fight, each on his own account.

Sun Tzu
The Art of War

Alexander the Great, James McDonnell, Napoleon, and other strategic geniuses realized that people within an organization who share in suffering, glory, rewards, recognition, and experiences act cohesively as one for the betterment of the common good. One of the first strategic steps of any organic corporation has always been an effective and progressive profit sharing plan. The organic Japanese corporation perhaps epitomizes this idea of strategic sharing. The strategic individual action of any corporate participant is shared by his or her colleagues and reinforced by them if necessary. In this way, individual initiative blends into organic action.

Strategic organic action is also made possible by constant and shared study. In Japan all the members of the group constantly study each other, the corporation, their competitors and potential competitors, and the world, and then ardently discuss the results. This allows the possible courses of joint, cohesive action to become clear. By studying and testing each other, each member of the group develops an idea of (1) how every other member

146

develops an idea; (2) how every other member might respond in any set of circumstances; and (3) whether or not these ideas involve a member's own actions. When taking individual action, any member has a good concept of how the rest of the group will react and of what support is available through this method of study. The possibilities and probabilities of successful action are maximized. The founders of ROLM, for example, started out playing poker with each other for quite a while before they discussed any ideas of launching a company.

Westerners are often perplexed by the long process through which the Japanese corporation makes a decision. What actually takes place is not merely a decision but the development and analysis of possible group strategies and related resources to carry out the decision; therefore, when the decision is made, all members of the group know what is expected of them and realize that they are openly committed to the decision. With many second wave organizations in the West, the decision is made and then must be sold. Following this, a strategy must be devised and resources must be found. The process is usually longer and is carried out less efficiently, a process Japanese businesses find equally if not more puzzling. If the decision is not sold, it is rejected. The Japanese find this even more perplexing because of the inefficient use of human capital, thought, and effort. One maxim adopted by the ROLM corporation is that the power released to achieve a decision is proportional to the number of people involved in making it.

GROUP SYNERGY

In studying, sharing, and discussing everyone's work, each member in the Japanese corporation can be helped with his or her deficiencies and can maximize his or her attributes to ensure a stronger and more dynamic group spirit and capability. The combined spirit and strength of the group gives the organization a competitive edge because it takes strategic action in unison. The spirit of the group, intrinsically linked by corporate culture, is often the deciding factor in any competitive endeavor.

Corporate spirit was the driving force that allowed APPLE to challenge IBM. There is another line of strategy that implies a company should seek to demoralize competitors by getting them to expend their resources on fruitless endeavors. For example, a corporation can invest in areas in which it might have a strong hidden advantage. When competitors open the market with products in that area, the corporation might take over the market with its hidden advantage. Many large-scale second wave corporations pursued this tactic by virtue of their size. During the third wave, corporations use this tactic by virtue of their superior information.

Hit 'em where they ain't.

General Douglas MacArthur

TIMING

In studying the world, its trends, and its changes, a group is able to plot various strategies in relation to potential opportunities and problems. By knowing this and its member interaction, the group is able to devise possible strategies and related timing. It is becoming increasingly true that the first company in a market has a decided, longer term strategic advantage. As markets and technologies constantly change with increasing rapidity, timing has become an essential component of success. In studying trends and political events, the group can see where it and its competitors are off balance, what adjustments might be necessary, and what aggressive thrusts might be made. In studying the corporation, the group is able to assess where it might serve the best possible long-term purpose within its internal market. The group should then be able to determine how best to interact with the various parts of the organism and what the organism needs.

Strategy is an evolutionary plan that requires constant attention from each participant because it represents a critical focused momentum, without which the corporation is at the mercy of the drifting tides of the environment that sooner or later would drive it onto the rocks.

STRATEGIC CORPORATE CULTURE

The corporate warp tells participants where they are going, why, and how to get there; consequently, a strategic corporate warp is necessary. It is important for participants to have a positive frame of mind and to believe that they can win. The principles and objectives of the corporate warp guide these beliefs. The realization that they are working with other good, outstanding people who know where they are going gives corporate participants adequate support and the belief that they can win. Belief in the ultimate win is carefully cultivated as is a general corporate commitment to certain moral principles, and both contribute to participant's ability to be superior and to trust others within the corporation. These moral principles enable participants to relate to others within the corporation and also to people in different businesses in various countries. Profits are secondary in most progressive firms, especially in many Silicon Valley firms.

Trust and interpersonal networks allow a corporation's human capital to maximize and pool its potential. The more human capital invested in strategy,

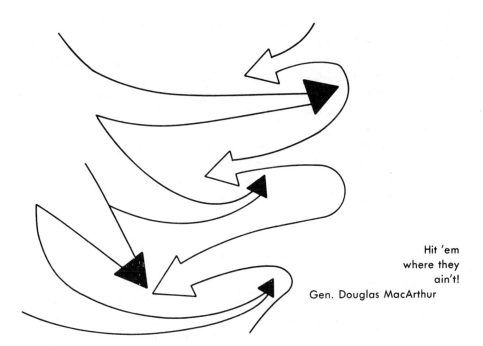

Hit 'em
where they
ain't!
Gen. Douglas MacArthur

EXHIBIT 10-2   Strategic confrontation, action, and reaction require a corporation to hit its competitors when they are off balance and do not expect a punch. Competitors will give way to the unexpected punch when they have strength to waste.

the more cohesive the group; the more focused the human capital, the more effective is the group; the more minds within the group, the more feedback; the more information within the group, the more computing power that can be usefully and continually applied.

Strategy operates best if the competition has no conception of what the strategy is. Organic strategy is the most desirable because it is not usually understood by competitors until action is taken. Traditional strategy, on the other hand, is predictable. Organic strategy is a real-time, current strategy that involves immediate, appropriate action, which is guided by an ever-evolving warp. Organic action gives a corporation a decided edge in dealing with corporations oriented toward a traditional straight-line tunnel vision type of mechanical strategy, which is often not quick or flexible enough to adapt to problems or opportunities as they arise.

Many second wave firms use their size as strategy, attempting to scare competitors away from "their" markets by what often was the myth of invincible size. This myth sufficed during the second wave because there were enough true stories of smaller firms being crushed. In the third wave, however, this tactic has lost much of its utility because information and human capital have become generally available. Many second wave myths have been destroyed, while new avenues of market penetration have opened for organic corporations. Instead of being an asset now, size has become an inflexible detriment in many cases.

Flexibility of strategic organic action allows the corporation to flow toward its objectives around natural and unnatural obstacles. Flexible action must also have high tensile strength, i.e., the various particles must act cohesively as the corporation twists and turns its way toward its goals. Strategic action within a corporation consists of (1) the kind of people and how they relate; (2) the intensity of the corporate warp; and (3) available and adequate resources. The moral and spiritual beliefs of the corporation's people is intrinsic to its strength of action.

CREATIVE COMPETITION

Nolan Bushnell, the aforementioned guru of Silicon Valley, said that time was the essence of success and consequent strategy. Do not let any time pass without using it to maximum utility. Using time efficiently constantly improves execution and precision. Thought and attention constantly improve efficiency and effectiveness because things are never as efficient or effective as they might be. The customer and the market are always looking for increased efficiency and effectiveness, which translate into a better product for less money, a product that will do more and be more reliable. The customer is always looking for an increased precision delivery of utility. Every individual should bear this in mind because the company that executes better than others always has the advantage.

During the second wave, corporate strategy could rely on the mass manipulation of factor inputs because of market control and a cheap and stable supply of raw materials. In the third wave environment of rapidly changing markets and accelerating costs, each individual must become a source of strategy and action. Everyone must learn how to develop and evolve interactive strategic plans and actions.

In the second wave, people assessed factors for their relevance in a specified market; in the third wave, individuals must not only learn how factors relate to the present corporate markets, but they must also think of how they might strategically relate to possible markets. Individuals must shift from three-dimensional time to four-dimensional time in thought and action. To do so, individuals must continuously gather as much information as possible and must study possible implications on a constant basis. They must attack information from all angles to evaluate potential problems and opportunities. Questions and answers must be formulated and reformulated, even after what seems to be a satisfactory conclusion is found because the process is continuous. The more possible actions taken, the more viable any action taken. This is the course taken by Lee Iacocca and the philosophy he has tried to instill in his people.

> Fighting with a large army under your command is nowise different from fighting with a small one: it is a question of (appropriate) signs and signals. . . . The value of a whole army—a mighty host of a million men—is dependent on one man alone; such is the influence of spirit.

> Sun Tzu
> *The Art of War*

Options for each individual and each corporation develop from a constantly defined base. What motivates each individual or each corporation? What business is each in? Neither the individual nor the corporation can afford to be in the security business. They must be in the business of growth because security lies in growth. Increases in feedback and risk follow increases in growth and change, forcing all individuals to become increasingly entrepreneurially oriented. For example, individuals who thought they were involved in secure industries, such as transportation and utilities, have found themselves members of a high-wire act, if they have not already been laid off.

Individuals and corporations must function at the competitive edge, at the points of confrontation where competitors meet each other. Often these points and the consequent points of advantage, although critical, are not clear. Through strategic organic action and thinking, the individual and the company can exploit areas of gray mist. For instance, a competitor may not be aware that the customer needs an added feature to the product. It is therefore possible for an individual to develop an advantage by digging out this piece of information. In so doing, the individual and the corporation can always keep one step ahead of the competition, as well as keep the competition off balance and guessing. Whoever is off balance and guessing is due for a fall.

The competition can be driven instead of the other way around. The entrepreneurially minded individual can push the competition into areas and actions for which it is not prepared and cannot cope. You can speed up the pace of product innovations and introductions, confusing the competition and making it run faster than it can. In this way, you hold the whip. It may even be possible to make the competition invest in areas of no profit or negative profit just because the competition thinks that it must match your moves. The competition will eventually fall.

151

CORPORATE IMAGE

In the customer's mind, image is another important strategic factor to which serious attention must be paid. For years competitors who claim to have identical products have marveled at how difficult it is to break into Procter & Gamble's markets, and how its customers are willing to pay a substantial premium for the Procter & Gamble product, even though it is "identical" to a cheaper product. As part of their strategy, individuals and corporations must strive to improve the image of the product in a customer's mind on a constant basis. Details, such as always wearing a clean pressed suit, smiling, and knowing everything about the product, impresses the customer or potential customer. Television advertising is not enough, although it must not be neglected; each individual and each product must create, on a constant basis, an improved corporate image.

One of the strong points of the IBM strategy is its image. A customer in Columbus, Ohio, once gave a large order to IBM, simply because he liked the corporate image better in an aesthetic sense, even though competitive bids were lower and more technologically advanced. Corporate spirit, corporate drive, and mission give momentum to the corporate image. If the individual considers the product worthwhile, if he or she has a proud self-image and image of the corporation, and if these feelings are reinforced, the individual will put forward maximum effort in promoting the product. Through its individuals, the corporation must constantly seek to improve its image of quality, efficiency, effectiveness, aesthetics, morality, and social consciousness.

CONCENTRATION

The onset of troops [should be] is like the rush of a torrent that will even roll stones along its course.

> Sun Tzu
> *The Art of War*

Almost everyday I am confronted with new possibilities that could result in a significant new business, on the order of 10 to 100 million annually. I am then forced to remember what businesses we are in and to concentrate our limited resources on them to remain viable and profitable.

> Daniel Fylstra
> Visicorp

(One of these new possibilities was, however, integrated software packages. The employee with the idea broke to form Lotus when he found he wasn't making any progress with it at Visicorp.)

One of the essential tenets of successful strategy is to pick an area of comparative advantage and strike quickly and hard, concentrating and maintaining an effort in the area while it remains profitable. Determining such areas is related to the quality and quantity of information. Shifting and spreading resources over a wide spectrum of opportunities create a management and financial control problem. Too often new ventures fail because they are underfinanced and undermanaged. Often management does not have the time nor the expertise because it has to deal with too many differing ventures and cannot develop an in-depth knowledge of any of them. Spreading yourself too thin lowers the fault tolerance level, exhausting human and physical resources; when problems arise resources are inadequate to their solution. This is apparently what happened to Baldwin United as the company spread itself in almost every direction that availed, stretching cash flow to the limit, until it finally broke.

Concentration to some extent may sound like a formula management strategy, in which overwhelming physical resources can be "concentrated," but it is not, as formula management relied upon excess resources. In organic management, concentration means information and brainpower. It is the concentration and interaction of brainpower and information that brings strategic success.

The National Geographic, in its February 1982 issue, explained Napoleon's victories in the following manner:

> How did he do it? "He had no formula," said historian Owen Connelly, a combat veteran himself. "Every battle was fresh. He always sought to concentrate his forces, but once a battle began, there was no pattern. What he really did was to sit back and wait for the enemy to make a mistake [for an opportunity to arise]. His policy: One engages, one waits, one sees. Austerlitz was a classic example. The Russians weakened their center to attack his flank, he saw the weakness, made his attack there, rolled them up."

Napoleon prepared his campaigns carefully. He was known to crawl over his maps on all fours, dividers in hand, measuring distances, studying terrain; so intent he sometimes bumped heads with his map expert, Bacler d'Albe, also on all fours. He would at times explode in anger: He demanded performance, refused to take "no" for an answer. He knocked one marshal's head against a stone wall, knocked another to the floor, hit others with his riding crop. And there was the memory, that intellect. "Read his letters," urged a French general. . . . "[Paris] would write 'Monsieur, you will please do all things which are deemed necessary so my glory will be served at its best.' Napoleon [in return] would write: 'Monsieur, you will ensure that 15,000 reserve horses will be in Prague 14 September. You will ensure that this order is fully executed and controlled. And I will check it myself.' Modern! Concise! Precise! Like mathematics, music, like Bach! And so victory followed victory!"

It was said that Napoleon carried with him Sun Tzu's, *The Art of War,* constantly. One of the key precepts of Sun Tzu was that a general must plan/prepare better and in more precise detail know the terrain, the environment, one's self and the enemy better than the enemy, so that he will be able to perceive an advantage, a weakness to be quickly exploited once the flow of battle began. In the flux of battle, weakness or opportunities appear often as brief windows, which just as quickly disappear. What may appear as a weakness may not be, requiring a precise perception by the commander as to what is and what is not, which cannot be had without intense planning and preparation. This is why many generals believe the winner of any battle is decided in the preparation phase and not on the battlefield itself.

It has been said of Jack Tramiel, the founder of Commodore and the hoped for rescuer of Atari, that he considers that "business is war," that he attacks along a broad front and exploits any break by concentration and pouring his resources through the breach, similar to Napoleon's tactics. Jack Tramiel apparently prefers quick decisive victories, like Napoleon. However, in war, as Lincoln pointed out, it is the last victory that decides the winner, as Napoleon found out at Waterloo. Many Japanese executives refer to business as a long war, where the army (employees) must be maintained, giving way where there is no clear advantage so that they may fight another day, and exploiting the enemy's weakness when shown. On the other hand Andy Grove, the founder of Intel, has been quoted as saying, "Business is sex, it's one on one,"—a confrontation, where both the "winner" and the "loser" can benefit.

STRATEGIC ASSETS

Physical assets as well as people must be of maximum flexibility in order for the corporation to react and adapt quickly to changes in the business environment. For example, in the early history of NCR, Patterson, the CEO, quickly adapted his cash register plant in Dayton, Ohio, to the manufacture of row boats when heavy floods hit. Japanese corporations have a competitive edge in many areas and have adapted so well to the third wave because they have been able to adjust their flow of assets quickly. When the rapid rise of raw material costs, triggered by the oil shortage, became apparent in the early seventies, the Japanese were able to increase the quality, efficiency, and effectiveness of their products and manufacturing by infusing new electronic and robotic features and materials into their production processes. These factors were the result of creative contingency thinking as they were for the most part ready for input when the need arose.

Human assets are the most valuable and flexible assets of the third wave, unlike the standardized and interchangeable assets of the second. In the third wave, each individual represents a key growing expertise of the firm. The Japanese look on all participants of a corporation in this manner. When American electronic firms laid off their people during the recession of the early seventies, the Japanese did not. After recovery, Japanese corporations had the people to seize the strategic advantage in many areas which they have not relinquished while American firms were trying to hire people. The people American firms hired or rehired were confronted by a lag in research and development that they found difficult to overcome.

STRATEGIC VISION

Strategic vision consists of seeing, often quite far into the future, what the possibilities are and what the competition cannot see or is not inclined to see. For instance, it took a great leap of faith for Sony and its Japanese followers to see the commercial possibilities of the videotape recorder. Sony is now one of the market leaders despite the fact that most of the technology is American. It took perhaps an even greater leap of vision for Honda, starting with the most primitive conditions after World War II, to become a substantial worldwide concern. Similarly Steve Jobs believed that there was a vast market for personal computers in spite of derision from many quarters, including established electronic firms. With the funds he got from selling his Volkswagen bus, he started APPLE. The individual outside the main stream of business who is not encumbered by any of its rituals often can see much more clearly what may after the fact seem to have been obvious opportunities. Olympia and York in Canada was able to visualize the return of New York City to economic health and invested heavily in city real estate, while everyone else considered New York to be falling apart. When New York recovered its economic health, Olympia and York's assets doubled.

STRATEGIC LIQUIDITY

To be able to move quickly and precisely, a corporation must have cash. Olympia and York had the cash with which to take action when it saw the opportunity. Both Robert Anderson of Atlantic Richfield and Andrew Carnegie ascribed their initial strategic advantage to having the "guts" to see a long-term opportunity and having the cash to invest. The key to flexible cash is cash-flow management, i.e., maximizing liquidity without investing unnecessarily in inventories, plants, services, or staff; being lean and mean, efficient, and effective; building up credit resources, developing growth and stock appreciation, and developing creative approaches to corporate finance. Alumax, for instance, was able to develop a larger stream of income from managing its finances than from its regular businesses when interest rates were high, while many of its competitors were suffering from the same high interest rates.

> Leadership is vision, creating a vision, being able to articulate it, being able to coalese a consensual vision—to create excitement around it. The best people are self-managing, they don't need to be managed. What they need is vision.

> Steve Jobs, chairman, APPLE
> "In Search of Excellence"
> PBS Broadcast, January 1985

Strategic Connections

Japanese and American firms have long understood the importance of connections, and have responded by hiring former government and military officials, but it is questionable whether they have done this with any strategy in mind. According to one former general, a firm which is being run by a former admiral is being poorly run, and the management needs to be replaced. Meanwhile the former general's former firm is also being accused of poor management and is passing on its excess costs to the government!

Conoco saved itself with its strategic connection to Du Pont. Martin Marietta saved itself from being absorbed by Bendix, Agee, and Cunningham by being closely knit to its particular defense fraternity. Saul Steinberg and Leaseco's rebuffed attempt to take over the Chemical Bank is another graphic illustration of how connections can prevent an "outsider" from entering into a protected area. A similar episode occurred in Canada when Robert Campeau tried to take over the Royal Trust and was prevented by a loosely knit set of connections called the Family Compact. More recently the executives of Getty Oil saved themselves (or so they thought) from Gordon Getty and early retirement by having some good friends at Texaco. And, the executives of Gulf Oil saved themselves from Boone Pickens by having a few good friends at Standard Oil of California, and along the way made themselves some money.

STRATEGIC EXCELLENCE

A company must understand the strategic importance of excellence. A champion runner may do well in a marathon but, when placed in a 100 yard sprint, lose whatever strategic value his or her excellence had in the marathon. Similarly, an excellent oil company may lose whatever value it had if it tries to enter the electronics field. The value of excellence lies in attaining or maintaining a dominance in a particular field or situation in which an individual or corporation is strategically placed. If you have some measure of excellence, place yourself in a race you have some chance of winning.

If you know the enemy and know yourself, you need not fear the result of a hundred battles. If you know yourself but not the enemy, for every victory gained you will also suffer a defeat. If you know neither the enemy nor yourself, you will succumb in every battle.

Sun Tzu
The Art of War

11

THE ROLE OF THE CHIEF EXECUTIVE OFFICER

Perceive those things which cannot be seen.

Miyamoto Musashi
A Book of Five Rings

The CEO is the inspirational point, the point of reference, for organic action and evolution within the organism. The evolutionary code or the DNA of the corporation naturally flows from the CEO. In many cases, the corporation becomes a mirror image of the person at the helm, and a few basic questions help to define that image.

Who is the chief executive officer? To answer that question, you need to know what that person's principles and philosophy are, what his or her values are and how they are projected. Or, using Jefferson's words, what are the CEO's virtues and talents? How does the corporation reflect the CEO's personality? What is the CEO's vision?

The essence of management is leadership, and of leadership, credibility and communication. They have got to know and believe in what I stand for. Management is mutual respect. My door is always open. They can come in and find out what I'm thinking and WHY.

> Don Shula, coach
> Miami Dolphins

When thermonuclear war comes there will be only two things left. Don Shula and Astro turf.

> Miami Dolphins' player

I work hard at being a good coach.

> John Young, CEO
> Hewlett-Packard

The chief executive officer is no longer primarily a manager; now a CEO is a genetic designer, an engineer of a living thing, an inspirer, a leader, a preacher, a catalyst, a high priest, a legend, a mystery, a coach, a mystic, an artist, a guide, and, most important, a creator. As Henry Mintzberg pointed out in his ground-breaking exploration of the myth of second wave management, the third wave CEO is not a formula manager, but is instead the role model of the corporation. Victor Kiam, head of Remington, said he once fired an executive because, even though the man made money for the corporation, he did not work hard enough; i.e., the executive was not the right role model.

The man that beat Don Shula in Super Bowl XIX, Bill Walsh of the San Francisco 49ers, has established a reputation as the *hardest working* and *hardest thinking* coach in the NFL. Men and women like Lee Iacocca, Frank Borman, Nolan Bushnell, Steve Jobs, Jim Treybig, Bob Noyce, Ed de Castro, Charlie Sporck, An Wang, and Mary Kay Ash have become legends in their own corporations and generally throughout the world.

Lee Iacocca

Lee Iacocca is a dramatic example of the third wave CEO. As early as the late sixties, he was held up to young engineers at Ford as an example of what could be achieved by hard work and hard thinking. He, however, did get fired because of an image that did not fit Henry Ford II's tastes, the Ford Company still being a second wave company. Iacocca moved into Chrysler at a crucial

Drawing by W. Miller; © 1983 The New Yorker Magazine, Inc.

moment, after the company had been raped by second wave management and was on the verge of spiritual and physical death. He took over Chrysler at the critical juncture of the second and third waves when the crises of transition began to hit all businesses.

Lee Iacocca worked his way up, by results, from where, as the Japanese are fond of saying, "the rubber meets the road." Consequently, he thoroughly knew everything about the automobile business. The crisis in which Chrysler found itself proved beneficial because everyone knew that change had to come if the company was to survive; therefore, everyone was pliable and willing to expend extraordinary efforts—a situation quite similar to that of Japanese corporations just after World War II.

Mr. Iacocca not only cut slack (employment dropped by almost half) and inefficient plants, he introduced a new ethic of hard work and collaboration, a new mind set. Hierarchy levels were cut in half. New, automated machinery, robots, were integrated into production. Mr. Iacocca developed a new working relationship with the union through which the union became part of the management team and had a seat on the board of directors. He emphasized the urgency and importance of the situation and the need for new quality products. He arranged new creative financing and new performance criteria. He set an example by his own hard work and long hours. In a sense, Lee Iacocca was also in a fortunate position because he could say realistically to all parties that they either did it his way and quickly or they could "walk the plank."

As a result, Chrysler did "walk through the valley of death" to become once again a prosperous and viable corporate organism. Perhaps the new ethic at Chrysler will survive as it has in Japan since the dark postwar days.

Mary Kay Ash

Mary Kay Ash, head of Mary Kay Cosmetics, is another good example of the third wave CEO. Although cosmetics is hardly a new technology, the company presents its products as a whole new way for women to see themselves.

The primary part Mary Kay Ash plays is one of inspirer, motivator, and role model. She gets people to believe in themselves, her, and the company, all of which, she states firmly, are on God's business. The company stages several seminar conventions a year, which have become gala events to rival the most extravagant Hollywood production. These events serve to motivate and inspire long after the participants have left. Recognition is constantly given and built. Hugs and kisses are used extensively. This sort of corporate evangelism is required to a greater or lesser degree depending upon the internal and external environment of the company.

The soul of the corporation

No one ever pats anybody on the back around here. If de Castro ever patted me on the back, I'd probably quit. . . . De Castro knows what makes me go . . . the bastard . . . some notion of insecurity and challenge, of where the edges are, of finding out what you can't do, all within a perfectly justifiable scenario. It's for the kind of guy who likes to climb up mountains.

Tracy Kidder's Tom West
The Soul of a New Machine, 1983

Tom West, the fictional hero upon whom the real events at Data General Corporation were based, is an example of a mystic and is referred to by his cohorts as the "Prince of Darkness." Ed de Castro, the CEO, is considered to be a combination of an ogre and a wizard. The motivational ways of Mary Kay would clearly fail at Data General, and vice versa. What is clear is that the CEO must know his or her company thoroughly, not just in terms of ledgers but in terms of the people in the business. What do they need?

TRADITIONAL CEOs AND MOTIVATION

Not too long ago, I was consulted by a major West Coast institution concerning the subject of productivity. The institution had undertaken a project on how to increase America's productivity in conjunction with the Department of Commerce and some major business leaders. They asked me to scan the list of business leaders and to give my opinions on the approaches they were taking. Upon scanning the list, I replied that most of the business leaders listed were CEOs of large second wave companies whom I did not believe would be of much help. In the typical hierarchical second wave firm, the CEO is much more concerned, perhaps by circumstance, with protecting his or her position and income in the immediate present rather than with the company's health, the national concern, or any altruistic motives. The second wave CEO feels compelled to protect his or her position because there are always a number of senior executives in various parts of the organization with many schemes to promote themselves into part or all of the CEO's position. Because of the nature of bureaucratic politics, such concerns are foremost in second wave companies. Such companies do not value people by what they have done for the company but by where they are in the hierarchy and by what political power they can wield. The main concern of the CEO in bureaucratic companies is to "play office." Too often they also unfortunately play "take the money and run," which is what has happened in many second wave companies, forcing some to seek assistance from the taxpayer.

I asked the gathered members of the institute why a CEO who was head of a corporation that was performing up to the shareholders', albeit low, expectations, who owned a large house in the suburbs and a country place should care at all about productivity? They could not answer. There may not be an answer.

It is not enough to specify what the role of the CEO in the new third wave company should be but also who he or she should be. A chief executive officer (1) must have a sense of purpose above and beyond the balance sheet; (2) must care about people and the company; (3) must not be too concerned with his or her own welfare, especially if he or she is going to try to put a second wave organization through transformation; (4) must to some degree be an idealist, a visionary; and (5) must measure achievements by the long-term health and progress of the company above all. To some extent, the CEO must be an unsung hero or heroine of the people and the republic. He or she should believe in a cause. Many dynamic third wave CEOs are the products of the social turmoil of the sixties and have put their idealism in a profitable economic and social value system. Such appears to be the case of the CEOs at APPLE, ROLM, and Tandem.

ATTRIBUTES OF THE NEW CEO

John Sculley, CEO of APPLE, spoke about the role and function of a CEO at the Stanford Business School. Mr. Sculley pointed out that if a company wants to be number one, it must look like number one. Its image reflects its CEO. Images are more than mirages—they are real and they stimulate action. A chief executive officer must generate decisions based upon strategy and related conceptual understanding of the parameters of the reality with which he or she is faced. Decisions should not be based upon financial analysis. The role of the CEO and top management is to provide the framework and resources for bright people to do great things without being hampered by the organization. Although the action may be spontaneous and organic, the context within which it takes place should be carefully planned and nurtured by the CEO. Making ideas and innovations effective is what moves organizations. A good idea without an equally good network and resources to implement it is worthless. The job of the CEO is to provide the network and resources.

A DYNAMIC THIRD WAVE CEO MEETS A CHAOTIC SECOND WAVE BUREAUCRACY

When Frank Borman went to work for Eastern Airlines, he found a bloated second wave bureaucracy battered by the third wave, plagued by politics, swamped with waste and negative morale, suffocated by a negative customer image, and functioning with obsolete equipment and no direction. Each day the airline was falling into greater chaos and toward bankruptcy.

If there ever was a man trained to think in the third wave terms, it is Frank Borman. He was trained by NASA as one of the astronauts who would go to the moon. The National Aeronautics and Space Administration is a forerunner of the third wave organization, necessarily functioning on the edge of efficiency, effectiveness, quality, and technology. All astronauts are picked on their ability to think, react, and act with quickness, innovation, and precision. These qualities are ingrained and enhanced in each candidate. The astronauts must constantly work to improve the effectiveness, efficiency, and quality of the mission. NASA is an organization with a mission, and a family with gigantic esprit de corps and great morale.

It was from the NASA environment that Frank Borman and his particular mind set entered Eastern Airlines as the number three man. For him the experience was painful. In the years leading up to his acquisition of the CEO position, he was under pressure from everyone and threatened to quit more than once; but he did learn what was wrong with the company and what had to be done to fix it.

Eastern Airlines was built by an autocratic, tough, but benevolent despot who started out flying as a combat ace when airplanes were literally strung together with wire. It was often said of Captain "Eddie" Vernon Rickenbacker, even in the recesses of Eastern, that he was a Neanderthal, a baffled nineteenth century man trying to cope with the twentieth century. He valued loyalty and conformity above all else. Captain Rickenbacker often said that he valued good judgment above all else, but when it came down to it, what he valued were people whom he thought liked him. He valued people who agreed with him. It was well understood that the surest way to get fired was to disagree with Captain Eddie; perhaps it was the only way. If an employee toed the line, it was unlikely that he or she would ever be fired regardless of what mistakes the employee might have made. In fact, if an employee made a serious enough mistake, he or she was usually promoted.

As indicated in *From The Captain to the Colonel,* by the time Frank Borman took over Eastern Airlines, there were close to seventy vice presidents, most of whom did very little if anything at all. Vast ranks of middle management multiplied. Many strata of management developed and many "empires" were created, which conflicted constantly. These empires tried to outdo each other, especially in spending and in executive privileges, pouring red ink onto Eastern's ledgers. The two chief empires existed in New York and Miami, each believing they were the headquarters. The red ink had some inverted justification because it allowed Eastern to push a stronger case for higher fares before the Civil Aeronautics Board (CAB). Customers flew competitive airlines whenever they could, but those who could not formed a serious organization to harass and criticize the airline. The only such consumer organization to arise was WHEAL (We Hate Eastern Airlines). After having flown Eastern in the early seventies, I can sympathize with WHEAL, especially since my seat once broke on takeoff. Morale at the airline was extremely bad. People at the bottom were treated like serfs and were told to work harder and to sacrifice while they watched executives sit in plush offices and clubs, ride in limousines, and take lavish junkets, including a memorable one that Captain Eddie himself led around Latin America. Waste, hypocrisy, and inefficiency were everywhere.

Frank Borman was more than awestruck by the airline. Fortunately, he had a few years to regain his composure and learn about the company before taking the reins. He was aghast at the waste and internecine strife after coming from the moon program in which teamwork was a question of life and death. He found that the airline had no conception of how much it cost to carry weight, even though the transport of weight was the company's main business. For instance, why did seats weigh what they did, and how much did they cost to transport?[1]

> We had seats attractive from a marketing standpoint but which weighed about forty pounds per seat more than necessary. Nobody thought that vital, last percentage of cost could make so much difference. I guess it was because fuel was so cheap that airlines didn't worry about carrying around heavy seats, and airstairs and containers. But I had just come out of a field where weight meant everything, where even the saving of a single ounce was important.

The internecine strife and the management style of pitting people against each other went totally against all those years Frank Borman worked as a member of a team, of a family. Being run by the latest Harvard Business School techniques may have worked well for ITT but not for an airline in which people are of the essence. Second wave management within the airline fought change with figures and analyses, which were not of any real utility to the company. Mr. Borman commented that he "found Eastern's stratified structure absolutely repugnant."[2]

Cliques had developed, so members in the company were promoted through seniority or through people whom they knew. Clique members protected each other's mistakes, and dangerous deadwood accumulated, choking the arteries and synapses of the airline. Bureaucracy was rampant. One night during an horrific tragedy Frank Borman saw that "The airline has some great people" who only needed the proper leadership.

The tragedy was the crash of Eastern Airlines L-1011 jet into the Florida Everglades. Frank Borman was at home in bed reading a book, but he quickly scrambled to the site and waded bootless through the Florida swamp helping other Eastern employees load blood-soaked semiconscious survivors onto helicopters. That night Eastern people did work as a team without questions. They gave money to survivors with no strings attached, flew relatives in from as far away as Tokyo, and visited each survivor in the hospital, even personally shaved some. The members of Eastern Airlines could not do enough, and nobody directed them to do it. When the tragedy occurred, Frank Borman decided to stay and assume leadership of Eastern even though he had several interesting offers outside the company.

He assumed the position of CEO and president on 16 December 1975. He consolidated headquarters in Miami and immediately executed a program to cut the number of executives, management levels, and management perks. (He quickly sold the executive Jetstar: "With over 250 jets what the hell do we need an executive jet for?!") He toned down the plushness of his own office. He cut the number of vice presidents by more than half. He cut management levels so that there were no more than two levels between himself and whoever was doing the work, instead of as many as twenty levels previously. About 800 executives' positions were cut in total. Most of those occupying these positions, however, found jobs at lower levels where they could make a contribution to the company.

> Being from the military and NASA, I was expecting a more austere operation, but instead I found it pretty plush and very structured, full of committees and policy groups which met only once a month. It was a long way from the management style I was used to at NASA, where the guy who had all the information and knowledge was directly involved in staff meetings—his information wasn't sifted through three levels of management. When we had a review of Gemini, the engineer who designed an individual system was sitting in the room with his boss, and we asked them whatever questions we wanted answered.[3]

Mr. Borman's attitude is not dissimilar to that of the Japanese executives who insist on involving whoever is "where the rubber meets the road" in the decision, because these are the people involved with the customer and they know what is going on. Frank Borman constantly tried to know what was going on and how it could be improved. Departments that were often two to three times the size of a comparable competitor were trimmed drastically. He sent the remaining executives out to work. To help with the holiday overflow one day, he sent his executives to help out at the airport, to work as ticket takers, reservation clerks, or wherever they were needed. He himself worked as a baggage handler right through lunch and until 6 P.M.; the other executives who could not stop until he did, complained, "When is that SOB gonna quit!" He even was offered the odd tip, which he refused.

Frank Borman is a risk-taker, an entrepreneur. Against the advice of all, he pursued the Miami–Mexico City route on which Pan Am was losing money. He used large L-1011s on the route, and made money with over an 80% occupancy. His largest risky venture, which he also pursued against major opposition, was the Airbus (A-300), costing close to $1 billion. This risk has also paid off.

Borman is quick to grasp a situation and quick to make a decision. Vice presidents who prepare a thirty-minute presentation are usually cut off after the first two, then a decision is made. Analyses and figures are no longer definitive arguments to sell a decision. He cut lavish expenditure where it was not needed and spent on quality equipment and people that worked. His biggest expenditure was on the A-300 and later on the Boeing 757, which reequipped an obsolete and uncompetitive fleet. He introduced a wage freeze and the industry's first profit sharing plan that he sold to the unions. The plan was more profitable for members in the end than straight salary was. Borman reasoned that members should share in any profits or losses incurred because they are the airline.

He walks around and always asks people what is going on not just at work but in their lives. His concern for people has become formalized in corporate stories, such as the one about how he gave up his seat on a full flight to a tired stewardess deadheading (flying as a passenger) back to Miami. One of the greatest challenges he faced was breaking the mind set—the "me tooism"—induced by Rickenbacker. He welcomed initiative, new ideas, and contrary opinions, but he did it by demonstration and by challenging his people. A human touch has been restored to Eastern. The employees smile, and work together as a team. A human spark, a corporate soul has developed. Some semblance of a family has been created, and all equipment works. It is Frank Borman's charisma, stimulation, genetic corporate redesign, and hard work that has turned the company around. He did, however, make the mistake of believing that a strategy could be planned rather than evolve from a dynamic organization and its interaction with the environment. That mistake was crucial because the company's strategy did not fit well with the organization, its culture, or its environment (which included deregulation), although Eastern Airlines did improve. Although this remains a problem, Borman did restore the company's spirit and will, which should no doubt serve to overcome any difficulties.

Political offers have come, which some astronauts have pursued, but Frank Borman has turned them down, saying that he believes in the mission of the airline and his family; indeed, when Borman was first recommended to Eastern by a director of NASA, it was said he had the rightest stuff of all.

Just as the triumphant Roman general on parade heeded the slave who stood behind him reminding him of his mortality, even "star" CEOs such as Borman should heed the old maxim that you have to be good *and* lucky. Eastern Airlines ranked near the bottom of the most admired corporations in America in *Fortune's* January 1985 survey, but it is still viable and, in the airline industry, that may be achievement enough.

A Hierarchical CEO Meets a Dynamic Third Wave Company

When Nolan Bushnell developed Atari into a going concern, it seems the potential of the company was not apparent. Steve Ross, chairman of Warner Bros., bought it for $27 million, a bargain basement price at the time. Included

167

in the price was a contracted promise by Mr. Bushnell not to enter the video game market for seven years. To make the company perform and to exploit its strategic position, Mr. Ross hired a Harvard Business School graduate, Ray Kassar, who specialized in marketing textiles. He wanted Kassar to sell the market the maximum amount of the product. Mr. Ross had evidently observed a tremendous marketing gap that could be exploited with the right approach. Up until this point, Atari had been driven by engineering and had developed some attractive technology and engineering talent, but the company did not know how to market effectively. Atari developed from a gunslinger-pioneer corporate form to the entrepreneurial form, but Kassar pushed it into a pressurized bureaucratic form, and Atari's people became driven by fear and greed.[4]

Atari was now organized and operated on the Harvard Business School model of managing by the numbers and creating competition, rather than teamwork, among management and employees. The short-term goal of the immediate bottom line was pursued almost to the exclusion of strategic long-term concern for the people or the company. Many executives left the company, and the feeling grew that status and authority were granted by Mr. Kassar for personal and/or political reasons. In three years, seventeen different presidents of the coin-operated consumer and computer divisions joined and left Atari.

Few employees knew what the company's objectives were, or how closely, if at all, they were being met. There was the feeling that objectives were changing rapidly, and that competition among employees was a goal in itself. Engineers and other employees were rarely consulted about what they were doing, or about what concerned them, in any productive way. As the company moved from concentration on engineering to concentration on marketing, employee morale fell, Atari lost its technological edge, and its market position finally gave way. In a third wave environment, new ideas and new technology are the currency of the market.

All this action had to have consequences. Many of the most productive employees left Atari, and those who remained appeared to be more involved in political maneuvering than in product development. Finally, early in 1983, Steve Ross flew up to Atari and spent three days "taking apart" Kassar and his top management. Kassar's resignation soon followed. Almost directly related to the Atari losses has been Warner's struggle against corporate takeover attacks, including one by Rupert Murdoch; but the "buzzards" were a bit premature. The CEO who desires power and a healthy and profitable organization while seeking to avoid such chaos would do well to heed the old Christian adage that the route to power is in serving others—their fellow employees and their customers.

Speaking on the PBS broadcast this year on "In Search of Excellence," Steve Jobs described the importance of having managers who can not only manage but who have an emotional stake in the enterprise and understand it well. Managing is not enough; a manager must know and care about the enterprise.

> The best managers are the contributors who have to manage because no one else can do it, can take care of the contribution. We went through the phase—Well, we are going to be a big company; we need to hire professional managers.
>
> They could manage, but they couldn't do anything. We fired both of them.

Dinosaurs and the new environment

Business schools evolved to serve the particular needs of society, as does any institution. Business schools sprang up when the second wave was dominant, and they therefore turned out what was demanded—second wave corporate bureaucrats, skilled in bureaucratic politics and in administering formulas. The very best at this time was the Harvard Business School (HBS).

Even before the advent of the third wave Robert Townsend, then CEO of Avis, implicitly referred to HBS as a future breeding ground for "dinosaurs" and a stone age ruin in *Up the Organization*. Like at Stonehenge, tourists would wonder what people did there. Dinosaurs do not do so well in an environment calling for warm-blooded, flexible, adaptable, and creative mammals. Many such individuals run the corporate dinosaurs that are trying to shift to the third wave. Preconceived notions of bureaucratic and autocratic style in third wave management have proved disastrous, as with Exxon's venture into the electronic information field. Since the transition to the third wave is not yet complete and since dinosaurs are not yet extinct and still on the loose, another sign might be posted at appropriate places in the corporate jungle:

WARNING—*TYRANNOSAURUS REX* STILL ON THE PROWL—HIDE YOUR CORPORATION.

A Wall Street mergers-and-acquisitions specialist who had a hand in the Bendix–Martin Marietta (Bendix–Cunningham) war and many others recently told me a story about one such second wave executive. "We were fishing for big game out in the Atlantic and then he fell overboard, and this giant shark which had been following us came straight for him but at the last moment swerved away. I asked him later why this strange thing happened. He replied with a grin, 'professional courtesy.'"[5] That's amusing, but thinking men have hunted both sharks and dinosaurs!

A Corporate CEO Meets a Gunslinger-Pioneer Company on the Verge of Chaos

Adam Osborne of Osborne Computer said that he needed a "square head," i.e., a traditional corporate manager trained with business school acumen, to come and manage his fast-growing company. He knew that Osborne had to make the transformation from the gunslinger-pioneer to the entrepreneurial-corporate organizational form.

Robert Jaunich, then CEO of the second wave Consolidated Foods Company, let it be known that he was tired of commuting from his home in San Francisco to his office in Chicago. Soon the match was made. Upon entering Osborne, Jaunich said that he believed in integrity. He meant not only the traditional truth and honesty in business dealings but also the structural integrity and order within the business. To any privy to its internal workings, Osborne did not make a great deal of sense. Robert Jaunich tried to restore order in a rapidly changing company that was already out of control. He deferred increased equity financing so that the offering would make corporate sense. This deferment would have worked well in a solid second wave industrial company in which time is not essential; but this threw Osborne into even more shambles.

To make the transition from a gunslinger-pioneer firm to an entrepreneurial firm, niches in the market must be targeted and controlled. Such niches are controlled with some new technology that can be thrown toward relevant competitors. Adam Osborne had a known aversion to "cutting edge technology" and eventually cut himself on the receding edge. The company let out word about a new improved product in an effort to combat leaked sales. This strategy had a reverse effect since most sales of the current product stopped while potential customers waited for the new one, which the company was not yet set up to produce. Osborne soon had a problem with cash flow and declared bankruptcy under chapter 11.

Although Robert Jaunich was sincere, he was not a third wave magician. What was needed was a mixture of someone halfway between Jaunich, Gandalf the wizard, and Genghis Khan. Adam Osborne is busy trying to start another company.

The Beginnings of the Fourth Wave CEO

On the very frontiers of the third wave as it currently exists, Japan has initiated a project to develop the fifth generation computer (ICOT), the computer that can think. The man they chose to run this project is Kazuhiro Fuchi.

"The sad part of being a dictator is that one has so few close friends and those few have to be watched very carefully."

Drawing by Handelsman; © 1983 The New Yorker Magazine, Inc.

Upon his shoulders may rest the future direction of Japan and perhaps the world. Mr. Fuchi does not fit the Japanese stereotype of the corporate CEO or any stereotype at all. He radiates electricity and, like the mythical hero Genji, "he brought pleasure to the eye and serenity to the heart, and made people wonder what bounty of grace might be his from former lives." It is his all-encompassing knowledge, his inner almost spiritual vision, and his deep commitment that impress his staff and any visitors. He knows what is going on

171

everywhere and in what direction the company is moving. He seems to be a man who enjoys the challenge of the occasional mountain that he can, one gets the impression, knock over with a flick of his mind. Myth and legend have grown around him. He cares nothing for convention or tradition, realizing that he knows better. He knows he will win; he will take Japan into the next level created by the fifth generation computer. His staff believes in him. The primitive beginnings of the fourth wave and of a fourth wave CEO may be in the works.

MANAGING AMBIGUITY

As change accelerates, ambiguity will naturally grow along side. I recently heard a former vice chancellor of the University of California system, which has one of the more ambiguous management situations, explain how he handled the rapid change and ambiguity:

> I managed best when I managed by a kind of personality cult that set the tone, and by getting the best people possible and giving them the freedom and responsibility to operate within the "tone" or framework. Where I fell down was when I started getting specialists in. They tried and are still trying to fit everything into boxes. They are always trying to bring some new level of clarity to every situation. The trouble is all they do is muddy the water. Things change quickly, yesterday's clarity is today's mud. I hired those specialists because I didn't know any better then. Specialists have a large stake in being right even when they are very wrong. They often persist in trying to impose their version of reality upon a situation even though it is totally irrational, and when they fail to they won't admit it.[6]

Kagemusha, the Shadow Warrior, a recent Japanese film, is about management like *The Seven Samurai* is. The warlord of a province under prolonged siege dies. Knowing that the troops would lose heart and spirit if they knew of his death, his close associates train a peasant who resembles the lord to act, speak (mostly grunts), and express himself like the deceased lord. For a time, all goes well as the army continues to draw strength, direction, and spirit from the image of the old warlord. The invaders are temporarily repulsed. As long as "the shadow warrior" continues to allow the action to flow naturally from his image, the troop's success continues because this image is the engine of their spirit. It is only when he tries to take an active part, to inject his own personality and to manage operations, does the army falter and fall. The chain and flow of organic action were broken.

GROWING THE CORPORATION

The third wave CEO may have to be someone with a natural affinity for growing the organism, someone with a "green thumb," prompting the notion that the third wave has engendered "the greening of American management," whereas in the second wave, it did not matter much if the CEO had a "brown thumb" because he or she was just manipulating a machine. Because the corporation is necessarily an evolving organism sensitive to its care and feeding, it needs a nurturing caretaker.

I think of myself as a gardener, as an arranger, as a creator of a climate.

> Renn Zaphiropoulos
> Xerox

During the fourth wave, the CEO may approach more completely the mystical and spiritual qualities now being ascribed to some who are able to generate a spiritual synergy and momentum. In *The Leader* Michael Maccoby describes the requisite third wave CEO as a "developer," someone concerned with developing the individual and the corporation, primarily because he or she enjoys the development. Mr. Maccoby based his analysis upon the works of Lao Tzu.

> The best of all leaders is the one who helps people so
>   that, eventually, they don't need him.
> Then comes the one they love and admire.
> Then the one they fear.
> The worst is the one who lets people push him around.
> Where there is no trust there is bad faith.
> The best leader doesn't say much, but what he says carries weight.
> When he is finished with his work, the people say,
> "It happened naturally."

> Lao Tzu
> *The Leader* (Michael Maccoby)

What the ancients called a clever fighter is one who not only wins, but excels in winning with ease. But his victories bring him neither reputation for wisdom nor credit for courage. For inasmuch as they are gained over circumstances that have not come to light, the world at large knows nothing of them, and he therefore wins no reputation for wisdom;

173

inasmuch as the hostile state submits before there has been any bloodshed, he receives no credit for courage.

> Sun Tzu
> *The Art of War*

Sun Tzu's writing further explains the role of natural leadership through which the organism takes on the direction and characteristics of the leader set forward by his example. The organization grows and prospers in the light that the leader showers upon it.

Although the developer is considered the ideal by Maccoby, he describes several other types useful in some circumstances. The prototypes typical of the seventies were the gamesmen, the "gamblers of high tech," who combined a sense of play, achievement, and talent. Other types combined a lust for power, greed, and domination, characterizing many of those who managed second wave firms. Some developers who dominated second wave structures, such as those who were "company" people, traded everything for security, including the company's future at times. The ideal developer in Maccoby's view combines the best of Jefferson's concept of virtue and talent.

Maccoby describes six outstanding "leaders," including the CEO of Volvo, Pehr Gyllenhammer or P. G. for short. P. G. was an imaginative, creative, and progressive man from the start. He placed members of the union on the board long before it became law. He initiated creative individualized work, such as the process introduced at the Kalmar plant, so that workers could actually create and take individual responsibility for each car coming off the assembly line. This approach, which challenged conventional second wave wisdom, has resulted in an approximate 20% improvement in productivity. P. G. sees the development of corporate strategy as ongoing and interactive, i.e., all are encouraged to participate, while he remains the guide and inspirational point. He is very sensitive to everything that goes on in the corporation, including the personal lives of his people. While pursuing human goals, he understands how important profits are to a company. The importance of profits also encompasses the human side of the equation because profits equal corporate and individual recognition, identity, applause, reinforcement, and momentum.

> In business you need victory, even small ones on a tack; otherwise it throws cold water on everyone.

> Pehr Gyllenhammer, CEO
> Volvo, 1982

Describing his first encounter with a second wave office environment P. G. said, "When I left the university and entered working life, I didn't know if I could work in an office. Everything was dull. I didn't know if I should read a book or fall asleep. Since I didn't want to do dull things or sleep, I had a problem. I would go home and explode." In terms of the rigid bureaucratic hierarchy he commented, "It is no problem for me to be loyal to friends, but not to an organization. If I am free, it is no problem; I can be loyal to a common cause and I can accept the rules of the game." P. G. can accept these rules as long as they further human and social goals. On the importance of vision he wrote, "Leadership is being able to draw new boundaries beyond the existing limits of ideas and activities. Only through this kind of leadership can we keep our institutions from drifting aimlessly to no purpose."[7] P. G. also feels that the undefinable and nonquantifiable, such as emotions and morale, are necessary considerations in any management decision.

THE FOCAL POINT OF THE ORGANIZATION

Maccoby also talks about the CEO as the focus of the organization. "The leader should be the focus of people's ideas and objectives, to bring out the best in them." It is this focus of ideals and objectives that allows the CEO to guide the organization, or if necessary to change it. During the second wave, organizations could be changed by manipulating numbers and drawing numerical strategies, an advance from "seat of the pants management," so everyone thought. Henry Ford II brought in the Whiz Kids, including Robert McNamara, to turn around and change his company, which they did over a number of years. There was also the "meat-axe" approach that took place in many companies. Today's executive finds it more efficient to focus on culture, to reengineer the company genetically by splicing in new ideas and people, and to focus and project images and values that drive the organization in the desired direction. The desired direction is developed from an analysis of all possible directions relative to the corporation's abilities and past evolutionary track. Where has this living creature been and where might it best go? As his or her primary role, the CEO guides, integrates, and synergizes this evolutionary strategy with the cultural evolution of the corporation. He or she senses the "rhythm of the corporation and the environment, adjusting its course organically so that things happen optimally and naturally.

John Sculley, president of APPLE, said in *Infoworld,* 1984, that the leader's responsibility and focus is to keep members energized.

> The way we have been successful is by having had small teams creating great products, and we have not been encumbered by a lot of structure.

175

The risk is that we can become just bigger and bigger, and suddenly, those people who enjoy working in little teams, such as those who created Lisa and APPLE IIe, don't want to work here anymore. That's my job and Steve Jobs' job—to make sure that never happens. One way to do it is to come up with organizational concepts that allow us to become good at getting the functional infrastructure in place. Our customers can then have confidence that we can back up our products, on the one hand, and that we can manage a complex, multiproduct business, on the other hand, still maintaining the small-team entrepreneurial environment.

People have asked me what we want to model APPLE after, and the answer is nobody. We want to create a new environment. There aren't any good examples.

Public Image of the CEO

The chief executive officer is not only the internal image and form maker. His or her major role is to project the firm's image to the government, to the consumer, and to the public. Depending upon this image, the government may give desirable treatment to the firm, the consumer may choose the firm's product over a competitor's, and the public may consider the company a good corporate citizen and not a target for special-interest lobbies. The firm may obtain better and easier financing if it has an outstanding image. Images are actions and are perceived as reality. This fact is illustrated by the sharp rise in the number of CEOs appearing on television commercials since 1970. Frank Borman is seen carrying luggage, Victor Kiam is seen shaving, and so on. Their images on the television screen project their companies. Chief executive officers are also appearing on talk shows and in department stores as guest celebrities. The art of public relations has taken on new importance and real meaning.

Chief executive officers are now increasingly in the public's eye and vice versa. To be successful in this role, a CEO must consider and do what would make him or her successful internally and externally—develop a set of values, objectives, spirit, culture, be consistent, and make them clear. This clear image and understanding of a corporation builds trust and credibility for the corporation with its constituents. Corporate profits and viability are built on trust and credibility.

For the CEO to retain and perform his or her role, the CEO must be sensitive yet remain independent. A chief executive officer "captured" or managed by managers is most dangerous to himself or herself and to the corporation. Only by remaining independent can a CEO maintain a realistic and objective view of what is happening to and in the corporation and where it may be heading. The chief executive officer should always try to see what the real problems and opportunities clearly are. Einstein once said of physics that there are only simple questions and simple answers. The same can be said of business. One of the CEO's primary jobs is to ask simple questions and to seek simple answers. It was said that when Alexander the Great marched into the city of Gordia in Asia Minor, he was confronted with a hopelessly entangled knot, the Gordian knot. According to legend, he who could untangle it would rule the world. Alexander cut it in two with a stroke of his sword.

Simplicity is the ultimate sophistication.

> Steve Jobs, chairman
> APPLE

Subtle and simple is the way of God.

> Albert Einstein

12

EDUCATION AND THE NEW ENVIRONMENT

The answer my friend is blowin in the wind

Bob Dylan

FORMULA EDUCATION

The answer is no longer to be found in the formula, yet the educational system is still geared to developing people through formula training and not through creative thinking. The context has changed, but we keep searching for a formula instead of trying to develop an interactive process that requires thinking.

Scholastic aptitude scores, the measure of academic success, seriously declined during this period of transition. This decline not only indicates that the educational system may be losing its ability to relate to third wave society and business, but perhaps that the system may not know what to measure. Several

178

colleges, such as Bates, have dropped the SAT as an entrance requirement, preferring to rely on longer term criteria.

The educational system is the origin of much of the difficulty experienced by many corporations as they attempt the transition. It has produced one-track minds that have blindly followed formulas and led their corporations toward the edge of disaster during the transition. This one-track formula mind set is the product of a second wave educational system that was geared to producing products for a mechanical hierarchy and formula management, and not for organic processes needed in the dynamic third wave. The educational system's failure to upgrade itself quickly is a primary impediment to individual as well as corporate adaptation to the third wave.

> Over 50% of the graduating U.S. high school seniors are functionally illiterate; that is, they do not have the minimum skills necessary to survive and prosper in today's economy. For example, many cannot even balance a checkbook. They can't make and follow a simple budget. They can't read an insurance policy and understand what they're paying for and what they're protected against. They have no keyboard skills, not even on typewriters, let alone [on] keyboards that we are going to be dealing with in the future.
>
> Dr. William Miller, president
> SRI, 1982

Today's graduates are not prepared for the third wave. The educational system must become organic and be geared to today's dynamic environment. To become organic, education must shift from producing obedient, docile products for mechanical hierarchies to turning out individuals who can become thinking and creative entrepreneurs. Education must shift from mass training to individual cultivation in which the emphasis is on self-learning, not rote formula regurgitation.

WORK FORCE REQUIREMENTS OF THE THIRD WAVE

The number of functional mechanical jobs will continue to decline as traditional manufacturing continues to be shifted to overseas countries entering the second wave. Corporations faced with the new determinants of the third wave—increasing costs, increasing competition, and increasing rates of change—will continue to pare down the number of employees while upgrading individual work force requirements. Corporate slack will gradually become

179

a thing of the past. Technology will make automation and robotics cheaper and more efficient and effective. Increased quality, efficiency, and effectiveness will require the manufacture of fewer products and related waste. Directed functions and formula jobs, whose only requirement was obedience, will continue to decline even in high-technology industries.

High technology will never support the number of jobs we are losing.

Sol C. Chaikin, president
International Ladies Garment Workers Union, 1983

High technology has not created that many jobs in the past decade and it won't in the coming decades.

Jack Metzger, computer specialist
Roosevelt University, 1983

In Silicon Valley itself, projections indicate that the growth in service jobs, janitorial and the like, will far outstrip any growth in high-technology jobs. People will have to think for themselves, to create their own futures, to become entrepreneurs. If the educational system does not prepare us for these new roles, it will have failed, and the economy and society will suffer.

The Most Valuable Resource

During the first wave, the bulk of education took place within the family and work place, which was usually the farm. Because the farms were owner operated, education was entrepreneurially oriented. The requirements of the second wave, calling for obedient and mechanically thinking servants, forced education into an institutional setting with institutional processes. The second wave educational institution became more of a training place than an educational center because mass training and mass thinking were fostered instead of individual thinking and initiative. The institution became a sieve through which only the obedient and less creative could pass. Fortunately for us, Thomas Edison was not exposed to much institutional training of this kind which would have stifled his creativity. Education and individual creative thinking have enjoyed a new premium since the initiation of the third wave. Personal computers for individualized learning are being placed in many progressive schools, although many second wave teachers still do not understand the new context.

Our most unique and valuable resource for growth, our ingenuity, is also our most plentiful.

Senator Gary Hart, 1983

Alexis de Toqueville said that Americans' superior ingenuity and sense of entrepreneurship gave them a competitive advantage in shipping because each American worked for his own enterprise to a much greater extent than each European did. Second wave processes and institutions seemed to have temporarily laid this spirit to rest. Thinkers like Ivan Illich have led a revolution against second wave training. Harvard University recently accepted an applicant taught by his parents, who had rejected the formal educational system. Recognizing the situation, parents, communities, and corporations are beginning to take an increasing share in the educational process.

CREATIVE THINKING VERSUS LEARNING BY ROTE

Early in his career, Soichiro Honda needed to learn something about casting techniques, so he took a course at the technical institute but deliberately skipped the final examination. When he was told that he could have gotten his diploma if he had taken the examination, he replied that the diploma did not guarantee anything, not even that he could think well enough to earn a living. Similarly, when considering any new graduate at his laboratory, Edison asked what was the volume of a light bulb. Anyone who proceeded to measure the bulb with instruments and to work a formula was rejected. The ones that filled the light bulb with water and then measured the water's volume were hired.

This is not to say that formulas do not have their uses. After all, Mr. Honda did go to the institute to learn about a formula. He and Edison point to the importance of being able to think creatively with any acquired knowledge, as opposed to having a piece of paper that states you know the formula by rote, but not necessarily how to use it.

YESTERDAY'S SYSTEM

As the change of events accelerates, the utility of specialized education decreases and the need for current learning increases. In an environment of fast change, the lag between education and reality must decrease. In an environment of slow change, such as the second wave, lags are not as significant. In today's environment of changing economic structures and changing values and technology, education must be ongoing. One possible adjustment might be to allow a charitable tax deduction, at appropriate rates, for time spent lecturing at local educational institutions by professionals and entrepreneurs. Students might also be given increasing credits for internships and entrepreneurial experiences. Educational organizations seeking to preserve and perpetuate themselves must move toward the prime purpose of serving society and not themselves.

Corporations must and are taking up more of the educational challenge by gearing their people to think more creatively and by repairing or substituting for an inadequate education. Increasingly companies are asked the question implied by Honda: Does the diploma mean that he or she knows how to think? Chief executive officers in many fast growth companies are adopting seemingly bizarre behavior in order to see who can think and who cannot. Only people who can think will ensure the survival and prosperity of most corporations in the current environment, not those whose sole asset is docile personal loyalty and obedience. Ongoing education and stimulation have become a primary corporate concern. Information systems and video and computer systems have become integral to the corporate educational process.

HUMAN CAPITAL

Wassily Leontieff, the Nobel prize winning economist, once did an analysis of just how much human capital and physical capital went into the products of developed versus developing countries. He did this partially to assess the claim that products from developed countries enjoyed a competitive advantage because they were (physical) capital intensive, and that the only competitive goods from developing countries were those that exploited human capital to the maximum. Much to his surprise and to the surprise of many others, he found that products from the developed countries were much more intensive in human capital than products from the undeveloped nations.

The amount of human capital invested in products is also different among developed countries. Although the differential is beginning to shrink, human capital in most Japanese products, especially in automobiles, is more intensive than human capital in American products in terms of engineering, quality control, testing, design, and maintenance. The more competitively developed nations are better at infusing information into their products. Japan has experienced an advantage in the infusion of information because the country has had a more efficient, effective, and intensive human capital system in its society and in its educational methods. For instance, Japan graduates many more engineers per capita than any other nation, and fewer lawyers and

Ph.D.s and virtually no MBAs. An Achilles' heel, however, is beginning to show in Japan's software lag.

Software: Artificial Intelligence

We are experiencing the automation of human capital in the software revolution of the third wave. Software and artificial intelligence systems are taking the place of the direct application of human capital to many engineering, production, quality control, design testing, and maintenance problems. The educational system will become even more critical because software cannot now or in the foreseeable future think creatively.

All clichés to the contrary, American society wagers more on human intelligence than it wastes on gadgets.

J. J. S. Servan-Schreiber
The American Challenge

Servan-Schreiber is pointing out that America's challenge and competitiveness was based upon a greater investment in human capital than Europe's was. American investment in human capital probably still exceeds the European investment, but the differential is receding. The Japanese have recognized that their competitive advantage in human capital is being challenged by developments in software and artificial intelligence; therefore, they have invested heavily in a project to create the fifth generation computer, one that can think, decipher meaning, but not create.

It is strange that Japanese investment and development in software is lagging. They possibly feel, and perhaps correctly, that the present competitive advantage in human capital will be adequate until the fifth generation computer gives them a decided advantage in the development and deployment of software. An additional strategy the Japanese are following is to shift production in some areas to lower cost countries that are entering the second wave, because Japan's competitive advantage in human capital in those areas may be inadequate to sustain a large market share.

Countries like the United Kingdom may be able to develop sophisticated software but be disadvantaged in its application and implementation because its social infrastructure has yet to adapt effectively to the needs of the third wave. Its educational system needs revamping. America played much of Japan's role during the latter half of the second wave in Europe, adapting many European inventions to mass production and profit. America may continue to slip into Britain's historic role, allowing Japan to exploit American inventions, if it does not reenergize its competitive advantage in creativity, application, and implementation of mass individualized marketing.

HUMAN CAPITAL GENERATION AND APPLICATION

By investigating the evolution of the telecommunications industry, Ira Magaziner and Robert Reich found that application costs, including software, doubled while manufacturing costs dropped by more than 100 percent as the industry shifted from mechanical switching to electronic switching. The corporation or country that can apply and generate human capital and information the most effectively and efficiently will have the competitive advantage during the third wave, just as those who developed the most efficient and effective manufacturing had the edge during the second. There will be increasing pressures upon technology poor, natural resource poor, and limited food producing countries such as Switzerland and West Germany and Japan to move further into the top quadrant. Conversely, resource rich countries will feel less pressure to move into the top quadrant. It is important to note that China is beginning its move toward the third wave, following the United States and Japan to the upper left quadrant. China is beginning to develop the mass manufacturing of microprocessors and a nationwide television network that will accelerate its production of human capital and help it catch up technologically. In this effort, China will draw from its "engines"—Hong Kong, Taiwan, Shanghai, and Canton. However, the high human capital countries such as the United States and Japan where design, engineering, style, marketing, and management originate will retain the major return from investment. The countries that can focus the maximum amount of effective per-unit customer value will lead in trade competitiveness and profit.

EDUCATION WITHIN THE CORPORATION

Corporations, like educational institutions, have been approaching education from the mechanical perspective of training functional products for second wave organizations. During the second wave, the educational establishment thought that scholarship had to be pursued and backed with quantification, numbers, and formulas in order to be respectible, "that for something to exist it must exist in some quantity," and therefore be quantifiable. Formulas became the rage. The pursuit of this ideal to the extreme and illogical end has resulted in the near bankruptcy of much scholarship.

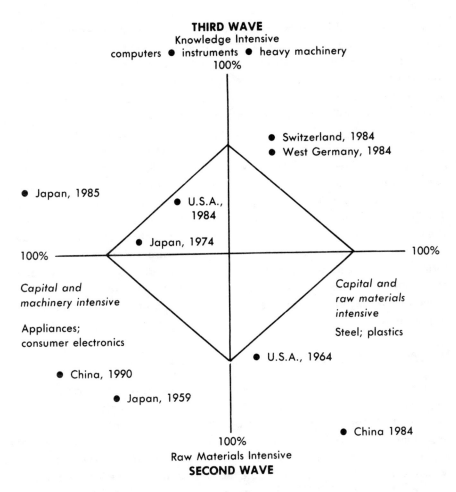

THIRD WAVE
Knowledge Intensive
computers ● instruments ● heavy machinery
100%

● Switzerland, 1984
● West Germany, 1984

● Japan, 1985

● U.S.A., 1984

● Japan, 1974

100% ———————————————— 100%

*Capital and
machinery intensive*

Appliances;
consumer electronics

● China, 1990

● Japan, 1959

*Capital and
raw materials
intensive*

Steel; plastics

● U.S.A., 1964

● China 1984

100%
Raw Materials Intensive
SECOND WAVE

EXHIBIT 12-1   Evolution of economic structures of different countries from second to third wave. If a country is scarce in resources or food, it must become intensive in human capital, knowledge, and technology in order to survive in the international business world.

Part of the problem is, no doubt, generated by the increasing political basis of academics. As a direct result of the political basis of academics, many academics and would-be academics find themselves being hired or retained not on the basis of their work but for pure political reasons. Many blame this on the "publish or perish" syndrome, claiming that this forces them to steal from their peers or students, put the proverbial knife in someone else's back, or even fabricate results, just to survive. To illustrate some of the cynicism and politics that have recently been at issue in a leading university: the "management" of the university, under pressure to hire at least one female, deliberately hired

185

someone who would clearly not be capable of it, which she knew and they knew. As a consequence she spends most of her time trying to keep above water and not pushing for equal treatment for her sisters in the hiring process. Needless to say, she has not given the "management" any trouble in any other areas either (this tactic is also common among large bureaucratic corporations). Much of academics has slipped into a pursuit of power and survival rather than truth and trust. Professors can be as often found discussing the extra bookcase one faculty member has or who is up or down this week in the hierarchy as they may be found discussing some new principle. Students subject to this sort of process learn it, and what they learn is the pursuit and creation of form rather than substance. Only when they go out into the market, do most people find that in the long run the market will not support form and demands substance. They will eventually find they are no longer in a state or foundation funded institution, or a large corporation with market control (which is a second wave form and on its way out), which can survive regardless of market demands. Many things that do exist cannot be measured, such as creativity, spirit, and drive, and if they exist in some quantity it is not a quantity we are yet able to comprehend.

FLUFF AND REALITY

There are few scholars now who will not show you tables and charts to back their theories, the result of the application of numerous statistical series or formulas to a sometimes enormous database. This form of research is most prevalent in the social sciences. When anyone points out that (1) the database is over fifteen years old; (2) has no relation to current reality; (3) is incomplete; (4) was gathered under questionable techniques; and (5) the formulas applied to its analysis were lacking and superficial, scholars will typically reply with irritation, "That is what I believe!" as though it were a question of faith, or simply shrug and say "That is the best I can do." No doubt the critic is branded a heretic, especially after questioning the consequence of what has been measured. Such spurious scholarship is rampant and has seeped into every cranny of the educational system.

However, it is not entirely the fault of the scholars. To a very large extent, they have been only reacting to what the market demanded of them. They have been the inheritors of a very long tradition, or market, that has included soothsayers and witchdoctors. All but the most naive advisors, planners, economists and so on in government and industry know that their analyses go to serve a decision that has usually already been made—a decision which may be based upon the fact that the chairman's aunt lives in the vicinity, or the president likes the golf course in the area, facts that cannot be sold to the shareholders, or voters, as the basis of decision. (Chiefs found also that the accumulation of witchdoctors added to their prestige and it also gave a status outlet for the ambitious who otherwise would seek to be the chief or a competing chief.) The role of the soothsayer was similarly to divine what the general wanted and interpret the entrails of the sheep accordingly, or in the case of the witchdoctor what the chief wanted and in relation what the voodoo bones said. Often what the general wanted was a decision dictated by the formula-analysis because he did not want to think about the problem himself. Generals and chiefs in the past, as they do now, found such "rigorous analysis" useful because people always seemed to go along better with a decision mandated by the "gods," or currently by "science," or by the formula. It was also useful when the decision went awry to blame it on fate, or a poor interpretation and thereby sacrifice the witchdoctor to satisfy public dis-satisfaction. (Analysis was and is also often useful as a substitute for decision— "We have the best people working on it.") Similarly today it is the planners and advisors who usually are the first to go in any downturn in the company's fortunes. The "best" or most popular soothsayers of the past were those like the Delphi Oracle who delivered analyses which could be interpreted in almost any way. Current practice recently confused a "developing country" which half in jest asked the responsible aid agency to send only one-handed economists in the future as the two-handed variety could never give a straight answer and were always confusing the issue by saying, "On the one hand . . . but on the other hand. . . ." This approach was possible in the second wave because reality could to some extent be manipulated or administered but this is no longer the case as reality has become less pliable and more critical, as the experience in Viet Nam with "rigorous analysis" and formula management showed us. Chiefs will have to increasingly think and decide for themselves, however much they may dislike it. Those who can't will go.

Reductionism is usually erroneous and misleading.

Tom Peters

EDUCATION FOR CREATIVE THINKING

We must get away from the idea that truth cannot exist if it cannot be measured, that scholarship must have numbers. Such ideas are not concurrent with the new realities of the third wave, if they were ever concurrent with reality at all. Perhaps the seeming inability of many people in corporate society to deal with reality because they prefer to associate with surreal numbers is somehow related. Many educational institutions have become expensive youth-minding agencies, not much different from summer camps, and at best functional training centers.

One of the bastions of second wave training has been the business school, which has sought to train corporate bureaucrats, in bureaucratic politics and manipulation skills. One of the first lessons learned in business school is not to trust anyone and to guard ideas, concepts, personal information, and thoughts zealously. These concepts are completely contrary to the third wave corporation's need for trust, ideas, communication, and interaction. What counted in the second wave corporation was the appearance of coming out on top. One of the surest ways to be superior was to undermine someone else's idea, plan, or position. This was usually done by pitting one person against another in order to stir up fears and jealousies, in other words by "killing two birds with one stone." This sort of corporate behavior created its own type of surrealism, with its own priorities and agenda that were not much related to external reality. Business schools have been teaching as their primary lessons not learned in the classroom but in the process. Such training has proved terribly damaging when it is carried through to many corporations.

SCHOLARSHIP AND REALITY

In terms of a positive change, scholarship must return to an honest basis, one concurrent with reality. This change may require as much courage in the educational establishment as the current business transformation requires in the corporate community. In a holistic sense, an educational process needs to replace the educational system, so that education can be the result of experiences, not rote training.

Education must exist for the present reality and for the future. Business education, for instance, must shift toward education for the third wave, as the dean of the University of California Business School at Berkeley implied, as Stanford is trying to do. ROLM and other progressive companies have undertaken intensive educational programs. The process consists of feeding participants' thoughts and actions back to them. Through this information, they can self-adjust and better align themselves with the ROLM philosophy and strategy and/or act as mirrors of the philosophy and strategy by putting positive action into the corporate culture.

With the advent of third wave technology and increased leisure time, education may increasingly be instigated and tailored by the individual to his or her own desires and needs. Once again a dynamic process of achievement may take place. Thomas Jefferson first designed the educational system to be a dynamic process whereby the most exceptional people in "virtue and talent" would advance to leadership. However, the educational system for the most part, declined to a sop for unemployment, a training program for industrial robots, a vent for spurious statistical findings, and, in some city schools, a breeding ground for criminals.

> They taught me a lot of formulas, to manipulate the symptoms of a problem, to keep things going for a while, but they never taught me how to reach into the causes of a problem, or grapple with underlying currents of opportunity—how to think about them. I'm not a mechanic and I resent having been trained to be one.

> Former MBA student

EDUCATION AS A CREATIVE PROCESS

While not neglecting the individual, corporate education should foster a unitary, holistic perspective. Because the people are the corporation, the education of the people, the self-interactive education should be promoted. An interactive synergy of evolutionary corporate knowledge may be constructed in this way. Such knowledge may be applied with increasing effectiveness toward its markets. The Japanese accomplish this interactive synergy by promoting personnel based upon the knowledge each has gained from mastering various tasks or jobs, as opposed to promoting personnel through bureaucratic politics or chance. With this process in place, the Japanese give eager employees every opportunity to try different but appropriate skills and to succeed at them. As stated previously, Japanese companies require members to carry a notebook in which to record (1) what they have learned and to where this new knowledge might lead; (2) how previous knowledge might be incorporated and applied into the framework of a new job; and (3) how they can improve a new situation as they move along. Participants are not only constantly learning, but they are constantly thinking and adding to their knowledge base, as well as applying new knowledge to it. This creates a continuing momentum of new knowledge within the company, which generates its competitive edge. It follows that the smarter, more outstanding people with whom a company begins, the heavier this momentum will be.

> We don't look for people in the standardized formula way of recruiting by the alphabet, or by university standing. Our recruiting is more organic. Every APPLE employee knows our business, is committed to our business, and is constantly on the lookout for the right recruits for our team, through

personal contact. This personal contact can start by doing some business with them.

APPLE employee, 1984

GETTING PEOPLE TO THINK FOR THEMSELVES

Steven Wozniak, cofounder of APPLE computer, recently wrote about his return to the University of California at Berkeley classroom after an absence of nine years. He mainly talks about what little creativity was generated or even tolerated in the classroom, even at Berkeley, and how formalized and formularized learning had become.

> One is directed to study problems by using only certain standard methods. I could not get good grades by being clever; I had to do it by learning given solutions. If I found a new way to solve a problem, it was not acceptable. . . . One cannot instruct a person to create a successful product, or to dream up good ideas. . . . When he's motivated to attain a goal, he'll work out the best way of getting there, but not because he is taught. . . . The best teaching role . . . is one of collaborator, friend. I'm not going to teach him the solution. The formal approaches to problem solving mean that students cannot take advantage of rapidly changing technology. Things change so quickly in computer science that a technology might appear and then be out of date within a few months. . . . The closed academic climate creates a prejudice against alternative philosophies of learning, and how academic scientists reflect that attitude in researching results that fit their views of the world.[1]

I certainly would have had stage fright in lecturing one of the instigators of the third wave on third wave technology, and would not have presumed to tell that person what the acceptable solutions were. Mr. Wozniak has only echoed what many feel. Wherever education may take place, be it in a corporation, in an institution, or at home, the process must return to education—getting people to think for themselves, and not training them to repeat formulas that they may well not understand or know how to use. We must understand that progress, security, and survival can only come from creative thinking, now that we can no longer control markets or stabilize markets. As situations change rapidly, education can serve the essential feedback process, allowing society to view itself, what it is doing right and wrong, and what it is following. The slower the feedback process moves in time, the slower society will be in maximizing the positives and in rectifying the negatives. In an environment of fast change and shrinking margins for error, such slowness may be extremely dangerous.

I know of no safe repository of the ultimate power of society but the people. And if we think them not enlightened enough, the remedy is not to take the power from them, but to inform them by education.

Thomas Jefferson

13

SOCIETY, CULTURE, AND THE CORPORATION IN THE THIRD WAVE

The most important change of the past decade is not technological advancement, but the virtual revolution that has occurred in our social awareness. After the turbulence, violence, and confrontation of the late sixties came a period of looking inward, as if our whole people, shocked, and deeply sobered by those years of uproar, began quietly to sort out the merits of all those causes. We have tried to heal divisions, both with insight, with effort, resulting in a qualitative change in our national attitude— our concern for the environment, job security for the work force, dignity for the handicapped, enhanced purpose for the aged and higher regard for the consumer. These causes are no longer considered controversial but society's unfinished business.

C. E. Meyer, Jr., president
TWA, 1978

SOCIAL AWARENESS AND INNER DIRECTION

Americans as individuals are once again taking charge of their political and economic futures. Political and economic problems are increasingly discussed and solved at the grass roots level. Politics is no longer the private preserve of the professional politician. Enterprise is no longer the private preserve of large corporations. People are becoming less "outer directed" and more "inner directed." There are significant channels for input into the political and economic whole. Electronic information technology has brought the reality of political action into every living room in America. Almost every issue, every injustice, and every decision come under the national microscope of television. Feedback loops are consummated by the rapid deployment of "single issue" lobby groups, on such issues as pollution, nuclear arms, or conservation, which respond immediately to any governmental action. The microcomputer and financial deregulation have opened many areas of enterprise to individuals. The microcomputer now allows the small business the capability of planning and running with increased precision, efficiency, and imagination. Microcomputers allow entrepreneurs an increased ability to develop and assess business plans. Individuals have significant ability to influence society in both economic and political ways. In *The Greening of America*, Charles Reich has reminded us that Bob Dylan has had more political influence than the vast bulk of second wave politicians.

POLITICAL ACTION AND INDIVIDUAL INITIATIVE

Big governments are recognizing that problems must be solved by local groups whenever possible. Government is restructuring funds and is allocating the majority of them to local levels. Big corporations are recognizing that people need to create their own futures and are funding new employee-generated ventures in some cases, such as Control Data is doing. Monsanto is funding new ventures with the purpose of learning how to generate and transfer some of the same energy and creativity. Profit sharing has become a widespread phenomenon. About 16 percent of all blue-collar workers are now included in some form of profit sharing, and over 435,000 American companies offer profit sharing. The increasing trend toward inner direction means that people are using more individual initiative as opposed to being directed by state or institutional agencies. Corporations are translating this ethic into their operations to allow freedom for individual initiative. This freedom must be provided in order to attract and motivate people. In turn, people will increasingly translate this ethic into community activity and the arts. As the arts grow in the national consciousness and in the importance awarded them by governments, more and more funds will be allocated to them. Value will not only be considered in terms of efficiency and effectiveness but also in terms of psychic satisfaction, in either creation or appreciation of the arts.

> There is a greatness in our national character, because we're healthy and growing. We are not the Latin language, which is dead!

> Robert Riddell, director
> USO, 1983

The New Yorker referred to Mr. Riddell as a person with the vision and psyche of someone from both the 1940s and the 1980s.[1] America is a healthy, growing nation, more healthy than others, and will continue to be if it maintains and enhances its diversity. Diverse people, values, and techniques are why America will always have that something extra with which to outdo its competitors, such as the Japanese who value cultural and racial homogeneity to an extreme.

SELF-ACTUALIZATION

A recent survey of what Americans valued most was indicative of this change. Among the most highly valued were interesting work, good health, and good friends. Among those things valued least were a lot of money and work that was related to making a lot of money. Although the results were surprising to some, they should not have been because these new values have led to increased interest in entrepreneurship and in self-actualization, especially in the arts. Entrepreneurs in the arts, who are investing in themselves, should be allowed to write off this investment at rates similar to industrial businesses investing in plant and equipment.

194

As hierarchies break down, giving way to individual and group responsibility, and as society's mechanical structures give way to new organic systems, new values rise to replace those that have crumbled. Under the previous hierarchical society, the amount of money a person made was usually a good indicator of the influence he or she had in society and the information he or she had access to. This, however, is no longer true in the free flux and flow of the third wave. Power and influence move in a flux of mostly indiscernible currents. A previously poor, unknown young lawyer can publish something attacking the automobile industry and become the major force of change in that industry overnight. An unknown can appear on a talk show and become an influential authority. A woman can whisper an idea into a friend's ear who, in turn, whispers the same idea into her husband's and in due course this idea becomes part of the party's presidential platform. Almost anyone can talk to anyone now, as opposed to hierarchical second wave society where access to certain individuals was precluded by the hierarchy. Money, position, and apparent power have become less important.

The new personal criteria

People, therefore, seek different and changing things from their lives and from corporate participation. Interesting work and people, healthy conditions, climate, purpose, meaning, love, care, and identity have all become important factors that are considered along with money. Not only are people into physical fitness, but the great mass of the population want to exercise and eat properly to maintain good health. The slogan of the new generation may well be: "No pain—no gain" added to "Work hard, play hard." People have become consumers of information, health, and experiences as much as or more than they have become consumers of products.

A person's income from corporate participation must now be assessed upon a multitude of factors and not just upon money. A person's corporate participation becomes less an endeavor to earn a living and more a continuous consumption of group activity and experience through which he or she receives the bulk of his or her identity reinforcement. Many individuals in the throes of the transition have found it difficult to make the transformation, however, primarily because they have been channeled into obsolete but still extant mechanical structures even though their needs have markedly changed. This dysfunction has perhaps been the major contributor to our drug and alcohol problems, the two largest and fastest growing single industries. Individuals who indulge in such practices often seek to escape their inability to make the requisite transformation. Some effort must be made to minimize this cost of transition.

The new status

The indicators of status have changed from the conspicuous consumption of large houses, large offices, and large cars, which are no longer reliable indicators of influence, to that of a good physique; good health; interesting friends; exciting corporate associations; information-rich neighborhoods and geographic locations in which to live, travel, and interact; and interesting hobbies. Status in third wave society has much less to do with where you are in the hierarchy than with who you are personally, your daring, determination, imagination, and entrepreneurship.

> I think the answer lies in entrepreneurial capitalism. We haven't sold out, we're taking over. . . . The most exciting battles are taking place inside political parties, corporations.
>
> Yuppies are challenging the ossified corporate structures, just as they once challenged the sacred traditions of academia, and forcing them into more imaginative solutions.
>
> Jerry Rubin, 1985
> Former Chicago 7 radical
> "Yuppie" Entrepreneur

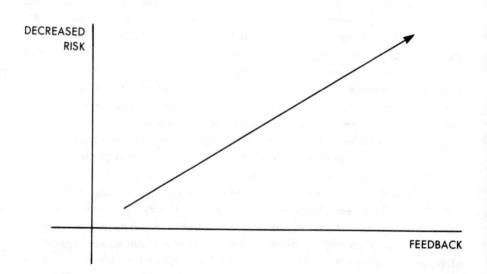

EXHIBIT 13.1   Risk and feedback increase as the speed of change increases.

The values and cultural shifts of the late sixties have become the accepted driving forces of social and corporate progress. The shock troops of the third wave who experienced and were part of the social revolution are accepting leadership positions through which they are and increasingly will be infusing new values and new structures into society. This dynamic force of healthy change has always been the hallmark of America since its inception. As Mr. Riddell has said, America is not dead like the Latin language!

PARTICIPATORY DEMOCRACY AND MANAGEMENT

All processes of American society are speeding up. Society itself is becoming more organic and less mechanical and hierarchical, resulting in increased feedback. This effect was referred to by Charles Reich as the "greening of America," which has in turn caused the "greening of American management." Alvin Toffler referred to this effect as "participatory democracy," a reparticipation of citizens in the day to day issues of democracy, which is reflected in spreading participatory management in turn.[2] Participatory management has commonly included workers and management. Recently management theorists, such as Peters and Waterman, have been essentially calling for the inclusion of the consumer in management, which is a logical extension. Beyond emphasizing consumer needs, quality, and ideas, a logical extension for corporations would be to give each purchaser of a major item, or of a substantial quantity, a share in the firm. With this share, a consumer could actually vote on corporate issues just as employees are entering into ownership participation and management.

THE NEW POWER OF THE CONSUMER

Tom Peters and Bob Waterman are right. American businesses have enjoyed virtual control of the marketplace for too many years. They grew fat, lazy, and dull, and treated the consumer as some kind of dumb cow to be milked at their will. Henry Ford's dictum was that the consumer could have any color as long as it was black. International competition has changed this picture, however, and will continue to do so. Consumer science has long been a neglected and ignored subject in most of our educational systems. It would be advantageous for American business to encourage the interactive education of an increasingly sophisticated and knowledgeable consumer, instead of allowing the consumer to learn from international competition. An interactive educational process in which consumers join the new participatory management would be a decided advantage on offshore competition and an excellent start.

197

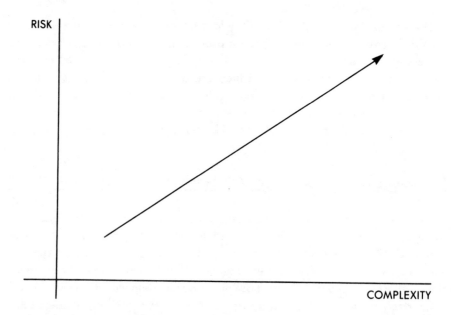

EXHIBIT 13.2   As risk and complexity increase so does the need for information, for filtering out noise, and for increasingly precise action as the margin for error steadily declines.

CORPORATE CONSCIOUSNESS

Charles Reich has discussed three different levels of consciousness in his seminal work *The Greening of America*.[3] Each of these is typical of a specific wave in society, although they all exist or existed concurrently. Consciousness I relates most strongly to the pioneering society of the first wave in which people carved out a life from the wilderness. The consciousness of society was independent, self-centered, creative, risk oriented, and entrepreneurial. Society attempted to conquer nature.

Consciousness I was succeeded by Consciousness II, which is typical of the industrial second wave. It was a programmed, formularized consciousness of the company person, which was oriented toward security, status, hierarchies, social acceptance, material possessions, and survival. This consciousness level naturally was rooted in the large corporations and the formula management of the second wave. Consciousness II people tried to control and master nature.

Consciousness III is the consciousness of the third wave in which people, instead of preprogrammed action, become interactive and synergistic networks and organisms. Men and women become more inner directed, focusing upon self-actualization, inner acceptance, and experiences rather than upon possessions, security, company friends, and hierarchical status. Consciousness III people seek to live in synergy and interact with nature and society. Indicative of this new type of consciousness, Bill Norris, CEO of Control Data, recently suggested "legislation that would compel companies to judge the merits of proposed mergers on the basis of whether they would serve or harm society."[4]

Consciousness III evolved with the breakdown of dominating power in large corporations and with the increased richness of information in the environment. The vast expansion of direct and indirect education during the mid-twentieth century, through television, books, and a growing educational plant, has created a new awareness and has increased education per capita, changing the social context dramatically.

THE ADMINISTRATORS AND THE ADMINISTERED

Society during the second wave was divided between the administrators and the administered. It had to deal with the vast influx of immigrants as well as organize a vast land and plentiful resources. Large numbers of immigrants were relatively uneducated and unversed in the traditions of democratic thought. Because of this, the administrators, who usually had some education, felt society to be divided between those that could be trusted, those with a strong upbringing based upon principle, and those that could not be, which is why loyalty to form was so valued. A long period of testing was required before any real administrative power could be assumed, regardless of a person's creative or managerial capability. The basic infrastructure of the nation had to be created as well.

Society took the tack of organizing large enterprises along the simplest possible lines. Because educational opportunities were lacking, especially for immigrants, enterprises required only obedience from its members, not education and thought. Very few employees had any education and some could not speak the language. People had to be programmed and directed in order for large corporations to harness America's natural resources, which included the immigrant masses. Corporations were not yet capable of interacting on a self-directed synergistic basis; they could not yet be organic.

THE WATERSHED

The third wave has changed all of this. Educational levels have increased, values have changed, and the country's infrastructure has been in place. New technologies have changed the nature of markets and the nature of business by requiring more precise actions and information. Mass marketing and mass production have turned to specialized and individual marketing and production, broadcasting to "narrow" casting, and mass magazines to specialized magazines.

As the third wave rose and gained momentum, people were no longer interested in second wave values, nor were they satisfied with merely carrying out orders. They wanted a piece of the creative action, they wanted self-actualization and meaning in their lives. Management styles, practices, and ideology had to change. Management could no longer be directive; to be effective it had to become organic. Directive action was less and less effective as educational levels increased and as markets became more demanding. Quick action required organic interaction, which could not wait for orders to be transmitted after lengthy analysis. Success is now part of creation and experience, not of possessions or hierarchy. Power is now a function of the capability of a network at a point in time, and not a prescribed position. Position and possessions in second wave success implied survival. Because survival is not at stake in the third wave, experiences and creativity are more desirable indicators of success. People discuss values and meaning everyday in conversation.

Obtaining or developing levels of responsibility is now more a function of evolution than of programmed testing. Advancement now depends on talent and virtue, whereas before it was largely a function of narrowly defined virtue, that is, who could be trusted and who had been around the longest. The process of the past rested upon a person's dependability in carrying out orders and in following formulas. Since formulas were relatively simple and because the mistakes in them were expected and could be buffered by slack, talent above a certain level did not matter. Success and survival were previously a function of hierarchical position, monetary income, and material possessions, whereas experiences, information, skill, networks, and knowledge now count for more. Monetary manipulation becomes less of a temptation, and bureaucratic politics become less rewarding.

GENESIS OF A NEW SOCIETY

Experiences, skill, and knowledge are generated within people and cannot be obtained by manipulation. The general level of education has also vastly improved. People, therefore, can and must be trusted with greater decision-making autonomy, changing the role of management from direction to facilitation. As people become more self-actualized, the organization becomes more organic and interactive, creating a dynamic system of values and cultures. The organization is closing its schism between those who are evaluated according to form and those who are evaluated according to results.

In Reich's terms, many organizations are becoming Consciousness III

200

organizations as the sensitivities of the new wave spread and take root. Such organizations would include most of the high-tech Silicon Valley firms, some airlines, and many telecommunications companies. There are also many Consciousness II organizations, such as oil, utility, and insurance companies. Some second wave firms are trying to transform their consciousness, many are not, and some are trying to fake a transformation. Many manufacturing and raw material-based companies remain at the Consciousness II level. A few organizations operate on the Consciousness I level, too. These include most farmers, small businesspeople, inventors, and some professionals.

Consciousness III firms are more competitive and act faster than the other two because they can more quickly focus information, human capital, and other resources. Third wave firms understand the new realities better—they can make and back decisions with more speed. This is why many Consciousness II companies are having problems in competing. Some have attempted to adopt or buy the new technology as an answer, without transforming their consciousness. The results are disastrous. After buying out Unimation–Robotics, Westinghouse lost most of the Unimation people because Consciousness III people could not coexist happily with Consciousness II people. Ed Land's problem at Polaroid may have been one of Consciousness I trying to coexist with Consciousness II and III. Rickenbacker's problems at Eastern Airlines may have been a problem of a Consciousness I type trying to impose his will on a Consciousness II organization. This indicates that organizations also must have a strategy for transforming their consciousness as well as their technologies.

In terms of the new heroes of third wave consciousness and values, there may not be a better example than Thomas Magnum, played by Tom Selleck. Magnum is a private investigator who owns nothing but has access to everything. He is entrepreneurial and has all the necessary interpersonal networks to put his ideas or "hunches" into play. He bends or breaks rules, often making fun of and fooling hierarchical institutions. Higgins, one of Magnum's sidekicks, is a perfect second wave foil. Magnum is trim, flexible, sensitive, and tolerant. He has a sense of humor and would rather think creatively than fight. He does what he does in pursuit of worthwhile experiences and to help people. Money does not seem to have any real significance to him, but self-actualization does. Clint Eastwood and his roles are another example of the new hero who is above all an individualist in conflict with bureaucracy.

The Consciousness II or second wave hero may be best summed up in John Wayne and the parts he played—United States marshall, cattle baron, or military officer. The characters Wayne brought to the screen did things according to the book, played by the rules and enforced them. They usually had little humor and were often insensitive, authoritarian, intolerant, and rigid. This character type no longer holds much attraction for third wave society.

201

CONSCIOUSNESS TRANSFORMATION IN THIRD WAVE CORPORATIONS

The Consciousness I corporation is usually the gunslinger-pioneer type or the early entrepreneurial type in which emphasis is placed on large and fast personal gains. Everything is focused upon quick wins.

The Consciousness II corporation is usually the bureaucratic or the corporate type in which emphasis is placed on who controls the corporation because the market is already being controlled to a desirable degree by the corporation. Everything is focused upon the acquisition of corporate power, bureaucratic politics, and clique loyalty.

The Consciousness III corporation is usually the entrepreneurial or entrepreneurial-corporate type in which emphasis is placed upon longer term corporate and social viability. Everything is focused upon serving the long-term needs of the corporation, its participants, and society. Focus is upon a creative and progressive corporate culture (warp) and interpersonal and intercommunity development.

THE NEW AGENDA

> The viable individual and corporation today must serve some real long-term social need. The age of corporate existence via marketing hype is over.
>
> Gene Richeson, founder
> ROLM Corporation

The difficulties of making the appropriate transition and transformation for many companies are enhanced by the aging phenomenon. In most industrialized countries, the average age of the population is higher than it has ever been before, as medicine prolongs life and contraception and changing values decrease births. This means that people in many corporations will stay there either because of decreased internal competition or because the pool from which their replacements can be drawn will simply be smaller. External competition, however, will mount from abroad as the younger corporations adapt their industries to mass, international marketing. Corporate aging and its direct relationship to declining competitive ability will become increasingly important.

Many second wave companies are experiencing increased difficulties resulting from this aging phenomenon because of their common practice of retiring in place (RIP) many of their no longer useful senior executives. This may be part of the corporate welfare-socialism phenomenon by which many of the costs shouldered by the public sector are increasingly being taken over by the private sector. The CEO of a major corporation has pointed out that because of the slow-moving structures of such organizations, many people at various corporate levels are able to retire themselves in place without telling the corporation or without being noticed.

However, as the aging phenomenon increases and advances, such costs, including medical costs, may become a significant burden for many companies if they are not already. Such climbing costs will put many companies in less competitive positions. One solution may be to help people who are no longer useful to achieve their ambitions and desires outside of the corporate framework, whether these desires be to return to school or to start a new business. New businesses may become contractees for the firm in time, thus enhancing its competitive position. Retiring in place, lavish "buy-offs," and other such practices are, in the final analysis, not only expensive but destructive to both the firm and the individual. Corporations cannot afford this practice in the longer term, and competitive firms cannot afford to become crippled by increasing corporate welfare costs. They must find a mutually humane and profitable way to retrack redundant people.

The aging phenomenon, encouraged by mindless corporate welfare, will also prolong the retention of the Consciousness II mind set in many firms. The proponents of quantum physics said that they would have to wait for the key people in the old order of science to die off before their scientific advances would be accepted, no matter how scientifically valid the new theories might be. They were largely proven to be right. Similarly, many corporations will not be able to make the necessary transformation and transition until certain key people disappear from the scene. The current structure of many corporations ensures that they will experience the aging phenomenon more acutely than others. People come in waves or generations like everything else, and those leading the wave will enter immediate targets of maximum opportunity, i.e., those firms that will give the most encouragement to their talents. Naturally those firms will be most likely to grow and prosper. Still, second wave remnants will cling tenaciously in many places and will not go without a fight.

Automate, Immigrate, or Evaporate

Part of the transformation process already apparent and affecting every facet of society is the, "automate, immigrate, or evaporate" (to quote a General Electric executive) process that every manufacturing corporation is facing. Many companies have been haphazardly, reluctantly, and frantically reacting to this pressure by laying people off en masse, or instituting only part of the process and crying in frustration when it does not work or does not give the required competitive edge.

> If the robot is the answer to high productivity, it would be easy for General Motors and Ford to catch up with the Japanese. All they need is to invest in robots and bring them in on the factory floor in large numbers. It's not that simple, however.
>
> Hideo Sugiura, executive vice president
> Honda

To successfully automate, the corporation must develop an organic process through which machines, participants, products, and customers can be linked in a chain of mutual satisfaction and harmony, enabling high-quality products to "flow like water." Robots are best placed where they can do the work of robots. They cannot replace people who make decisions; they *can* replace those who do much of the spiritually damaging but necessary mechanical work. Automation will allow many of the "working" people to become more concerned with values, self-fulfillment, and other third wave concerns instead of with scratching out an existence.

Successful and increasing automation is a pervasive, inescapable fact of society. More and more people will need to upgrade their skills and find other employment. Upgraded skills will allow them to increase their incomes and standards of living in turn. More precise information will require fewer people to accomplish certain tasks as information technology spreads. Governments and corporations must pay increasing attention to reintegrating such displaced people.

NEW CONDITIONS/NEW METHODS

Government must also seek more and better ways for people to be productive members of society rather than use the second wave techniques of throwing money and formulas at problems, which results in wastes and climbing costs. When people do not fit into the unnatural structures of the second wave, their talents and creativity are confined and suppressed. One approach government might take, which avoids increased bureaucracy, is through the tax structure. Any educational expense applicable to work, even if not current, could be deducted against income. Individual retirement accounts (IRAs) could be structured in such a way that people could draw from them for educational purposes without incurring a penalty. An educational insurance fund, like the unemployment insurance fund, could be started. Employer and employee would jointly contribute to this fund, which would cover the employee up to and through the time when he or she needs it. Reduced interest loans could be expanded and collected through the tax structure.

Such government and corporate initiatives are essential to a successful transition, which maintains and increases a competitive edge. Government's primary role is to create the conditions that allow the best natural evolution of society and the individual, not to support the creation of wasteful and large administrative bureaucracies.

Consciousness III is not an attack against reason as some quasi second wave thinkers believe. Consciousness III is an attempt at reason, reality, and natural truth against a lie.

A little revolution now and then is a good thing.

Thomas Jefferson

14

THE CYBERNETIC WAVE

"THE FOURTH WAVE"

The responsibility for [constructive] change therefore lies with us. We must begin with ourselves, teaching ourselves not to close our minds to the novel, the surprising, the seemingly radical. This means fighting off the idea-assassins who rush forward to kill any new suggestion on grounds of its impracticality, while defending whatever now exists as practical, no matter how absurd, oppressive, or unworkable it may be.

Alvin Toffler, 1980
The Third Wave

THE TECHNOLOGY OF THE WAVES

The first wave was generated by the application of agricultural technology to nature; the second wave by the application of mechanical technology to manufacture and raw materials extraction; and the third wave by the application of electronic technology to human capital. The fourth wave will evolve from the application of thought to electronic technology or vice versa.

The first public, albeit rudimentary and primitive, application of fourth wave technology has already been exhibited. It is a video game activated by thought waves. Attached to the head of the player are sensors that perceive thought wave patterns, which in turn move the cursor on the video screen. No doubt there may be more advanced applications of such technology under military development. At a recent Silicon Valley party, I got into a conversation with some engineers who were working on the current frontiers of voice recognition. They were discussing how a word, a "phoneme," could be imprinted upon a laser electronically, then could be "shot" through so many tiny crystal holograms until it ran across a hologram that matched. The match would trigger an electrical impulse, allowing a computer to recognize the word. I asked them if the same could be done for the electronic imprint of a thought pattern. They said it would be more difficult, but it could eventually be done.

In relationship to this, some futurists are now postulating that within forty years devices may be connected to the brain that will allow it to be directly linked into a computer network. Such a bond would create the possibility of unlimited memory, computing power, linkage of many minds, and direct creation (computers controlled by thought). This facility will no doubt be assisted by current research upon the "biochip" and optoelectronics. Direct creation will also be assisted by fusion reaction, another initial fourth wave breakthrough. The first experimental fusion reaction has been achieved. More energy is produced from the union of atomic nuclei than is used to induce the reaction, thereby accelerating the development of a cheap and inexhaustible source of energy.

DIRECT CREATION THROUGH CHEAP ENERGY AND PRODUCTS

Direct creation will result from the linkage of the third or fourth generation automated programmable factory with the thought process. The current automated factory relies upon rudimentary robotics without much software or artificial intelligence, very much the first generation. In the second generation, robotics will be more touch sensitive and flexible and will require more software. Third generation robotics will have speech recognition and artificial intelligence that will be capable of "learning" and receiving verbal direction. In

207

the fourth generation, robotics will be capable of receiving thought commands much as the cursor in the video game, allowing direct creation. Designs, thoughts, and concepts could be quickly modeled and translated into a prototype.

Direct creation, the foundation of the fourth wave, will make inexpensive products and services possible. Almost all products and services will be "tailor made" for precise individual requirements of delivered utility. As the juncture of electronic technology and human thought, the fourth wave could be described as the *cybernetic wave*, just as the third wave has been referred to as the computer wave, the juncture of software and electronics. A transitional cybernetic wave will come into being with the perfection of voice recognition.

CYBERNETICS

Cybernetics was first coined by Norbert Wiener at MIT to describe the coming juncture of thought and electronics. The word comes from a Greek term meaning to steer. Many originally interpreted this science of "steersmanship" literally as the function of mechanically steering, which is not surprising considering that the second wave was still dominant. It was the era of mechanical cybernetics. With the advent of the third wave, however, cybernetics has evolved to what Wiener and the Greeks originally meant, i.e., to govern or steer through a natural, interactive organic process. Wiener did develop his perspective from the study of medical science. Some have incorrectly used the term to describe the third wave, which is really the union of written software and electronics, not thought and electronics. Dr. Wiener heralded the cybernetic wave as a potentially beneficial development for mankind, freeing mankind, as "labor that accepts the conditions of competition with slave labor (machines) accepts the conditions of slave labor and is essentially slave labor." [1] Hewlett-Packard uses a caterpillar that turns into a beautiful flying butterfly in its advertisement for its personal computer. The implicit message is that Hewlett-Packard technology will set you free and will transform you in the new environment.

Herman Kahn, the founder of the Hudson Institute, considered the fourth wave as the culmination of "the great transition," the transition from a period of pervasive poverty, the first wave, through the transitional second and third waves, to a period of pervasive affluence, the fourth wave. The fourth wave will also be the culmination of the trend back to a form of unitary free enterprise and individual freedom. Systems will be in place that will allow the entrepreneur to have ideas assessed, financed, contracted, produced, and marketed quickly. Systems will also be in place for any individual's complaints to be assessed and acted upon, for his or her political views to be channeled to appropriate parties or agencies. Fusion energy will be perfected, making available cheap and plentiful energy.

THE CYBERNETIC CORPORATION

The fourth wave will see the rise of the integrated organic corporation, the cybernetic corporation. The corporation will be integrated through the nervous systems of computer networks and telecommunications, often directly tied into the minds of the participants much as today's teleconferencing attempts to do in a very primitive form. The corporation will be a sort of noncorporation in that each participant will function primarily as an individual entrepreneur and pioneer with loose alliances. Each entrepreneur or participant will directly receive the results of his or her own efforts, plus a portion of the benefits arising from the synergy of combined efforts.

INFORMATION AND NOISE IN DECISION MAKING

In these early phases of the third wave, technology has produced an explosion of data and information. Data and information that are not useful quickly become noise, however. Information is useful and intelligible data. Data are intelligible signals related to the environment. Noise is unintelligible signals.

In the second wave, the approach was to hire excess staff. Executives believed that somewhere in the mass of numbers there was something useful, some valid information, as well as a substantial amount of noise. The system was one of trial and error, i.e., various bits of data were used until something worked or partially worked. If a formula did not work, there was enough slack to absorb the mistakes. The amount of information applied (information minus noise) is inversely proportional to amount of raw materials and capital used. The reason for the considered economic shallowness (rapid drop off in productivity) of information investment is related to several factors. First, in any set of circumstances that define an environment the amount of information (useful data) that can be mined from that specific environment drops off as investment increases. The most "easily" accessible information is "mined" first, subjecting further investment to diminishing returns in productivity. Further investment, however, is under pressure to show a return and often churns up noise (not useful data) disguised as information. While information generation decreases, noise generation increases, negating information and eventually investment produces a net product of noise. Second, investment is also structurally rigid in that it "mines" information in a relatively static framework or

209

rigid direction so that as the set of circumstances change (parameters), as the environment changes, the specific investment becomes increasingly less productive. If a way can be found both to dampen noise and to change the direction of investment as the environment changes, information investment productivity would increase rapidly. That way is probably AI—artificial intelligence.

In the third wave, the appropriate information must be applied as soon as possible or you might not get a second chance, and you do not have the slack to absorb the mistakes. It was often believed, and with some reason, that the more data one waded through, the more likely that better information would be found and, therefore, the better the decision made. In relation the more important the person making the decision, the more staff, computers, and databases he or she had control of or access to, whether the decision maker needed them or not. In most cases, people could not tell whether they needed more assistance or a different process. As we have seen, this confusion led to poor decision making. The mass of information was ignored because there was no way of separating out the noise efficiently or because the generation of

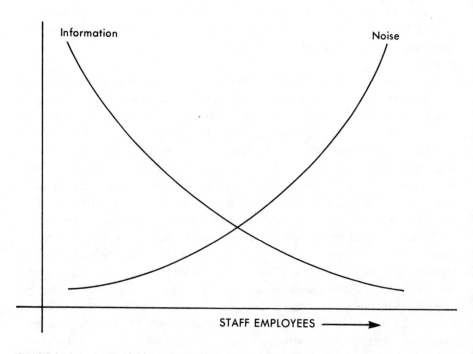

EXHIBIT 14.1   Units of information generated by each additional staff employee in a second wave organization.

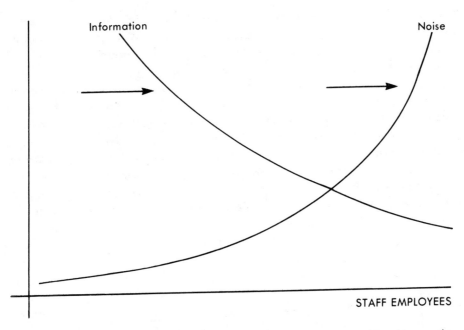

EXHIBIT 14.2   With the computing technology of the third wave, it is possible to increase the efficiency of information and application, but eventually the problem of diminishing returns and noise generation develops.

information became a purpose in itself. Over time, the original objective of making a decision was forgotten. The "conspicuous" consumption and generation of information, coined by James March of Stanford, often was a substitute and subterfuge for risky actions or decisions; in some organizations this meant almost any decision or action. In many cases, data production became a kind of "white noise" that would hide those responsible until attention was turned elsewhere. This kind of nondecision often was the correct choice because there was no way of differentiating the necessary information. This tactic became less and less viable as change accelerated and as information became sharper. The consequences were more serious. Benjamin Franklin's maxim of "a decision postponed is a decision half solved" became less and less applicable in the third wave context.

INFORMATION FROM DATA

How can relative information be targeted? How can informational relevance and meaning be assessed? Where is information useful? To whom? To what? How is the interactive accumulation of knowledge and information built and generated? The critical task of artificial intelligence (AI) is to organize information and target it into appropriate areas. Without AI, we will be swamped with flows of information that would quickly become noise, clogging up the arteries and synapses of the corporation.

Artificial intelligence allows the interactive evolution and application of knowledge in *target* areas. Napoleon well understood that resources had to be concentrated in specific areas to achieve an objective. In the second wave, vast quantities of basic resources were targeted at specific areas, resulting in effectiveness but also in vast quantities of waste. In the third wave, AI targets vast amounts of information at specific points, maximizing the efficiency and effectiveness of basic resources. In the fourth wave, evolving areas of knowledge will be targeted at specific areas for maximum efficient and effective use of information.

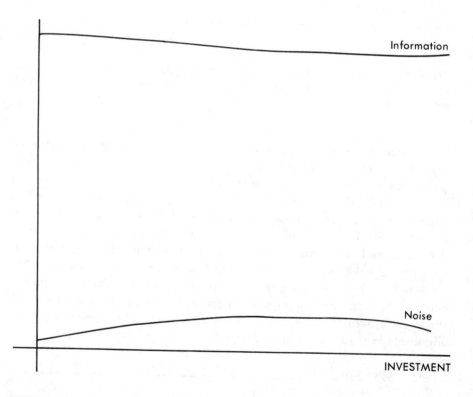

EXHIBIT 14.3 The institution of interactive artificial intelligence in the fourth wave will allow for the continuous information productivity of investment in staff or thinking computers.

212

A possible interactive network

The continuous generation of interactive information, which builds evolutionary focused knowledge, will spur spontaneous innovation and creation. An early primitive example is the experiment based upon the ARPANET system developed by Xerox Parc. At the time, Xerox Parc was wrestling with the problem of accelerating and improving the design of VLSI (very large systems integration) chips.

Lynn Conway of Xerox Parc and her collaborators came up with the idea of creating and sending a superior course on the design of VLSI chips, which included the design of such chips on an integrated, interactive basis, to a number of universities. The designs would be put on the ARPANET system for all to see. Specific and related areas would be brought to the attention of the relevant parties. The designs would be added to and tested in increments and eventually would evolve in an interactive way into the final design that would be quickly manufactured, using the latest automated techniques. The new chips would then be mass-produced and distributed for creative use. In this way, an evolutionary system for the creation of knowledge in the area of chip design came into being. Ms. Conway discusses how individuals will be able to follow a similar process on an enhanced national computer grid by exploring and pioneering evolutionary knowledge on an interactive basis in a new unlimited frontier, creating an unimaginable acceleration in the increase of knowledge and applied information.

The mind set of nations in the fourth wave

Although the information on AI projects is scant, the money and resources devoted to these projects are not. The Japanese and the British have committed about \$500,000,000, and the United States government and a private American consortium have given about twice that much. In the United States, Lynn Conway heads the research and development of the fifth generation computer that will be able to "think."

There are a number of other approaches being made on a smaller scale by France, Germany, Canada, Singapore, Korea, and Brazil. It is not clear what the Russians are doing, although they obviously cannot rely upon stealing to win this race because even a lag of a few months will be critical, if not terminal. The race is not just for first development of the fifth generation computer but more importantly for what it will mean. Achievement is not the only measure as it is for the international space race. In this instance, achievement will give the winner an edge in every field of knowledge and technology, an edge the losers may never overcome. It is the race to establish the first interactive national nervous system, the first effectively organic country. Fiber optic cables will be a primary medium for this nervous system.

In order to win the race, to enter a new field of technology, to commit funds, and to attempt the transition is not enough without a corresponding change in mind set, in the nature of interactions, and in the national style of management. This is why Britain's effort will fail, even if the project succeeds, because the national mind set will not have evolved sufficiently to use the results. Britain has not learned or seen the necessity to evolve its rigid society, due partially to the cushion of North Sea oil (which is, in the long run, a curse) and partially to its remaining large sums of capital. Emerging from World War II without capital or a creative mindset, the Japanese adopted an evolutionary system of change with American guidance. France is actively attempting to evolve its society and mind set while it pursues technology. Germany is not and may be left to continue developing quality mechanical products. Russia will probably lag because of its mired social evolution. The United States seems to be undergoing a schizo-phrenic evolution. Some elements of society are accelerating while others are retreating. It may require a challenge, such as Japan's realization of the first fifth generation computer, for the entire nation to pull in the same direction.

Artificial intelligence will open up another frontier—the commercial settle-ment of space. By using AI and robotics, humans will be able to settle not only nearby planets but other planetary systems. Intelligent robots, using a "space sling" to mine specimens and send them back to earth, should be in place soon after the AI puzzle is solved. Artificial intelligence, the ability of a machine to distinguish relevant information, will make the integrative corporation and country possible, not only within themselves but with nature and the fourth wave.

A PROLOGUE OF THE FUTURE SEEN FROM THE PAST

To look adequately into the future, as many have done, we must look back to the past. An analysis of past events and data indicates that Toffler's wave construct comprises a period of approximately 125 years, plus or minus 10 years, for each wave in North America. In Japan, the time period for each succeeding wave has been much shorter. For other countries, such as China, Korea, and Singapore, the projected period of each succeeding wave may be shorter still. The waves were of a much longer duration in Europe, especially the industrial second wave, than they were in North America; and they were much longer in North America than in Japan.

The construct of each wave appears as follows: A spurt of invention creates

214

the new parameters or potential boundaries of expansion for a new wave, and innovations proceed to fill this new frontier until it becomes saturated, causing economic growth to level off. The resources devoted to filling out the potential of the wave are utilized less fully and are rechanneled toward creative invention.

CREATIVE INNOVATION AND NEW PARAMETERS

Creative invention begins to contribute to the deterioration of the previous wave through a process described by Schumpeter as creative destruction, i.e., the socioeconomic infrastructure is devalued and a recession or a depression occurs. The period of invention is most significant from the time the previous wave levels off. Resources begin to be rechanneled until the period of primary innovation occurs, which is the beginning of the new wave. The period of primary innovation also acts to devalue the socioeconomic structure currently in place, causing another recession or depression during which a new socio-economic infrastructure is built. Recessions or depressions can be seen as society's efforts to realign and restructure its socioeconomic system to take advantage of the parameters and potential of the new wave. This period of primary innovation is a period of transition and turmoil, as the old wave crumbles and the new wave struggles to dominate. The primary innovation period appears to encompass approximately 25 years (again there could be plus or minus ten years at either end). During this time, new innovations are expensive and aimed at the high end of the market.

A period of secondary innovation begins after the new wave has gained dominance. Innovations become available at a medium price range. This secondary stage also causes a recession or depression and lasts for about 25 years. After the old wave has totally crumbled, a period of tertiary innovations follows. Innovations become generally available and relatively inexpensive (a period also of about twenty-five years plus or minus ten at each end). A recession may occur but should be relatively mild because the socioeconomic system should have been realigned sufficiently to take full advantage of the new wave. The new wave begins to level off and decline following these three stages. Between the rise of a new wave and the loss of dominance of the old wave, about 50 years lapse, roughly corresponding to that of the "Kondratieff" wave, the period between major depressions or recessions.

COMPOSITE TECHNOLOGIES AND PRODUCT LIFE CYCLES

Within each wave, composite technological products engender smaller waves. Each product created has a life cycle along with the subsequent wave it engenders. The frequency of these smaller waves and cycles is different for

215

each major wave. In the first or agricultural wave, technology, such as ploughing, remained relatively at the forefront of available technology for a long time. Any innovation in the shape of the plough for instance, remained relatively advanced for a long time. Invention and innovation were so infrequent that they were hardly noticeable. With the advent of the second wave and the market, however, composite technology waves and product life cycles became apparent. They appeared to be noticed by the general public only when the market became observably saturated.

In the third wave, the frequency of new composite technologies and markets appear rapidly, and usually long before the market for the old product or old technology has become saturated. Creative destruction and creative construction become relatively constant instead of periodic. It is not yet clear

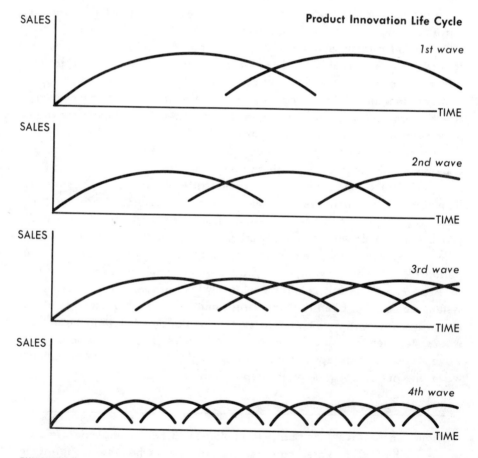

EXHIBIT 14.4

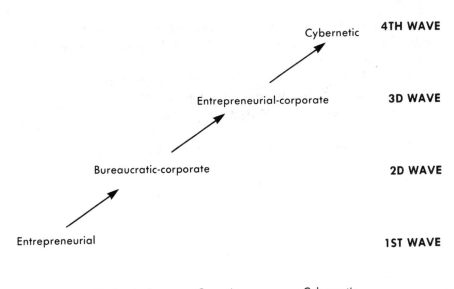

Organic	Mechanical	Organic	Cybernetic
Nature dependent	Nature "independent"	Nature interdependent	Nature integrative
Thinking	Obedience	Thinking + software	Thinking + AI (artificial intelligence)

EXHIBIT 14.5   American evolution of dominant organizational forms.

whether the third wave will follow the same periodic instances of depressions. It appears that economic downturns may follow as serious recessions at most, because of the new and constant destruction and construction phenomenon of the socioeconomic infrastructure. Consequently, parameters for potential development are expanding constantly. Research indicates that this may well be the trend because the rate of innovation and the length of the innovative period has more than doubled with each primary period of innovation.

A Chronicle of the Third Wave

If the present pattern and rate of creative invention and destruction are followed, the period of primary innovation should last until approximately 1995, when the third wave clearly becomes dominant. A serious downturn could occur then, followed by a period of high growth as secondary innovation takes off, lasting to 2020, again about 25 years. The secondary innovation stage would be followed by about 25 years of tertiary innovation. This would bring us to the year 2045, at which time the economy would begin to level off and decline, ushering in the fourth wave. The fourth wave, in turn, would reach dominance by about 2070.

Whatever happens, the future will be a time of rapidly increasing change in values, technologies, lifestyles, and management. We must constantly prepare for the speed of change if we are to realize our potentials.

Things do not happen—they are made to happen.

John F. Kennedy

15

HOW CAN YOU BREAK INTO THE THIRD WAVE?

We can lift ourselves out of ignorance, we can find ourselves as creatures of excellence and intelligence and skill. We can be free! We can learn to fly!

Richard Bach
Jonathan Livingston Seagull

DEVELOPING A PERSONAL STRATEGY

By now you have read most of the words in this book, and perhaps you have had some insights. What will you do about them? What will you do with them?

Perhaps you may only wish to ponder them on some mystic beach, or you may want to put them to use.

The most important insights a corporation or an individual may learn from this dialogue are: Know where the environment is going and where you are going in relation. Do you really want to go there? If not, where do you want to go and how do you want to get there? Are you prepared in body, resources, mind, and spirit? If not, how must you adapt given the environmental parameters of the third wave? The needed insights are not too different from the advice I received from a former coach of mine.

> Those who are merely content to drift with the tide [with circumstance], those who do not have a spirited conception of themselves and where they want to be, are doomed to failure and eventual extinction. When you are in a contest, you must want more than any other contestant to win. You must know the competition. You must know the race and what the race is about. You must know why you need to win. You must have a plan, and you must constantly be thinking.[1]

ASSESSING YOUR OWN HUMAN CAPITAL

In developing a personal strategy once you have developed the right mental attitude, you must first assess where you are in relation to where you want to be. What are your assets and weak points? You must be on the offensive and work hard with your assets. You must strengthen your weak points without excessive effort. Your assets must be flexible and liquid and have a maximum personal utility. It is a good rule to (1) never buy when you can rent [this rule also helps personal mobility and flexibility]; (2) never have things that you cannot use often; (3) maximize your access to useful information through magazines, newspapers, books, and databases; (4) maximize your ability to work—use information through software, personal alliances, and continuous education; and (5) know how hard your assets are working and shift them quickly if a more profitable use can be found.

In the third wave, the creation and use of artificial intelligence or software in a publishable form can work the hardest for you because it can be multiplied easily and applied in so many places without its originator ever coming near the site of application. It is your thoughts that work hardest and are potentially worth most. Books, computer programs, patents, designs, art, entertainment, and articles are good examples of thought applied to creation.

As a first priority, you must assess your own human capital. Does it have the appropriate channels for full realization? With the rapid increase in telecommunications, world population and related markets, and internationalization of the economy, there will be markets for any significant human capital. A recent humorous and telling comment in the entertainment industry has been, "He's not much here but he's very big in Japan!" While I was a graduate student in Europe, I noticed some inventions and country and western singers originally from North America. They were very popular there but virtually unknown back home.

The large sums possible from the world application of human capital are much different from the relatively small returns possible from the restrictive application of human capital within a second wave corporate environment. In the second wave corporation, human capital can only be more widely applied and rewarded as an individual advances up the hierarchy. In the third wave organic organization, every bit of relevant human capital has an immediate chance of being applied and rewarded. If an individual cannot become a full-fledged entrepreneur, he or she may find it more profitable to join or to remain in a third wave organic corporation. If a person is at the top or near the top in a second wave hierarchy, he or she may be more inclined to be more concerned with the status quo rather than with progress; but this is delusionary because the forces of change will reach this person also. An individual, like a retiring chairperson of a railroad, may be content as one of the last of a dying breed of dinosaurs, however, if that brings meaning to his or her life.

THE ENTREPRENEURIAL OPPORTUNITY

If you have the talent and wish to become an entrepreneur, you should consider becoming a software entrepreneur because the application of your human capital is restricted and must be relevant to a specific corporation and its warp, even if the corporation is organic. As an entrepreneur, you would be free to seek the application of your human capital on the world market and with any corporations that may desire your services. As a service entrepreneur under contract, you may become a part of multiple corporations or of a series of corporations or alliances in succession.

You should develop your networks, working relations, and interpersonal knowledge conscientiously because it is through such networks that you can act upon ideas and gain profit. Your image also will aid in your development of such networks without your active participation, so you should also continuously assess your image and make any necessary adjustments. Remember President Reagan's advice: "Perception is reality"[2] and reality is action. A decided advantage of any political or businessperson in the media is that he or she has already developed many and various interpersonal networks. People already know them. As the saying goes, "Work hard and advertise."

221

James Treybig, one of the most successful third wave entrepreneurs, said recently that the most vital asset of an entrepreneur is personal fitness, as well as intelligence. Physical fitness will allow you to weather the inevitable stresses of competition and of life in general. Physical fitness allows you to be more efficient and effective, to be more alert and flexible, to be more quickly proactive and reactive, and to think better. Pressures for increasing efficiency, effectiveness, and quality will continually mount, so you should demand such increases from yourself—your body, your mind, and your spirit. You will not only remain competitive but will participate as part of the corporate whole if you keep yourself personally fit.

Purpose and Competition

When I run, I can feel His [God's] pleasure.

Chariots of Fire

One of the main postulations made by many psychologists and the ancient Greeks is that each individual has a need to be all that he or she can be to satisfy a primary need for personal happiness. The need to achieve is referred to as self-actualization. In the movie *Chariots of Fire*, the protagonist needed to run faster than anyone else. What do you need to achieve? Whatever it may be, it requires some entrepreneurial action on your part.

It is will and determination that make anything happen whether it's on the part of a corporation, an individual, or a country.

If you want to be as good or better than anyone else, you better be as fit as them. And when you're fit and talented, [it is] determination that differentiates the good player from the great player.

Tony O'Reilly, CEO
Heinz
Business Week, December 17, 1984

While there has been a lot of justified derision of financial results as indicators of corporate health, financial controls and results properly understood remain the primary indicators of a corporation's determination, drive, and discipline. George Lucas, properly referred to as a creative genius for his films which include *Star Wars*, was said to have been made happiest when he discovered that in all his films less than $100 had slipped between the cracks.

222

A CHIEF EXECUTIVE

If you are a chief executive, you should first examine the messages you have been generating and their actual effects. Are they what you intended to relate? What is your image and what should it be? How does it effect the corporate warp and objectives? How does it effect strategy?

As a chief executive, you should carefully assess the company's strategy in relation to the environment. Know the history and philosophy of the environment and society as it originated from the founding fathers. Know how the environment is evolving. How can principle and history be applied to generate motivating energy? Know that money as a motivating force has gone from subsistence in the first wave, to salaries in the second, and to profit sharing in the third.

Those who will prosper in the third wave are those who are not only increasing their own efficiency and effectiveness at a maximum rate but those who are *delivering* quality, efficiency, and effectiveness to the customer in a durable and reliable product. Those industries in the electronic information markets will be on the fastest track because increased efficiency and effectiveness are a function of the amount of information and human capital infused into a product or applied to a service. Where is your company in relation to this capability? If it is far out in left field, you had better think quickly about a strategy for transition and transformation in order for the company to be competitive.

In considering transition and transformation, however small, you should look carefully at the market and its future. The future of the market may be generated by cross-referencing the present ones with the past ones. Where are the segments or niches that you could fill in order for your company to have a comparative advantage? What is your transitional capability? Are your plant and equipment obsolete and heavily financed? Are participants capable of making the transition? What is their flexibility? Do you have members with a wide range of skills at your disposal? How are your finances? Can your corporate culture be changed quickly? Can you design a new corporate warp, or do you need help with a new strategy and warp design? Can you hire a consultant to help? Machiavelli once suggested to a prince in a position similar to a chief executive's that he go for outside help. If the strategy did not work, the prince could hold the consultant responsible.

You should carefully plan for a transition and transformation because they go hand in hand. Do you know the company's culture and business well enough? Study them over and over again. What is your company's image? How is it evolving? What social role are you and your corporation playing in reality? What is your longer term legacy? What is your leadership? What meaning are

223

you engendering for yourself, the corporation, and society? What are the clearest, simplest questions you can ask? What are their answers? Are you up to the task you have outlined, in body, mind, and spirit?

AN EXECUTIVE

An executive has a crucial role in developing and implementing strategy according to the corporate warp and the environment. Do you, the executive, understand and know all you need to know about the warp and the environment? Study and think about it consistently and constantly. The environment and the corporate culture are both dynamic and evolutionary, and you have a part to play in their evolution. Do questions about the corporate warp need to be raised? How can strategies be improved, developed, and assessed? How can internal efficiency and effectiveness be improved? How can delivered efficiency and effectiveness be improved? How is your corporate interpersonal net growing? With whom do you need to develop a working relationship and how can you do this? What is the capability of your net? What should it be? Keep questioning yourself and your perceptions. One moment's correct assessment in a rapidly changing environment may be a "landmine" in the next.

A MIDDLE MANAGER

If you are a middle manager, you are the spark that keeps the organism running and charged; therefore, you must know the corporation. You must know the warp, which includes culture and objectives, and you must know the general strategy. This is the "energy" with which you charge corporation members. Within this framework, what are the projects you have been pursuing? Do they make sense in relation to the warp and strategy of the corporation? What new projects are on *your* drawing boards?

Do you keep a detailed note pad and write up a description of your function and the functions of your projects from these notes on a regular basis? Where can improvements be made? How are you and your projects contributing to increased efficiency and effectiveness for the company and the customer? Do you have a plan? Is the plan evolutionary and dynamic? You *are* a corporate politician. You must develop, mobilize, and stimulate people and resources, using a positive political style.

ONE OF THE TROOPS

If you are one of the troops, you should realize that the corporate warp is generated from you. The corporate values are an aggregation of your values, and the corporate objectives are a function of your capabilities. Your self-

224

actualization is in achieving the values and objectives of the corporation because they are also yours. Do you know the corporate warp or culture and objectives well enough? Are they in line with your beliefs? Do you study them and keep notes on a constant and consistent basis.

How can you improve yourself and, therefore, the corporation? Keep notes on all your tasks; you may be able to generate and transfer new productive ideas. Think about how new improvements can contribute to the efficiency and effectiveness of the company and the customer. Push to your maximum capability. Execute with style and quality. Advertise subtly. Consistently work on your education and your human capital. Realize that a fit body and mind are indicators of creativity, flexibility, and adaptability. Growth, new ideas, and new profits come from your fitness rather than from the traditional dark suit and white shirt, which indicate loyalty to form and formula.

Develop your own corporate net of working relationships. What is it now capable of and where do you want these relationships to lead you in the future? Who are you? Who do you want to be?

A GOVERNMENT PARTICIPANT

If you work in government, your mandate and role evolve from the first act of American independence. Know your history and the principles that it is based upon thoroughly. The ideology and principles of the founders are still the corporate warp of government and the nation. If you are not willing to support and extend this "warp," you're in the wrong line of work.

The objectives are still access to life, liberty, and the pursuit of happiness. The key word is *access*. How can you increase the access of as many citizens as possible? How can you increase your access to the channels and networks that give your role meaning? What is your official and unofficial role? How does your role relate to the current administration's interpretation of the corporate warp? How does your role relate to the strategy through which this interpretation is pursued? You should not maintain your position if you do not agree with either the strategy, the interpretation, or both, as no one should in a private corporation.

Can you define a niche or area in which you can play a useful role within a general strategy or policy? Can you improve a program or refine a policy? Can you help a specified constituency? In almost any position of significance in government, you are a politician. To do your job, you must build a following or constituency, so you can mobilize the necessary resources, people, energy, and credibility. Develop a growing network and constantly assess it. Know that the principles of the nation and the administration's interpretation and strategy are

225

the waves upon which you ride. Keep a journal and also make it a philosophical extension of yourself and everyone with whom you interact, so you can have an idea of where you are headed. Know why you are working in government. Benefits and a pension are not enough. What do you want to achieve? The basic ethic of your work should always be service to the people.

Wherever you may be on the ideological spectrum, you need to develop a full and continuing understanding of the third wave, organic interaction, and organic management. The third wave is moving much faster than its predecessor and is accelerating all the time. It is a new dimension in which opportunities appear and disappear and do not wait to be accessed. Problems appear and compound rapidly, requiring immediate and appropriate attention and feedback before they get out of hand. Many utility companies are finding this to be true as they make the transition to nuclear technology. The third wave is one of intensifying and complex information that surrounds and seeps through every pore in our environment. Such information needs to be sorted and usefully applied before it turns into noise and pollutes and jams our surroundings.

Responsibility and a sense of responsibility are increased on the part of institutions, politicians, corporations, individuals, and families. "Computer literacy" and access to computers are a requirement for almost everyone in order for society to cope adequately with this fast-paced, information-rich environment. New technology constantly breaks the surface. No sooner is a new computer technology introduced when a new one supersedes it. Costs of physical materials will continually escalate; but with an individual's increasing store of human capital, he or she may be able to access information stored in products so that the actual cost of delivered utility will continue to decline.

In the third wave, networks will grow in importance, and power will become increasingly transitory and related to a particular network configuration at a particular time. Official or formal position will no longer indicate people's actual power and status in corporations, institutions, or governments. Organic interaction is the genesis of networks and the activation of people, energy, and resources.

Organic management is a natural outgrowth of organic law and interaction, a prerequisite of management in the third wave. It is a form of management that seeks to guide the natural evolution of networks forming a corporation, institution, or government. Management senses and monitors the natural rhythm of participants in the organism and their network interactions. It seeks to guide participants in directions that are increasingly viable both for the organism and for the society, and treats all organizations as living, interacting systems that seek mutual viability.

MANAGEMENT EDUCATION AND RESEARCH

Peter Drucker wrote recently, in *New Management*, that business schools have become irrelevant to the profession because they have become popular places to learn the latest popular techniques, and not to learn the art of management. They are like the popular musical academies of the eighteenth century which could train students to produce effective minuets, but could not create students who could produce a beautiful sonata, he went on to write.[3] They, like current business students, knew technique very well but knew very little about the nature of music.

Management education must shift from training to emphasizing the self and continuous education. During the second wave, managers administered for the most part. They administered relatively static, mechanical organizations according to the formulas in which they had been trained. Second wave managers were good corporate and government bureaucrats. In most instances, it did not matter who was in a management position as long as that individual knew the rules and the formulas. Administration is no longer possible because administrated prices are no longer possible. The second wave has been referred to as the age of administration, but the third wave is the age of management because people have to be considered as interacting human organisms and not as parts in a machine.

Business schools traditionally have trained graduates to be administrators, not managers. The degrees given are masters in business administration or doctorates in business administration, not management, which is not surprising because most business schools had their genesis during the second wave. A new personal and institutional approach is needed now. A new accelerated, intensive stream of education that could be referred to as the management stream rather than the administrative stream should be developed. The degrees conferred on management majors should be masters in business management or doctorates in business management.

Education must consist of experience with interactive networks that react on an organic and dynamic basis. The candidates selected should be those who are natural leaders and innovators in tune with change. The time actually spent on campus initially should be short, say nine months. All the candidates should be incorporated within interactive networks in order for the self and the organic system of education to be maximized. Individuals should return to the campus for an intensive update every year for a week. Each candidate should be supplied with a personal computer, a printer, a modem, and software upon entering. The personal computer would be used to develop interactive networks.

227

After leaving the campus, students could access courses and data from the university using the computer and telecommunications lines. This would necessitate that the university put most of its library and courses on accessible electronic databases. With telecommunication networks, continuing students could have access to each other and to willing professors for data and advice on any real-world problems they might encounter. In this way, an interactive, evolving core of applicable knowledge might be developed, while generating a continuing "real time" education for participants.

Most of the research conducted by doctoral students has also been part of the administrative stream. Increasing research must be devoted to the dynamic, organic, and management aspects of business. Candidates devoted to the doctorate in business management would do so, bringing in more aspects of theology, psychology, anthropology, cybernetics, and biology. Such research would shed light on the organization as a dynamic, organic whole. Doctors of business administration should serve more precisely as "organizational doctors." Each candidate should also be supplied with a personal computer with which he or she could develop interactive research on a national basis by having access to as many databases as possible. The first electronic business journal, which will serve many diverse markets and interests, should not be too far off. Applicable business research and education then will have proceeded into the third wave, making it easier for us all to adapt.

CORPORATE VIABILITY

Corporations need to assess themselves on a continuous basis and seek their comparative long-term advantage accordingly. For most corporations, a long-term comparative advantage and strategy will involve some facet of electronic information technology as well as technological transition. Such a transformation requires that the corporation change its mind set and strategic framework.

A strategic, evolutionary plan composed of people is needed to genetically splice or rewire the corporation on a continuous organic basis. A first step in any such plan should be to cut the number of middle managers and levels and to give those that remain more autonomy, trust, and creative freedom. Middle managers also must make the transition from rule enforcers and information gatherers to entrepreneurs and motivators. With electronic information technology, managers can assess and model options and progress. The fewer management levels and the better information/computer systems, the faster and better information will flow, allowing more precise and rapid decision making.

As we have seen in the Atari example, profit is no longer a useful indicator of corporate health. Profits can always be greater if a company is well managed. Losses, as seen from our review of Delta Airlines, are no longer good indicators of poor management or corporate viability either. In Delta's case, the length employees are willing to give, sacrifice, and help the company through its troubles may be a better indicator of corporate viability. Management and strategy must undergo thorough and constant assessment. Is the corporation getting the best out of all its people and assets? Is everyone doing and being all that he or she can?

The Buddha, the Godhead, resides quite as comfortably in the circuits of a digital computer or the gears of a motorcycle as he does at the top of a mountain or in the petals of a flower. To think otherwise is to demean the Buddha—which is to demean oneself.

> Robert M. Pirsig
> *Zen and the Art of Motorcycle Maintenance,* 1984

16

FAITH AND BUSINESS IN THE THIRD WAVE

Beware the yeast of the Pharisees.

Jesus Christ
Matthew 16:6

THE STRUCTURE OF THIRD WAVE SOCIETY

The essential framework of effective corporate philosophies is based upon universal truths tested through time and pronounced most effectively by Jesus Christ and others thousands of years ago. Hal Levitt of Stanford University's Business School has said that Christ was "the greatest teacher ever—a teacher with a capital T." Such natural truths are the corporate warp of world civilization. The Declaration of Independence begins with the words, "We hold these truths to be self-evident. . . ." By acting in concert with the truth, with nature, with natural law, and with reality a corporation or an individual will succeed. As Shakespeare echoed Christ in *Hamlet*, "This above all: to thine ownself be true."

John Opel, CEO of IBM, speaking at Stanford, replied to a question as to the primary rules for success: "Be honest. Be honest with yourself, with others and society. Create something of true utility [value] that serves, and associate with quality people." These tenets are reflected in the corporate warp of IBM. The corporate warps of successful corporations, like ROLM, Honda, Tandem, and Hewlett-Packard, succeed because, like the Declaration of Independence and the Constitution, they deal with clear, natural and self-evident truths that evolve with nature and reality. It is plausible to relate American ideology that is implicit in corporate ideology to the ideology made clear by Jefferson and his colleagues in the Declaration of Independence and in the Constitution. These two documents set out to establish the framework of organic law, under which the new organism, the nation, would operate and be managed. Efforts by the Congress to translate the principles of the Declaration into constitutional law were described by its members as efforts to develop organic law, to develop the natural law of reason and truth.

THEOLOGY AND THE NATION

Jefferson and his colleagues set out in this virginal land to develop the natural conditions under which "God's plan" for mankind could unfold. This is the original and true "manifest destiny" theme of America described by the founding fathers, which was somehow confused with conquest and industrial business during the second wave. Jefferson and his colleagues based much of their ideology upon intensive research into the theology and religion of Jesus Christ. Jefferson undertook this research into what Christ was trying to say after failing to get Joseph Priestly, whom he thought was better qualified, to do so.

The newly revealed evolutionary values and knowledge Christ developed eventually took the place of the old static structures of Roman society and contributed to the fall of Rome. The old social hierarchy, sensing a threat from Christ, sought to break his will and beliefs, but only succeeded in breaking him physically and destroying itself in the process. A new organic evolutionary force then replaced the old formularized structures. As has often been said, and with reason, Christ was and is the most effective natural, evolutionary revolutionary. Once it thought it had control over the immediate environment, the Roman Empire became a bureaucracy forsaking creation, expansion, innovation, and idealism. The Empire turned to bureaucratic politics, clique loyalty, and moral,

231

political, and intellectual dissipation, and the ideas of the Christians gradually rose and built upon the ruins of Roman civilization. More recent examples of such a "renaissance" of values have occurred in Japan, where a new society has been built upon the ruins of militarism, and in China, where a new society has been built upon the ruins of feudalism.

Many organizations have developed into bureaucracies, much as the Roman and later the British Empires and their societies did. Such territories are fertile grounds for a Messiah, a Gandalf, a Thatcher, a Jefferson, or an Iacocca. The important thing is that these "revolutionaries" realize what state they are in and seek what they need. They must do so relatively quickly because the determinants of third wave changing technology, increasing competition, and rising costs occur rapidly. The leeway to create change is less and thus change is more difficult. The "window" you may be able to jump through today may not and probably will not be there tomorrow.

To a large extent, religion has been the keeper of the essential flame of the organic warp, even through the darkness of the first wave's medievalism and the second wave's industrialism. Religion guides the growth of a world civilization that has little conception of its ultimate power or purpose.

INTEGRITY

Humans are not meant to be automatons, machines, or industrial serfs. They can think, perform, and initiate the best for themselves, the corporation, and society. Thomas Murphy, the retired chairman of General Motors, said recently that it is possible to be a good businessperson and a good Christian. He might have added it is a most viable and profitable approach, something that John D. Rockefeller would have agreed with. Rockefeller claimed that his success was "God's will" (although, he might not have consistently participated in the ritual).

One of religion's most relevant teachings is that the honest and caring person in business is one who gains the customer's trust, and consequently is one who generates the most business. In order to be honest and caring, the business-person must understand the reality of his or her environment. One of the richest Japanese businessmen today started out by selling used clothes to an impoverished population with the promise that he would never sell a used item for 10% more than he paid for it. He was deluged with business.

Jean Riboud, the CEO of Schlumberger, recently observed that businesses are once again becoming institutions of meaning and religion. A Berkeley business professor claims that his research has shown that entering some of the more progressive firms is equivalent to entering a religion.

FACING REALITY

> The difference between a good and a bad manager is his willingness and ability to face and deal with reality.
>
> Syd Glucksman, CEO
> Lehman Brothers KL, 1984

Bill Coors, CEO of Coors Brewing, categorically states that his main job is to sense the reality of the environment and to help the company deal with it. In relationship to this, he is fond of telling the following story: "They found in a laboratory experiment that if you take a frog and put him in a pot of hot water he will jump out, but if you put him in a pot of cold water and gradually warm it up, what you will get is—boiled frog. My job is to sense these subtle changes and see that the corporation doesn't end up as a 'boiled frog.'"

To face and deal with reality and to avoid the consequences of becoming a "boiled frog," a manager first might have to understand that he or she is not managing well. Either the manager is not facing reality or perceptions are clouded for one reason or another. To become a good manager, a person must face his or her perceptions. A blind person must first recognize that he or she is blind. A "good" consultant or a new member of the team might help the manager to realize blind spots. A good consultant is one who helps the manager understand his or her environment, reality, and how to deal with it.

In the general transitional period we are all now experiencing, it is important first that the transition not be delayed (international competition will make us sorry if it is); and second that displaced people and plants be found new and productive places within the new economy. While the third wave sectors—electronics/information and service—of the economy are "booming," the first wave sector—mining and agriculture—and the second wave sector—basic manufacturing—are suffering all the signs of depression. These two sectors are suffering from the increased efficiency of the third wave, which requires less in basic inputs because increased precision causes less waste and therefore less demand. Efforts should not be made to delay the transition in the first two sectors but to assist those displaced to find new productive careers. Reality should not and cannot be hidden.

Hewlett-Packard generally has been acknowledged as the premiere organic corporation with a human approach. The company's approach has been to find challenges for each individual consistent with his or her evolving capabilities and ambitions. This is one of management's primary tasks. In order to accomplish this task, management must listen and observe extremely well.

233

Managers are responsible for the personal well-being of each employee, to see that each is appropriately rewarded and cared for through benefits, activities, and health protection and insurance. David Packard recently recounted an early episode in the company's history when a good employee and his family were financially devastated by tuberculosis, an event Mr. Packard did not want repeated. A company health plan was therefore introduced. A progressive salary and profit sharing plan has also been initiated.

THE FREEDOM TO FAIL

Thomas Watson of IBM told a similar story about a murder-suicide incident that occurred after an employee was fired. This convinced Watson that an appropriate place must always be found for a no longer needed employee willing to work. There is a substantial amount of corporate human capital invested in each employee. If a member is no longer suitable for one position and is willing to work, he or she should be placed more appropriately. To dispense with a member altogether wastes a substantial amount of human capital. The corporation should try to give the employee a useful position within the warp.

People must have the freedom to fail and learn from their mistakes if they and the corporation are going to succeed. Failing, in many instances, is a learning process on the road to success. Alf Powis, CEO of NORANDA, was once asked how many mistakes he allowed his executives. He replied, "Oh, quite a few, as long as they don't make the same ones twice."

Peter Drucker recently wrote, in *New Management,* that one of the most important tasks of management was the management of potential evil, that is, the tendency of most of us when imbued with power to use it to excess. Drucker believes that the role of management is not to create employees in its own image but to bring out the best in fellow participants—not to get them to do a certain task but to get them to do what they can.

It is said that we have been at war too long, and we have. The war is over. No longer do we need to work to survive and to be accepted socially. We work now because we search for meaning, for some way to fulfill our sense of social obligation, for a mission, and for self-actualization. To be fired or to quit merely indicates that a person and the inherent ethic of the organization in which he or she works are not synchronized. The individual needs to search for meaning and self-actualization elsewhere. Most progressive organizations understand this and search consistently to give their people expanded opportunities for self-actualization and increased meaning. They know that poor performance, theft, and sabotage can be traced to an individual's lack of self-actualization in the work environment.

If a member cannot find meaning in one place in a large organization, he or she can find it in another. The company thereby conserves and enhances valuable human capital, as well as developing cross-fertilization. The psychological care and feeding of organization people is gaining importance and relevance because psychological support helps members to achieve corporate objectives. Corporations are realizing the necessity and meaning of recognizing that everyone in the organization counts.

THE INTEGRATED ORGANIZATION

As time progresses, most organizations are becoming increasingly integrated organisms. Interpersonal networks are becoming larger and more interconnected, and electronic nervous systems are growing and spreading. Atlantic Richfield spent over $17 million on a video conferencing system that it maintains, without considering any gains in efficiency or effectiveness, will pay for itself within a year just from savings in travel costs. The size and number of electronic databases (corporate memories) are growing. Such integration allows the organization to act faster, more efficiently, and more effectively; to apply more information; to develop more feedback; and to sense its environment better than ever before. Such integration also increases the psychological and human aspects of the organization, requiring new and more precise skills from management.

The new organic corporation is now considered a living being whose responsibilities are no longer solely to provide profits for the shareholders or bonuses to management but also to answer to its constituents and to society at large. The third wave corporation no longer lives by "bread alone" but also creates and defines meaning and social purpose. The organic "lean and mean" organization has some similarities to the JIT production system that is incorporated into many of their manufacturing operations. Projects and ideas move through the system quickly. All characteristics of a project are constantly monitored much as products are in the JIT system.

The active thoughts and emotions of all participants is integral to the process, as well as whatever muscle and rote training is necessary. The corporation cannot exist without the hearts, minds, and energy of its people. Within the "quality circle," which could be called the "strategy circle," participants involve their minds and hearts in the quest of increased flexibility, fulfillment, effectiveness, and efficiency, and a sharpened competitive edge. Andy Grove of Intel says that the organization must become a precisely targeted organic flow, a flexible process rather than a rigid machine. Once that process is developed, bureaucracy can be seriously cut, and costly slack will not impede corporate operation. Dana Corporation cut bureaucracy by more than half

235

while increasing productivity, revenues, and output by more than a factor of three.

There is little or no slack in the new organic corporation. Every participant is a store of precise and applicable human capital, while retaining maximum flexibility to quickly swing in any direction. Participants are humans, not dinosaurs lumbered with excess weight and size who were, therefore, inefficient in many circumstances.

Governments and the educational system must assist corporate transformation in the third wave. A tax credit or accelerated write-off should be allowed to companies incurring the additional costs from an honest attempt to make the transformation. Progressive executives who give of their time to lecture about their successes and failures, especially about entrepreneurship, should be able to write off this time as a charitable contribution at the appropriate dollar value.

THE EDGE OF THE PRECIPICE

Many organizations stand at the edge of the precipice in terms of adapting to the new wave, the new technology, the new markets, and the new values.

They will not find the answers in formulas (as *Business Week* described some *In Search of Excellence* devotees who put principles on flash cards, or in lengthy computer printouts or even in books such as this). They will only find their answers by thinking long and hard.

While there has been a needed derision of numbers and overreliance on them, proper (MIS systems) financial controls, properly understood, are more important than ever in a period of transition and fast change where the corporation might easily "fall off the track." When Lee Iacocca took over Chrysler, he found an archaic, chaotic, almost feudal bureaucracy with various "war lords" and their own fiefdoms, with no financial controls and no ideas as to where the company was headed. The company morale and discipline had, apparently, almost completely broken down. The first thing he did was to bring in a required financial system and first-rate financial people.

Financial systems provide the hard skeleton upon which the living body of the corporation operates. In a time of flux and change, it is of primary importance to know the current state of the corporation and where it is going.

Will corporations meet the challenge with courage, determination, and intelligence, strapping on the new technology and new values of the third wave? Will they soar like a glider riding a powerful updraft or fall to the valley floor like an autumn leaf? To know the truth is to face reality, and to face reality is the first required step toward survival and success. In the final analysis, there is no clear choice among doing things the Japanese way, the American way, or some other way. The only requirement is to do what is necessary.

God sleeps in rocks
God awakens in plants
God walks in animals
God thinks in man

Ancient Sanskrit writing

Notes

Chapter 1

1. Alexis de Tocqueville, *Democracy in America*, vol. 1. Garden City, N.Y.: Doubleday, 1969.
2. Gardner Means, "The Administered Price Thesis Reconfirmed," *American Economic Review*, June 1972.
3. de Tocqueville, *Democracy in America*.
4. Inquiry into the events at Three Mile Island, Nuclear Regulatory Commission hearings, 1983.

Chapter 2

1. "Meet the Lean Mean New IBM," *Fortune*, June 13, 1983, p. 68.
2. Tetsou Sakiya, *Honda: The Men, the Management, the Machines*, Tokoyo: Kodanska International, Ltd., pp. 118, 119, 123, 125.
3. See Chrysler Corporation public relations.
4. "Timex Quits the Computer Race," *Business Week*, March 1984, p. 46.
5. "GM's Unlikely Revolutionist," *Fortune*, March 19, 1984, p. 106.
6. "ATT," *Time*, January 16, 1984, p. 52.
7. "Embattled Kodak Enters the Electronic Age," *Fortune*, August 1983, p. 120.
8. "Playing the Last Card: International Harvester," *Forbes*, January 28, 1985, p. 135.
9. "Profile: Jean Riboud (Schlumberger)," *The New Yorker*, June 13, 1983, p. 135.
10. *Ibid.*
11. "View from the Top," Stanford University lecture, 1983.
12. "TI: Shot Full of Holes and Trying to Recover," *Business Week*, November 5, 1984.
13. "View from the Top," Stanford University lectures, 1984, 1985.
14. "MCI versus Bell," *Fortune*, January 24, 1983, p. 31.
15. "Management by Bankruptcy, Continental Airlines," *Fortune*, October 1983, p. 69.
16. See SP-SF public relations.
17. See Jaguar public relations.

Chapter 3

1. "U.C. Re-Tooling MBA Program," *San Francisco Chronicle*, September 22, 1983.
2. "View from the Top," Stanford University lecture, 1983.
3. See Ferranti Electronics, United Kingdom, public relations.
4. Conversation with Nolan Bushnell, outside Brooks Hall, San Francisco, Spring 1985.
5. "View from the Top," Stanford University lecture, 1983.
6. Tetsou Sakiya, *Honda: The Men, the Management, the Machines*, Tokyo: Kodanska International, Ltd., p. 147.
7. *Ibid.*, p. 210.
8. ROLM philosophy; see ROLM public relations.
9. *Ibid.*
10. *Ibid.*
11. Hewlett-Packard philosophy; see Hewlett-Packard public relations.
12. *Ibid.*

Chapter 4

1. "Ford," *San Francisco Chronicle,* July 13, 1983, p. 24.
2. See Tandem Corporation public relations.
3. See *The Writings of Plutarch.*
4. See U.S. Supreme Court Archives.
5. Robert Sobel, *IBM: Colossus in Transition,* New York: Times Books, 1981, pp. 58–63.
6. *Ibid.*
7. See IBM advertising department; IBM public relations.

Chapter 5

1. "Profile: Jean Riboud (Schlumberger)," *The New Yorker,* June 13, 1983, p. 135.
2. Letter from the White House to the Governor of New Hampshire, 1984.
3. See APPLE advertising department; APPLE public relations.

Chapter 6

1. Japanese embassy report, 1948.
2. United States Declaration of Independence.
3. W. MacNeal Dixon, Gifford Lectures, St. Andrews University, 1957.
4. Tom Peters and Robert Waterman, *In Search of Excellence,* New York: Harper & Row, 1982, p. 289.
5. Conversation with visiting Japanese delegation, Spring 1985.

Chapter 7

1. Steve Brandt, *Entrepreneuring,* Reading, Mass.: Addison-Wesley, 1982, p. 98.
2. "Thomas Jefferson," *Presidents,* Washington, D.C.: American Heritage, 1968, p. 110.

Chapter 8

1. Gerald Barney, *The Global 2000 Report,* Harmondsworth, UK: Penguin, 1982, pp. 6–42.
2. *Ibid.*

Chapter 9

1. Michael Maccoby, *The Leader,* New York: Ballantine Books, 1981, pp. 188–191.
2. United Technologies public relations department.
3. Lord Elgin, Elgin Archives, Ottawa, Canada.
4. Maccoby, p. 96.
5. Personal conversation.

Chapter 11

1. Robert Serling, *From the Captain to the Colonel,* New York: Dial Press, 1980, pp. 117–143, 173–204, 416–417.

2. *Ibid.*, pp. 373, 443–447.
3. *Ibid.*, pp. 454, 468–523.
4. "What Went Wrong at Atari, West," *San Jose Mercury News*, November 6, 1983, p. 14.
5. Personal conversation.
6. "View from the Top," Stanford University lecture, 1983.
7. Michael Maccoby, *The Leader*, New York: Ballantine Books, 1981, pp. 146–147.

Chapter 12

1. Steve Wozniak, "Learning," *California Living*, November 6, 1983, p. 9.

Chapter 13

1. Robert Riddell, "Director USO," *The New Yorker*, 1983.
2. Alvin Toffler, *The Third Wave*, New York: William Morrow, 1980, pp. 427–431.
3. Charles A. Reich, *The Greening of America*, New York: Random House, 1971, pp. 233–235.
4. See Control Data Corporation public relations.

Chapter 14

1. Norbert Weiner, *The Human Use of Human Beings*, Garden City, N.Y.: Anchor Books, 1954, p. 8.

Chapter 15

1. Personal conversation.
2. Letter from the White House to the Governor of New Hampshire, 1984.
3. Peter Drucker, *New Management*, Graduate School of Management, University of Southern California, second quarter, 1985.

BIBLIOGRAPHY

Ashby, W. Ross. *An Introduction to Cybernetics.* London: Chapman and Hall, 1956.
———. *Design for a Brain.* London: Chapman and Hall, 1960.
Bain, J. S. *Barriers to New Competition.* Cambridge: Harvard University Press, 1955.
———. *Industrial Organization.* New York: John Wiley & Sons, 1968.
———. *Essays on Price Theory and Industrial Organization.* Boston: Little, Brown, 1972.
Barney, Gerald. *The Global 2000 Report / Entering the 21st Century.* New York: Penguin Books, 1982.
Beer, Stafford. *Cybernetics and Management.* London: English University Press, 1959.
———. *Brain of the Firm.* New York: John Wiley & Sons, 1972.
Bell, Daniel. *The Coming of Post-Industrial Society.* New York: Basic Books, 1976.
———. *The Cultural Contradictions of Capitalism.* New York: Basic Books, 1976.
Berelson, Bernard, and Gary A. Steiner. New York: Harcourt Brace & World, 1964.
Boskin, Michael, ed. *The Economy in the 1980s.* New Brunswick, Canada: Transaction, 1980.
Boulding, Kenneth E. *The Organizational Revolution.* Chicago: Quadrangle, 1953.
Bourne, Russell, ed. "200 years." *U.S. News & World Report,* 1975.
Brandt, Ronald S., ed. *Staff Development / Organization Development.* Alexandria, Va.: ASCD, 1981.
Brandt, Steven. *Entrepreneuring.* Reading, Mass.: Addison-Wesley, 1982.
Brunner, John. *The Shockwave Rider.* New York: Ballantine Books, 1975.
Buckley, Walter. *Sociology and Modern Systems Theory.* Englewood Cliffs, N.J.: Prentice-Hall, 1967.
Burns, Arthur. *The Decline of Competition.* New York: McGraw-Hill, 1936.
Buskirk, Richard H. *Modern Management and Machiavelli.* New York: Mentor, 1974.
California Commission on Industrial Innovation / Winning Technologies. *A New Industrial Strategy for California and the Nation.* Report to the governor, Sacramento.
Chamberlain, Edward. *The Theory of Monopolistic Competition: A Re-Orientation of The Theory Of Value.* Englewood Cliffs, N.J.: Prentice-Hall, 1964.
Churchman, C. West. *The Systems Approach.* New York: Laurel, 1968.
Clair, Wilcox. *Public Policies Toward Business.* Homewood, Ill.: Richard D. Irwin, 1971.
Cole, Robert C. *Work, Mobility and Participation.* Berkeley: University of California Press, 1980.
Cousins, Norman. *In God We Trust.* New York: Harper, 1958.
Cunliffe, Marcus. *The American Heritage History of The Presidency.* New York: American Heritage, 1968.
Cyert, Richard, and Kalman Cohen. *Theory of the Firm.* Englewood Cliffs, N.J.: Prentice Hall, 1965.
Dannefield, Karl H. *The Renaissance.* Boston: D. C. Heath, 1959.
Darendorf, Ralf. *Class and Class Conflict in Industrial Society.* Stanford: Stanford University Press, 1959.
Darwin, Charles. *The Origin of the Species.* New York: Avenel, 1979.
Davis, John P. *Corporations.* New York: Capricorn, 1961.
Deal, Terrence E., and Allan A. Kennedy. *Corporate Cultures.* Reading, Mass.: Addison-Wesley, 1982.
De Bono, Edward. *Lateral Thinking.* New York: Harper Colophon, 1973.
Dore, Ronald. *British Factory-Japanese Factory.* (Berkeley: University of California Press, 1973.
Drucker, Peter F. *The Concept of the Corporation.* Boston: Beacon Press, 1960.
———. *The Age of Discontinuity.* New York: Harper & Row, 1968.
Ehrlich, Paul R. *The Population Bomb.* New York: Ballantine Books, 1968.
———. *The End of Affluence.* New York: Ballantine Books, 1974.
Emery, F. E. *Systems Thinking.* New York: Penguin Books, 1976.
Feather, Frank. *Through the 80's.* Washington, D.C.: World Futures Society, 1980.

Feigenbaum, Edward A., and Pamela McCorduck. *The Fifth Generation*. Reading, Mass.: Addison-Wesley, 1983.

Forbes, John, and Douglas Stettinius, Sr. *Portrait of a Morgan Partner*. Charlottesville: University Press of Virginia, 1974.

Fowles, Jib., ed. *Handbook of Futures Research*. Westport, Conn.: Greenwood Press, 1978.

Galbraith, John Kenneth. *The New Industrial State*. New York: Signet, 1967.

———. *Economics and the Public Purpose*. New York: Mentor, 1975.

Gaster, Theodor H. *The Dead Sea Scriptures*. Garden City, N.Y.: Doubleday-Anchor, 1956.

George, F. H. *Cybernetics, Automation and Society*. London: Linden Hill, 1962.

Getty, J. Paul. *How to Be a Successful Executive*. New York: Playboy Press, 1971.

Green, Arnold W. *Sociology/An Analysis of Life in Modern Society*. New York: McGraw-Hill, 1952.

Green, Mark J., James M. Fallows, and David R. Zwick. *Who Runs Congress*. New York: Bantam Books, 1972.

Hacker, Louis M. *The Triumph of American Capitalism*. New York: Columbia University Press, 1947.

Hamilton, Alexander, James Madison, and John Jay. *The Federalist Papers*. New York: Mentor, 1961.

Hanson, Dirk. *The New Alchemists*. Boston: Little, Brown, 1980.

Harman, Willis W. *An Incomplete Guide to the Future*. San Francisco: San Francisco Book Co., 1976.

Heilbroner, Robert L. *The Economic Transformation of America*. New York: Harcourt Brace Jovanovich, 1977.

Helmer, Olaf. *Social Technology*. New York: Basic Books, 1966.

Henderson, Bruce D. *Henderson on Corporate Strategy*. New York: Mentor, 1979.

Hitch, Charles J., and Roland N. McKean. *The Economics of Defense in the Nuclear Age*. New York: Atheneum, 1978.

Hollister, C. Warren. *River through Time/The Course of Western Civilization*. New York: John Wiley & Sons, 1975.

Humble, John W., ed. *Management by Objectives in Action*. New York: McGraw-Hill, 1970.

Hunter, A. *Monopoly and Competition*. New York: Penguin Books, 1968.

Jenkins, Elizabeth. *Elizabeth the Great*. New York: Times Books, 1958.

Johnson, Chalmers, ed. *Change in Communist Systems*. Stanford: Stanford University Press, 1969.

Judson, Horace Freeland. *The Eighth Day of Creation*. New York: Touchstone Press, 1979.

Kahn, Herman, and Anthony J. Wiener. *The Year 2000*. New York: Macmillan, 1967.

Kanter, Rosabeth Moss. *The Change Masters*. New York: Simon & Schuster, 1983.

Keene, Donald. *The Japanese Discovery of Europe, 1720–1830*. Stanford: Stanford University Press, 1969.

Kefauver, E. *In a Few Hands*. New York: Pantheon Books, 1965.

Kidder, Tracy. *The Soul of a New Machine*. New York: Avon Books, 1982.

Korda, Michael. *Power!* New York: Random House, 1975.

Kroeber, A. L. *Anthropology: Culture Patterns and Processes*. New York: Harvest, 1948.

Laski, Harold. *Reflections on the Revolutions of Our Time*. New York: Viking Press, 1943.

Lawrence, Douglas H., and Leon Festinger. *Deterrents and Reinforcement*. Stanford: Stanford University Press, 1962.

Leiderman, P. Herbert, and David Shapiro, eds. *Psychobiological Approaches to Social Behavior*. Stanford: Stanford University Press, 1964.

Li, Dun J. *The Civilization of China*. New York: Charles Scribner's Sons, 1975.

Lindaman, Edward B. *Thinking in the Future Tense*. Nashville, Tenn.: Boardman, 1978.

Lundberg, Ferdinand. *The Rich and the Super-Rich*. New York: Bantam Books, 1968.

Maccoby, Michael. *The Gamesman*. New York: Ballantine Books, 1976.

242

————. *The Leader.* New York: Ballantine Books, 1981.

Maclean, Fitzroy. *Eastern Approaches.* New York: Times Books, 1950.

Malchlup, Fritz. *The Production and Distribution of Knowledge in the United States.* Princeton: Princeton University Press, 1962.

Mansfield, Edwin. *The Economics of Technological Change.* New York: W. W. Norton & Co., 1968.

————. *Microeconomics.* New York: W. W. Norton & Co., 1970.

————. *Monopoly Power and Economic Performance.* New York: W. W. Norton & Co., 1971.

Massie, Robert K. *Peter the Great.* New York: Ballantine Books, 1980.

Maurer, John G. *Open Systems Approaches/Readings in Organization Theory.* New York: Random House, 1971.

Miles, Ian. *The Poverty of Prediction.* Westmead, U.K.: Saxan Books, 1975.

Miller, John C. *Origins of the American Revolution.* Stanford: Stanford University Press, 1943.

Mintzberg, Henry. *Power in and Around Organizations.* Englewood Cliffs, N.J.: Prentice-Hall, 1983.

Moffit, Donald, ed. *The Wall Street Journal Views America Tomorrow.* Princeton, N.J.: Dow Jones Books, 1977.

Moynihan, Daniel P. *Coping/On the Practice of Government.* New York: Random House, 1973.

Musashi, Miyamoto. *A Book of Five Rings.* New York: Overlook Press, 1982.

Naisbitt, John. *Megatrends.* New York: Warner Books, 1982.

Nef, John U. *The Conquest of the Material World.* Chicago: University of Chicago Press, 1964.

Ohmae, K. *The Mind of the Strategist.*

Orwell, George. *Animal Farm.* New York: Signet, 1946.

————. *1984.* New York: New American Library, 1949.

Otten, C. Michael. *Power, Values and Society.* Glenview, Ill.: Scott Foresman, 1981.

Ouchi, William G. *Theory Z.* New York: Avon Books, 1982.

Packard, Vance. *The Status Seekers.* New York: David Mackay, 1959.

————. *The Waste Makers.* New York: Pocket Books, 1964.

Pascale, Richard Tanner, and Anthony G. Athos. *The Art of Japanese Management.* New York: Warner Books, 1981.

Perlo, Victor. *The Unstable Economy.* New York: International, 1973.

Peters, Thomas J., and Robert H. Waterman. *In Search of Excellence.* New York: Harper & Row, 1982.

Pfeffer, Jeffrey. *Organizational Design.* Arlington Heights, Va.: AHM, 1978.

————. *Power in Organizations.* Boston: Pitman, 1981.

————. *Organizations and Organizational Theory.* Boston: Pitman, 1982.

Pirsig, Robert M. *Zen and the Art of Motorcycle Maintenance.* New York: Bantam Books, 1975.

Plato. *The Republic.* Viking Press, 1968.

Reich, Charles A. *The Greening of America.* New York: Random House, 1971.

Reich, Robert B. *The Next American Frontier.* New York: Times Books, 1983.

Reich, Robert B., and Ira Magaziner. *Minding America's Business.* New York: Harcourt Brace Jovanovich, 1982.

Reischauer, Edwin O. *The United States and Japan.* Cambridge: Harvard, University Press, 1965.

Ricardo, David. *The Principles of Political Economy and Taxation.* New York: E. P. Dutton, 1937.

Rifkin, Jeremy, and Randy Barber. *The North Will Rise Again.* Boston: Beacon Press, 1978.

Rothenberg, Albert, and Carl R. Hausman, eds. *The Creativity Question.* Durham, N.C.: Duke University Press, 1976.

Rozak, Theodore. *The Makings of a Counter-Culture.* Garden City, N.Y.: Doubleday, 1969

Sakiya, Tetsuo. *Honda Motor/The Men, The Management, The Machines.* Tokyo: Kodansha International, 1982.

Sale, Kirkpatrick. *Human Scale.* New York: Coward, McCann & Geoghegan, 1980.

Sampson, Anthony. *The Sovereign State of ITT.* New York: Stein Day, 1973.

243

Sansom, G. B. *Japan, A Short Cultural History.* Stanford: Stanford University Press, 1978.

Scherer, F. M. *Industrial Market Structure and Economic Performance.* New York: Rand McNally, 1970.

Schoenberg, Robert J. *The Art of Being a Boss.* New York: Mentor, 1978.

Schurmann, Franz, and Orville Schell. *Communist China.* New York: Vintage, 1967.

Serling, Robert J. *From the Captain to the Colonel.* New York: Dial Press, 1980.

Servan-Schreiber, J. J. *The American Challenge.* New York: Avon Books, 1967.

Sewell, John W. *The United States and World Development.* New York: Praeger, 1980.

Shapiro, David. *Neurotic Styles.* New York: Basic Books, 1965.

Sisk, Henry L. *Management and Organization.* Palo Alto, Calif.: South-West Publishing Co., 1977.

Skinner, B. F. *Walden II.* New York: Macmillan, 1962.

Smith, Adam. *Paper Money.* New York: Dell, 1981.

Steiner, Gary A. *The Creative Organization.* Chicago: University of Chicago Press, 1965.

Stigler, George. *The Theory of Price.* New York: Macmillan, 1966.

Theobald, Robert. *An Alternative Future for America's Third Century.* Chicago: Swallow Press, 1976.

Thomas, Lewis. *The Lives of a Cell.* New York: Bantam Books, 1974.

———. *The Medusa and the Snail.* New York: Bantam Books, 1979.

Tinbergen, Jan. *RIO/A Report to the Club of Rome.* New York: E. P. Dutton, 1976.

Toffler, Alvin. *Future Shock.* New York: Bantam Books, 1971.

———. *The Third Wave.* New York: William Morrow, 1980.

———. *Previews and Premises.* Boston: South End, 1984.

Tolkien, J. R. R. *The Lord of the Rings.* London: Allen and Unwin, 1968.

Townsend, Robert. *Up the Organization.* Greenwich, Conn.: Fawcett, 1970.

Trebling, H. M. *Essays on Public Utility Pricing and Regulation.* Lansing: Michigan State University Press, 1969.

Tzu, Sun. *The Art of War.* Edited by James Clavell. New York: Delacourt, 1983.

United States Senate. *Our Third Century: Directions.* Washington, D.C.: U.S. Government Printing Office, 1976.

Vogel, Ezra F. *Japan as Number One.* New York: Harper Colophon, 1980.

Weber, Max. *Economy and Society.* Berkeley: University of California Press, 1978.

Wells, Alan. *Mass Media and Society.* Palo Alto, Calif.: Mayfield, 1972.

White, Richard M. *The Entrepreneur's Manual.* Radnor, Pa.: Chilton, 1977.

Wiener, Norbert. *Cybernetics.* Cambridge: MIT Press, 1948.

———. *The Human Use of Human Beings.* Garden City, N.Y.: Anchor Press, 1954.

Williamson, Oliver E. *Corporate Control and Business Behavior.* Englewood Cliffs, N.J.: Prentice-Hall, 1970.

———. *The Economics of Discretionary Behavior: Managerial Objectives in a Theory of the Firm.* Englewood Cliffs, N.J.: Prentice-Hall, 1964.

Wright, J. Patrick. *On a Clear Day You Can See General Motors.* New York: Avon Books, 1979.

WAR WITH
RUSSIA?

Other Books by Stephen F. Cohen

WAR WITH RUSSIA?

FROM PUTIN & UKRAINE TO TRUMP & RUSSIAGATE

STEPHEN F. COHEN

HOT BOOKS
an imprint of Skyhorse Publishing, Inc.
New York, NY

Hot Books may be purchased in bulk at special discounts for sales promotion, corporate gifts, fund-raising, or educational purposes. Special editions can also be created to specifications. For details, contact the Special Sales Department, Skyhorse Publishing, 307 West 36th Street, 11th Floor, New York, NY 10018 or info@skyhorsepublishing.com.

Hot Books® and Skyhorse Publishing® are registered trademarks of Skyhorse Publishing, Inc.®, a Delaware corporation.

Visit our website at www.hotbookspress.com.

10 9 8 7 6 5 4

Library of Congress Cataloging-in-Publication Data is available on file.

ISBN: 978-1-5107-4581-0
eBook: 978-1-5107-4582-7

Cover design by Brian Peterson

Printed in the United States of America

With loving gratitude to Katrina, who, while "not fully" agreeing with the contents and enduring some slings and arrows, made this book possible.

Table of Contents

To My Readers

THIS BOOK IS UNLIKE OTHERS I have published. Above all, it evolved during the years since 2014 when US-Russian relations were becoming more dangerous than they had ever been—and then made even worse by the allegations known as Russiagate. How this happened and what these unprecedented realities mean are ongoing themes in the pages that follow.

War With Russia? is also different in another respect. Over the years, I have written several kinds of books for other scholars and general readers— biography, narrative and interpretive political history, collections of essays and columns. The contents of this volume, however, were not originally intended to be a book. Nor were the words initially written. They began as radio broadcasts.

In 2014, the host of *The John Batchelor Show*, a popular nation-wide news program based at WABC AM in New York City, offered me a weekly segment on Tuesdays at 10 pm for one hour—about 40 minutes of discussion apart from commercial breaks. I had previously known John, a novelist and historian, and considered him to be one of the most erudite, intellectual, and, despite his formal role as a "conservative," ecumenical hosts in American talk radio. I accepted.

There was an equally important consideration. I had been arguing for years—very much against the American political-media grain—that a new US-Russian Cold War was unfolding, driven primarily by politics in Washington, not in Moscow. For this perspective, I had been largely excluded from influential print, broadcast, and cable outlets where I had previously been welcomed.

Virtually alone among major US media figures, John Batchelor—whose show has some 2.7 million listeners a week across the United States as well as 5 million downloaded podcasts a month here and abroad—evidently agreed with my general perspective, or at least thought it important enough to follow. "The New US-Russian Cold War" became, and remains, the rubric of our broadcasts, though subjects sometimes range more widely.

Our procedure changed over the years. Initially, John and I broadcast live, but due to our schedules began taping the night's discussion around 7 pm, when we already had the US and Russian "news" of the day. From the beginning, the podcast was posted the next day on the website (TheNation.com) of *The Nation* magazine, where I had been a contributor for many years. In 2014-2015, because I was writing articles for the magazine, the podcast was accompanied by only a brief paragraph listing the topics of the broadcast. Beginning in January 2016, as the new Cold War grew more perilous, I began writing longer commentaries expanding on each of my contributions to the Batchelor program—I did so very quickly overnight, sometimes with little regard for literary polish—and posting them with the podcast.

Inadvertently, I became a weekly web columnist, resuming an experiment in scholarly journalism I had undertaken in the 1980s in a monthly column, "Sovieticus," for *The Nation*. Then and now again, I wanted to provide essential historical context missing in news reports and analysis. Most of the weekly broadcasts and my commentaries—John and I skipped a few weeks due to holidays or scheduling problems on my part—were done in New York City, but some where I occasionally found myself on Tuesdays, from my hometown in Kentucky to Moscow.

Part I of this book is composed of four abridged articles I wrote for *The Nation* in 2014 and 2015. All of the articles in the Prologue and sections II, III, and IV are selected from almost 150 of my web "columns." Except for the Prologue, written in late 2018, they appear in chronological order as an analytical narrative of ongoing events. The date under each title is the day it was posted at TheNation.com. The commentaries appear here largely as posted, though for the book I polished the language somewhat, added some clarifying information, and combined a few related commentaries into one or two.

I also made some deletions in order to avoid unnecessary repetition. But repetition of large themes and ongoing subjects became unavoidable, indeed necessary, for the purpose of my weekly commentaries—and of this book: to make accessible to general readers an alternative, dissenting narrative of what I think are among the most fateful developments of our time. Whether I have succeeded or not is for readers to judge.

Quite a few writers in mainstream publications disliked what I was writing. Their agitated responses were noted in a November 24, 2017 feature article about me in *The Chronicle Review*, the magazine supplement of The Chronicle of Higher Education. It was subtitled "The Most Controversial Russia Expert in America." My scholarly work—my biography of Nikolai Bukharin and essays collected in *Rethinking the Soviet Experience* and *Soviet Fates and Lost Alternatives*, for example—has always been controversial because it has been what scholars term "revisionist"—reconsiderations, based on new research and perspectives, of prevailing interpretations of Soviet and post-Soviet Russian history.

But the "controversy" surrounding me since 2014, mostly in reaction to the contents of this book, has been different—inspired by usually vacuous, defamatory assaults on me as "Putin's No. 1 American Apologist," "Best Friend," and the like. I never respond specifically to these slurs because they offer no truly substantive criticism of my arguments, only ad hominem attacks. Instead, I argue, as readers will see in the first section, that I am a patriot of American national security, that the orthodox policies my assailants promote are gravely endangering our security, and that therefore we—I and others they assail—are patriotic heretics. Here too readers can judge.

I should add that emails and letters I received over the years from listeners and readers lauding my commentaries, for which I remain grateful, far out-numbered the public slurs. But slurring any Americans who think differently about US policy toward Russia has silenced too many skeptics and contributed to another theme of this book—a new and more dangerous Cold War without any real public debate in our mainstream politics or media.

Part of the animus against me seems to be due to my criticism of mainstream media malpractice in covering Russia, yet another recurring subject in the pages that follow. As I explained in a previous book, *Failed Crusade: America and the Tragedy of Post-Communist Russia* (2000), readers should not mistake my media criticism for ivy-tower resentment or contempt.

On the contrary, I have long combined my vocation as a university scholar with my own contributions to mainstream journalism. So much that in the late 1970s, while I was a tenured Princeton professor, the *New York Times* offered me a position as one of its correspondents in Moscow. (I declined for family reasons and because I sensed that big changes in the Soviet Union were still some years away.) Moreover, my subsequent *Nation* "Sovieticus" column was frequently reprinted in influential newspapers. And from the late 1980s, I was for many years a prominent on-air consultant for CBS News.

In short, no professional or personal antipathies underlie my criticism of mainstream media, only my conviction that violations of their own professional standards in reporting and commenting on Russia and relations between Washington and Moscow have contributed to this new and more dangerous Cold War. Hence my weekly efforts, and now in this book, to offer readers an alternative narrative and explanation of how it came about.

***

All writers have help along the way, I perhaps more than many due to the wide range of my weekly subjects. Three people regularly helped me with information and, equally important, critical feedback: James Carden, Lev Golinkin, and Pietro Shakarian. My research assistant, Mariya Salier, provided expertise, both technical and substantive, well beyond that of the usual assistant. David Johnson's daily email digest, *Johnson's Russia List*, which includes non-mainstream articles and other materials, has been invaluable, as it is for anyone occupied with Russia. Also valuable is the website of the American Committee for East-West Accord (eastwestaccord.com), of which I am a board member, edited by James Carden.

Farther away, my longtime friend Dmitri Muratov, chief editor of Russia's most important independent newspaper, *Novaya Gazeta*, made my views accessible to readers in that country by translating and publishing a number of the articles in this book. (Reactions, not surprisingly, were mixed but nonetheless valuable.)

At *The Nation*, Ricky D'Ambrose, an innovative filmmaker in his other life, played an indispensable role every Wednesday by shepherding each weekly commentary from my computer to the website and in the process by making important editorial improvements.

And at the end, despite my missed deadlines, Tony Lyons, Oren Eades, and the team at Skyhorse Publishing turned my manuscript into this book with remarkable speed and skill.

I am very grateful to all of these people. And, of course, to John Batchelor, who gave me a national platform and made my evidently distinctive voice widely recognized from shops and restaurants to airports and a hospital operating room.

But the book would not have been possible in any way without the support of my wife, Katrina vanden Heuvel, who is Editor and Publisher of *The Nation*. I owe her much more than gratitude. My commentaries put her in an unenviable position. That she did not "fully agree" or "only partially agreed" with many of them was customary in our thirty-year marriage. That some

Prologue

The Putin Specter—Who He Is Not

"Putin is an evil man, and he is intent on evil deeds."
—Senator John McCain[1]

"[Putin] was a KGB agent. By definition, he doesn't have a soul."
"If this sounds familiar, it's what Hitler did back in the 1930s."
—2016 Democratic Presidential Nominee Hillary Clinton[2,3]

T HE SPECTER OF AN EVIL-DOING VLADIMIR PUTIN HAS loomed over and
undermined US thinking about Russia for at least a decade. Inescapably,
it is therefore a theme that runs through this book. Henry Kissinger deserves
credit for having warned, perhaps alone among prominent American political figures, against this badly distorted image of Russia's leader since 2000:
"The demonization of Vladimir Putin is not a policy. It is an alibi for not
having one."[4]

But Kissinger was also wrong. Washington has made many policies strongly influenced by the demonizing of Putin—a personal vilification far exceeding any ever applied to Soviet Russia's latter-day Communist leaders. Those
policies spread from growing complaints in the early 2000s to US-Russian
proxy wars in Georgia, Ukraine, Syria, and eventually even at home, in
Russiagate allegations. Indeed, policy-makers adopted an earlier formulation
by the late Senator John McCain as an integral part of a new and more
dangerous Cold War: "Putin [is] an unreconstructed Russian imperialist and

K.G.B. apparatchik. . . . His world is a brutish, cynical place. . . . We must prevent the darkness of Mr. Putin's world from befalling more of humanity."[5]

Mainstream media outlets have played a major prosecutorial role in the demonization. Far from atypically, the *Washington Post's* editorial page editor wrote, "Putin likes to make the bodies bounce. . . . The rule-by-fear is Soviet, but this time there is no ideology—only a noxious mixture of personal aggrandizement, xenophobia, homophobia and primitive anti-Americanism."[6] Esteemed publications and writers now routinely degrade themselves by competing to denigrate "the flabbily muscled form" of the "small gray ghoul named Vladimir Putin."[7,8] There are hundreds of such examples, if not more, over many years. Vilifying Russia's leader has become a canon in the orthodox US narrative of the new Cold War.

As with all institutions, the demonization of Putin has its own history. When he first appeared on the world scene as Boris Yeltsin's anointed successor, in 1999–2000, Putin was welcomed by leading representatives of the US political-media establishment. The *New York Times'* chief Moscow correspondent and other verifiers reported that Russia's new leader had an "emotional commitment to building a strong democracy." Two years later, President George W. Bush lauded his summit with Putin and "the beginning of a very constructive relationship."[9]

But the Putin-friendly narrative soon gave away to unrelenting Putin-bashing. In 2004, *Times* columnist Nicholas Kristof inadvertently explained why, at least partially. Kristof complained bitterly of having been "suckered by Mr. Putin. He is not a sober version of Boris Yeltsin." By 2006, a *Wall Street Journal* editor, expressing the establishment's revised opinion, declared it "time we start thinking of Vladimir Putin's Russia as an enemy of the United States."[10,11] The rest, as they say, is history.

Who has Putin really been during his many years in power? We may have to leave this large, complex question to future historians, when materials for full biographical study—memoirs, archive documents, and others—are available. Even so, it may surprise readers to know that Russia's own historians, policy intellectuals, and journalists already argue publicly and differ considerably as to the "pluses and minuses" of Putin's leadership. (My own evaluation is somewhere in the middle.)

In America and elsewhere in the West, however, only purported "minuses" reckon in the extreme vilifying, or anti-cult, of Putin. Many are substantially uninformed, based on highly selective or unverified sources, and motivated by political grievances, including those of several Yeltsin-era oligarchs and their agents in the West.

By identifying and examining, however briefly, the primary "minuses" that underpin the demonization of Putin, we can understand at least who he is not:

• Putin is not the man who, after coming to power in 2000, "de-democratized" a Russian democracy established by President Boris Yeltsin in the 1990s and restored a system akin to Soviet "totalitarianism." Democratization began and developed in Soviet Russia under the last Soviet leader, Mikhail Gorbachev, in the years from 1987 to 1991.

Yeltsin repeatedly dealt that historic Russian experiment grievous, possibly fatal, blows. Among his other acts, by using tanks, in October 1993, to destroy Russia's freely elected parliament and with it the entire constitutional order that had made Yeltsin president. By waging two bloody wars against the tiny breakaway province of Chechnya. By enabling a small group of Kremlin-connected oligarchs to plunder Russia's richest assets and abet the plunging of some two-thirds of its people into poverty and misery, including the once-large and professionalized Soviet middle classes. By rigging his own reelection in 1996. And by enacting a "super-presidential" constitution, at the expense of the legislature and judiciary but to his successor's benefit. Putin may have furthered the de-democratization of the Yeltsin 1990s, but he did not initiate it.

• Nor did Putin then make himself a Tsar or Soviet-like "autocrat," which means a despot with absolute power to turn his will into policy. The last Kremlin leader with that kind of power was Stalin, who died in 1953, and with him his 20-year mass terror. Due to the increasing bureaucratic routinization of the political-administrative system, each successive Soviet leader had less personal power than his predecessor. Putin may have more, but if he really is a "cold-blooded, ruthless" autocrat—"the worst dictator on the planet"[12]—tens of thousands of protesters would not have repeatedly appeared in Moscow streets, sometimes officially sanctioned. Or their protests (and selective arrests) been shown on state television.

Political scientists generally agree that Putin has been a "soft authoritarian" leader governing a system that has authoritarian and democratic components inherited from the past. They disagree as to how to specify, define, and balance these elements, but most would also generally agree with a brief Facebook post, on September 7, 2018, by the eminent diplomat-scholar Jack Matlock: "Putin . . . is not the absolute dictator some have pictured him. His power seems to be based on balancing various patronage networks, some of which are still criminal. (In the 1990s, most were, and nobody was controlling them.) Therefore he cannot admit publicly that [criminal acts] happened without his approval since this would indicate that he is not completely in charge."

• Putin is not a Kremlin leader who "reveres Stalin" and whose "Russia is a gangster shadow of Stalin's Soviet Union."[13,14] These assertions are so far-fetched and uninformed about Stalin's terror-ridden regime, Putin, and Russia today, they barely warrant comment. Stalin's Russia was often as close to unfreedom as imaginable. In today's Russia, apart from varying political liberties, most citizens are freer to live, study, work, write, speak, and travel than they have ever been. (When vocational demonizers like David Kramer allege an "appalling human rights situation in Putin's Russia,"[15] they should be asked: compared to when in Russian history, or elsewhere in the world today?)

Putin clearly understands that millions of Russians have and often express pro-Stalin sentiments. Nonetheless, his role in these still-ongoing controversies over the despot's historical reputation has been, in one unprecedented way, that of an anti-Stalinist leader. Briefly illustrated, if Putin reveres the memory of Stalin, why did his personal support finally make possible two memorials (the excellent State Museum of the History of the Gulag and the highly evocative "Wall of Grief") to the tyrant's millions of victims, both in central Moscow? The latter memorial monument was first proposed by then-Kremlin leader Nikita Khrushchev, in 1961. It was not built under any of his successors—until Putin, in 2017.

• Nor did Putin create post–Soviet Russia's "kleptocratic economic system," with its oligarchic and other widespread corruption. This too took shape under Yeltsin during the Kremlin's shock-therapy "privatization" schemes of the 1990s, when the "swindlers and thieves" still denounced by today's opposition actually emerged.

Putin has adopted a number of "anti-corruption" policies over the years. How successful they have been is the subject of legitimate debate. As are how much power he has had to rein in fully both Yeltsin's oligarchs and his own, and how sincere he has been. But branding Putin "a kleptocrat"[16] also lacks context and is little more than barely informed demonizing.

A recent scholarly book finds, for example, that while they may be "corrupt," Putin "and the liberal technocratic economic team on which he relies have also skillfully managed Russia's economic fortunes."[17] A former IMF director goes further, concluding that Putin's current economic team does not "tolerate corruption" and that "Russia now ranks 35th out of 190 in the World Bank's Doing Business ratings. It was at 124 in 2010."[18]

Viewed in human terms, when Putin came to power in 2000, some 75 percent of Russians were living in poverty. Most had lost even modest legacies of the Soviet era—their life savings; medical and other social benefits; real wages; pensions; occupations; and for men life expectancy, which had fallen well below the age of 60. In only a few years, the "kleptocrat" Putin had mobilized enough wealth to undo and reverse those human catastrophes and put billions of dollars in rainy-day funds that buffered the nation in different hard times ahead. We judge this historic achievement as we might, but it is why many Russians still call Putin "Vladimir the Savior."

• Which brings us to the most sinister allegation against him: Putin, trained as "a KGB thug," regularly orders the killing of inconvenient journalists and personal enemies, like a "mafia state boss." This should be the easiest demonizing axiom to dismiss because there is no actual evidence, or barely any logic, to support it. And yet, it is ubiquitous. *Times* editorial writers and columnists—and far from them alone—characterize Putin as a "thug" and his policies as "thuggery" so often—sometimes doubling down on "autocratic thug"[19]—that the practice may be specified in some internal manual. Little wonder so many politicians also routinely practice it, as did US Senator Ben Sasse: "We should tell the American people and tell the world that we know that Vladimir Putin is a thug. He's a former KGB agent who's a murderer."[20]

Few, if any, modern-day world leaders have been so slurred, or so regularly. Nor does Sasse actually "know" any of this. He and the others imbibe it from reams of influential media accounts that fully indict Putin while burying a nullifying "but" regarding actual evidence. Thus another *Times* columnist: "I realize that this evidence is only circumstantial and well short of proof. But it's one of many suspicious patterns."[21] This, too, is a journalistic "pattern" when Putin is involved.

Leaving aside other world leaders with minor or major previous careers in intelligences services, Putin's years as a KGB intelligence officer in then–East Germany were clearly formative. Many years later, at age 67, he still spoke of them with pride. Whatever else that experience contributed, it made Putin a Europeanized Russian, a fluent German speaker, and a political leader with a remarkable, demonstrated capacity for retaining and coolly analyzing a very wide range of information. (Read or watch a few of his long interviews.) Not a bad leadership trait in very fraught times.

Moreover, no serious biographer would treat only one period in a subject's long public career as definitive, as Putin demonizers do. Why not instead the period after he left the KGB in 1991, when he served as deputy to the mayor of St. Petersburg, then considered one of the two or three most democratic leaders in Russia? Or the years immediately following in Moscow, where he saw first-hand the full extent of Yeltsin-era corruption? Or his subsequent years, while still relatively young, as president?

As for being a "murderer" of journalists and other "enemies," the list has grown to scores of Russians who died, at home or abroad, by foul or natural causes—all reflexively attributed to Putin. Our hallowed tradition puts the burden of proof on the accusers. Putin's accusers have produced none, only assumptions, innuendoes, and mistranslated statements by Putin about the fate of "traitors." The two cases that firmly established this defamatory practice were those of the investigative journalist Anna Politkovskaya, who was shot to death in Moscow in 2006; and Alexander Litvinenko, a shadowy one-time KGB defector with ties to aggrieved Yeltsin-era oligarchs, who died of radiation poisoning in London, also in 2006.

Not a shred of actual proof points to Putin in either case. The editor of Politkovskaya's paper, the devoutly independent *Novaya Gazeta*, still believes her assassination was ordered by Chechen officials, whose human-rights abuses she was investigating. Regarding Litvinenko, despite frenzied media claims and a kangaroo-like "hearing" suggesting that Putin was "probably" responsible, there is still no conclusive proof even as to whether Litvinenko's poisoning was intentional or accidental. The same paucity of evidence applies to many subsequent cases, notably the shooting of the opposition politician Boris Nemtsov, "in [distant] view of the Kremlin," in 2015.

About Russian journalists, there is, however, a significant overlooked statistic. According to the American Committee to Protect Journalists, as of 2012, 77 had been murdered—41 during the Yeltsin years, 36 under Putin. By 2018, the total was 82—41 under Yeltsin, the same under Putin. This strongly suggests that the still–partially corrupt post-Soviet economic system, not Yeltsin or Putin personally, led to the killing of so many journalists after 1991, most of them investigative reporters. The former wife of one journalist thought to have been poisoned concludes as much: "Many Western analysts place the responsibility for these crimes on Putin. But the cause is more likely the system of mutual responsibility and the culture of impunity that began to form before Putin, in the late 1990s."[22]

• More recently, there is yet another allegation: Putin is a fascist and white supremacist. The accusation is made mostly, it seems, by people wishing to deflect attention from the role being played by neo-Nazis in US-backed Ukraine. Putin no doubt regards it as a blood slur, and even on the surface it is, to be exceedingly charitable, entirely uninformed. How else to explain Senator Ron Wyden's solemn warnings, at a hearing on November 1, 2017, about "the current fascist leadership of Russia"? A young scholar recently dismantled a senior Yale professor's nearly inexplicable pro-pounding of this thesis.[23] My own approach is compatible, though different.

Whatever Putin's failings, the fascist allegation is absurd. Nothing in his statements over nearly 20 years in power are akin to fascism, whose core belief is a cult of blood based on the asserted superiority of one ethnicity over all others. As head of a vast multi-ethnic state—embracing scores of diverse groups with a broad range of skin colors—such utterances or related acts by Putin would be inconceivable, if not political suicide. This is why he endlessly appeals for harmony in "our entire multi-ethnic nation" with its "multi-ethnic culture," as he did once again in his re-inauguration speech in 2018.[24]

Russia has, of course, fascist-white supremacist thinkers and activists, though many have been imprisoned. But a mass fascist movement is scarcely feasible in a country where so many millions died in the war against Nazi Germany, a war that directly affected Putin and clearly left a formative mark on him. Though he was born after the war, his mother and father barely survived near-fatal wounds and disease, his older brother died in the long German siege of Leningrad, and several of his uncles perished. Only people who never endured such an experience, or are unable to imagine it, can con-jure up a fascist Putin.

There is another, easily understood, indicative fact. Not a trace of anti-Semitism is evident in Putin. Little noted here but widely reported both in Russia and in Israel, life for Russian Jews is better under Putin than it has ever been in that country's long history.[25]

• Finally, at least for now, there is the ramifying demonization allega-tion that, as a foreign-policy leader, Putin has been exceedingly "aggressive" abroad and his behavior has been the sole cause of the new cold war.[26] At best, this is an "in-the-eye-of-the-beholder" assertion, and half-blind. At worst, it justifies what even a German foreign minister characterized as the West's "war-mongering" against Russia.[27]

In the three cases widely given as examples of Putin's "aggression," the evidence, long cited by myself and others, points to US-led instigations, pri-marily in the process of expanding the NATO military alliance since the late 1990s from Germany to Russia's borders today. The proxy US-Russian war in Georgia in 2008 was initiated by the US-backed president of that coun-try, who had been encouraged to aspire to NATO membership. The 2014 crisis and subsequent proxy war in Ukraine resulted from the longstanding effort to bring that country, despite large regions' shared civilization with Russia, into NATO. And Putin's 2015 military intervention in Syria was done on a valid premise: either it would be Syrian President Bashar al-Assad in Damascus or the terrorist Islamic State—and on President Barack Obama's refusal to join Russia in an anti-ISIS alliance. As a result of this history, Putin is often seen in Russia as a belatedly reactive leader abroad, as a not sufficiently "aggressive" one.

Embedded in the "aggressive Putin" axiom are two others. One is that Putin is a neo-Soviet leader who seeks to restore the Soviet Union at the expense of Russia's neighbors. He is obsessively misquoted as having said, in 2005, "The collapse of the Soviet Union was the greatest geopolitical catastrophe of the twentieth century," apparently ranking it above two World Wars. What he actually said was "a major geopolitical catastrophe of the twentieth century," as it was for most Russians.

Though often critical of the Soviet system and its two formative leaders, Lenin and Stalin, Putin, like most of his generation, naturally remains in part a Soviet person. But what he said in 2010 reflects his real perspective and that of very many other Russians: "Anyone who does not regret the break-up of the Soviet Union has no heart. Anyone who wants its rebirth in its previous form has no head."[28,29]

The other fallacious sub-axiom is that Putin has always been "anti-Western," specifically "anti-American," has "always viewed the United States" with "smoldering suspicions."—so much that eventually he set into motion a "Plot Against America."[30,31] A simple reading of his years in power tells us otherwise. A Westernized Russian, Putin came to the presidency in 2000 in the still prevailing tradition of Gorbachev and Yeltsin—in hope of a "strategic friendship and partnership" with the United States.

How else to explain Putin's abundant assistant to US forces fighting in Afghanistan after 9/11 and continued facilitation of supplying American and NATO troops there? Or his backing of harsh sanctions against Iran's nuclear ambitions and refusal to sell Tehran a highly effective air-defense system? Or the information his intelligence services shared with Washington that if heeded could have prevented the Boston Marathon bombings in April 2012?

Or, until he finally concluded that Russia would never be treated as an equal and that NATO had encroached too close, Putin was a full partner in the US-European clubs of major world leaders? Indeed, as late as May 2018, contrary to Russiagate allegations, he still hoped, as he had from the beginning, to rebuild Russia partly through economic partnerships with the West: "To attract capital from friendly companies and countries, we need good relations with Europe and with the whole world, including the United States."[32]

Given all that has happened during the past nearly two decades—particularly what Putin and other Russian leaders perceive to have happened—it would be remarkable if his views of the West, especially America, had not changed. As he remarked in 2018, "We all change."[33] A few years earlier, Putin remarkably admitted that initially he had "illusions" about foreign policy, without specifying which. Perhaps he meant this, spoken at the end of 2017: "Our most serious mistake in relations with the West is that we trusted you too much. And your mistake is that you took that trust as weakness and abused it."[34]

If my refutation of the axioms of Putin demonization is valid, where does that leave us? Certainly, not with an apologia for Putin, but with the question, "Who is Putin?" Russians like to say, "let history judge," but given the perils of the new Cold War, we cannot wait. We can begin at least with a few historical truths. In 2000, a young and little-experienced man became the leader of a vast state that had precipitously disintegrated, or "collapsed," twice in the twentieth century—in 1917 and again in 1991—with disastrous consequences for its people. And in both instances it had lost its "sovereignty" and thus its security in fundamental ways.

These have been recurring themes in Putin's words and deeds. They are where to begin an understanding. No one can doubt that he is already the most consequential "statesman" of the twenty-first century, though the word is rarely, if ever, applied to him in the United States. And what does "consequential" mean? Even without the pseudo-minuses spelled out above, a balanced evaluation will include valid ones.

For example, at home, was it necessary to so strengthen and expand the Kremlin's "vertical" throughout the rest of the country in order to pull Russia back together? Should not the historic experiment with democracy have been given equal priority? Abroad, were there alternatives to annexing Crimea, even given the perceived threats? And did Putin's leadership really do nothing to reawaken fears in small East European countries victimized for centuries by Russia? These are only a few questions that might yield minuses alongside Putin's deserved pluses.

Whatever the approach, whoever undertakes a balanced evaluation should do so, to paraphrase Spinoza, not in order to demonize, not to mock, not to hate, but to understand.

Part I

THE NEW COLD WAR ERUPTS

2014–2015

Patriotic Heresy vs. Cold War

August 27, 2014

(Adapted from a talk given in Washington, DC, on June 16, 2014.)

WE MEET TODAY DURING THE WORST and potentially most dangerous American-Russian confrontation in many decades, probably since the 1962 Cuban Missile Crisis. The Ukrainian civil war, precipitated by the unlawful change of government in Kiev in February, is already growing into a proxy US-Russian war. The seemingly unthinkable is becoming imaginable: an actual war between US-led NATO and post-Soviet Russia.

Certainly, we are already in a new Cold War that Western sanctions will only deepen, institutionalize, and prolong—one potentially more dangerous than its 40-year predecessor, which the world barely survived.

We—opponents of the US policies that have contributed so woefully to the current crisis—are few in number, without influential supporters, and unorganized. I am old enough to know our position was very different in the 1970s and 1980s, when we struggled for what was then called détente. We were a minority, but a substantial minority with allies in high places, including in Congress and the State Department. Our views were solicited by mainstream newspapers, television, and radio. In addition to grassroots support, we had our own well-funded lobbying organization in Washington, the American Committee on East-West Accord, whose board included corporate CEOs, political figures, prominent academics, and statesmen of the stature of George Kennan.

We have none of that today. We have no access to the Obama administration, virtually none to Congress, now a bipartisan bastion of Cold War politics, and very little to the mainstream media. We have access to important alternative media, but they are not considered authoritative, or essential, inside the Beltway. In my long lifetime, I do not recall such a failure of American democratic discourse in any comparable time of crisis.

I want to speak generally about this dire situation—almost certainly a fateful turning point in world affairs—as a participant in what little mainstream media debate has been permitted but also as a longtime scholarly historian of Russia and of US-Russian relations and informed observer who believes there is still a way out of this terrible crisis.

Regarding my episodic participation in the very limited mainstream media discussion, I will speak in a more personal way than I usually do. From the outset, I saw my role as twofold.

Recalling the American adage "There are two sides to every story," I sought to explain Moscow's view of the Ukrainian crisis, which is almost entirely missing in US mainstream coverage. What, for example, did Putin mean when he said Western policy-makers were "trying to drive us into some kind of corner," "have lied to us many times" and "have crossed the line" in Ukraine? Second, having argued since the 1990s, in my books and *Nation* articles, that Washington's bipartisan Russia policies could lead to a new Cold War and to just such a crisis, I wanted to bring my longstanding analysis to bear on today's confrontation over Ukraine.

As a result, I have been repeatedly assailed—even in purportedly liberal publications—as Putin's No. 1 American "apologist," "useful idiot," "dupe," "best friend," and, perhaps a new low in immature invective, "toady." I expected to be criticized, as I was during nearly twenty years as a CBS News commentator, but not in such personal and scurrilous ways. (Something has changed in our political culture, perhaps related to the Internet, but I think more generally.)

Until now, I have not replied to any of these defamatory attacks. I do so today because I now think they are directed at many of us in this room and indeed at anyone critical of Washington's Russia policies, not just me. Re-reading the attacks, I have come to the following conclusions:

None of these character assassins present any factual refutations of anything I have written or said. They indulge instead in ad hominem slurs based on distortions and on the general premise that any American who seeks to understand Moscow's perspectives is a "Putin apologist" and thus unpatriotic. Such a premise only abets the possibility of war.

Some of these writers, or people who stand behind them, are longtime proponents of the twenty-year US policies that have led to the Ukrainian crisis. By defaming us, they seek to obscure their complicity in the unfolding disaster and their unwillingness to rethink it. Failure to rethink dooms us to the worst outcome.

Equally important, these kinds of neo-McCarthyites are trying to stifle democratic debate by stigmatizing us in ways that make our views unwelcome on mainstream television and radio broadcasts and op-ed pages—and to policy-makers. They are largely succeeding.

Let us be clear. This means that we, not the people on the left and the right who defame us, are the true American democrats and the real patriots of US national security. We do not seek to ostracize or silence the new cold warriors, but to engage them in public debate. And we, not they, understand that current US policy may have catastrophic consequences for international and American security.

The perils and costs of another prolonged Cold War will afflict our children and grandchildren. If nothing else, this reckless policy, couched even at high levels in a ritualistic demonizing of Putin, is already costing Washington an essential partner in the Kremlin in vital areas of US security—from Iran, Syria, and Afghanistan to efforts to counter nuclear proliferation and international terrorism.

But we ourselves are partially to blame for the one-sided, or nonexistent, public debate. As I said, we are not organized. Too often, we do not publicly defend each other. . . . And often we do not speak boldly enough. (We should not worry, for example, as do too many silent critics, if our arguments sometimes coincide with what Moscow is saying. Doing so results in self-censorship.)

Some people who privately share our concerns—in Congress, the media, universities, and think tanks—do not speak out at all. For whatever reason—concern about being stigmatized, about their career, personal disposition—they are silent. But in our democracy, where the cost of dissent is relatively low, silence is no longer a patriotic option.

We should, however, exempt young people from this imperative. They have more to lose. A few have sought my guidance, and I always advise, "Even petty penalties for dissent in regard to Russia could adversely affect your career. At this stage of life, your first obligation is to your family and thus to your future prospects. Your time to fight lies ahead." Not all of them heed my advice.

Finally, in connection with our struggle for a wiser American policy, I have come to another conclusion. Most of us were taught that moderation in thought and speech is always the best principle. But in a fateful crisis such as the one now confronting us, moderation for its own sake is no virtue. It becomes conformism, and conformism becomes complicity.

I recall this issue being discussed long ago in a very different context—by Soviet-era dissidents when I lived among them in Moscow in the 1970s and 1980s. . . . A few people have called us "American dissidents," but the analogy is imperfect: my Soviet friends had far fewer possibilities for dissent than we have and risked much worse consequences.

Nonetheless, the analogy is instructive. Soviet dissidents were protesting an entrenched orthodoxy of dogmas, vested interests, and ossified policy-making, which is why they were denounced as heretics by Soviet authorities and media. Since the 1990s, beginning with the Clinton administration, exceedingly unwise notions about post-Soviet Russia and the political correctness of US policy have congealed into a bipartisan American orthodoxy. The natural, historical response to orthodoxy is heresy. So let us be patriotic heretics, regardless of personal consequences, in the hope that many others will join us, as has often happened in history.

I turn now, in my capacity as a historian, to that orthodoxy. The late Senator Daniel Patrick Moynihan famously said: "Everyone is entitled to his own opinions, but not to his own facts." The US establishment's new Cold War orthodoxy rests almost entirely on fallacious opinions. Five of these fallacies are particularly important today.

Fallacy No. 1: Ever since the end of the Soviet Union in 1991, Washington has treated post-Communist Russia generously as a desired friend and partner, making every effort to help it become a democratic, prosperous member of the Western system of international security. Unwilling or unable, Russia rejected this American altruism, emphatically under Putin.

Fact: Beginning in the 1990s with the Clinton administration, every American president and Congress has treated post-Soviet Russia as a defeated nation with inferior legitimate rights at home and abroad. This triumphalist, winner-take-all approach has been spearheaded by the expansion of NATO—accompanied by non-reciprocal negotiations and now missile defense—into Russia's traditional zones of national security, while excluding Moscow from Europe's security system. Early on, Ukraine and, to a lesser extent, Georgia were Washington's "great prize."

Fallacy No. 2: There exists a "Ukrainian people" who yearn to escape centuries of Russian influence and join the West.

Fact: Ukraine is a country long divided by ethnic, linguistic, religious, cultural, economic, and political differences—particularly its western and eastern regions, but not only those. When the current crisis began in late 2013, Ukraine was one state, but it was not a single people or a united nation. Some of these divisions were made worse after 1991 by a corrupt elite, but most of them had developed over centuries.

Fallacy No. 3: In November 2013, the European Union, backed by Washington, offered Ukrainian President Viktor Yanukovych a benign association with European democracy and prosperity. Yanukovych was prepared to sign the agreement, but Putin bullied and bribed him into rejecting it. Thus began Kiev's Maidan protests and all that has since followed.

Fact: The EU proposal was a reckless provocation compelling the democratically elected president of a deeply divided country to choose between Russia and the West. So too was the EU's rejection of Putin's counterproposal for a Russian-European-American plan to save Ukraine from financial collapse. On its own, the EU proposal was not economically feasible. Offering little financial assistance, it required the Ukrainian government to enact harsh austerity measures and would have sharply curtailed its longstanding and essential economic relations with Russia. Nor was the EU proposal entirely benign. It included protocols requiring Ukraine to adhere to Europe's "military and security" policies—which meant in effect, without mentioning the alliance, NATO. Again, it was not Putin's alleged "aggression" that initiated today's crisis but instead a kind of velvet aggression by Brussels and Washington to bring all of Ukraine into the West, including (in fine print) into NATO.

Fallacy No. 4: Today's civil war in Ukraine was caused by Putin's aggressive response to the peaceful Maidan protests against Yanukovych's decision.

Fact: In February 2014, the radicalized Maidan protests, strongly influenced by extreme nationalist and even semi-fascist street forces, turned violent. Hoping for a peaceful resolution, European foreign ministers brokered a compromise between Maidan's parliamentary representatives and Yanukovych. It would have left him as president, with less power, of a coalition reconciliation government until early elections in December. Within hours, violent street fighters aborted the agreement. Europe's leaders and Washington did not defend their own diplomatic accord. Yanukovych fled to Russia. Minority parliamentary parties representing Maidan and, predominantly, western Ukraine—among them Svoboda, an ultranationalist movement previously anathematized by the European Parliament as incompatible with European values—formed a new government. Washington and Brussels endorsed the coup and have supported the outcome ever since. Everything that followed, from Russia's annexation of Crimea and the spread of rebellion in southeastern Ukraine to the civil war and Kiev's "anti-terrorist operation," was triggered by the February coup. Putin's actions were mostly reactive.

Fallacy No. 5: The only way out of the crisis is for Putin to end his "aggression" and call off his agents in southeastern Ukraine.

Fact: The underlying causes of the crisis are Ukraine's own internal divisions, not primarily Putin's actions. The essential factor escalating the crisis has been Kiev's "anti-terrorist" military campaign against its own citizens, mainly in Luhansk and Donetsk. Putin influences and no doubt aids the Donbass "self-defenders." Considering the pressure on him in Moscow, he is likely to continue to do so, perhaps even more directly, but he does not fully control them. If Kiev's assault ends, Putin probably can compel the rebels to negotiate. But only the Obama administration can compel Kiev to stop, and it has not done so.

In short, twenty years of US policy have led to this fateful American-Russian confrontation. Putin may have contributed to it along the way, but his role during his fourteen years in power has been almost entirely reactive—a complaint frequently directed against him by more hardline forces in Moscow.

* * *

In politics as in history, there are always alternatives. The Ukrainian crisis could have at least three different outcomes. The civil war escalates and widens, drawing in Russian and possibly NATO military forces. This would be the worst outcome: a kind of latter-day Cuban Missile Crisis. In the second outcome, today's de facto partitioning of Ukraine becomes institutionalized in the form of two Ukrainian states—one allied with the West, the other with Russia. This would not be the best outcome, but neither would it be the worst.

The best outcome would be the preservation of a united Ukraine. It will require good-faith negotiations between representatives of all of Ukraine's regions, including leaders of the rebellious southeast, probably under the auspices of Washington, Moscow, the European Union, and eventually the UN. Putin and his foreign minister, Sergei Lavrov, have proposed this for months. Ukraine's tragedy continues to grow. Thousands of innocent people have already been killed or wounded.

Alas, there is no wise leadership in Washington. President Barack Obama has vanished as a statesman in the Ukrainian crisis. Secretary of State John Kerry speaks publicly more like a secretary of war than as our top diplomat.

The Senate is preparing even more bellicose legislation. The establishment media rely uncritically on Kiev's propaganda and cheerlead for its policies. American television rarely, if ever, shows Kiev's military assaults on Luhansk, Donetsk, or other Ukrainian rebel cities, thereby arousing no public qualms or opposition.

And so we patriotic heretics remain mostly alone and often defamed. The most encouraging perspective I can offer is to remind you that positive change in history frequently begins as heresy. Or to quote the personal testimony of Mikhail Gorbachev, who said of his struggle for change in the late 1980s inside the even more rigidly orthodox Soviet *nomenklatura*: "Everything new in philosophy begins as heresy and in politics as the opinion of a minority." As for patriotism, here is Woodrow Wilson: "The most patriotic man is sometimes the man who goes in the direction he thinks right even when he sees half of the world against him."

Distorting Russia

February 12, 2014

THE DEGRADATION OF MAINSTREAM AMERICAN PRESS coverage of Russia, a country still vital to US national security, has been under way for many years. If the recent tsunami of shamefully unprofessional and politically inflammatory articles in leading newspapers and magazines—most recently about the Sochi Olympics, Ukraine, and, as usual, Russian President Vladimir Putin—is an indication, this media malpractice is now pervasive and the new norm.

There are notable exceptions, but a general pattern has developed. Even in the venerable *New York Times* and *Washington Post*, news reports, editorials, and commentaries no longer adhere rigorously to traditional journalistic standards, often failing to provide essential facts and context; make a clear distinction between reporting and analysis; require at least two different political or "expert" views on major developments; or publish opposing opinions on their op-ed pages. As a result, American media on Russia today are less objective, less balanced, more conformist, and scarcely less ideological than when they covered Soviet Russia during the preceding Cold War.

The history of this degradation is also clear. It began in the early 1990s, following the end of the Soviet Union, when the US media adopted Washington's narrative that almost everything President Boris Yeltsin did was a "transition from communism to democracy" and thus in America's best interests. This included Yeltsin's economic "shock therapy" and oligarchic looting of essential state assets, which destroyed tens of millions of Russian lives; armed destruction of a popularly elected Parliament and imposition of a "presidential" Constitution, which dealt a crippling blow to democratization and now empowers Putin; brutal war in Chechnya, which gave rise to terrorists in Russia's North Caucasus; rigging of his own reelection in 1996; and leaving behind in 1999, his approval ratings in single digits, a disintegrating country laden with weapons of mass destruction. Indeed, most American journalists still give the impression that Yeltsin was an ideal Russian leader.

Since the early 2000s, the media have followed a different leader-centric narrative, also consistent with US policy, that devalues multifaceted analysis for a relentless demonization of Putin, with little regard for facts. If Russia under Yeltsin was presented as having entirely legitimate politics and national interests, we are now made to believe that Putin's Russia has none at all, at home or abroad—even on its own borders, as in Ukraine.

Russia today has serious problems and many repugnant Kremlin policies. But anyone relying on mainstream American media will not find there any of their origins or influences in Yeltsin's Russia or in provocative US policies since the 1990s—only in the "autocrat" Putin who, however authoritarian, in reality lacks such power. Nor is he credited with stabilizing a disintegrating nuclear-armed country, assisting US security pursuits from Afghanistan and Syria to Iran, or even with granting amnesty, in December, to more than 1,000 jailed prisoners, including mothers of young children.

Not surprisingly, in January *The Wall Street Journal* featured the widely discredited former president of Georgia, Mikheil Saakashvili, branding Putin's government as one of "deceit, violence and cynicism," and the Kremlin as the "nerve center of the troubles that bedevil the West." But wanton Putin-bashing is also the dominant narrative in centrist, liberal, and progressive media, from the *Post*, *Times*, and *The New Republic* to CNN, MSNBC, and HBO's *Real Time with Bill Maher*, where Howard Dean, not previously known for his Russia expertise, recently declared, to Maher's and his panel's great approval, "Vladimir Putin is a thug."

American media therefore eagerly await Putin's downfall—due to his "failing economy" (some of its indicators are better than US ones), the valor of street protesters and other right-minded oppositionists (whose policies are rarely examined), the defection of his electorate (his approval ratings remain around 65 percent), or some welcomed "cataclysm." Evidently believing, as does the *Times*, for example, that democrats and a "much better future" will succeed Putin (not zealous ultranationalists growing in the streets and corridors of power), US commentators remain indifferent to what the hoped-for "destabilization of his regime" might mean in the world's largest nuclear country.

* * *

For weeks, this toxic coverage has focused on the Sochi Olympics and the deepening crisis in Ukraine. Even before the Games began, the *Times* declared the newly built complex a "Soviet-style dystopia" and warned in a headline, "Terrorism and Tension, Not Sports and Joy." On opening day, the paper found space for three anti-Putin articles and a lead editorial, a feat rivaled by the *Post*. Facts hardly mattered. Virtually every US report insisted that a record $51 billion "squandered" by Putin on the Sochi Games proved the funds were "corrupt." But as Ben Aris of *Business New Europe* pointed out, as much as $44 billion may have been spent "to develop the infrastructure of the entire region," investment "the entire country needs."

Overall pre-Sochi coverage was even worse, exploiting the threat of terrorism so licentiously it seemed pornographic. The *Post*, long known among critical-minded Russia-watchers as Pravda on the Potomac, exemplified the media ethos. A sports columnist and an editorial page editor turned the Olympics into "a contest of wills" between the despised Putin's "thugocracy" and terrorist "insurgents." The "two warring parties" were so equated readers might have wondered which to cheer for. If nothing else, American journalists gave terrorists an early victory, tainting "Putin's Games" and frightening away many foreign spectators, including some relatives of the athletes.

The Sochi Games will soon pass, triumphantly or tragically, but the potentially fateful Ukrainian crisis will not. A new Cold War divide between West and East may now be unfolding, not in distant Berlin but in the heart of Russia's historical civilization. The result could be a permanent confrontation fraught with instability and the threat of a hot war far worse than the proxy one in Georgia in 2008. These dangers have been all but ignored in highly selective, partisan, and inflammatory US media accounts that portray the European Union's "Partnership" proposal benignly as Ukraine's chance for democracy, prosperity, and escape from Russia thwarted only by a "bullying" Putin and his "cronies" in Kiev.

Perhaps the largest untruth promoted by most US media is the claim that "Ukraine's future integration into Europe" is "yearned for throughout the country." Every informed observer knows—from Ukraine's history, geography, languages, religions, culture, recent politics, and opinion surveys—that the country is deeply divided as to whether it should join Europe or remain close politically and economically to Russia. There is not one Ukraine or one "Ukrainian people" but at least two, generally situated in its Western and Eastern regions.

Such factual distortions point to two flagrant omissions. . . . The now exceedingly dangerous confrontation between the two Ukraines was not "ignited," as the *Times* claims, by President Viktor Yanukovych's duplicitous negotiating—or by Putin—but, as I pointed out, by the EU's reckless ultimatum, in November 2013, that the democratically elected president of a profoundly divided country choose between Europe and Russia. Putin's proposal instead for a tripartite EU-Ukraine-Russia trade arrangement, rarely if ever reported, was flatly rejected by US and EU officials.

But the most crucial media omission is Moscow's reasonable conviction that the struggle for Ukraine is yet another chapter in the West's ongoing, US-led march toward post-Soviet Russia, which began in the late 1990s with NATO's eastward expansion and continued with US-funded NGO political activities inside Russia, a US-NATO military outpost in Georgia, and missile-defense installations near Russia. Whether this longstanding Washington-Brussels policy is wise or reckless, it—not Putin's December 2013 financial offer to save Ukraine's collapsing economy—is deceitful. The EU's "civilizational" proposal, for example, includes "security policy" provisions, almost never reported, that would apparently subordinate Ukraine to NATO.

Any doubts about the Obama administration's real intentions in Ukraine should have been dispelled by the recently revealed taped conversation between a top State Department official, Victoria Nuland, and the US ambassador in Kiev. The media predictably focused on the source of the "leak" and on Nuland's verbal "gaffe"—"Fuck the EU." But the essential revelation was that high-level US officials were plotting to "midwife" a new, anti-Russian Ukrainian government by ousting or neutralizing Yanukovych, the democratically elected president—that is, a coup.

Americans are left with a new edition of an old question. Has Washington's twenty-year winner-take-all approach to post-Soviet Russia shaped today's degraded news coverage, or is official policy shaped by the coverage? Did Senator John McCain stand in Kiev alongside the well-known leader of an extreme nationalist party because he was ill-informed by the media, or have the media deleted this part of the story because of McCain's folly? Whatever the explanation, as Russian intellectuals say when faced with two bad alternatives, "Both are worst."

Why Cold War Again?

April 2, 2014

THE EAST-WEST CONFRONTATION OVER UKRAINE, WHICH led to Moscow's annexation of Crimea but long predated it, is potentially the worst international crisis in more than fifty years—and the most fateful. A negotiated resolution is possible, but time is running out.

A new Cold War divide is already descending in Europe—not in Berlin but on Russia's borders. Worse may follow. If NATO forces move toward Poland's border with Ukraine, as is being called for in Washington and Europe, Moscow may send its forces into eastern Ukraine. The result would be a danger of war comparable to the Cuban Missile Crisis of 1962.

Even if the outcome is a non-military "isolation of Russia," today's Western mantra, the consequences will be dire. Moscow will not bow but will turn, politically and economically, to the East, as it has done before, above all to fuller alliance with China. The United States will risk losing an essential partner in vital areas of its own national security, from Iran, Syria, and Afghanistan to threats of a new arms race, nuclear proliferation, and more terrorism. And—no small matter—prospects for a resumption of Russia's democratization will be greatly diminished for at least a generation.

Why did this happen, nearly twenty-three years after the end of Soviet Communism, when both Washington and Moscow proclaimed a new era of "friendship and strategic partnership"? The answer given by the Obama administration, and overwhelmingly by the US political-media establishment, is that Russian President Putin is solely to blame. According to this assertion, his "autocratic" rule at home and "neo-Soviet imperialist" policies abroad eviscerated the partnership established in the 1990s by Presidents Bill Clinton and Boris Yeltsin. This fundamental premise underpins the American mainstream narrative of two decades of US-Russian relations, and now the Ukrainian crisis.

But there is an alternative explanation, one more in accord with the facts. Beginning with the Clinton administration, and supported by every subsequent Republican and Democratic president and Congress, the US-led West has unrelentingly moved its military, political, and economic power ever closer to post-Soviet Russia. Spearheaded by NATO's eastward expansion, already encamped in the former Soviet Baltic republics on Russia's border— now augmented by missile defense installations in neighboring states—this bipartisan, winner-take-all approach has come in various forms.

They include US-funded "democracy promotion" NGOs more deeply involved in Russia's internal politics than foreign ones are permitted to be in our country; the 1999 bombing of Moscow's Slav ally Serbia, forcibly detaching its historic province of Kosovo; a US military outpost in former Soviet Georgia (along with Ukraine, one of Putin's previously declared "red lines"), contributing to the brief proxy war in 2008; and, throughout, one-sided negotiations, called "selective cooperation," which took concessions from the Kremlin without meaningful White House reciprocity, and followed by broken American promises.

All of this has unfolded, sincerely for some proponents, in the name of "democracy" and "sovereign choice" for the many countries involved, but the underlying geopolitical agenda has been clear. During the first East-West conflict over Ukraine, occasioned by its 2004 "Orange Revolution," an influential GOP columnist, Charles Krauthammer, acknowledged, "This is about Russia first, democracy only second.... The West wants to finish the job begun with the fall of the Berlin Wall and continue Europe's march to the east.... The great prize is Ukraine." The late Richard Holbrooke, an aspiring Democratic secretary of state, concurred, hoping even then for Ukraine's "final break with Moscow" and to "accelerate" Kiev's membership in NATO.

That Russia's political elite has long had this same menacing view of US intentions makes it no less true—or any less consequential. Formally announcing the annexation of Crimea on March 18, 2014, Putin vented Moscow's longstanding resentments. Several of his assertions were untrue and alarming, but others were reasonable, or at least understandable, not "delusional." Referring to Western, primarily American, policy-makers since the 1990s, he complained bitterly that they were "trying to drive us into some kind of corner," "have lied to us many times," and in Ukraine "have crossed the line." Putin warned, "Everything has its limits."

The Détente Imperative and Parity Principle

April 14, 2015

(Adapted from a talk given in Washington, DC, on March 26, 2015.)

W HEN I SPOKE AT THIS FORUM nine months ago, in June 2014, I warned that the Ukrainian crisis was the worst US-Russian confrontation in many decades. It had already plunged us into a new (or renewed) Cold War potentially even more perilous than its forty-year US-Soviet predecessor. . . . I also warned that we might soon be closer to actual war with Russia than we had been since the 1962 Cuban Missile Crisis.

Today, the crisis is even worse. The new Cold War has been deepened and institutionalized by transforming what began, in February 2014, as essentially a Ukrainian civil war into a US/NATO-Russian proxy war; by a torrent of inflammatory misinformation out of Washington, Moscow, Kiev, and Brussels; and by Western economic sanctions that are compelling Russia to retreat politically, as it did in the late 1940s, from the West.

Still worse, both sides are again aggressively deploying their conventional and nuclear weapons and probing the other's defenses in the air and at sea. Diplomacy between Washington and Moscow is being displaced by resurgent militarized thinking, while cooperative relationships nurtured over many decades, from trade, education, and science to arms control are being shredded. And yet, despite this fateful crisis and its growing dangers, there is still no mainstream debate about, still less any effective political opposition to, the US policies that have contributed to it.

Indeed, the current best hope to avert a larger war is being assailed by political forces, especially in Washington and in US-backed Kiev, that seem to want a military showdown with Russia's unreasonably vilified president, Vladimir Putin. In February, German Chancellor Angela Merkel and French President Francois Hollande brokered in Minsk a military and political agreement with Putin and Ukrainian President Petro Poroshenko that, if implemented, would end the Ukrainian civil war.

Powerful enemies of the Minsk accord—again, both in Washington and Kiev—are denouncing it as appeasement of Putin while demanding that President Obama send $3 billion of weapons to Kiev. Such a step would escalate the war in Ukraine, sabotage the ceasefire and political negotiations agreed upon in Minsk, and possibly provoke a Russian military response with unpredictable consequences. While Europe is splitting over the crisis, and with it perhaps the vaunted transatlantic alliance, the recklessness in Washington is fully bipartisan, urged on by four all-but-unanimous votes in Congress.

* * *

A new Washington-Moscow détente is the only way to avert another prolonged and even more dangerous Cold War. For this, we must relearn a fundamental lesson from the history of the 40-year US-Soviet Cold War and how it ended, a history largely forgotten, distorted, or unknown to many younger Americans. Simply recalled, détente, as an idea and a policy, meant expanding elements of cooperation in US-Soviet relations while diminishing areas of dangerous conflict, particularly, though not only, in the existential realm of the nuclear arms race. In this regard, détente had a long, always embattled, often defeated, but ultimately victorious history.

Leaving aside the first détente of 1933, when Washington officially recognized Soviet Russia after fifteen years of diplomatic non-recognition (the first Cold War), latter-day détente began in the mid-1950s under President Dwight Eisenhower and Soviet leader Nikita Khrushchev. It was soon disrupted by Cold War forces and events on both sides.

The pattern continued for thirty years: under President John Kennedy and Khrushchev, after the Cuban Missile Crisis; under President Lyndon

Johnson and Soviet leader Leonid Brezhnev, in the growing shadow of Vietnam; under President Richard Nixon and Brezhnev in the 1970s; and briefly under Presidents Gerald Ford and Jimmy Carter, also with Brezhnev. Each time, détente was gravely undermined, intentionally and unintentionally, and abandoned as Washington policy, though not by its determined American proponents. (Having been among them in the 1970s and 1980s, I can testify on their behalf.)

Then, in 1985, the seemingly most Cold War president ever, Ronald Reagan, began with Soviet leader Mikhail Gorbachev a renewed détente so far-reaching that both men, as well as Reagan's successor, President George H.W. Bush, believed they had ended the Cold War. How did détente, despite three decades of repeated defeats and political defamation, remain a vital and ultimately triumphant (as it seemed at the time to most observers) American policy?

Above all, because Washington gradually acknowledged that Soviet Russia was a co-equal great power with comparable legitimate national interests in world affairs. This recognition was given a conceptual basis and a name: "parity."

It is true that "parity" began as a grudging recognition of the US-Soviet nuclear capacity for "mutually assured destruction" and that, due to their different systems (and "isms") at home, the parity principle (as I termed it in 1981 in a *New York Times* op-ed) did not mean moral equivalence. It is also true that powerful American political forces never accepted the principle and relentlessly assailed it. Even so, the principle existed—like sex in Victorian England, acknowledged only obliquely in public but amply practiced—as reflected in the commonplace expression "the two superpowers," without the modifier "nuclear."

Most important, every US president returned to it, from Eisenhower to Reagan. Thus, Jack F. Matlock Jr., a leading diplomatic participant in and historian of the Reagan-Gorbachev-Bush détente, tells us that for Reagan, "détente was based on several logical principles," the first being "the countries would deal with each other as equals."

Three elements of US-Soviet parity were especially important. First, both sides had recognized spheres of influence, "red lines" that should not be directly challenged. This understanding was occasionally tested, even violated, as in Cuba in 1962, but it prevailed. Second, neither side should interfere excessively, apart from the mutual propaganda war, in the other's internal politics. This too was tested—particularly in regard to Soviet Jewish emigration and political dissidents—but generally negotiated and observed.

And third, Washington and Moscow had a shared responsibility for peace and mutual security in Europe, even while competing economically and militarily in what was called the Third World. This assumption was also tested by serious crises, but they did not negate the underlying parity principle.

Those tenets of parity prevented a US-Soviet hot war during the long Cold War. They were the basis of détente's great diplomatic successes, from symbolic bilateral leadership summits, arms control agreements, and the 1975 Helsinki Accords on European security, based on sovereign equality, to many other forms of cooperation now being discarded. And in 1985-1989, they made possible what both sides declared to be the end of the Cold War.

* * *

We are in a new Cold War with Russia today, and specifically over the Ukrainian confrontation, largely because Washington nullified the parity principle. Indeed, we know when, why, and how this happened.

The three leaders who negotiated an end to the US-Soviet Cold War said repeatedly at the time, in 1988-90, that they did so "without any losers." Both sides, they assured each other, were "winners." But when the Soviet Union itself ended nearly two years later, in December 1991, Washington conflated the two historic events, leading the first President Bush to change his mind and declare, in his 1992 State of the Union address, "By the grace of God, America won the Cold War."

Bush added that there was now "one sole and pre-eminent power, the United States of America." This dual rejection of parity and assertion of America's pre-eminence in international relations became, and remains, a virtually sacred US policy-making axiom, one embodied in the formulation by President Bill Clinton's secretary of state, Madeleine Albright, that "America is the world's indispensable nation." It was echoed in President Obama's 2014 address to West Point cadets: "The United States is and remains the one indispensable nation."

This official American triumphalist narrative is what we have told ourselves and taught our children for nearly twenty-five years. Rarely is it challenged by leading American politicians or commentators. It is a bipartisan orthodoxy that has led to many US foreign policy disasters, not least in regard to Russia.

For more than two decades, Washington has perceived post-Soviet Russia as a defeated and thus lesser nation, presumably analogous to Germany and Japan after World War II, and therefore as a state without legitimate rights and interests comparable to America's, either abroad or at home, even in its own region. Anti-parity thinking has shaped every major Washington policy toward Moscow, from the disastrous crusade to remake Russia in America's image in the 1990s, ongoing expansion of NATO to Russia's borders, non-reciprocal negotiations known as "selective cooperation," double-standard conduct abroad, and broken promises to persistent "democracy-promotion" intrusions into Russia's domestic politics.

Two exceedingly dangerous examples are directly related to the Ukrainian crisis. For years, US leaders have repeatedly asserted that Russia is not entitled to any "sphere of influence," even on its own borders, while at the same time enlarging the US sphere of influence, spearheaded by NATO, to those borders—by an estimated 400,000 square miles, probably the largest such "sphere" inflation ever in peacetime. Along the way, the US political-media establishment has vilified Putin personally in ways it never demonized Soviet Communist leaders, at least after Stalin, creating the impression of another orientation antithetical to parity—the delegitimization of Russia's government.

Moscow has repeatedly protested this US sphere creep, loudly after it resulted in a previous proxy war in another former Soviet republic, Georgia, in 2008, but to deaf or defiant ears in Washington. Inexorably, it seems, Washington's anti-parity principle led to today's Ukrainian crisis. Moscow reacted as it would have under any established national leader, and as any well-informed observer knew it would.

Unless the idea of détente is fully rehabilitated, and with it the essential parity principle, the new Cold War will include a growing risk of actual war with nuclear Russia. Time may not be on our side, but reason is.

Part II

US Follies and Media Malpractices

2016

Secret Diplomacy On Ukraine

January 20

DIPLOMATIC ACTIVITY BY WASHINGTON, PARIS, GERMANY, Moscow, and Kiev since early January, largely unreported in the American media, may be the last, best chance to end the Ukrainian crisis. Russian President Vladimir Putin appointed two trusted and experienced associates as his personal representatives to Kiev and to the anti-Kiev rebels in Donbass. A few days later, on January 13, President Barack Obama placed a call to Putin, the man he had vowed to "isolate" in international affairs, with Ukraine a priority of their discussion. Two days later, a leading American and Russian opponent of negotiations, Victoria Nuland and Vyacheslav Surkov, met privately in a remote Russian enclave. On January 18–19, representatives of German Chancellor Angela Merkel and French President Francois Hollande met with Ukrainian President Petro Poroshenko in Kiev.

At issue were two essential elements of the Minsk Accords, drafted by Merkel and Hollande and ratified by Putin and Poroshenko but resisted for many months by Poroshenko: constitutional legislation in Kiev granting the rebel regions a significant degree of home rule; and the legitimacy of forthcoming elections in those regions. All sides reported significant progress, though Poroshenko said he lacked sufficient votes in the Ukrainian Parliament, a tacit admission he fears the possibility of a violent backlash by armed ultranationalist forces.

Dire problems at home have compelled all of these leaders to undertake the intense negotiations, problems ranging from Europe and Syria to Russia's economic woes, as well as their own political standing at home. In this context, the US media-political narrative is wrong about what Putin wants in

Ukraine: not a permanently destabilized country, as is incessantly reported, but a peaceful neighbor that does not threaten Russia's vital economic or security interests—or permanently divide millions of inter-married Russian-Ukrainian families.

These negotiations face many obstacles—in particular, powerful opposition in Washington and NATO. But the secret diplomacy represents a possible turning point, a fork in the road, one that will test the qualities of the leaders involved and could shape their historical reputations, first and foremost those of Presidents Obama and Putin.

The Obama Administration Escalates Military Confrontation With Russia

February 3

THE PENTAGON HAS ANNOUNCED IT WILL quickly quadruple the positioning of US-NATO heavy weapons and troops near Russia's western borders. The result will be to further militarize the new Cold War, making it more confrontational and more likely to lead to actual war.

The move is unprecedented in modern times. Except for Nazi Germany's invasion of the Soviet Union during World War II, Western military power has never been positioned so close to Russia, thereby making the new Cold War even more dangerous than was the preceding one.

Russia will certainly react, probably by moving more of its own heavy weapons, including new missiles, to its Western borders, possibly along with tactical nuclear weapons. This should remind us that a new and more dangerous US-Russian nuclear arms race has also been under way for several years. The Obama administration's decision can only intensify it. The decision will have other woeful consequences, undermining ongoing negotiations by Secretary of

State John Kerry and Russian Foreign Minister Sergei Lavrov for cooperation on the Ukrainian and Syrian crises and further dividing Europe, which is far from united on Washington's increasingly hawkish approach to Moscow.

We can only despair that these ongoing developments have barely been reported in the US media and publicly debated not at all, not even by current American presidential candidates or raised by moderators of their "debates." Never before has such a dire international situation been so ignored in a US presidential campaign. The reason may be that everything which has happened since the Ukrainian crisis erupted in 2014 has been blamed solely on the "aggression" of Russian President Putin—a highly questionable assertion but an orthodox media narrative.

Another Turning Point in the New Cold War

February 24

U KRAINE REMAINS THE POLITICAL EPICENTER OF the new Cold War, but Syria is where it may become a hot war. The Syrian ceasefire agreement—brokered by Secretary of State Kerry and his Russian counterpart Lavrov, and emphatically endorsed by Russian President Putin but less so by President Obama—offers hope on several levels, from the suffering Syrian people to those of us who want a US–Russian coalition against the Islamic State and its terrorist accomplices, and thus the possibility of diminishing the new Cold War.

The actual chances of a successful ceasefire are slim, due partly to the number of combatants and lack of a monitoring mechanism, but mainly to powerful forces opposed to the ceasefire both in Washington and Moscow. American opposition is already clear from statements by leading politicians, from Secretary of Defense Ashton Carter's clear dissatisfaction with Kerry's negotiations with Moscow and from anti-ceasefire reports and editorials in the establishment media.

At the same time, Putin's unusual personal ten-minute announcement of the ceasefire on Russian television suggests that some of his own military-security advisers are opposed to the agreement, for understandable reasons. They want to pursue Moscow's military success in Syria achieved since it intervened in September 2015. The ceasefire is now Putin's own diplomatic policy, leaving him vulnerable to the commitment of President Obama, who has previously violated agreements with the Kremlin, most recently and consequentially by disregarding his pledge not to pursue regime change in Libya.

In Ukraine, President Poroshenko continues to demonstrate that he is less a national leader than a compliant representative of domestic and foreign political forces. Having again promised Germany and France that he would implement the Minsk Accords for ending Ukraine's civil war, which they designed, he promptly reneged, bowing to Ukrainian ultra-right movements that threaten to remove him. And having called for the ouster of his exceedingly unpopular Prime Minister Arseny Yatsenyuk—"our guy," as the US State Department termed him in 2014 and still views him—Poroshenko then instructed members of his party to vote against the parliamentary motion, leaving Yatsenyuk in office, at least for now.

With Washington, and Vice President Joseph Biden in particular, widely seen to be behind this duplicity, Poroshenko increasingly resembles a pro-consul of a faraway great power. At the same time, on the second anniversary of the violent Maidan protests that brought to power the current US–backed government, the State Department hailed the "glories" of what is now becoming a failed Ukrainian state and ruined country.

The Obama Administration Attacks Its Own Syrian Ceasefire

March 2

T HE US-RUSSIAN-BROKERED CEASEFIRE IN SYRIA PRESENTS an opportunity to deal a major blow to the Islamic State, greatly diminish the Syrian civil war, and generate cooperation between Washington and Moscow elsewhere, including in Ukraine. The agreement is, however, under fierce attack on many fronts. US "allies" Turkey and Saudi Arabia are threatening to disregard the ceasefire provisions by launching their own war in Syria. In Washington, Secretary of Defense Carter and his top generals informed the White House and Congress that Secretary of State Kerry's agreement with Moscow is a "ruse," and that Putin's Russia remains the "No. 1 existential threat" to the United States—charges amply echoed in the American mainstream press.

Much is at stake. The "Plan B" proposed by Carter apparently means a larger US military intervention in Syria to create an anti-Russian, anti-Assad "safe zone" that would in effect partition the country. Viewed more broadly, this would continue the partitioning of political territories that began with the end of the Soviet Union and Yugoslavia in the 1990s and now looms over Syria, Ukraine, and possibly even the European Union.

Moreover, though today's severe international crises get scant attention in the ongoing US presidential campaigns, candidate Hillary Clinton has a potentially large and highly vulnerable stake in the Syrian crisis. As documented by a two-part *New York Times* investigation, then-Secretary of State Clinton played the leading role in the White House's decision to topple Libyan leader Moammar Gaddafi in 2011. That folly led to a terrorist-ridden failed state and growing bastion of the Islamic State. Clinton's campaign statements suggest that she does not support Kerry's initiatives but instead a replication of the Libyan operation in order to remove Syrian President Assad—a version, it seems, of Carter's "Plan B."

Meanwhile, there is the familiar (and meaningless) accusation that Putin has "weaponized information," including about Syria. A critical-minded reader should ask whether US mainstream information is any more reliable than Russia's.

Was Putin's Syria Withdrawal Really a "Surprise"?

March 16

W HY HAVE PURPORTED US EXPERTS BEEN repeatedly surprised by what President Vladimir Putin does and does not do? Clearly, they do not read or listen to him.

When Putin began the air campaign in Syria in the fall of 2015, he announced that it had two purposes. To bolster the crumbling Syrian Army so it could fight terrorist groups on the ground and prevent the Islamic State from taking Damascus. And thereby to bring about peace negotiations among anti-terrorist forces. Putin said he hoped to achieve this in a few months.

In short, mission, in Putin's words, now "generally accomplished," though you would not know it from American media reports. US policy- makers and pundits seem to believe their own anti-Putin propaganda, which for years has so demonized him that they cannot imagine he seeks anything other than military conquest and empire building. Nor can they concede that Russia has legitimate national security interests in Syria.

They similarly do not understand what Putin hopes to achieve: a de-militarization of the new Cold War. In particular, if the end of Russia's Syrian bombing campaign abets peace negotiations under way in Geneva or anywhere else, the diplomatic process could spread to Ukraine, another militarized conflict between Washington and Moscow.

Also unnoticed, Putin's decision to withdraw militarily from Syria, even though only partially, exposes him to political risks at home, where he is, we need to recall, considerably less than an absolute dictator. Hard-liners in the Russian political-security establishment—de facto allies of Washington's own war party—are already asking why he stalled the achieved Russian-Syrian military advantage instead of taking Aleppo, pressing on toward the Syrian-Turkish border, and inflicting more damage on ISIS. Why, they ask, would Putin again seek compromise with the Obama administration, which has repeatedly "betrayed" him, most recently in Libya in 2011 and by its anti-Russian coup in Kiev in 2014? And why, they also ask, if Washington perceives the Syrian withdrawal as "weakness" on Putin's part, will the United States not escalate its "aggression" in Ukraine?

All this comes as Russia's economic hardships have enabled Putin's political opponents at home, the large Communist Party in particular, to try to mount a new challenge to his leadership. But the gravest threat to his clear preference for diplomacy over war is less his domestic critics than the Obama administration, which seems not to have decided which it prefers.

Trump vs. Triumphalism

March 23

W HATEVER ELSE ONE MAY THINK ABOUT Donald Trump as a presidential candidate, his foreign policy views expressed, however elliptically, in a *Washington Post* interview this week should be welcomed. They challenge the bipartisan neocon/liberal interventionist principles and practices that have guided Washington policy-making since the 1990s—with disastrous results.

That policy-making has involved the premise that the United States is the sole, indispensable superpower with a right to intervene wherever it so decides by military means and political regime changes. In the process, Washington has used select NATO members ("coalitions of the willing") as its own United Nations and rule-maker. In recent years, from Iraq and Libya to Ukraine and Syria, the results have been international instability, wars (unilateral, proxy, and civil), growing terrorism, failed "nation building," mounting refugee crises, and a new Cold War with Russia.

Trump seems to propose instead diplomacy ("deals") toward forming partnerships, including with Russia; rethinking NATO's mission; urging Europe to take political and financial responsibility for its own crises, as in Ukraine; and perhaps diminishing America's military footprint in the world. In effect, a less missionary and militarized American national-security policy.

Trump may be calling on an older Republican foreign policy tradition. In any event, he appears to be advocating two realist perspectives. The world is no longer unipolar, pivoting around Washington; and the United States must share and balance power with other great powers, from Europe to Russia and China.

The orthodox bipartisan establishment, Republicans and Democrats alike, have reacted to Trump's proposals as though he is the foreign policy anti-Christ, leveling all-out assaults on his remarks. It is possible that this confrontation might lead, if the mainstream media do their job, to the public debate over US foreign policy that has been missing for twenty years, certainly during the 2016 presidential campaign.

A Fragile Mini-Détente In Syria

March 30

BY REGAINING CONTROL OF PALMYRA, A major and ancient city, the Syrian army and its ground allies, backed by Russian air power, have dealt ISIS its most important military defeat. The victory belies the US political-media establishment's allegations that President Putin's six-month military intervention was a sinister move designed to thwart the West's fight against terrorism. Instead, it has gravely wounded the Islamic State, whose agents were behind recent terrorist assaults on Paris and Brussels.

This comes in the context of fledgling US–Russian cooperation in Syria, a kind of mini-détente brokered by Secretary of State Kerry and Russian Foreign Minister Lavrov. Not surprisingly, these positive developments are being assailed by the US policy-media war party, which has redoubled its vilification of Putin. Preposterously, for example, he is accused of "weaponizing the migration crisis" in Europe, even though the crisis began long before Russia's intervention in Syria. (If the intervention continues to be successful, it might eventually diminish the number of immigrants fleeing that war-torn, terror-ridden country.)

Putin is clearly behind Lavrov's initiatives, even meeting with Kerry several times. Obama's position, however, remains unclear. And neither he nor the US commander of NATO congratulated or otherwise applauded the Russian-Syrian victory in Palmyra, while Obama again went out of his way to insult Putin personally (twice).

With White House backing, the Kerry-Lavrov mini-détente might extend to the political epicenter of the new Cold War, Ukraine. Instead, Washington is seeking to make the US-born Natalie Jaresko prime minister of Ukraine, putting an American face on the ongoing Western colonization of the Kiev government. Jaresko is also the candidate of the US-controlled IMF, on which Kiev is financially dependent but whose demands for austerity measures and "privatization" of state enterprises will almost certainly further diminish the government's popular support, abet the rise of ultra-right-wing forces, and worsen Kiev's conflict with Russia.

Donald Trump has emerged as the only American presidential candidate to challenge the bipartisan policies that contributed so greatly to this new Cold War. Predictably, the US national security establishment has reacted to Trump with a version of the preceding Cold War's red-baiting. Thus, Hillary Clinton charged that Trump's less militarized proposals would be like "Christmas in the Kremlin." The mainstream media have taken the same approach to Trump, thereby continuing to deprive America of the foreign policy debate it urgently needs.

"Information War" vs.
Embryonic Détente

April 6

THE KREMLIN IS CHARGING THAT A spate of Western news allegations against President Putin are designed to disrupt US-Russian relations at a critical point. The allegations include not only the Panama Papers investigation of Kremlin offshore investments but also apartments purchased for Putin's daughters, his "suspected" involvement in the Washington death of a former top Russian official, and even a rumored romance between the Russian president and Rupert Murdoch's ex-wife.

Whether or not this is an organized "information war" is unclear, but similar anti-Kremlin "news" appeared regularly during the preceding 40-year Cold War when relations seemed headed toward détente. This is such a moment in the new Cold War, as negotiations between Secretary of State Kerry and Russian Foreign Minister Lavrov suddenly seem promising, especially in regard to the Syrian ceasefire and possibly even Ukraine.

Why, then, in the aftermath of the Syrian-Russian victory over the Islamic State at Palmyra and elsewhere, are "moderate oppositionists" backed by the United States, Saudi Arabia, and Turkey violating the ceasefire agreement by attacking Syrian forces? And why the sudden spate of news reports, apparently inspired by the Obama administration, about Putin's alleged personal "corruption?" They can only be intended to present him as an unfit US ally in Syria or anywhere else.

But the Panama Papers did more political damage to Petro Poroshenko, president of the Washington-backed government in Kiev. They revealed that he had personally established offshore accounts and, still worse, while his Ukrainian army was suffering a humiliating defeat at the hands of the Russian-backed rebels in Eastern Ukraine in August 2014. (Unlike Putin, Poroshenko and his offshore accounts were named in the investigation.)

With the Kiev government already in deep political and economic crisis, this is a further blow to Poroshenko's standing with the Ukrainian elite and people. There are already calls for his impeachment. How will the Obama administration deal with this latest crisis of its "Ukrainian project," as it is sometimes derisively termed, which has all but wrecked Washington's relations with Moscow?

Among the current American presidential candidates, only Donald Trump continues to say anything meaningful and critical about US bipartisan foreign policy. In effect, he has asked five fundamental (and dissenting) questions. Should the United States always be the world's leader and policeman? What is NATO's proper mission today, 25 years after the end of the Soviet Union and when international terrorism is the main threat to the West? Why does Washington repeatedly pursue a policy of regime change—in Iraq, Libya, Ukraine, and now in Damascus, even though it always ends in "disaster"? Why is the United States treating Putin's Russia as an enemy and not as a security partner? And should US nuclear-weapons doctrine adopt a no–first use pledge?

Trump's foreign policy questions are fundamental and urgent. Instead of engaging them, his opponents (including President Obama) and the mainstream media dismiss them as ignorant and dangerous. Some of his outraged critics are even branding him "the Kremlin's Candidate"—thereby anathematizing alternative views and continuing to shut off the debate our country so urgently needs.

The Crisis of the US "Ukrainian Project"

April 13

U KRAINE REMAINS THE POLITICAL EPICENTER OF a new Cold War that prevents Washington and Moscow from cooperating on issues of vital national security, most recently mounting threats of terrorism, potentially nuclear terrorism, in Europe and, soon no doubt, elsewhere.

Petro Poroshenko, president of the US-backed Kiev government, has suffered a recent succession of political blows, including right-wing and "liberal" threats to overthrow him; an inability to appoint a new prime minister; a Dutch referendum vote against giving his government the European Union partnership he wants; the Panama Papers revelations about his personal offshore accounts; and more. The US political-media establishment blames Poroshenko's problems on Ukraine's rampant financial corruption and on the "aggression" of Russian President Putin, but the underlying cause is the real political history of Poroshenko's "Maidan Revolution" regime.

As the second anniversary of Ukraine's civil war (and US-Russian proxy war) approaches, we need to recall some of the disgraceful episodes of the proclaimed "Revolution of Dignity." That history includes the following episodes:

• The violent overthrow of Ukraine's constitutionally elected president, Viktor Yanukovych, in February 2014.

• Kiev's refusal to seriously investigate the "Maidan snipers," whose killings precipitated Yanukovych's ouster, assassins who now seem to have been not his agents, as initially alleged, but those of right-wing Maidan forces.

• The new government's similar refusal to prosecute extreme nationalists behind the subsequent massacre of pro-Russian protesters in Odessa shortly later in 2014.

• And the new Maidan government's unwillingness to negotiate with suddenly disenfranchised regions of Eastern Ukraine, which had largely voted for Yanukovych, and instead to launch an "anti-terrorist" military assault on them.

• Even Poroshenko's subsequent election as president was questionably democratic, opposition regions and parties having been effectively banned.

All this was done, and not done, officially in the name of "European values" and in order to "join Europe," and with the full support of the West, particularly the Obama administration. Two years later, the Ukrainian civil war has taken nearly 10,000 lives, created perhaps 2 million refugees, empowered armed quasi-fascist forces that threaten to overthrow Poroshenko, and left the country in near economic and social ruin.

The Dutch referendum was not the first sign that the European Union is wearying of the disaster it helped to create. Two of its top officials had already stated that Kiev actually had no chance of joining the European Union for "20 to 25 years." More and more Europeans are asking why their leaders forced Kiev in 2013 to choose between the EU and its traditional trading partner, Russia, instead of embracing Putin's proposal for a three-way economic arrangement that would have included Russia.

In Cold-War Washington and its media, the question as to why the Obama administration also imposed the choice on Ukraine is not even raised. There is only more blaming of "Putin's Russia" for a tragedy that continues to unfold. For a truer understanding, look back to its origins.

Is War With Russia Possible?

May 4

D URING THE PAST TWO WEEKS, THE Obama administration appears to have been undermining cooperation with Moscow on three new Cold War fronts.

It has refused to accept President Putin's compelling argument that the Syrian army and its allies are the only "boots on the ground" fighting the Islamic State effectively, currently around the pivotal city of Aleppo. Instead, Washington and its compliant media are condemning the Syrian-Russian military campaign against "moderate" anti-Assad fighters in the area, many of them actually also jihadists. At risk are the Geneva peace negotiations brokered by Secretary of State Kerry and Russian Foreign Minister Lavrov.

Regarding the confrontation over Ukraine, where Kiev's political and economic crisis grows ever worse, the best hope for ending that civil and proxy war, the Minsk Accords, was virtually sabotaged at the UN, where US Ambassador Samantha Power claimed the accords require Russia returning Crimea to Ukraine. In fact, Crimea is not even mentioned in the Minsk agreement.

And in Europe, where opinion mounts favoring an end to the economic sanctions against Russia—as evidenced by the Dutch referendum against admitting Ukraine to the European Union and by the French Parliament's vote in favor of ending the sanctions—the Obama administration (not only Ambassador Power but President Obama himself) is lobbying hard against such a step when the issue comes up for a vote this summer.

Meanwhile, US-led NATO continues to increase its land, sea, and air build-up on or near Russia's borders. Not surprisingly, Moscow responds by sending its planes to inspect a US warship sailing not far from Russia's military-naval base at Kaliningrad. Preposterously, having for two decades steadily moved NATO's military presence from Berlin to Russia's borders, and now escalating it, Washington and Brussels accuse Moscow of "provocations against NATO." But who is "provoking"—"aggressing" against—whom? The NATO buildup can only stir in Russians memories of the Nazi

German invasion in 1941, the last time such hostile military forces mobilized on the country's frontier. Some 27.5 million Soviet citizens died in the aftermath.

Though not reported in the US media, an influential faction in Kremlin politics has long insisted, mostly but not always behind closed doors, that the US-led West is preparing an actual hot war against Russia, and that Putin has not prepared the country adequately at home or abroad. During the past two weeks, this conflict over policy has erupted in public with three prominent members of the Russian elite charging, sometimes implicitly but also explicitly, that Putin has supported his "fifth column" government headed by Prime Minister Dmitri Medvedev. Critics are not seeking to remove Putin; there is no alternative to him and his public approval ratings, exceeding 80 percent, are too high.

But they do want the Medvedev government replaced and their own policies adopted. Those policies include a Soviet-style mobilization of the economy for war and more proactive military policies abroad, especially in Ukraine. In this context, we should ask whether US and NATO policy-makers are sleepwalking toward war with Russia or whether they actively seek it.

Stalin Resurgent, Again

June 1

IN ANOTHER EXAMPLE OF UNINFORMED COVERAGE of Russia, American media are misrepresenting the current upsurge of pro-Stalin sentiments as unique to the Putin era. In public opinion surveys, nearly 60 percent of Russians asked now view the despot as a positive figure in their country's history.

Having studied and written about the Stalin era and its legacy for many decades, most recently in my book *The Victims Return*, I have often explained that Russia has been deeply divided over Stalin's historical role ever since his death in 1953, 63 years ago.

Looking back, Russians see two towering mountains, each informed by contested history. On one side, a mountain of Stalin's achievements in the form of industrialization and modernization in the 1930s, however draconian, that prepared the county, they insist, for the great victory over Nazi Germany in 1941–1945. And on the other, a mountain of human victims resulting from Stalin's brutal forced collectivization of the peasantry and Great Terror with its Gulag of torture prisons, mass executions, and often murderous forced labor camps, both of which killed millions of people.

Russian and Western historians, with access since the 1990s to long closed archives, are still trying to strike a scholarly balance, but for ordinary Russians the balance is more directly affected by their perceptions of their own well-being at home and of Russia's national security. Positive views of Stalin do not mean they want a new Stalin in the Kremlin or a recapitulation of Stalinism, but that the despot is for many a historical, and still relevant, symbol of a strong state, law and order, and national security.

These conflicts over Stalin's reputation began publicly long ago, in the 1950s under Soviet leader Nikita Khrushchev, who assailed the personal cult created by Stalin. They continued under Leonid Brezhnev when the disputes were muffled by tightened censorship. They burst fully into the open during Gorbachev's attempted anti-Stalinist reformation known as glasnost and perestroika in the late 1980s and during the Yeltsin 1990s, when economic and social hard times afflicted most Russian citizens and caused Stalin's popular ratings to surge again. And, of course, they continue under Putin.

There are three American media misrepresentations regarding the most recent resurgence of pro-Stalin sentiments. Under Putin, the Stalinist past is not again being censored. Anti-Stalinist historians, journalists, filmmakers, TV producers, and others continue to present their work to the public. Today, the horrors of the Stalin era are widely known in Russia. Second, nothing remotely akin to historical Stalinism is present or unfolding in Russia today, contrary to assertions by several leading US newspapers.

And third, Putin, who has had to try politically to straddle and unite profoundly conflicting eras in Russian history—Tsarist, Soviet, and post-Soviet—is not himself, in words or deeds, a Stalinist. To the contrary, due to his personal support there is now in Moscow a large, modern State Museum of the History of the Gulag and currently under construction a national monument memorializing Stalin's victims, first called for by Khrushchev in 1961, but never even begun under any of Putin's predecessors. (For perspective, note that in Washington there is still no national monument dedicated to the victims of American slavery.)

Nor is Stalin merely an historical issue in Russia. Intensified moments during the preceding Cold War always inflated pro-Stalin sentiments in Soviet Russia. This is happening again today in response to NATO's perceived military encirclement of Russia, from the Baltics to Ukraine and Georgia, and in response to the Western sanctions that have contributed to economic hardships for many Russians. How this will affect Putin's leadership and own popular support (still well above 80 percent) remains to be seen. But it is worth noting that the Russian Communist Party, the second largest in the country and itself somewhat divided over the Stalinist past, has decided to put Stalin's image on its campaign materials for the forthcoming parliamentary elections in September.

Has Washington Gone Rogue?

June 22

WHAT IS THE MEANING OF THE recent escalation of Washington's anti-Russian behavior? Consider only its growing NATO military buildup on Russia's western borders, refusal to cooperate with Moscow against the Islamic State in Syria, and the Obama administration's unwillingness to compel the US-backed government in Kiev to implement a negotiated settlement of the Ukrainian civil war. Is an undeclared US war against Russia already underway? Given that many US allies are unhappy with these developments, has Washington gone "rogue"? And does the recent spate of US warfare "information" reflect this reality?

Undoubtably, there is some alarming evidence. NATO's "exercises" on Russia's borders on land, sea, and in the air are becoming permanent. The Obama administration refuses to separate its "moderate oppositionists" in

Syria from anti-Assad fighters who are affiliated with terrorist groups, despite having promised to do so. There is the unprecedented public demand by 51 State Department "diplomats" that Obama launch air strikes against Assad's Syrian army, which is allied with Moscow, even if it might mean "military confrontation with Russia." And we have the questionable allegation that the Kremlin hacked files of the Democratic National Committee followed by a NATO statement that hacking a member state might now be regarded as war against the entire military alliance, requiring military retaliation.

Some of Washington's European and other allies clearly are unhappy with these developments, even opposed to them. The German Foreign Minister, for example, denounced NATO's ongoing buildup as "war-mongering." Several major European countries, which (unlike the United States) are suffering the reciprocal costs of economic sanctions on Russia are expressing discontent with them. There is the relative success of Russia's international economic conference in St. Petersburg last week, hosted by President Putin personally, whom the Obama administration continues to try to "isolate." There is even a growing political and security relationship between Israeli Prime Minister Benjamin Netanyahu and the Russian president.

Whether or not Washington's behavior constitutes undeclared war, Putin warned, at the international conference, that if such US conduct continues it will mean "war." As a result, Moscow is preparing for the worst, bringing the two nuclear superpowers closer to their worst confrontation since the 1962 Cuban Missile Crisis.

Some American pundits think warlike steps by Washington will benefit Hillary Clinton in the presidential election. She has long and clearly associated herself with hardline US policies toward Russia, but the question is larger. Even though a presidential election is supposed to feature the best aspects of American democracy, including full public discussion of foreign policy, the mainstream media have largely deleted these vital questions from their election coverage. Given full coverage, including of Donald Trump's foreign-policy views, which are significantly unlike those of Clinton, especially regarding Russia, we might learn two important things. Would Trump's less hawkish positions appeal to American voters? And will those voters see through and reject establishment media cheerleading for, in effect, Washington's rogue-like flirting with war with Russia?

Blaming Brexit on Putin and Voters

June 29

FOR YEARS, I AND OTHERS HAVE pointed to the gradual disintegration of what Washington calls "the post–Cold War world order," even though Russia, the world's largest territorial country, was excluded by the expansion of NATO and the (in effect) US-led European Union. And even though multiple crises of this US-led "order"—from economic inequality and Europe's refugee crisis to the Ukrainian civil war—were abetted by Washington's own policies. Brexit is the most recent manifestation of this ongoing historic process.

But instead of reconsidering Western policies, the US political-media establishment is blaming Brexit on Putin for "ruthlessly playing a weak hand," as did a *New York Times* editorial on June 26, and on "imbecilic" British voters, as did *Times* columnist Roger Cohen on June 28. In fact, Putin took a determinedly neutral stand on Brexit throughout, partly because Moscow, unlike Washington, is hesitant to meddle so directly in elections in distant countries. But also because the Kremlin was—and remains—unsure as to whether Brexit might be on balance a "plus or minus" for Russia.

Judging by the debate still under way in Russian media, Moscow worries Brexit will be a "minus" due to adverse economic consequences for Russia. In addition, the Kremlin worries that with the UK soon to be outside the EU, the United States and its traditionally Russophobic British partner will now increase NATO "aggression" against Russia, as indeed a *Washington Post* editorial urged on June 27. Therefore, contrary to the legion of American cold warriors, Brexit evoked no "celebration in the Kremlin," only wait-and-see concern.

The denigration of British voters, who mostly voted their working and lower-middle class economic and social interests, as they saw them, is perhaps even more shameful. It reveals Western elite attitudes toward democracy and "imbecilic" citizens. Not surprisingly, the UK establishment, with US encouragement, is desperately seeking a way to reverse the Brexit referendum, much as the Republican establishment is trying to deprive Donald Trump of the presidential nomination he won democratically in the primaries.

This is not the first time ruling elites have shown their contempt for democratic process. Twenty-five years ago, in 1991, the Soviet nomenkla-tura, in pursuit of state property, disregarded a national referendum that by a much larger majority than in the Brexit case favored preserving the Soviet Union.

There's also some irony here. During the week that Brexit furthered the disintegration of the EU, Putin was further integrating Russia's economy and security with China and with the multinational Shanghai Cooperation Organization, which may soon include India and Pakistan. Considering the size of those economies and of their populace, who is being "isolated"—Putin or the American president who announced his determination "to isolate" him?

Considering the largely negative US role in world affairs since the end of the Soviet Union, not the least of which is its new Cold War against Russia, it may be time for an American Exit (Amexit) from Washington's ceaseless quest for international hegemony.

The Imperative of a US-Russian Alliance vs. Terrorism

July 6

PRESIDENT OBAMA'S GENERALS HAVE REPEATEDLY INSISTED that Russia under Vladimir Putin is the "number-one existential threat" in the world today. This is a virtually impeachable misconception of national security.

The evidence cited is mostly bogus—for example, that Putin is planning a military takeover of the three small Baltic states, perhaps also Poland, and that he seeks to break up the European Union. In reality, Putin needs a stable and prosperous EU as an essential Russian trading partner. And he wants security guarantees for Russia, instead of NATO's ongoing buildup, from the Baltics to the Black Sea, which will be ratified and made permanent at NATO's Warsaw summit on July 6-7. Any actual Russian threats today are primarily of the West's own making—reactions to US-led policies in recent years.

The real "number-one" threat, from the Middle East and Europe to the American homeland, is international terrorism. Today's terrorist organizations are a new phenomenon, no longer loners or tiny groups with a gun or a bomb, but a highly organized menace with state-like funding, armies, technology, modern communications, and a capacity to recruit adherents. Still worse, they are in search of radioactive materials to enrich their already highly destructive explosives, which could make areas they strike uninhabitable for many years. Imagine the consequences if the planes of 9/11 had had such materials aboard.

Russia—because of decades fighting terrorism at home and abroad and its geopolitical location both in the West and in the Islamic world—is America's essential partner in the struggle against this new terrorism. Moscow has experience, intelligence, and other assets that Washington and its current allies lack. It should be enough to remember that Moscow informed Washington about the Boston Marathon bombers months before they struck, but the warning was disregarded.

And yet, Washington has steadfastly excluded a willing Kremlin from its own ineffectual and often counter-productive "war against terrorism," refusing systematic cooperation with Moscow. For their part, mainstream media "analyses" about what to do, after each new terrorist act, rarely if ever even mention a role for Russia. This despite the considerable damage inflicted on the Islamic State in Syria by Putin's air campaign allied with Syrian Army and Iranian "boots on the ground"—an achievement only denigrated, when noted at all, by the US political-media establishment. It does so partly because of its Cold War against Russia, reflected in NATO's provocative build-up on Russia's Western borders, and because of Washington's self-defeating obsession with overthrowing Syrian President Assad.

There may be, however, a positive development. According to sources close to Obama, the president now wants at least a partial rapprochement with Russia before leaving office as part of his presidential legacy, beginning in Syria. Related reports were published by the *Washington Post*, though only to express strong opposition, inspired, it seems, by Secretary of Defense Ashton Carter, to any kind of détente with Putin.

American Cold Warriors understand that cooperation in Syria could spread to resolving the Ukrainian crisis and other US-Russian conflicts— that is, to ending or at least winding down the new Cold War. For his part, Putin recently made several public statements expressing his readiness for large-scale cooperation with Obama—"We do not hold grudges," he remarked—and in particular for a "broad anti-terrorism front."

The same sources also report that in this regard Obama is virtually alone in high-level Washington circles, even among his own White House security advisers. If so, there is yet another irony: Obama, who once vowed to "isolate" Putin—probably the world's busiest international statesman in recent months—may now find himself isolated in his own administration.

The Friends and Foes of Détente

July 20

IN RECENT WEEKS, THERE HAS BEEN a behind-the-scenes diplomacy on behalf of full US-Russian military cooperation against the Islamic State in Syria. With Secretary of State Kerry's visit to Moscow last week, the proposal became public. Understanding that a mini-détente in Syria could spread to US-Russian conflicts elsewhere—particularly to the NATO buildup on Russia's border, the conflict over Ukraine, and nuclear-weapons policies—political forces in the American establishment escalated their opposition. They further demonized Putin, charging Obama with "appeasement," and threatened to ban Russia from the upcoming Olympic games in Rio de Janeiro.

The failed coup in Turkey may be an important factor in this struggle, though as with the failed coup against Soviet leader Mikhail Gorbachev 25 years ago, in August 1991, we may not learn the full story for some time. Nonetheless, Turkish President Recep Tayyip Erdoğan, increasingly alienated from the EU and fellow members of NATO, is likely now to resume his previously close relationship with Moscow. If so, he may end his obstruction of the proposed alliance against the Islamic State in Syria.

At the same time, Obama's formal condemnation of the coup has unnerved the US-backed government in Kiev, which came to power in 2014 by overthrowing a president who had also been popularly elected. In response, there is some evidence that Ukraine's current president, Petro Poroshenko, is escalating his military attacks on rebel Donbass, presumably to revive his fading political support in the West.

Meanwhile, at the Republican National Convention in Cleveland, Trump representatives rejected an attempt by cold warriors to write into the party platform a promise to increased US military aid to Kiev—Obama has long refused to do so despite considerable public and private pressure—reinforcing earlier statements by Trump that he, unlike Hillary Clinton, is pro-détente. In response, cold warriors confirmed that there is indeed a new Cold War by echoing an ugly feature of the preceding one—McCarthyism. They accused the Trump campaign of being in cahoots with Putin, even having received money from Moscow.

I have argued for more than 10 years that Washington policy was leading to a renewed Cold War with Moscow. The return of Cold-War Olympic politics and McCarthy-like slurs should eliminate any doubt about the nature of today's US-Russian relations and the vital importance of a new détente.

Neo-McCarthyism

July 27

HAVING ENTERED ACADEMIC RUSSIAN STUDIES IN the 1960s, I recall that even then the field was still afflicted by remnants of the self-censorship bred by the McCarthyism of the 1940s and 1950s. Cold War brings with it this kind of limitation on free speech, so I am not surprised that it may be happening again as a result of the new Cold War with "Putin's Russia." This time, however, it is coming significantly from longstanding liberals who purported to protect us against such civil liberties abuses.

Many liberals and their publications have recently branded Donald Trump as Putin's "puppet" (Franklin Foer), "de facto agent" (Jeffrey Goldberg),

"Kremlin client" (Timothy Snyder). *New York Times* columnist Paul Krugman spells out the implication that Trump "would, in office, actually follow a pro-Putin foreign policy, at the expense of America's allies and her own self-interest." These disgraceful allegations are based on little more than a mistranslation of a casual remark Putin made about Trump, Trump's elliptical suggestions that he may favor détente with Moscow, his tacit endorsement of Obama's refusal to escalate the military conflict in Ukraine, and Russian business relations of Trump's "associates" of the kind eagerly sought since the late 1980s by many American corporations, from ExxonMobil to MacDonald's.

This is, of course, an ominous recapitulation of McCarthy's accusations, which seriously damaged American democracy and ruined many lives. Still worse, this Kremlin-baiting of Trump is coming from the Clinton campaign, which most of the liberals involved support, as reflected in a page-one *Times* story headlined "A Trump-Putin Alliance." Clinton apparently intends to run against Trump-Putin. If so, the new Cold War can only become more dangerous, especially if she wins and if this neo- McCarthyite tactic reflects her hawkish views on "Putin's Russia."

Perhaps not unrelated, Obama's proposal for a US-Russian alliance against the Islamic State in Syria, with its potential for easing the conflict in Ukraine and NATO's buildup on Russia's borders, is now being openly opposed by Secretary of Defense Carter. As a result, it seems, the original proposal to Putin was withdrawn for one that would compel Moscow to accept the longstanding US policy of removing Syrian President Assad. Not surprisingly, it was rejected by Putin, though Secretary of State Kerry has resumed negotiations with his Russian counterpart Lavrov. Where the silent President Obama stands on this vital issue—as Russian and Syrian forces stand ready to take the crucial city of Aleppo, long held by jihadists—is unclear.

Cold-War Casualties From Kiev to the *New York Times*

August 17

T HE PRECEDING 40-YEAR COLD WAR WAS accompanied by intense high-level factional politics for and against US-Soviet Cold War relations. Sometimes the politics played out behind the scenes, sometimes openly, if obliquely, in the media. It is happening again, perhaps more dangerously and disgracefully.

Last week's still somewhat mysterious episode in Crimea was an important example. Russian President Putin declared that Kiev had sent agents with terrorist intent to (now) Russia's Crimean peninsula. They were captured and one or more Russian security agents killed. Putin said the episode showed that Kiev had no real interest in the Minsk peace talks and that he would no longer participate in them, the other participants being the leaders of Germany, France, and Ukraine. Kiev said the episode was a Russian provocation signaling Putin's intent to launch a large-scale "invasion" of Ukraine.

As must always be asked when a crime is committed, who had a motive? Putin had none that are apparent. Kiev, on the other hand, is in a deepening economic, social, and political crisis and losing its Western support, especially in Europe. It is fully possible that Kiev staged the episode to rally that flagging support by (yet again) pointing to Putin's impending "aggression." Washington seemed to support Kiev's version, raising the question as to whether a faction in the Obama administration was also involved, especially since Europe, particularly Germany, openly doubted Kiev's version. If Putin is serious about quitting the Minsk negotiations, a larger war is now the only way to resolve the Ukrainian civil and proxy war—a way apparently favored by some factions in Washington, Kiev, and possibly in Moscow.

Factional politics were even clearer regarding Syria, where President Obama had proposed military cooperation with Russia against the Islamic State—in effect, finally accepting Putin's longstanding proposal—along with important agreements that would reduce the danger of nuclear war. The *Wall Street Journal* and the *Washington Post* had reported strong factional opposition to both of Obama's initiatives—in effect, a kind of détente with Russia.

Both initiatives have been halted, whether temporarily or permanently is unclear. We may soon know because Putin needs a decision by Obama now, as the crucial battle for Aleppo intensifies. Under his own pressure at home, Putin seems resolved to end the Islamic State's occupation of Syria, Aleppo being a strategic site, without or with US cooperation, which he would prefer to have.

Meanwhile, the *New York Times* continues to make its own factional contributions to the new Cold War, and to Hillary Clinton's presidential campaign, at the expense of its own journalistic standards. Consider its recent article about Paul Manafort, in effect Donald Trump's campaign manager. It alleges that Manafort committed pro-Russian and corrupt dealings on behalf of Ukraine's now deposed President Viktor Yanukovych when Manafort served him as a well-paid political adviser. The *Times* has already printed a number of neo-McCarthyite articles against Trump and his associates, labeling them Putin's "agents."

The Manafort article is another telling example. It violates several journalistic standards. Its source for Manafort's financial corruption in Ukraine came from Kiev's "Anti-Corruption Committee," which even the IMF regards as an oxymoron and a reason the funding organization has not released billions of dollars pledged to Kiev. Even if Manafort was corrupt, The *Times* must have known the questionable nature of the source when it received the "documents," but readers were not told.

More important politically, when working to rebrand Yanukovych as a presidential candidate after his earlier electoral defeat, Manafort was hardly "pro-Russian." Putin profoundly distrusted and personally disliked Yanukoyvch at that time.

One reason was fundamental. Manafort urged Yanukovych, in order to broaden his appeal from his electoral base in southeast Ukraine, to strike a pro-Western economic arrangement with the European Union instead of with Putin's Eurasian Economic Union. Yanukovych tried to do so and almost succeeded. (The last-minute collapse of EU negotiations detonated the Ukrainian crisis in November 2013.) Assuming the *Times* knew this well-known history—admittedly an assumption when it involves *Times* coverage of Russia—this too it did not tell its readers.

The paper's expose of Manafort was also highly selective. However financially corrupt he may have been, Manafort did no more politically in Ukraine, indeed considerably less, than had other well-paid American electoral advisers in other countries. All we need do, though the *Times* did not, is recall the 1996 reelection campaign of then Russian President Boris Yeltsin.

So desperate was the Clinton administration to save the failing but compliant Yeltsin from his Communist Party opponent, it arranged for American election operatives to encamp in Moscow to help manage his campaign. (The administration also arranged for billions of IMF dollars to be sent to enable Yeltsin to pay pensions, wages, and other arrears, some of which was stolen by Yeltsin's associates and diverted to a New York bank.) So large was the role of the American "advisers" in Yeltsin's (purported) victory that *Time* magazine bannered it, "Yanks to The Rescue," on its July 15, 1996 cover and ShowTime made a feature film, "Spinning Boris," about their heroic exploits as late as 2003. No one asked, as we should, whether any Americans should be so intimately involved in any foreign elections.

Finally, the revelation that Manafort had financial dealings with Russian "oligarchs" is ludicrous—and also highly selective. Which of the scores of American corporations doing business in Russia and neighboring countries, from ExxonMobil to McDonald's and Ford, have not, given Russia's oligarchic economic system?

The degradation of the *Times*—in effect, announced on its front page last week in a declaration that it would suspend its own journalistic standards in covering Trump and his presidential campaign—is especially lamentable. In the past, the *Times* set standards for aspiring young journalists. Judging by the growing number of young "journalists" who assail critics of US policy toward Russia as Kremlin "apologists," "stooges," and "useful idiots," rather than actually study the issues and report disagreements even-handedly, the *Times* is no longer an exemplar. Unprofessional, unbalanced journalism remains another casualty of this new Cold War.

More Lost Opportunities
September 7

THREE SIGNIFICANT BUT LITTLE-NOTED DEVELOPMENTS OCCURRED at the G20 meeting in China last week.

Following a private meeting with Russian President Putin, President

Obama retreated from their agreement for joint military action against the Islamic State in Syria. Obama blamed a lack of trust in Putin, but clearly he had capitulated to powerful opposition in Washington to any rapprochement with Moscow. Obama said talks would continue, but yet another lack of resolve on his part was more likely to reinforce Putin's lack of trust in the American president and make it harder for him to sell any such agreement to his own political elite in Moscow.

At the same time, Obama also withdrew his own proposals that would have made nuclear war considerably less likely. They entailed a mutual US-Russian declaration of a doctrine of no-first-use of nuclear weapons; and taking nuclear warheads off high-alert, giving both sides more than the current 14 minutes or so to determine whether or not the other had actually launched a nuclear attack and to decide whether or not to retaliate. Obama was said to have been persuaded by Strangelovian arguments by advisers that such a wise decision, long called for by experts, would undermine US national security.

And in Kiev, President Poroshenko unilaterally reversed the order of steps spelled out in the Minsk Accords to end the Ukrainian civil and proxy war. He declared that returning control of the Eastern border with Russia to Kiev had to be the first step of implementation, not the final step as spelled in the Minsk agreements. In effect, Poroshenko's announcement betrayed German Chancellor Merkel and French President Hollande, who had brokered the Minsk agreements.

Unless Poroshenko relents, he has ended the only existing option for negotiating an end to the Ukrainian conflict. It is hard to imagine that Poroshenko took this step without the permission of the Obama administration, particularly of Vice President Joseph Biden, who has been in charge of the "Ukrainian project" at least since 2014.

There was other largely unreported news at the G20 meeting. Two years ago, Obama declared his intention to "isolate" Putin in world affairs. At the G20 meeting, the Russian president was the most sought-after leader by other world leaders. Obama, on the other hand, seemed marginalized apart from the formal ceremonies. Whether this was because he is a "lame duck" president or is no longer taken seriously as a foreign-policy leader, or both, is a matter of interpretation.

Unlike in the American political-media establishment, there was little evidence at the G20 meeting of the demonization of Putin, which has been a central feature of US policy toward Russia for several years. In this regard, America under Obama hardly seems to be the "leader of the free world."

Despite their pro-forma stances, other countries, including European ones, may continue to drift away from Washington in their actual relations with Russia.

As for the current US presidential campaign, there was little evidence at the G20 meeting that other capitals took seriously Washington charges (all without actual evidence) that Putin's Kremlin was trying to disrupt or decide the outcome of the election. In Europe, for example, a full debate is under way about relations with Russia, while in the US establishment anyone who proposes better relations, particularly Donald Trump, is subjected to neo-McCarthyite charges of being a "Kremlin client" or "Putin puppet."

Undeterred, Trump renewed his call for what once meant "détente," arguing that it would be better to have "friendly" relations with Russia, even a partnership, than today's exceedingly hostile relationship. In effect, Trump has become the pro-détente candidate in the 2016 presidential election, a position previously also taken by other Republican presidents—Eisenhower, Nixon, and Reagan. The pro–Cold War party's refusal to engage Trump on these vital issues, instead of Kremlin-baiting him, continues to be detrimental to US national security and to American democracy.

Another Endangered Chance to Diminish the New Cold War

September 14

TWO POSSIBLE DIPLOMATIC BREAKTHROUGHS, INVOLVING SYRIA and Ukraine, might end or substantially reduce the US-Russian proxy wars in those countries and thus the new Cold War itself.

Representing their respective bosses, Presidents Obama and Putin, Secretary of State Kerry and Foreign Minister Lavrov have announced a plan that, if implemented in the next seven days, would lead to joint US-Russian operations against the terrorist organizations ISIS and Al-Nusra in Syria. If so, the result could be an American-Russian military alliance, the first since World War II, that might end both the war in Syria and the dangerous escalation of the new Cold War elsewhere.

The nearly simultaneous announcements of a unilateral cease fire by Donbass rebels and of a willingness to move on home-rule legislation for Donbass by Ukrainian President Poroshenko, which he has previously refused to do, strongly suggested that this possible diplomatic breakthrough, in effect implementing the Minsk peace accords, was timed to coincide with the one regarding Syria. Given the vital role of Syria and Ukraine in the Cold War, this two-front détente diplomacy represents a fateful opportunity, to be seized or lost as were previous ones.

But opposition to the Obama-Putin Syrian diplomacy is fierce, especially in Washington. It is openly expressed by Department of Defense Secretary Carter and faithfully echoed in leading media, particularly the *Washington Post*, the *New York Times*, and MSNBC. The primary tactic is to further vilify Putin as an unworthy American partner in any regard—an approach driven by years of Putin-phobia and now by an awareness that cooperation in Syria would mark Russia's full return as a great power on the world stage.

Much now depends on whether or not Obama will fight for his own anti–Cold War diplomacy, as President Reagan did in the 1980s but as Obama repeatedly has failed to do. His foreign-policy legacy is at stake, as are international relations.

Opposition to a diplomatic breakthrough in Ukraine is also fierce and potentially dangerous for Poroshenko. Heavily armed ultra-right Ukrainian forces continue to threaten to overthrow him if he yields to European pressure to grant more home rule to rebel Donbass. Under pressure from France, Germany, and possibly the White House, Poroshenko may now think he has no choice, or he may be playing for time, as some observers think. Either way, the Ukrainian conflict is at a turning point, for better or worse, as is the one in Syria.

Unavoidably, these developments are spilling over into the American presidential campaign. However ironically, Donald Trump has, in his own way, like Obama, called for US-Russian military cooperation in Syria. Certainly, his position in this regard is considerably closer to that of President Obama (no matter what the latter unwisely continues to say publicly about Putin) than is that of Hillary Clinton, who thus far has maintained her considerably more hawkish positions both on Russia and Syria.

A full debate on these fateful issues is long overdue in American politics, especially in a presidential electoral year. The mainstream media has all but banned it with neo-McCarthyite allegations against Trump. Will the mainstream media now play their obligatory role or continue to promote the new Cold War?

Who's Making US Foreign Policy?

September 21

THE PRECEDING 40-YEAR COLD WAR WITNESSED many instances of high-level attempts to sabotage détente policies of US and Soviet leaders. It is happening again in the new Cold War, as evidenced when American war planes unexpectedly attacked Syrian Army forces.

The attack blatantly violated preconditions of the Obama-Putin plan for a US-Russian alliance against terrorist forces in Syria. Considering that US military intelligence knew the area very well and that the Department of Defense, headed by Ashton Carter, had openly expressed opposition to the Obama-Putin plan, the attack was almost certainly not "accidental," as DOD claims and as American media similarly reports.

If the attack was intentional, we are reminded of the power of the American war party, which is based not only in DOD but in segments of the intelligence agencies, State Department, Congress, and in the mainstream media, notably the *Washington Post*. Judging by Ambassador Samantha Power's tirade against Russia at the UN, not even Obama's own team fully supports his overtures to Moscow, undertaken in part perhaps to enhance his desultory foreign policy legacy.

Why is the war party so adamantly opposed to any cooperation with Russia anywhere in the world when it is manifestly in US interests, as in Syria? Several considerations play a role. Among them, only Russian President Putin, of major foreign leaders, has politically opposed the neocon/liberal interventionist aspiration for a US-dominated "world order." Hence the incessant demonizing of Putin.

Still more, Russia's return as an international great power, 25 years after the end of the Soviet Union, contradicts and offends the ideological premises of this aspiration. Another but little-noted example is Moscow's recent plan to mediate the decades-long Israeli-Palestinian conflict, a diplomatic initiative based on increasingly warm relations between Putin's government and Israel. Any cooperation with Moscow would therefore validate the "resurgent Russia" phenomenon so resented by the American war party.

One way American cold warriors challenge Russia's role in world affairs today is to denigrate its elections, as though they are mere replicas of Soviet-era charades. Several little-noted results of the September Russian parliamentary (Duma) elections are therefore worth emphasizing.

The elections were relatively "free and fair." (As everywhere, such judgments should be in the context of a country's own history, not our own.) This said while understanding that going back to the "democratic" Yeltsin years, the Kremlin has regularly redistributed some 5 to 10 percent of the votes to its own party or to other parties it wishes to play a minority role in the Duma.

This time those votes seem to have been taken from the only real nationwide opposition party, the Communist Party, which probably received closer to 20 percent of the votes than the just over 13 percent registered, and given to the Kremlin party and to a minority party. (The latter, unlike the Communists, habitually votes for the Kremlin's economic and social legislation.) Contrary to most preelection polling, the Kremlin party got 54 percent, a "constitutional majority," as it is called, suggesting that the Putin leadership may be planning major policy changes at home.

One other result should be emphasized. The several "liberal," pro-Western parties, without any help or harm by the Kremlin, garnered a total of barely 4 percent of the vote. This may be the most authentic result of the election: there is no longer any electoral base for such politics in Russia.

Most American commentators blame the outcome on Putin's repression, but a much larger factor has been US Cold War policies, which are deeply resented by a large majority of Russians. Indeed, a number of independent Russian commentators concluded that the electoral results were a reaffirmation of popular support for Putin and against US-led assaults on his leadership and reputation.

Slouching Toward War?

October 6

THE OBAMA ADMINISTRATION HAS TERMINATED MONTHS-LONG negotiations with Moscow for a joint US-Russian campaign against jihad terrorist forces in Syria. Cooperation in Syria would have been the first major episode of détente in the new Cold War, indeed the first US-Russian military alliance since World War II. Its spirit might have spread to the dangerous conflicts in Ukraine and on Russia's border with Eastern Europe, where NATO continues to build up its forces.

The Syrian agreement was sabotaged not by Russia, as is alleged in Washington and by the mainstream media, but by American enemies of détente, first and foremost in the Department of Defense. DOD's opposition was so intense that one of its spokesmen told the press it might disobey an Obama presidential order to share intelligence with Moscow, as called for by the agreement.

It was a flagrant threat to disregard the US constitution. A *New York Times* editorial not only failed to protest the threat but appeared to endorse it. Other major media seemed not even to notice the possibility of a constitutional crisis, another indication of how badly the new Cold War, and the demonization of Russian President Putin, has degraded the US political-media establishment.

The consequences of thwarted diplomacy in Syria are already evident. American politicians and media are calling for military action against Russian-Syrian forces, in particular, imposition of a "no-fly zone," which would almost certainly lead to war with Russia. Others call for more economic sanctions against Russia, perhaps to ward off growing West European attitudes favoring an end to existing sanctions.

In any event, developments in Syria have now deepened the new Cold War in words and deeds. This is the case in Moscow as well. Putin, who has long pursued negotiations with the West over the objections of his own hardliners, now seems resolved to destroy the jihadist forces encamped in Aleppo without the American partner he had hoped for. Meanwhile, talk of war also fills Russian media, and the Putin government has just begun a highly unusual nation-wide "civil defense" exercise to prepare the country for that eventuality.

In short, the collapse of diplomacy in Syria has fully remilitarized US-Russian relations and brought the countries closer to war than at any time since the Cuban Missile Crisis. Unlike during the preceding Cold War, none of this is being discussed critically in establishment American media. The *New York Times* and the *Washington Post*, for example, publish articles and editorials, one after the other, declaring Putin to be an "outlaw" and "rogue" leader unfit to be an American partner on any front. In the mainstream, no one proposes or is permitted to propose any rethinking of US policies that may have contributed to this dire situation.

No one asks, for example, if the Kremlin might be right in insisting that the overthrow of the Assad government, the primary US goal, would only strengthen terrorist forces in Syria, whose defeat is Moscow's primary objective. In this connection, Moscow charges that détente in Syria failed in large part because Washington and its allies continue to arm and coddle, directly or indirectly, Syrian terrorists and their "moderate" anti-Assad abettors.

This factor, for which there is considerable evidence, also is not explored or discussed in the US media, even in a presidential election year. Instead, CBS News' *60 Minutes*, which, like the *Times*, was once a gold standard of professional American journalism, recently broadcast a nuclear warmongering segment giddily marveling that the United States would soon have more "usable" nuclear weapons to deploy against Russia.

Again, where was the publicly silent President Obama while his proposed détente was being killed by members of his own administration? Russians and West Europeans are also asking this question.

Washington Warmongers, Moscow Prepares

October 12

WE SHOULD BE "SHOCKED" LESS BY Donald Trump's sexual antics or by Hillary Clinton's misdeeds as secretary of state than by the entire US political-media establishment's indifference to Washington's drift toward war with Russia.

Since the breakdown of the Obama-Putin agreement to cooperate militarily against terrorists in Syria—a failure for which the Obama administration is primarily responsible—Washington has escalated its warfare rhetoric against the Kremlin and particularly Russian President Putin. The man with whom the Obama administration proposed to partner with in Syria only two weeks ago is now denounced as a "war criminal" for Russia's fight against terrorists in Aleppo, which was to be "liberated" by the now aborted US-Russian military alliance. The ever-bellicose *Washington Post* was more specific, publishing a leaked account of how Putin might be arrested outside of Russia and put on trial.

But the first victim might have been Secretary of State Kerry, who negotiated and advocated the proposed alliance and who now must level "war crimes" accusations against Russia, dealing a considerable blow to his own reputation. Putting another nail in the coffin of its jettisoned cooperation with the Kremlin, the White House also officially accused the Putin leadership of trying to undermine the American electoral system through systematic hacking, though it presented no real evidence.

Meanwhile, mainstream media continue to base their coverage of US national security in this regard on unrelenting vilification of Putin, not on actual US interests. Any talk of partnership with Russia, though still advocated by Donald Trump, is being widely traduced as "insanity," as, for example, by MSNBC's unabashedly Russophobic Rachel Maddow.

Moscow is reacting in kind to Washington's words and deeds. The reaction includes unusually harsh speeches by Putin and Foreign Minister Lavrov (formerly Kerry's partner); an unusual nationwide civil-defense exercise; a proposal to give military officials control over regional political leaders in the event of war; and a beefing up of Russian ground-to-air missile defense systems in Syria. While Lavrov spoke of an American policy driven by "aggressive Russophobia," Putin said normal relations could be restored only by Washington reversing all of its Cold War policies in recent years, from NATO expansion to Russia's borders to economic sanctions. Though clearly Putin did not mean this literally, it seems to have been his most expansive condition to date.

For those of us with historical memory, there is a precedent for a way out in dark times in US-Russian relations. Only a generation ago, in the mid- and late 1980s, President Ronald Reagan decided to meet halfway in very fraught times repeatedly with Soviet leader Mikhail Gorbachev. A breakthrough as achieved by Reagan and Gorbachev is urgently needed, but no such leader seems likely to occupy the White House any time soon, unless it might be Trump.

Did the White House Declare War on Russia?

October 19

A STATEMENT BY VICE PRESIDENT JOSEPH BIDEN on NBC's *Meet the Press* on October 16, pre- released on October 14, stunned Moscow, though it was scarcely noted in the American media. In response to a question about alleged Kremlin hacking of Democratic Party headquarters in order to disrupt the presidential election and throw it to Donald Trump, Biden said the Obama administration was preparing to send Putin a harsh "message," presumably in the form of some kind of cyber-attack.

The Kremlin spokesman and several leading Russian commentators characterized Biden's announcement as a virtual "American declaration of war on Russia" and as the first ever in history. At this potentially explosive stage in the new Cold War, Biden's statement, which must have been approved by the White House, could scarcely have been more dangerous or reckless.

Biden was reacting, of course, to official US charges of Kremlin political hacking. No actual evidence for this allegation has yet been produced, only suppositions or, as Glenn Greenwald has pointed out, "unproven assertions." While the political-media establishment has uncritically stated the allegation as fact, a MIT expert, Professor Theodore Postol, has written there is "no technical way that the US intelligence community could know who did the hacking if it was done by sophisticated nation-state actors." Instead, the charges, leveled daily by the Clinton campaign as part of its neo-McCarthyite Kremlin-baiting of Trump, are mostly political. We should ask why some US intelligence officials have permitted themselves to be used for this unprofessional purpose.

Still more, the warlike context includes a stunning reversal of the American political-media establishment's narrative of the ongoing battle for the Syrian city of Aleppo. Only a few weeks ago, as I pointed out, President Obama had agreed with Putin on a joint US-Russian military campaign against "terrorists" in Aleppo. That agreement collapsed primarily due to an attack by US warplanes on Syrian forces. Russia and its Syrian allies continued their air assault on east Aleppo but now, according to Washington and its mainstream media, against anti-Assad "rebels."

Where have the jihad terrorists gone? They have been deleted from the US narrative, which now accuses Russia of "war crimes" in Aleppo for the same military campaign in which Washington was to have been a full partner. Equally obscured is that west Aleppo, largely controlled by Assad's forces, is also being assaulted—by "rebels"—and children are dying there as well.

And why is there no US government or media concern about the children who will almost certainly die in the American-backed campaign to recapture Mosul, in Iraq? Here too the stenographic American media has gone from the fog of cold war to falsification.

Trump Could End the New Cold War

November 16

WILL, OR CAN, A PRESIDENT TRUMP enact a policy of détente—replacing elements of conflict with elements of cooperation—in US relations with Russia? As we saw earlier, détente had a long 20th-century history. Indeed, its major episodes were initiated by Republican presidents, from Eisenhower and Nixon to, most spectacularly, Reagan in 1985.

The history of détente teaches that at least four prerequisites are required: a determined American president who is willing to fight for the policy against fierce mainstream political opposition, including in his own party; a leader who can rally some public support by prominent figures who did not support his presidential candidacy; a president with like-minded appointees at his side; and A White House occupant who has a pro-détente partner in the Kremlin, as Reagan had with Soviet leader Gorbachev.

Whether or not he knows the history of détente, Trump seems determined. During his primary and presidential campaigns, he alone repeatedly called for cooperation with Moscow for the sake of US national security and refused to indulge in today's fact-free vilification of Russian President Putin. Trump also seems little impressed by the bipartisan foreign-policy establishment, even contemptuous of its record during the preceding two decades. The establishment's certain opposition is unlikely to deter him.

Less clear is whether or not many of Trump's previous opponents in either party will support détente or whether he will have in his inner circle of appointees—particularly a secretary of state and ambassador to Moscow— who will wisely advise and assist him in this vital pursuit, as Reagan had. As for a partner in the Kremlin, Putin is clearly ready for détente. He has said and demonstrated as much many times, contrary to commentary about him in the American media.

In many respects, as we have seen, the new Cold War is more dangerous than was the preceding 40-year Cold War. Three of its current fronts— Ukraine, the Baltic region, and Syria—are ever more fraught with the possibility of hot war. Détente succeeds, however, when mutual national interests are agreed upon and negotiated.

The Ukrainian civil and proxy war has become a disaster for Washington,

Moscow, and for the Ukrainian people themselves. Ending it is therefore a common interest, but perhaps the most difficult to negotiate. NATO's ongoing buildup up in the Baltic region and in Poland, and Russia's counter-buildup on its Western borders, are fraught with accidental or intentional war. Avoiding war, as Reagan and Gorbachev agreed, is an existential common interest.

If Trump is determined, he has the power to end the buildup and even reverse it, though the new eastern-most members of NATO will loudly protest. On the other hand, despite claims to the contrary, Russia represents no military threat to these countries, as wise Trump advisers will assure him. Agreement on Syria should be the easiest. Both Trump and Putin have insisted that the real threat there is not Syrian President Assad but the Islamic State and other terrorists. The first major step of a new détente might well be the US-Russian military alliance against terrorist forces that even President Obama once proposed but abandoned.

There are, of course, other new Cold War conflicts, large and smaller ones. Some could be easily and quickly negotiated in order to build elite and popular support for détente in the US. This could begin with the "banomania" both sides have enacted since 2014. For example, Putin could end the ban on American adoptions of Russian orphans, which wrecked the hopes of scores of American families and Russian children. Such a good-will step would give détente a human face and soften opposition in the US.

The largest ban is, of course, US and European economic sanctions on Russia, which Putin wants ended. A more complex issue, this is likely to come to the fore only if or when détente progresses. On the other hand, a number of European countries, which have suffered economically from Russia's counter-sanctions, also want them ended. Trump will not be without allies if he moves in this direction.

There are other considerations. History shows that successful, stable détente requires the give-and-take of diplomacy, something not practiced by the White House with Russia for several years. The standard version of why Obama's détente ("reset") failed, to take an often-cited example, is untrue. Putin did not wreck it. The Obama administration took Moscow's major concessions while making almost none of its own. In this regard, Trump's businessman model of negotiations may be an asset. Businessmen understand that a mutual interest (profit) is gained only when both sides make concessions.

There is also a larger question. As I explained previously, détente rests on what was formerly called "parity," in particular recognition that both sides

have legitimate national interests. For many years, due largely to the demonization of Putin, the American political-media establishment has implied
that Russia has no legitimate national interests of its own conception, not
even on its borders. Trump seems to think otherwise, but as with many of his
other elliptical statements, time will tell.

And there is this. Reagan and Gorbachev began with nuclear and other
military issues. Trump and Putin might do so as well—for example, by agreeing to take nuclear warheads off high-alert and adopting a mutual doctrine
of no-first-use of nuclear weapons, which Obama also briefly proposed but
also abandoned. Given current toxic relations between the two countries,
however, more political steps may be needed first.

Whether or not Trump vigorously pursues détente with Russia may tell us
more about his presidency generally if only because an American president usually has more freedom of action in foreign affairs than in other policy realms.
And no issue is now more important than the state of US-Russian relations.

The Friends and Foes of Détente, II

November 23

ANTI-DÉTENTE OPPOSITION HAS QUICKLY EXPRESSED ITSELF in response
to President-elect Trump's still elliptical indications that he may seek
a strategic partner in Russian President Putin. The opposition is led in the
Senate by the usual Cold-War bipartisan axis that includes John McCain,
Lindsay Graham, and Benjamin Cardin, and in the print media by the *New
York Times* and the *Washington Post*. Their thinking and goals are expressed
by one of their stenographers, *Post* columnist Josh Rogin. He warns readers
that détente is both impermissible and unattainable because of Putin's "long-
term strategy to undermine the stability and confidence of liberal Western
democracies."

There is, of course, no evidence that this is Putin's goal. The allegation merely recapitulates existential language of the preceding 40-year Cold War, as though the Soviet Union never ended. Rogin concludes by assuring readers that these American foes of détente are readying a campaign, here and abroad, to "stop the next Russian reset [the term Obama used for détente] before it even begins." If Trump is determined to reduce or even end the new Cold War, another historic struggle over détente has thus begun.

There is, however, a new important factor. Europe is playing a larger and more active role in this Cold War than it did in the preceding one, and there the friends and foes of détente are more evenly divided. Socially, politically, and electorally, a growing number of European countries are increasingly opposed to confronting and trying to isolate Russia. For economic reasons, they are also eager to end the economic sanctions imposed on Moscow by the West.

Non-anti-Russia governments (not necessarily "pro-Russian" ones) have recently come to power in Moldova and Bulgaria. More are possible within a year or so in Austria, Italy, and elsewhere, even in Germany. The Netherlands, Greece, Cyprus, and Spain have already expressed discontent with the sanctions and with the stalemated war in Ukraine. And one exceedingly anti-Russian government, the United Kingdom, has left the European Union via Brexit.

In this respect, Europe may be diminishing its political deference to the United States, currently the most anti-Russian, pro–Cold War of the major powers, along with the UK, and finally edging toward its own foreign policy. If so, what this means for the heralded "transatlantic alliance" may depend on whether or not Trump reaches out for pro-détente allies in Europe.

Just how much relations with Russia are in flux is indicated even by outgoing President Obama. He recently stopped referring to the United States as "the indispensable nation" in world affairs and termed it instead "an indispensable nation," suggesting America might have equal partners. And whereas he once dismissed Russia as a weak "regional power," he has revised that formulation considerably. Now, according to Obama, "Russia is an important country. It is a military superpower... It has influence around the world. And in order for us to solve many big problems around the world, it is in our interest to work with Russia and obtain their cooperation." This is the traditional language of détente.

False Narratives, Not "Fake News," Are the Danger

November 30

Dᴇꜱᴘɪᴛᴇ ᴛʜᴇ (ʟᴀʀɢᴇʟʏ ʙᴏɢᴜꜱ) ꜰᴜʀᴏʀ ᴏᴠᴇʀ "fake news," entrenched false narratives of the new Cold War are the real threat to US national security and to the détente policies that President-Elect Trump suggests he might pursue. I have commented on them intermittently in recent years, but it is important at this crucial political moment to reiterate five of them:

1. That Russian President Putin is solely responsible for the new Cold War and its growing dangers on several fronts, from the confrontation over Ukraine to Syria. If this is true, there is no need for Washington to rethink or change any of its policies, but it is not true.

2. That President Obama's declared intention, in 2014, to "isolate Putin's Russia" in international affairs has been successful, and therefore Putin is desperate to be released from the political wilderness. This too is untrue. Since 2014, Putin has been perhaps the busiest national leader of any major power on the world stage, from China and India to the Middle East and even Europe. Arguably, the world is changing profoundly, and Putin is more attuned to those changes than is the bipartisan US foreign-policy establishment.

3. That Washington's Cold War policies toward Russia have strengthened the vaunted US-European "transatlantic alliance," as exemplified by NATO's buildup on Russia's western borders. In reality, a growing number of European countries are trending away from Washington's hard-line policies toward Moscow, among them France, Austria, The Netherlands, Italy, Hungary, and others, perhaps even Germany. And this does not include Brexit, which removed hard-line London from European policy-making. This does not mean these countries are becoming "pro-Russian," as crude media coverage would have it, but less anti-Russian for the sake of their own national interests.

4. That "Russia's aggression," its "invasion," is the primary cause of the Ukrainian crisis, which is still the political epicenter of the new Cold War. In reality, the underlying cause is a civil war that grew out of Ukraine's diverse history, politics, social realities, and culture. This means that negotiations, not more war, are the only solution.

5. The orthodox US narrative of the Syrian civil war has, on the other hand, suddenly changed. While Obama was negotiating with Putin for joint US-Russian military action in Syria, "terrorists" were said to be entrenched in Aleppo and other anti-Assad strongholds. Since that diplomacy failed, the *New York Times*, the *Washington Post*, CNN, and other mainstream media have rewritten the narrative to pit Syrian, Russian, and Iranian forces against benign anti-Assad "rebels" and "insurgents." In Iraq, in Mozul, however, the US-led war is said to be against "terrorists" and "jihadists." Thus, in Aleppo, Russia is reported to be committing "war crimes" while in Mozul these are called "collateral damages."

All of us live according to the stories we tell ourselves. When policy-makers act according to false narratives, the result is grave dangers, as we are now experiencing in the new Cold War. To escape these dangers, Washington must first get the history right, particularly of its own role in creating it.

Cold War Hysteria vs. National Security

December 15

SINCE THE PRESIDENTIAL ELECTION, ALLEGATIONS HAVE grown that Kremlin cyber-invasions of the Democratic National Committee and dissemination of its materials severely damaged Hillary Clinton's campaign and contributed to Donald Trump's victory. Thus far, no actual evidence has been made public to support these unprecedented and exceedingly dangerous charges.

Nor are the motives being attributed to Russian President Putin credible. Why would a Kremlin leader whose mission has been to rebuild Russia with economic and other partnerships with the West seek to undermine the political systems of those countries, not only in America but also in Europe, as is being alleged?

Judging by the public debate among Russian policy intellectuals close to the Kremlin, it is not clear that it so favored the largely unknown, inexperienced, and unpredictable Trump. But even if Putin was presented with the possibility of stealing and publicizing DNC emails, he certainly would have understood that such crude Russian interference in a US election would become known and thus work in favor of Clinton, not Trump.

Nonetheless, these Trump-Putin allegations are inspiring an alarming Cold War hysteria in the American political-media establishment, still without facts to support them. One result is more neo-McCarthyite slurring of people who dissent from this narrative. A December 12 *New York Times* editorial alleged that Trump had "surrounded himself with Kremlin lackeys." And Senator John McCain ominously warned that anyone who disagreed with his longstanding political jihad against Putin "is lying."

A kind of witch hunt may be unfolding of the kind the *Washington Post* tried to instigate with its now discredited "report" of scores of American websites said to be "fronts for Russian propaganda." It could spread to higher levels. For example, Trump's nominee for secretary of state, Rex Tillerson, is charged with being "a friend of Putin" as a result of having struck a major deal for ExxonMobil for Russian oil reserves. Surely Tillerson was obliged to do this as the company's CEO.

Several motives seem to be behind this bipartisan campaign against the President-elect, who is being associated with all manner of Russian misdeeds. One is to reverse the Electoral College vote. Another is to exonerate the Clinton campaign from its electoral defeat by blaming Putin instead and thereby trying to maintain the Clinton wing's grip on the Democratic Party. Yet another is to delegitimize Trump even before he is inaugurated. And no less important, to prevent the détente with Russia that Trump seems to want.

We therefore face the growing possibility of two profound and related crises. One is an ever more perilous Cold War with Russia. The other is a new American president so politically paralyzed he cannot cope with such dangers as previous presidents have done.

Part III

UNPRECEDENTED DANGERS

2017

Did Putin Really Order a "Cyber–Pearl Harbor"?

January 4

CONFRONTATIONS BETWEEN WASHINGTON AND MOSCOW — NOW EXTENDING from the Baltic region, Ukraine, and Syria to the American political system itself—are becoming more dangerous than was the US-Soviet nuclear confrontation over Cuba in 1962. Unlike in 1962, when the Kennedy administration made public evidence of Soviet missile silos under construction on the neighboring island, the Obama administration has presented no concrete evidence that the Kremlin, directed by President Putin, hacked the Democratic National Committee and arranged for damaging materials to be disseminated in order to put Donald Trump in the White House.

Nonetheless, even as a number of independent cyber experts doubt the plausibility of White House intelligence reports, powerful political interests are inflating the story to imply that a US warlike act of retaliation is required. A *Washington Post* editorial on Dec. 31, for example, declared that America had suffered "a real cyber-Pearl Harbor" at Putin's hands. The motives of these political interests vary, as we have seen, from exonerating Hillary Clinton of her defeat to crippling Trump before he even enters the White House. In resolving the Cuban Missile Crisis wisely, President Kennedy did not have to cope with these kinds of debilitating public divisions and toxic allegations.

Today's hysteria, suffused with growing neo-McCarthyism and a witch hunt–like search for "Putin's friends" in the United States, first and foremost, of course, Trump himself, are making any rational, fact-based discourse nearly impossible. Public discussion is urgently needed regarding NATO's buildup on Russia's western borders, the civil/proxy wars in Ukraine and Syria, and more generally a less confrontational US policy toward Russia. With the *New York Times*, the *Washington Post*, and their echo chambers on cable-TV networks labeling anyone who rethinks US policy a "Trump apologist" and "Putin apologist," civil discourse so vital to democratic resolutions, and to US national security, has become nearly impossible.

Trump and Putin have tried to diminish the hysteria. Putin's attempt, declining to adopt the traditional Cold War tit-for-tat approach of immediately expelling 35 American "intelligence operatives" from Russia, raises a question about the Obama administration. Did whoever advised the president to expel 35 Russians and their families within 72 hours understand the order would violate the hallowed tradition of Russian New Year's Eve, the most sentimental of holidays, which families spend together at home, not in clubs or otherwise dispersed? If so, it was a malicious decision that enabled Putin to be magnanimous toward the American families affected in Russia. On the other hand, if Obama's advisers did not know this simple fact, it may explain his disastrous Russia policies since taking office.

Meanwhile, Putin has his own political problems. His generals, tasked with taking the Syrian city of Aleppo, had already protested his repeated "humanitarian ceasefires" as thwarting their mission. Now hard-liners are asking why Putin gave such a "soft" response to Obama's sanctions and expulsions as retaliation for Russia's purported role in the US presidential election. This too Obama should have been made to understand by his advisers. Was he? Or was Obama determined to prevent Trump from changing the soon-to-be former president's approach to Russia?

The Real Enemies of US Security

January 11

NOT SURPRISINGLY, NOW THERE IS MORE: allegations that the Kremlin possesses compromising materials, from sexual to financial, that would enable it to "blackmail" President-elect Trump. The leaked "documents" were first gleefully trumpeted by CNN on January 10 and quickly followed by a tsunami of echoing media stories. The allegedly incriminating documents themselves were then published by *BuzzFeed*—all raising serious questions about the sub-tabloid reporting of admittedly "unsubstantiated," even "unverifiable," allegations, though few people raised any. More importantly, who planned this obviously coordinated strike against Trump, and why?

At least two conflicting interpretations are possible. Either Trump is about to become a potentially treasonous American president. Or powerful domestic forces are trying for other reasons to destroy his presidency before it begins. Even if the allegations are eventually regarded as untrue, they may permanently slur and thus cripple Trump as a foreign-policy president, especially in trying to cope with the exceedingly dangerous new Cold War with Russia. That itself would constitute a grave threat to American national security—one created not by Trump or Putin but by whoever is responsible for these new "revelations."

Their timing is suspicious. They come on the heels of the just-released "Intelligence Community's" utterly vacuous "Assessment" that Kremlin leader Putin directed a campaign, including hacking of the Democratic National Committee, intended to discredit Mrs. Clinton and put Trump in the White House. Anti-Trump media widely trumpeted this story. But even the determinedly anti-Trump, anti-Putin *New York Times* "analysis", by Scott Shane on January 7, initially had reservations. It found that the much awaited "intelligence community" report was "missing…hard evidence to back up the agencies' claims"—that there was an "absence of any proof".

The anti-Trump "dossier" said to have been compiled by a former British intelligence agent, Christopher Steele, and leaked to CNN and *BuzzFeed*, is no more convincing. Despite Steele's claims of "Kremlin sources," it seems culled from long circulating Russian, American, UK, and other NATO scuttlebutt, of the "Intel" variety.

Even before the latest "revelations," there has been an unprecedented media campaign to defame Trump as a would-be traitor in his relations with Russia. On the evening of January 4, a CNN paid contributor characterized the next president as a Russian "fifth columnist." No one on the panel dissented or demurred. Subsequently, *Washington Post* columnists warned that Trump might commit "treason" as president or even replicate with Putin the notorious 1939 Nazi-Soviet Pact. Another columnist set out the articles of Trump's impeachment even before his inauguration. Here too nothing so poisonous, or potentially detrimental to national security, or to the institution of the presidency itself, has occurred in modern American history, if ever.

Predictably, anti-Trump media are warning him, and the public, against being "skeptical" about the quality and motives of US intelligence agencies.

Given the long history of the CIA's misleading American presidents into disastrous wars, from the Bay of Pigs and Vietnam to Iraq and Libya, why would anyone think this is sound advice? National security requires a president who is able to evaluate critically intelligence reports or have people around him who can do so.

All this comes on the eve of Rex Tillerson's hearings for confirmation as secretary of state. Few doubt that Tillerson was a successful CEO of the global ExxonMobil Corporation, though some are charging that in doing so he too became "a friend of Putin."

This unfortunate occasion is a moment to make a somewhat related point. The United States does not need a "friend" in the Kremlin, as President Bill Clinton liked to boast he had in the often compliant and intoxicated Boris Yeltsin, but a national-security partner whose nation's interests are sufficiently mutual for sustained cooperation—for détente instead of Cold War. In this regard, Tillerson, whose professional success was based on reconciling national economic interests, would appear to be well qualified, though he too is being defamed for suggesting any kind of cooperation with Moscow, no matter the benefits to US national security.

What might Putin himself think about this political uproar in the United States? His own leadership motives are usually and wrongly surmised solely from the fact that he is "a former KGB agent," which appears to be his middle name in US media coverage. However formative that biographical circumstance may have been, it does enable Putin to analyze intelligence reports and understand politics inside national intelligence agencies.

His reaction to the US Intelligence Community Assessment may therefore have been shock over the embarrassing paucity of the report. He might even have reconsidered his long-sought cooperation between Russian and US intelligence in the fight against international terrorism. Putin might now conclude, they need us more than we do them. Considering the recent antics of US "Intel," he might not be wrong.

Ukraine Revisited

February 8

WITH FIGHTING HAVING ESCALATED BETWEEN THE US-backed Kiev government and Russian-backed rebels in Donbass, we must focus yet again on Ukraine's pivotal role in the new Cold War since 2013–2014. Here again, as we have seen elsewhere, widely disseminated false narratives obscure what really happened.

The orthodox US account that Russian President Putin alone is responsible for the new Cold War hangs largely on his alleged unprovoked "aggression" against Ukraine in 2014 and ever since. (The narrative is sustained in part by the near-total absence of American mainstream reporting of what is actually happening in Kiev-controlled or rebel-controlled territories.) In fact, Putin's actions both in Donbass, where an indigenous rebellion broke out against the overthrow of the legally elected president in Kiev three years ago, and in Crimea, which had been part of Russia for more than 200 years (about as long as the United States has existed), was a direct reaction to the longstanding campaign by Washington and Brussels to bring Ukraine into NATO's "sphere of influence."

That itself was a form of political aggression against the centuries of intimate relations between large segments of Ukrainian society and Russia, including family ties. At the very least, it was reckless and immoral for Washington and the European Union to impose upon Kiev a choice between Russia and the West, thereby fostering, if not precipitating, civil war. And to flatly reject Putin's counter-proposal for a three-way Ukrainian-Russian-EU economic relationship. In this regard, Washington and the EU bear considerable responsibility for the 10,000 who have died in the ensuing Ukrainian civil and proxy war. They have yet to assume any responsibility at all.

A false narrative also quickly emerged to explain the recent escalation of fighting along the ceasefire zone in Ukraine. There are no facts to support the US political-media establishment's contention that Putin initiated the escalation—all reported facts point to Kiev—or any logic whatsoever. Why would Putin, who has openly welcomed Trump's détente initiative, seek to provoke or challenge the new American president at this critical moment? Whether or not Kiev was actively encouraged by anti-détente forces in

Washington is unclear, but a real possibility. (Inflammatory remarks made by Senators John McCain and Lindsay Graham in Ukraine, in January, now circulating on a video, may be telling evidence.) If so, the blood of the 40 or more who died in the January–February fighting is on their hands as well.

What are the chances of Trump-Putin cooperation to end the Ukrainian crisis? If the country is not to fragment into two, three, or more parts, a united Ukraine will have to be militarily non-aligned (that is, not a member of NATO) and free to have prosperous economic relations with both Russia and the West.

The Minsk Accords, drafted by Germany and France and endorsed by Moscow and Kiev, would have moved Ukraine in this direction, but have been repeatedly thwarted, primarily by Kiev. Whether or not full backing for Minsk by both Trump and Putin, particularly the provision giving rebel territories some degree of home rule, would end the Ukrainian civil war is far from certain. It might even result in the overthrow of the current Kiev government by well-armed ultranationalist forces. But for now there is no peaceful alternative.

Even if Trump and Putin adopt a wise joint policy toward Ukraine, neither leader has much political capital to spare at home. Trump is opposed by virtually across-the-political-spectrum opposition to any kind of agreements with Russia, not the least regarding Ukraine. And Putin can never be seen at home as "selling out" Russia's "brethren" anywhere in southeast Ukraine. Whether the two leaders have the wisdom and determination to end Ukraine's tragic and utterly pointless war, which has left the country nearly in ruins, remains to be seen.

Kremlin-Baiting President Trump

February 15

THE TSUNAMI OF ALLEGATIONS THAT PRESIDENT Trump has been seditiously "compromised" by the Kremlin continues to mount. *New York*

Times guru-columnist Thomas Friedman repeated the charge yet again on February 15. He too did so without any verified facts. The lack of any non-partisan high-level protest against this Kremlin-baiting of Trump is deeply alarming. It has become, it seems, politically correct.

Promoted by Hillary Clinton's campaign in mid-2016 and even more after her defeat, and exemplified now by the strident innuendos of MSNBC's Rachel Maddow and almost equally unbalanced CNN panels and newspaper editorial pages, the practice is growing into a kind of latter-day McCarthyite red-baiting and hysteria. Such politically malignant practices are to be deplored anywhere they appear, without exception, whether on the part of conservatives, liberals, or progressives. Whatever the motives, the slurring of Trump, which is already producing calls for his impeachment, poses grave threats to US and international security and to American democracy itself.

One or more of the allegations against Trump may turn out to be true, as might be almost anything in politics, but no actual evidence has been presented for any of the allegations. Without facts, all of us—professors, politicians, doctors, journalists, pundits—are doomed to malpractice or worse. A special investigation might search for such facts, but it is hard to imagine a truly objective and focused probe in the current political atmosphere.

For now, there are no facts or logic to support the following six related allegations that Trump has been treasonously "compromised" by Putin's Kremlin:

1. Trump has "lavished praise" on Putin, as the *Times* charged on February 12, echoing many other media outlets. All Trump has said is that Putin is "a strong leader" and "smart" and that it would be good "to cooperate with Russia." These are empirically true statements. They pale in comparison with, for example, FDR's warm words about Stalin, Nixon's about Leonid Brezhnev, and particularly President Bill Clinton's about Russian President Boris Yeltsin, whom he compared favorably with George Washington, Abraham Lincoln, and FDR. Only against the backdrop of unrelenting US media demonizing of Putin could Trump's "praise" be considered "lavish." Unlike virtually every other mainstream American politician and most media outlets, Trump has simply refused to vilify Putin—as in declining to characterize him as "a killer," for which there is also no evidence.

2. Trump and his associates have had, it is charged, business dealings in Russia and with Russian "oligarchs." Perhaps, but so have scores of major American corporations, from Delta Airlines, McDonald's, Wendy's, KFC, and Starbucks to Ford, Procter & Gamble, and several energy giants. Unavoidably, some of their Russian partners are "oligarchs." Moreover, unlike many international hotel chains, Trump tried but failed to build his own affiliate, or anything else permanent, in Russia. The "Russian assets" about which his son once spoke evidently referred to condos and coops in the United States sold to cash-bearing Russians in search of a luxury brand and who did not need mortgages. New York City and South Florida are among those prime and entirely legitimate markets. It is said that Trump's tax returns, if revealed, would expose incriminating Russian money. Perhaps— but also an allegation, not a fact.

3. Trump's "associate," and briefly campaign manager, Paul Manafort, is alleged to have been "pro-Russian" when he advised Ukrainian President Victor Yanukovych, who was subsequently deposed unconstitutionally during the Maidan "revolution" in February 2014. As I already pointed out, this, to be polite, is uninformed. A professional political "adviser," Manafort was well paid, like many other American electoral experts hired abroad. But his advice to Yanukovych was to move politically and economically toward the ill-fated European Union Partnership Agreement, away from Russia, as Yanukovych did in order to get votes beyond his constituency in southeastern Ukraine. (Nor was the unsavory Yanukovych, whom Putin loathed for this and other reasons, considered pro-Russian in Moscow prior to his crisis in late 2013, when Putin got stuck with him.)

4. In January, as we know, a "dossier" of "black" or "compromising" material purporting to document how the Kremlin could blackmail Trump was leaked to CNN and published by *Buzzfeed*. Compiled by a former British intelligence official, Christopher Steele, whose shadowy partners in various countries abetted his commercial projects, the "report" was initially contracted by one of Trump's Republican primary opponents and then taken up and paid for by the Clinton campaign. Its 30-odd pages are a compilation of the entirely innocent, unverified, preposterous, and trash for sale in many political capitals, including London, Moscow, Kiev, Baltic capitals, and Washington. More recently, CNN exclaimed that its own intelligence leakers had "confirmed" some elements of the dossier, but thus far nothing that actually compromises Trump. Generally, more fact checking is done at tabloid magazines, lest they be sued for libel. (Nonetheless, Senator John McCain, a rabid opponent of any détente with Russia, acquired and gave a copy of the dossier to the FBI. No doubt the agency already had copies, bits of which had been floating around for months, but understood McCain wanted it leaked. And so it was, by someone.)

5. But the crux of pro-Kremlin allegations against Trump was, and remains, the charge that Putin hacked the DNC and disseminated the stolen

emails through WikiLeaks in order to put Trump in the White House. A summary of these "facts" was presented in the declassified report released by the US "Intelligence Community" and widely published in January 2017. Though it has since become axiomatic proof for Trump's political and media enemies, as I pointed out earlier, virtually nothing in the "Assessment's" some 13 pages of text (or Steele's dossier) is persuasive—or entirely logical. For example, would Trump, a longtime hotelier, really commit "acts of sexual perversion" in a VIP suite he did not control, especially in Moscow, where audio and video bugging had long been rumored? Indeed, those who accept the Intelligence Community Assessment (ICA) as canon seem not to have noticed the nullifying disclaimer its authors buried at the end: "Judgments are not intended to imply that we have proof that shows something to be a fact."

In reality, about half the ICA pages are merely assumptions—or "assessments"—based on surmised motivations, not factual evidence of a Kremlin operation on behalf of Trump. The other half is a pointless and badly outdated evaluation deploring broadcasts by the Kremlin-funded television network RT. Not addressed is the point made by a number of American hacking experts that Russian state hackers would have left no fingerprints, as US intelligence claimed they had. Indeed, the group Veteran Intelligence Professionals for Sanity believes that the damaging DNC documents were not hacked but leaked by an insider. If so, it had nothing to do with Russia. (The NSA, which has the capacity to monitor the movement of emails, was only "moderately confident" in the report it co-signed, while the CIA and FBI were "highly confident," even though the FBI inexplicably never examined the DNC computers.)

There is another incongruity. At his final presidential press conference, Obama referred to the DNC scandal as a leak, not a hack, and said he did not know how the emails got to WikiLeaks—this despite allegations by his own intelligence agencies. (No one seems to have asked Obama if he misspoke!) On the other side of this alleged conspiracy, nor is it clear that Putin so favored the clearly erratic Trump that he would have taken such a risk, which if discovered, as I also pointed out earlier, would have compromised Trump and greatly favored Clinton. (Judging from discussions in Kremlin-related Russian newspapers, there was a serious debate as to which American presidential candidate might be best—or least bad—for Russia.)

6. Finally, there is the resignation (or firing) of General Michael Flynn as Trump's national security adviser for having communicated with Russian representatives about the sanctions imposed by Obama just before leaving the White House and before Trump was inaugurated. Flynn may have misled Vice President Mike Pence about those "back-channel" discussions, but they were neither unprecedented nor incriminating, so far as is known.

Other American presidential candidates and presidents-elect had communicated with foreign states before taking office—as Richard Nixon seems to have done to prevent a Vietnam peace agreement that would have favored Hubert Humphrey, and as Ronald Reagan seems to have done with Iran to prevent release of its American hostages before the election. In fact, this was and remained a common practice. Obama's own top Russia adviser, Michael McFaul, told the *Washington Post* on February 9 that he visited Moscow in 2008, before the election, for talks with Russian officials. The *Post* reporter characterized this as "appropriate conduct." Certainly, it was not unprecedented.

Nor was Flynn's. More generally, if Flynn's purpose was to persuade the Kremlin not to overreact to Obama's December sanctions, which were accompanied by a provocative threat to launch a cyber attack on Moscow, this was wise and in America's best interests. Unless our political-media establishment would prefer the harshest possible reaction by Putin, as some of its Cold War zealots apparently do.

All this considered, it is less Putin who is threatening American democracy than is the Kremlin-baiting of President Trump without facts. Less Putin who is endangering US and international security than are the American enemies of détente who resort to such practices. Less Putin who is degrading US media with "fake news" than is the media's fact-free Kremlin-baiting of Trump. And less the "former KGB thug" who is poisoning American politics than are US intelligence leakers at war against their new president.

President Eisenhower eventually stopped Joseph McCarthy. Who will stop the new McCarthyism before it spreads even more into the "soul of democracy"? Facts might do so. But in lieu of facts there are only professional ethics and patriotism.

Putin's Own Opponents of Détente

February 22

THE RUSSIAN POLICY ELITE CLOSELY FOLLOWS US publications, especially "leading" papers like the *New York Times*. It would have reacted strongly—as should American readers—to a series of articles in the *Times* from February 16 through February 19 on the theme of a "Trump-Putin axis" in the White House, as columnist Paul Krugman so elegantly phrased it on February 17. Indeed, the entire February 19 *Times Sunday Review* was substantially devoted to this extraordinary, though now commonplace, allegation.

But Russian analysts would have focused even more—as should we—on an ominous statement quoted approvingly by *Times* columnist Nicholas Kristof, on February 16, that "the bigger issue here is why Trump and people around him take such a radically different view of Russia than has been the case for decades." The clear message: any critical thinking about US policy toward Russia since the 1990s is now under suspicion—and perhaps criminal. No wonder some members of the Russian elite have concluded that the slurring of the new US president and all American proponents of better relations means there will be no new détente.

This can only please Putin's own opponents of "cooperation" with the United States. There is, of course, a spectrum of policy views in the Russian political elite. Some strongly favor a new détente with Washington, but we should not discount those—rarely, if ever, noted in US media—that equally strongly do not. Generally known as "state nationalist patriots," these Russians insist that détente has been historically catastrophic for Russia and thus is unpatriotic.

Their opposition echoes in part the centuries-long divide between Russian Westernizers and traditionalist Slavophiles, but it is also pointedly contemporary. Today's Russian foes of détente argue that the Gorbachev-Reagan-Bush rapprochement of the late 1980s and early 1990s led to the end of the Soviet Union and Russia's collapse as a great power. And that the Yeltsin-Clinton "partnership" during the 1990s resulted in a decade of Russia's humiliation at home and abroad.

They add, not incorrectly, that the US repeatedly lied or broke promises to Gorbachev and Yeltsin and even to Putin himself during Moscow's détente-like "reset" with Washington, and will do so again under President Trump. If nothing else, Putin must not be seen at home as following in the tradition of Gorbachev and Yeltsin. (Yes, to make the point again, this means that Putin is not an "autocrat" whose will despotically becomes policy.)

Embracing Trump as a détente partner would pose other problems for Putin. As head of a vast multi-ethnic state, with some 20 million Muslim citizens, Putin cannot be associated with anti-Muslim aspects of Trump's immigration policies. Nor can he consider as a "bargaining chip" Moscow's increasingly close relations with China or even Iran. (The "China card," played by Henry Kissinger on behalf of President Richard Nixon, is no longer applicable.) Even nuclear-weapons reductions, the most attainable détente achievement, along with cooperation in Syria, is no longer so straight-forward. For Putin, it is inextricably tied to the missile-defense systems Washington is installing around Russia. Trump would need to revise this Obama policy as well.

There is another historical echo in the new struggle over détente. As during the 40-year Cold War, those known as "hardliners" or "hawks" both in Washington and Moscow have again formed an unholy, if inadvertent, axis.

The "Fog of Suspicion"

March 8

ONCE RESPECTABLE AMERICAN MEDIA ARE RECKLESSLY feeding neo-McCarthyist impulses inherent in the Russiagate frenzy. This could indeed become a political witch hunt ensnaring Americans with legitimate "contacts" with Russia—scholars, corporate executives and independent business people invested in Russia, diplomats, performers, journalists themselves, and many others.

On March 6, for example, the *New York Times'* Charles Blow, echoing his fellow columnists, applauded the "gathering fog of suspicion" in the hope it will bring down President Trump. MSNBC contributed a two-hour kanga-roo tribunal on "The Trump-Putin Power Play" (no question mark) featuring "experts" without any doubts (or much actual knowledge) on their minds. A CNN "documentary" on Putin—"The Most Powerful Man in the World"—provided the kind of elliptical narrative needed to explain his "war" on America, and to inspire more hysteria. Both MSNBC and CNN regularly feature prosecutorial "former intelligence officials" whose misinformed state-ments about Russia's leadership can only give the CIA and US "Intel" gener-ally a bad reputation. Specialists with dissenting analyses and points of view are effectively excluded. In this enveloping "fog," the accompanying clamor for "investigations" may only make things worse.

Not surprisingly, the "fog of suspicion" is chilling, even freezing, public discourse about worsening US-Russian relations, which should be a compel-ling media subject. As the political-media establishment "redirects" Trump away from his campaign promise of détente with Russian President Putin, some university scholars, think-tank specialists, and journalists are reluctant to speak candidly, at least publicly. As are US CEOs in pursuit of profits in Russia, who would normally welcome Trump's détente as their predeces-sors embraced the Nixon-Kissinger détente with Soviet Russia in the 1970s. Also not surprisingly, only one or two members of Congress have publicly expressed any principled alarm over the mounting hysteria. Most seem will-ing to accept the anti–national security mission of Senator Lindsay Graham to make 2017 "the year of kicking Russia in the ass."

This absence of statesmanship prevails in Washington even as three new Cold War fronts become more fraught with the possibility of hot war. In the Baltic and Black Sea regions, on Russia's borders, where NATO's unprec-edented buildup continues and is provoking equally dangerous forms of Russian "brinkmanship." In Syria, where the growing number of American troops are increasingly in military proximity to the Russian-Syrian alliance, another realm of lethal mishaps waiting to happen. And in Ukraine, where recent developments show again that the US-backed Kiev government is hostage to armed ultranationalists and where that civil and proxy war could easily become a much larger conflagration with Russia.

There is also the wildly hyperbolic charge that Putin, like his worst Soviet predecessors, is now at war against the entire "liberal world order," including the European Union. This too is trumpeted by influential American media, but for this too there are no facts or logic. Why would Putin want to destroy the EU, an essential trading partner? Why would he undermine European politicians who favor ending sanctions against Russia, as is being alleged?

More generally, is Putin really the cause of Europe's multiple crises today in ways that the superpower Soviet Union never was? And what is this international "order" that has featured so many wars, many of them US ones, since the Soviet Union ended in 1991?

The blaming of Russia for America's domestic shocks—for Hillary Clinton's defeat and for President Trump, in particular—is political evasion now being projected onto the entire "liberal world order." This is indeed a "fog," but not the one of "suspicion" the *Times*, the *Washington Post*, cable "news," and other mainstream media are busy promoting.

Neo-McCarthyism Is Now Politically Correct

March 22

I HAVE BEEN SHARPLY CRITICIZED, PARTICULARLY BY self-professed liberal and progressive Democrats, for warning that Russiagate allegations against President Trump, whatever their still unverified validity, are growing into a kind of widespread Russophobic neo-McCarthyism. Recall that the original premise of McCarthyism was the existence of a vast Soviet Communist conspiracy inside America. Now consider, in addition to previous examples I have already given, more recent echoes of that era.

At recent House hearings, Democratic Representative Adam Schiff warned of a "Russian attack on our democracy." He meant the Kremlin's alleged hacking of the DNC and allegations that the Trump campaign had "colluded"—that is, conspired—with the Kremlin.

As the session unfolded, representative after representative, most of them Democrats, demanded the "unmasking" of Americans who had or have "contacts" with Russia. Under suspicion, it seemed, was anyone who traveled frequently to Russia, married a Russian, written or spoken critically about

US policy toward Russia (as the *New York Times*' Nicholas Kristof warned in an example I cited earlier), or, as another Democrat put it, otherwise done "Putin's bidding." He was referring to the new Secretary of State Rex Tillerson in his previous role as CEO of ExxonMobil.

Most alarming perhaps was the spectacle of FBI Director James Comey emerging in the role of his distant predecessor J. Edgar Hoover as a great authority on Russian malignancies—in this case, on the politics of "Putin's Russia" and Putin himself, including his personal motives, plans, and more. And yet, when asked what he thought about Gazprom—Russia's giant natural gas company, producer of more than a third of Europe's energy, and very often cited as a major pillar of Putin's power—Comey said he had not heard of it. And there was the spectacle of Schiff, who elaborating on the purported "collusion" as "one of the most shocking betrayals of our democracy in history," seemed to morph into McCarthy himself.

Congress, of course, was not acting in a political vacuum. For months, mainstream media, mostly associated with the Democratic Party—from the *Times* and the *Washington Post* to the *New Yorker*, *Politico*, MSNBC, CNN, and NPR—have promoted the theme of a Trump-Putin conspiracy and now a "Trump-Putin regime" in the White House.

Little wonder that related aspects of neo-McCarthyism have become politically correct. On March 20, MSNBC's Chris Matthews declared that loyal "Americans don't go to Russia." In a tweet on March 14, the *Atlantic's* David Frum proposed that someone "should stake …out" a Russian Embassy concert, in Washington, in memory of the Red Army Choir that perished in a plane crash and "photograph who attends."

Adumbrations of the 1950s are bipartisan. For a disagreement in the Senate, John McCain accused his fellow Republican Senator Rand Paul of "working for Vladimir Putin." And Trump's new UN ambassador, Nikki Haley, proclaimed, "We should never trust Russia." (If implemented, her diplomatic axiom would invalidate decades of US nuclear arms control agreements with Moscow.)

Lest anyone think the present danger is any less than was that of Soviet Russian Communism, we have *Post* columnist Dana Milbank warning, on March 21, of "the red menace of Vladimir Putin's Russia." Considering recent American media coverage, he might well think Communists still control the Kremlin.

The political logic inherent in all of this is obvious—and ominous. The question is how many influential Americans, if any, will at long last stand publicly against it.

Yevtushenko's Civic Courage

April 5

Y EVGENY YEVTUSHENKO, RUSSIA'S GREAT POET-DISSENTER, DIED on April
1. I may not be fully objective about him, having known him for many
years. Not well in the late 1970s and early 1980s, when I lived off and on in
Moscow among Soviet-era dissidents, though a bit from our encounters there
and in New York. But very well from 1985, when Mikhail Gorbachev began
the perestroika reforms and I regained my Soviet entry visa, denied since
1982. So well that Zhenya, as his friends called him, was the godfather of my
younger daughter, born in 1991.

Mindful of the adage that a great writer in Russia is more than a writer,
Yevtushenko was for decades the nation's—and perhaps the world's—most
famous and popular poet. He used his talent and position to champion the
cause of historical and political justice and then a Soviet democratic reformation, as attempted by Gorbachev in the late 1980s. Long before Gorbachev's
"glasnost" summoned radical reformers into public action, Yevtushenko
acted boldly at great political and personal risk.

Western observers not known for protesting anything in their own countries often criticized Yevtushenko for having been officially tamed and corrupted by privilege, and still do so. They do not know the scores of writers,
dissidents, and cultural works his private interventions helped, even saved.
Or the impact of his (not so) private letter to Soviet leader Leonid Brezhnev
protesting the Soviet invasion of Czechoslovakia in 1968. Many of his
poems, and his riveting public readings, inspired at least two generations of
Soviet reformers, including Gorbachev, as he later acknowledged.

At least two of Yevtushenko's most famous poems had a direct impact on
public affairs. "The Heirs of Stalin" warned the nation in 1962 that powerful
forces behind the scenes were seeking to overthrow Soviet leader Nikita
Khrushchev, in part for his anti-Stalinist revelations, as they finally did in
1964. And "Babi Yar" broke the official Soviet taboo against discussion of
the Jewish Holocaust.

Zhenya's death causes me to wonder again why established American figures—in the media, Congress, universities, cultural life, and elsewhere—have
not protested abuses now engulfing US politics in a wave of McCarthy-like

hysteria. They have far less to lose than did Yevtushenko. A torrent of fact-free allegations and slurring of people has flowed for months from leading newspapers and television networks, but exceedingly few, if any, Americans in a prominent position to protest have done so.

When *New York Times* columnist Charles Blow declares that "the Russians did interfere in our election. This is not a debatable issue"—why does no one protest that it is in fact debatable? Or when Blow slurs Secretary of State Rex Tillerson as a compromised friend of Russian President Putin? Or when other baseless allegations are made almost nightly by MSNBC and CNN hosts and panelists? Or when hyperbolic claims of a vast "Russian threat" to democracy everywhere were declared at the Senate "investigation" earlier this month? Some prominent Americans have grave doubts about this political and media conduct, but they are silent. Do they lack the civic courage that Yevtushenko exhibited for decades while treading a political razor's edge?

Such behavior, along with large policy issues, were exhibited in another way by the US response to the recent terrorist act on a St. Petersburg subway. Downplaying it generally, too many American commentators suggested that Putin was himself behind the explosion that killed or maimed scores of Russian citizens—in order, it was said, to deflect attention from public protests against official financial corruption. Again, there is no evidence or plausible logic for these shameful innuendoes.

They also directly threaten US national security. Ever since the 9/11 actual attack on America, inescapably recalled by subsequent attacks on European cities, the imperative of a US-Russia alliance against international terrorism has been abundantly clear. So are the readiness and capabilities of Russia—which has suffered in this regard more than any other Western nation—to help. Time and again such an alliance has been thwarted, primarily by powerful forces in the US establishment.

President Trump indicated he wanted this alliance. The tragedy in St. Petersburg should have been occasion enough to warrant one. But it may again be thwarted, now by the Kremlin-baiting of Trump and the nearly indifferent reaction by the US political-media establishment to the most recent act of terrorism in Russia.

When Yevgeny Yevtushenko turned his pen against the powerful, repressive forces of Soviet neo-Stalinism and anti-Semitism, he risked his life and his family's. What do privileged Americans who understand the ongoing folly but remain silent have to lose?

"Words Are Also Deeds"

April 12

THE US POLITICAL-MEDIA ESTABLISHMENT HAS EMBRACED three fraught narratives for which there is still no public evidence, only "Intel" allegations. One is, of course, "Russiagate," as it is being called: that Kremlin leader Putin ordered a hacking of the DNC and disseminated its emails to help put Donald Trump in the White House. The second is that Syrian President Assad, Putin's ally, ordered last week's chemical-weapons attack on Syrian civilians, including young children. A new third faith-based narrative, promoted by MSNBC in particular, now links the other two: Trump's recent missile attack on a Syrian military air base was actually a Putin-Trump plot to free the new American president from the constraints of "Russiagate" investigations and enable him to do Putin's bidding.

In addition to the absence of any actual evidence for these allegations, there is no logic. The explanation that Putin "hated Hillary Clinton" for protests that took place in Moscow in 2011 is based on a misrepresentation of that event. (The protested parliamentary election actually resulted in Putin's party losing its constitutional majority in the Duma.) And why would Assad resort to the use of chemical weapons, thereby risking all the military, political, and diplomatic gains he has achieved in the past year and half, and while he had Russian air power at his disposal as an alternative? The emerging sub-narrative that Putin lied in 2013, when he and President Obama agreed Assad would destroy all of his chemical weapons, is based on another factual misrepresentation. It was the United Nations and its special agency that verified the full destruction of those weapons, not Putin.

The Russian adage "words are also deeds" is true, it seems. Trump's missile attack on Moscow's ally Syria probably had a domestic political purpose—to disprove the narrative that he is somehow "Putin's puppet." If so, the American mainstream media that has promoted this narrative for months is deeply complicit. Meanwhile, the Kremlin, which watches these narratives unfold politically in Washington, has become deeply alarmed, resorting to its own fraught words. The No. 2 leader, Prime Minister Dmitri Medvedev, declared that US-Russian relations have been "ruined," a statement I do not recall any previous Soviet or post-Soviet leader ever having made. Medvedev added that the two nuclear superpowers are at "the brink" of war.

Understanding that Medvedev is regarded as the leading pro-Western figure in Putin's inner circle, imagine what the other side—state patriots, or nationalists, as they are called—is telling Putin. Still more, the Kremlin is warning that Trump's missile attack on Syria crossed Russia's "red lines," with all the warfare implications this term has in Washington as well. And flatly declaring the mysterious use of chemical weapons in Syria to have been a "provocation," Putin himself warned that forces in Washington were planning more such "provocations" and military strikes. In short, while the Kremlin does not want and will not start a war with the United States, it is preparing for the possibility.

Meanwhile, Trump's new secretary of state, Rex Tillerson, had just arrived in Moscow for talks with Russian leaders. Whether or not Putin himself would met with Tillerson was still uncertain. Putin may be an authoritarian leader, the "decider," but influential forces were strongly against him meeting with an American secretary of state in the immediate aftermath of such a US "provocation." Whatever the case, Tillerson's visit is vitally important.

Tillerson is well known to Putin and other Kremlin leaders. On behalf of ExxonMobil, he negotiated with them one of Russia's largest energy deals, granting access to the nation's vast oil resources beneath frozen seas. Putin personally approved the agreement, which oil giants around the world had sought. He would not have done so had he not concluded that Tillerson was a serious, highly competent man. (For this achievement on behalf of a major American corporation, US media continue to slur Tillerson as "Putin's friend.")

The Kremlin will therefore expect candid answers from Tillerson to questions related to the looming issue of war or peace. Are the fact-free narratives now prevailing in Washington determining factors in Trump's policy toward Russia? Are they the reason Trump committed the "provocation" in Syria? Does this mean Trump no longer shares Russia's essential strategic premise regarding the civil and proxy war in Syria—that the overthrow of Assad would almost certainly mean ISIS or another terrorist army in Damascus, an outcome the Kremlin regards as a dire threat to Russia's national security?

And, most fundamentally, who is making Russia policy in Washington: President Trump or someone else? Putin, it should be recalled, asked the same question publicly about President Obama, when the agreement he and Obama negotiated for military cooperation in Syria was sabotaged by the US Department of Defense.

The answers that the experienced Tillerson—he had his own corporate global state department and intelligence service at ExxonMobil—gives may do much to determine whether or not the new Cold War moves even closer to the brink of hot war in Syria. To avert that dire possibility, American mainstream media should return to their once professed practice of rigorously fact-checking their narratives with an understanding that words are indeed also deeds.

Wartime "Tears" in Moscow, Cold War Inquisition in Washington

May 10

GROWING UP IN SMALL-TOWN KENTUCKY IN the aftermath of World War II, I looked forward to the annual V-E (Victory in Europe) Day remembrance, on May 8, particularly the parades featuring floats and veterans in their uniforms. Apparently it is no longer observed as a major American holiday across the United States. In sharp contrast, Victory Day, May 9, remains the most sacred Russian holiday, a "holiday with tears."

And so it was this year. The day was marked by commemorations across the vastness of Russia, not only by the traditional military parade on Moscow's Red Square. A remarkable new feature, "The Immortal Regiment," has recently been added—millions of people, among them President Putin, walking together through a myriad of streets bearing portraits of family members who fought in what is known as The Great Patriotic War, very many of whom did not return. The annual events are promoted by the government, as US media unfailing point out, but the "holiday with tears" is profoundly authentic for an overwhelming majority of the Russian people, and for understandable historical reasons.

Most Americans today believe "we defeated Nazi Germany," as President

Obama wrote on the 70th anniversary of the end of World War II. It is a misconception fostered by Hollywood films that portray the US landing at Normandy in June 1944 as the beginning of the destruction of Hitler's Germany.

In truth, America won the war in the Pacific, against Japan, but the Soviet Union fought and destroyed the Nazi war machine on the "Eastern Front" almost alone from 1941 to 1944, from Moscow, Kursk, and Stalingrad, and eventually to Berlin in 1945. Some 75 to 80 percent of all German casualties were suffered on the Eastern Front. By the time US and British forces landed at Normandy, Hitler had insufficient divisions to withstand the invasion, too many of them destroyed or still fighting oncoming Soviet forces from the east.

Soviet losses were almost unimaginable. More than 27 million citizens died, 60 to 70 percent of them ethnic Russians. Some 1700 cities and towns were all but destroyed. Most families lost a close or extended member. Perhaps most tellingly, only three of every hundred boys who graduated from high school in 1941–42 returned from the war. This meant that millions of Soviet children never knew their fathers and that millions of Soviet women never married. (They were known as "Ivan's widows," more than a few doomed to lonely lives in the often-harsh post-war Soviet Union.)

This is an enduring part of Russia's "holiday with tears." This is in large measure why so many Russians, not just the Kremlin, have watched with alarm as NATO has crept from Germany to their country's borders since the late 1990s. Why they resent and fear Washington's claims on the former Soviet republics of Ukraine and Georgia. And why they say of NATO's ongoing buildup within conventional firing range of Russia, "Never has so much Western military power been amassed on our borders since the Nazi invasion in June 1941." This is the "living history" that underlies Russia's reaction to the new Cold War.

Again in sharp contrast, on May 8 and 9 in Washington, today's Russia was being portrayed at renewed Senate hearings as an existential threat, as having committed an "act of war against America" by "hijacking" the 2016 presidential election on behalf of President Trump. By end of day on May 9, Trump's firing of FBI Director James Comey was said to be an attempt to cover up that collusion.

After nearly a year, no actual facts have yet been presented to support the allegation. On the other hand, evidence has appeared that for more than a year elements of the US Intelligence Community—almost certainly the CIA and FBI—have been engaged in shadowy operations designed to link Trump to Putin's Kremlin. I've called this "Intelgate" and urged it be investigated first and foremost. Intel leaks and "reports," in evident "collusion" with the failed Clinton campaign, have driven the Russiagate narrative from the outset, amplified almost daily by a mainstream media that shows no interest at all in Intelgate.

Which brings us to Trump's (and before him Obama's) thwarted effort to forge an anti-terrorist alliance with Moscow. Russia has suffered more from jihadist terrorism than has any other Western country. For many Russians, it is becoming an existential threat reminiscent of German fascism in the 1930s. Therefore, they naturally want another wartime alliance with the United States. But Russia's tearful memories and real present-day perils do not interest Russiagate zealots, who are focused on Trump's firing of Comey. (Considering his acts detrimental to her campaign, a President Hillary Clinton would almost certainly also have replaced Comey.)

None of this seems to matter to representatives of the Democratic Party or to Washington's bipartisan cold warriors. They prefer pursuing still fact-free allegations. On May 8-9, they should instead have gone to Moscow to commemorate the historic allied victory in World War II. But they were following recent precedent: President Obama pointedly boycotted the 70th anniversary commemoration in Moscow in 2015.

Terrorism and Russiagate

May 31

IT CANNOT BE EMPHASIZED TOO OFTEN: international terrorism—a modern-day phenomenon that controls territory, has aspects of statehood, commands sizable fighting forces and agents in many countries, and is in pursuit of radioactive materials to make its bombings incalculably more lethal—is the No. 1 threat to the world today. Coping with this existential danger requires an international alliance of governments, first and foremost between the United States and Russia.

President Trump has suggested, publicly and privately, an anti-terrorism coalition with Russian President Putin. At each stage of the negotiations, the media's Russiagate (no need for quote marks) narrative—has intervened in ways that jeopardize, if not sabotage, the diplomatic process.

We now have more instances. Allegations that Trump betrayed intelligence secrets to Russian Foreign Minister Lavrov during an Oval Office meeting and discussed with him his firing of FBI Director Comey. And that the president's son-in-law and aide, Jared Kushner, participated in an attempt to establish a secret "back channel" of communication with Moscow prior to Trump's inauguration. These allegations, like many others, are uninformed.

Putin has repeatedly sought a US-Russian anti-terrorism alliance for nearly 17 years, at least since the 9/11 attacks on America. Each time the prospect seemed real, at least to Moscow, it was thwarted by forces in Washington.

This time, therefore, especially given misgivings by some of his senior advisers, Putin needed from Trump personally, via Lavrov, answers to two questions. Did the two sides agree about the exchange of high-level intelligence required for such an alliance? Trump responded by sharing a piece of classified information about a terrorist threat to American and Russian passenger airliners. In doing so, Trump did nothing unprecedented, improper, or probably even revelatory. (The source involved Israel, whose intelligence agencies work closely with their Russian counterparts on matters involving terrorism.)

Second, Putin needed to know whether Trump, reeling under accusations of being a "Kremlin puppet" and facing a myriad of investigations at home, could be a reliable anti-terrorism partner. Trump responded by saying he had fired Comey, whom he thought, not unreasonably, had been inspiring some of the allegations against him. However inelegantly expressed by Trump, these were necessary discussions with Lavrov if the US-Russian alliance against terrorism was to proceed.

Nor was the Trump team's search for a back channel of communications with Moscow, whether through Russian officials or private American citizens, as Kushner then was, unprecedented or improper for a President-elect, as I previously detailed. The former diplomat Jack Matlock has said he did it for President-elect Jimmy Carter, as did then–private citizen Michael McFaul for President-elect Obama—in Moscow, no less. It is likely that Henry Kissinger, whom Putin knows and trusts, was also involved on behalf of President-elect Trump. (It's worth recalling that President John F. Kennedy used both a private American citizen and the Soviet ambassador in Washington as a back channel during the Cuban Missile Crisis.)

Trump, however, had a special problem. Regular communications with the Kremlin eventually end up, of course, both in official Russian and American channels. Convinced that US intelligence agencies had been behind the allegations against him since the summer of 2016, and particularly the steady stream of leaks to the media, Trump reasonably worried about initiating his back channel through any US institution or agency. Hence attempts by Kushner, and possibly others, to begin privately with the Russian ambassador to Washington. Not unreasonably, not improperly, though perhaps ineptly.

The real issue Americans must decide is what is more compelling: the need for a US anti-terrorism alliance with Russia or the still-undocumented allegations called Russiagate? The lethal bombings in Manchester and in a St. Petersburg metro station are more evidence, if any is still needed, that American subways and arenas are not immune.

"Details After the Sports"

June 21 / June 28

THE LATE COMEDIAN GEORGE CARLIN HAD a still telling routine. A local radio newscaster begins his report: "Nuclear war in Europe. Details after the sports." Consider some recent "details" you may have missed in leading American media.

On June 18, a US plane shot down a Syrian military aircraft. Allied with Syria and fighting there at its government's official invitation, unlike American forces which are there in violation of international law, Moscow regarded this as a provocative act of war. After a nearly 24-hour pause while the Putin leadership debated its response, the Russian military command announced that henceforth any US aircraft flying where Russia and Syria were conducting operations would be "targeted"—that is, warned to leave immediately or be shot down.

A red line had been crossed by the United States, as the Soviet Union had done in Cuba in 1962. This time, Washington wisely retreated, as Moscow did in the Cuban Missile Crisis. The Department of Defense announced it would "reposition" its war planes away from Russian-Syrian operations.

But this does not mean the danger of a Cuba-like crisis has been eliminated in Syria (or elsewhere). The Trump administration is threatening to attack Syria if President Assad "again" uses chemical weapons, thereby creating the real risk of a "false flag." Independent investigators, notably Seymour Hersh and Theodore Postol, have raised serious doubts as to whether Assad actually used chemical weapons previously, in 2013 or this April. Their findings were nowhere explored in the American mainstream media.

Nor was another recent episode. A NATO warplane above the Baltic Sea came perilously close to a Russian aircraft carrying Minister of Defense Sergei Shoigu, probably Russia's most popular political figure after President Putin. Had something worse happened, it too might well have led to war between the two nuclear superpowers.

Such "details" in current US-Russian relations are deleted or obscured by the media's fixation on Russiagate—allegations that Trump and Putin "colluded" to put Trump in the White House. Here too there are important new "details" you may have missed. Russiagate's core allegation is based officially—leaving aside the private and easily disputed Steele "dossier"—on the January 2017 US "Intelligence Community Assessment." We now know this report was not based on a consensus of all "seventeen US intelligence agencies," as implied, but on "handpicked analysts," possibly from only the CIA.

We learn this directly from former CIA Director John Brennan and former Director of National Intelligence James Clapper. Brennan, we also now know, was hardly an objective CIA director, having explained in his recent House testimony that any Americans who have contacts with Russians can embark "along a treasonous path" and "do not know they are on a treasonous path until it is too late."

Brennan's contempt for the trustworthiness of Americans was matched by Clapper's contempt for Russians. He told NBC's *Meet the Press*, on May 8, that "Russians ... are typically, almost genetically driven to co-opt, penetrate ..." and thus "genetically driven" to attack American democracy. No mainstream media have explored these revelations about President Obama's apparently paranoid CIA director and ethnically biased National Intelligence director.

Instead, they have continued to parrot what is now an established falsehood. The most indicative example is Maggie Haberman, a leading *New*

York Times reporter on Russiagate and regular CNN panelist. On June 26, she wrote that President Trump "still refuses to acknowledge a basic fact agreed upon by 17 American intelligence agencies … Russia orchestrated the attacks and did it to help get him elected." But it is Ms. Haberman and the *Times* that refuse "to acknowledge a basic fact." And they are far from alone. On June 26, *Washington Post* columnist Richard Cohen repeated the same falsehood about "17 American intelligence agencies," as do almost daily CNN and MSNBC.

On June 25, the *Post* added another dubious "detail" that went unnoticed. Buried in an interminable "investigative" article claiming to prove Putin's "crime of the century," was something meant to be a bombshell: Obama's White House knew about Putin's personal role in Russiagate from a mole—either human or technical—in his Kremlin inner circle. Logic alone discredits the story. If US Intel had acquired a listening source in Putin's closed circle, it would be one of the great espionage feats in history—a present and future asset so precious that no official would dare leak it (a treasonous capital crime) to the *Washington Post*.

One day, all of these reckless media malpractices may be critically exposed by historians and schools of journalism, though they do not do so today. One day we may learn, to use an expression I first heard from a former British intelligence agent more than 40 years ago, that documents like the ICA report and Steel's dossier are mostly "rubbish in and rubbish out." In real time, however, such "details"—with their deletions, distortions, and distractions—are a major reason why we are slouching toward war with Russia, as in Syria.

Cold-War News Not "Fit to Print"

July 19 / August 9

THE MAINSTREAM NARRATIVE OF THE NEW Cold War, now including Russiagate, continues to exclude important elements that do not conform to its orthodoxies. Typically, the narrative is driven by stories in the *New York Times* and the *Washington Post*, often based on anonymous Intel sources, and amplified for hours, even days, on CNN and MSNBC. As for the exceptionally influential *Times*, its front-page credo, "All the News That's Fit to Print," seems to have become "All the News That Fits." Here are more recent examples:

News that Trump and Putin met privately after their formal "summit" meeting in Hamburg earlier in July was treated as a sinister development. Omitted was the history of previous summit meetings. For example, Reagan and Gorbachev met alone with their translators in February 1986, when they agreed that the abolition of nuclear weapons was a desirable goal. That did not happen, but the following year they became the first and only leaders ever to abolish an entire category of those weapons. Moreover, in the long history of summits, advisers of American, Soviet, and post-Soviet leaders frequently thought it wise to arrange some "private time" for their bosses so they could develop a political comfort level for the hard détente diplomacy that lay ahead.

History is also frequently missing in other media accounts. When it turned out that a Russian lawyer wanted to speak to Donald Trump Jr. about "orphans," at a now infamous meeting at Trump Tower, this was derided as a laughable Russiagate cover-up. But the issue is serious both in Russia and for some in the United States. In 2012, Putin signed a bill banning future American adoptions of Russian orphans. (Thousands had been adopted by American families since the 1990s.) It was generally thought to have been Putin's retaliation for the US Congress' Magnitsky Act, which sanctioned Russian "human rights violators."

Several other aspects of this saga are rarely, if ever, reported. One is that the account of the Magnitsky affair given by William Browder, a onetime American financial operator in Russia who spearheaded the US legislation, uncritically repeated by US media, has been seriously challenged. Another is that Putin was already, prior to the Magnitsky Act, under considerable Russian public and elite pressure to end American adoptions because several adopted children had died in the United States. Yet another is the pain of more than 40 American families who had virtually completed the formal adoption process when the ban was enacted, leaving their children stranded in Russia.

Still more, there is the possibility that Putin might enable at least some of these Russian children to come to their would-be American families as a détente concession to Trump. But similarly unreported, Putin needs a "sanctions" concession from Trump.

In December 2016, on his way out of the White House, President Obama seized two Russian diplomatic compounds in the United States, both Russian private property, and expelled 35 Russian diplomats as intelligence agents. Putin has yet to retaliate tit for tat, as has long been traditional in such matters, by seizing American facilities in Moscow and expelling an equal number of US diplomats. Here too Putin is under Russian public and elite pressure—lest he look "soft"—to retaliate. US media reporting on Russiagate, however, probably makes it politically impossible for Trump to reverse any of Obama's sanctions, even if it helped to avoid yet another crisis in US-Russian relations and abet the détente he seems to want.

Other facts and context were missing from reports of Trump Jr.'s meeting with the Russian lawyer, which was initiated by an offer of "Kremlin dirt" on Hillary Clinton and thus portrayed as exceptionally sinister. But at that very time, June 2016, the Clinton campaign was already paying the former British intelligence officer, Christopher Steele, to collect "Kremlin dirt" on Trump—an enterprise that became known as the anti-Trump or Steele "dossier" and a foundation of Russiagate. In addition, by then, a staffer at the Clinton campaign or the DNC was collecting "black" information on Trump from officials of the US-backed Ukrainian government. Both acts of "opposition research," however commonplace in American politics, may have been deplorable, but only Clinton's was actually operationalized and productive. Nothing of the sort seems to have come of Trump Jr.'s meeting.

Consider also the US Senate's proposed economic sanctions against Russia, applauded by mainstream media. Largely uninformed, as are most of Congress' contributions to the new Cold War, they would penalize European energy corporations, and possibly American ones as well, involved in any vital (or profitable) undertakings that include Russian energy companies. Heavily dependent on Russian energy, European governments are furious over the Senate sanctions. This looming rift in the transatlantic alliance has barely been reported here, though it is a major story in Europe.

Ignorance or Russiagate spite has also obscured, perhaps entirely undermined, a potentially vital development. In Hamburg, Trump and Putin agreed that the two sides should work toward regulating cyber technology, including hacking, in international affairs. Certain that Putin had "hacked American democracy" in 2016, though still without any evidence, the US political-media establishment protested so vehemently that Trump seemed to withdraw from this agreement. But it is urgently needed, if only because cyber-hacking, with its capacity to penetrate strategic infrastructures, increases the chances of nuclear war by mishap or intent. Here too orthodox media coverage of "Russiagate" has become a direct threat to American and international security.

What's fit to print also ignores the possible significance of new French President Emmanuel Macron's decision to hold state visits both with Putin and then Trump. American commentary has offered trivial explanations without considering that Macron may be trying to adopt the tradition of the founder of the Fifth Republic, Charles de Gaulle—aloof from both Moscow and Washington, and even NATO, during the preceding Cold War. If so, this too would not fit the US media's orthodox narrative.

Finally, there is Russia's own internal politics, no longer reliably reported by US media. A recent trip to Moscow confirmed my own perception that the political situation there is also worsening due primarily to Cold War fervor in Washington, including Russiagate and proposed new sanctions. Contrary to US opinion, Putin has long been a moderate, restraining force in his own political establishment, but his space for moderation is shrinking. Thus far, his response to various US sanctions was the least he could have done. Much harsher political and economic counter-measures are being widely discussed and urged on him. For now, he resists, explaining, "I do not want to make things worse."

But as always happens in times of escalating Cold War, the pro-American faction in Russian politics is being decimated by Washington's policies. And the space for anti-Kremlin and other opposition is rapidly diminishing. This too appears to be news not fit to print.

Historical Monuments, From Charlottesville to Moscow

August 17

CONFRONTATIONS OVER MEMORIAL REMNANTS OF THE Confederacy, in Charlottesville and elsewhere, revived a theme that has long interested me: similar political legacies of American slavery and of Stalin's Great Terror, which engulfed the Soviet Union from the mid-1930s until the despot's death in 1953. Having grown up in the Jim Crow South and later become a historian of the Stalinist and post-Stalinist eras, I understand, of course, profound differences between the black victims of slavery and the victimization caused by the Stalinist Terror. But I also see some similar historical and political consequences. Notably:

• Both events victimized many millions of people and were formative chapters in the histories of the two political systems and societies.

• For decades, in both countries, subsequent generations were not taught the stark truth about these monstrous historical events. I did not learn in Kentucky schools, for example, that many founding fathers of American democracy had been slave owners. Similarly, the beginning of partial truth-telling about Stalin's Terror began in the Soviet Union only in the mid-1950s and early '60s, under Nikita Khrushchev, and was then stopped officially for another 20 years until Mikhail Gorbachev's rise to power in 1985, when the Terror was fully exposed as part of his glasnost, or truth-telling, reforms.

• Both traumas—great and prolonged crimes, to be exact—produced citizens with very different life experiences and conflicting narratives of their own lives and their nation's history. The result was constant political, social, and even economic conflicts during the course of many years, some of them dramatic and violent. Eventually, descendants both of the victims and the victimizers were in the forefront. (My book *The Victims Return* focuses on this dimension of the Stalinist Terror and its aftermath.)

• One aspect of the controversy in both countries has been conflict over existing monuments and other memorializing sites established decades ago honoring leading victimizers in the American slave and Soviet Stalinist eras, and what to do about them in light of what is now known about these historical figures. Recent events in Charlottesville are only one example, as are ongoing Russian controversies about sites that still honor Stalin—notably his bust behind the Lenin Mausoleum on Red Square—and his "henchmen."

• A profound, even traumatic, historical-political question underlies these conflicts in both countries. How to separate the "crimes" committed by the historical figures still honored from glorious national events with which their names are also associated—in the American case, with the founding of American democracy; in the Russian case, with the great Soviet victory over Nazi Germany, led by Stalin? And if the "crimes" are paramount, who else, and what else, should be deleted from places of honor in the respective national histories? No consensus regarding this ramifying question has been achieved in either society. Both have their consensus-seekers and their "alts," with no resolution in sight.

Which brings us, very briefly, to Putin, whose place in this saga needs to be considered more fully later on. Since coming to power in 2000, he has played an essential but little-understood role in trying to cope with this decades-long controversy in Russia. It has not been, contrary to widespread opinion in American media, the role of a neo-Stalinist.

In order to rebuild a Russian state that would never again disintegrate, as it had in 1917 and again in 1991, Putin needed an effective degree of historical consensus about the conflicting Tsarist, Soviet, and post-Soviet pasts. Unlike many previous Kremlin rulers, Putin has not sought to impose a new historical orthodoxy through censorship and the educational system but to let society—through historians, journalists, broadcast and movie producers, and others—sort out history by presenting their rival perspectives. As a result, there is almost no historical censorship in Russia today.

Even more telling symbolically is the matter of memorials. In America, it bears repeating, there is still no national museum or memorial dedicated solely to the history of slavery. In 2015, there opened in Moscow, with Putin's essential political and financial backing, a large, modern-day State Museum of the History of the Gulag, the penal labor camps in which millions of Stalin's victims languished virtually as slaves and often died. Still more, on October 30, Putin will personally commemorate the first-ever national monument, in the center of Moscow, memorializing the memory of Stalin's victims.

Many Russians will not approve. A recent survey of opinion found Stalin to be "the most admired figure in history." Americans should not be surprised. As William Faulkner reminded us, such past eras are never really past.

The Lost Alternatives of Mikhail Gorbachev

August 24

THE YEAR 2017 MARKS THE 30TH anniversary both of Gorbachev's formal introduction of his democratization policies in the Soviet Union and of the Intermediate-Range Nuclear Forces Treaty he signed with President Reagan, the first—and still only—abolition of an entire category of nuclear weapons.

For me personally, 2017 also marks the anniversary of my first meeting with Gorbachev, in Washington in November 1987. Over the years, our relationship has grown into a personal family friendship. It has included many private discussions about politics, past and present. The most recent, three hours over dinner, was in late July at a restaurant near Gorbachev's home, about a 50-minute drive from Moscow. Also present were my wife Katrina vanden Heuvel—publisher and editor of *The Nation*—and Dmitri Muratov, editor of the independent newspaper *Novaya Gazeta*, of which Gorbachev is a minority owner.

I asked Gorbachev, on this multiple 30th anniversary, whether he felt his legacies, and his place in history, had been lost in light of events after 1987 and especially since he left power in 1991. He has addressed variations of these questions many times over the years, often in English translation.

Now 86 and in poor health, but mentally as engaged as ever, Gorbachev reiterated two points he has made before. Regarding democracy in Russia, it is a long process with forward and backward stages, but ultimately inevitable because more than one generation of Russians now adheres to the democratic values he promoted while in power. Regarding the new Cold War, he ascribes the largest responsibility to US and European leaders, particularly American ones, who failed to seize the opportunity he (and Reagan) left behind. My own thoughts on these issues will not surprise readers.

Circumstances today, certainly in the US political-media establishment, could hardly be more unlike they were when Gorbachev was Soviet leader and shortly after. Hopes for a strategic partner in the Kremlin have given way to nearly consensual assertions that the current Kremlin leader, Vladimir Putin, poses a worse threat to democracy everywhere and to US national security than did even his Soviet Communist predecessors. Hopes 30 years ago for a world without Cold War and nuclear buildups on both sides have been vaporized by unrelenting Cold War politics in Washington and by inclinations, both in Washington and Moscow, favoring another nuclear arms race. The alternatives presented by Gorbachev are no longer discussed, or even remembered, lost in a haze of historical amnesia.

Nor is there any meaningful public discussion in the United States of who—how, when, and why—those alternatives were squandered during the past 30 years. To the extent they are discussed, the nearly unanimous American explanation is that Putin's "aggressive" policies abroad and undemocratic ones at home were, and remain, solely responsible.

As I have argued, this is an exceedingly unbalanced explanation that requires deleting many causal factors that unfolded before and after Putin came to power in 2000. Among them, Washington's decision to expand NATO eastward to Russia's borders after the Cold War purportedly ended; President George W. Bush's unilateral withdrawal from the Anti-Ballistic Missile Treaty; the West's annexation of Kosovo, which the Kremlin cited as a precedent for its annexing of Crimea; and regime-change policies by several US presidents, from Iraq and Libya to, more surreptitiously, Ukraine in 2014.

None of this is discussed in the US mainstream media, partly because of the exclusion of opposing voices and partly because any Americans suggesting these alternative explanations for the new Cold War are being traduced as "pro-Kremlin" and "Putin apologists," even in progressive publications that once deplored such defamatory discourse.

Which should remind us of another great achievement by Gorbachev in the late 1980s, the introduction of glasnost—unfettered journalism and history writing in the Soviet Union—that led to the end of Soviet censorship but also to "more glasnost" impulses around the world, including in the US media. This too seems to have been lost, displaced by secrecy, a pervasive lack of candor, and other media malpractices in the United States. What we have been told, and not told, for example, about Russiagate allegations reflects a lack of glasnost at the top and lack of willingness in the mainstream media to ferret out anything that does not suggest the culpability of President Trump. Almost everything else is ignored, marginalized, or maligned, even when put forth by well-credentialed observers.

Analyzing the end of Gorbachev's democratization policies in post-Soviet Russia is more complex. Having set out my interpretation in my book *Soviet Fates and Lost Alternatives*, I will note only several factors that also unfolded before Putin came to power.

They included the undemocratic way the Soviet Union was ended surreptitiously in December 1991; the all-but-unprecedented decision by Russia's first post-Soviet president, Boris Yeltsin, to use tank cannons to abolish a popularly elected parliament—indeed, an entire constitutional order—in October 1993 and to replace it with one with fewer checks on what became a super-presidency; Yeltsin's brutal wars against the breakaway province of Chechnya; the rigging of his reelection in 1996; and the oligarchic plundering of Russia and attendant impoverishment of a majority of Russian citizens while he was in power. Again, these, and other developments under Yeltsin in the 1990s, are the essential starting point for any analysis of Putin's role in the reversal of Russia's democratization initiated by Gorbachev. For many American commentators, however, the Yeltsin 1990s remain a rose-tinted period of "democratic transition" and US-Russian solidarity.

Are Gorbachev's lost alternatives retrievable? It's hard to be optimistic. We are probably closer to actual war with Russia today than ever before in history. President Trump, who seemed to want to reverse bipartisan US policies that contributed so significantly to the new Cold War, is said to have been defeated or dissuaded in this regard by "adults" who themselves represent those previous policies.

The absence of debate and glasnost in the mainstream American media encourages silent opponents of Washington's Cold War policies to remain mute. Western Europe may, for various reasons, eventually rebel against Washington's anti-Russian policies and adopt its own approach to Moscow. But as Gorbachev demonstrated, leaders are needed for transformational alternatives. And time is running out.

Meanwhile, Mikhail Sergeevich Gorbachev, having lived long beyond his greatest achievements, watches and hopes, however faintly.

Does Putin Really Want to "Destabilize the West"?

September 6

A T THE CENTER OF RUSSIAGATE AND near abolition of US diplomacy toward Russia today is the accusation that Putin wants to "destabilize

Western democracies," from America to Europe. As with so many other new Cold War narratives, there is no persuasive historical evidence or political logic for this sweeping allegation.

Putin came to power in 2000 with the expressed mission of rebuilding, modernizing, and stabilizing Russia, which had collapsed into near-anarchy and widespread misery during the decade following the end of the Soviet Union. He sought to do so, in very large measure, through expanding good political and economic relations with democratic Europe.

Until the Ukrainian crisis erupted in 2014, much of Putin's success and domestic popularity was based on an unprecedented expansion of Russia's economic relations with Europe and, to a lesser extent, with the United States. Russia provided a third or more of the energy needs of several European Union countries while thousands of European producers, from farmers to manufacturers, found large new markets in Russia, as did scores of US corporations. As late as 2013, the Kremlin was employing an American public-relations firm and recruiting Goldman Sachs to help "brand" Russia as a profitable and safe place for Western investment. Along the way, Putin emerged, despite some conflicts, as a partner among European leaders and even American ones, with good working relations with President Bill Clinton and (initially) with President George W. Bush.

Why, then, would Putin want to destabilize Western democracies that were substantially funding Russia's rebirth at home and as a great power abroad while accepting his government as a legitimate counterpart? Putin never expressed such a goal or had such a motive. From the outset, in his many speeches and writings, which few American commentators bother to read—even though they are readily available in English at Kremlin.ru—he constantly preached the necessity of "stability" both at home and abroad.

Putin's vilifiers regularly cite questionable "evidence" for the allegation that he has long, even always, been "anti-American" and "anti-Western." They say he previously had a career in the Soviet intelligence services. But so did quite a few Western-oriented Russian reformers during the Gorbachev years. They say Putin opposed the US invasion of Iraq. But so did Germany and France. They say he fought a brief war in 2008 against the US-backed government of the former Soviet republic of Georgia. But a European investigation found that Georgia's president, not the Kremlin, began the war.[35]

Putin is also accused of pursuing a number of non-Western and thus, it is said, anti-Western policies at home. But this perspective suggests that all foreign "friends" and allies of America must be on America's historical clock, sharing its present-day understanding of what is politically and socially "correct." If so, Washington would have considerably fewer allies in the world, not only in the Middle East. Putin's reply is the non-Soviet principle of national and civilizational "sovereignty." Each nation must find its own way at home within its own historical traditions and current level of social consensus.

In short, had Putin left office prior to 2014, he would have done so as having been, certainly in the Russian context, a "pro-Western" leader—a course he generally pursued despite NATO's expansion toward Russia's borders, US regime -change policies in neighboring countries, and criticism in high-level Russian circles that he had "illusions about the West" and was "soft" in his dealings with it, especially the United States.

Everything changed with the Ukrainian crisis in 2014, as a result of which, it is asserted, Russia "aggressively" annexed Crimea and supported Donbass rebels in the ensuring Ukrainian civil war. Here began the sweeping allegation that Putin sought to undermine democracy everywhere, and eventually the American presidential election in 2016. Here too the facts hardly fit, as we have already seen but need to recall.

Throughout 2013, as the European Union and Washington wooed Ukraine's elected president, Viktor Yanukovych, with a bilateral economic partnership, Putin proposed a tripartite agreement including Russia, Ukraine's largest trading partner. The EU and Washington refused. The crisis erupted when Yanukovych asked for more time to consider the EU's financial terms, which also included ones involving adherence to NATO's policies.

Putin watched as initially peaceful protests on Kiev's Maidan Square devolved by February 2014 into Western-applauded armed street mobs that caused Yanukovych, still the constitutional president, to flee and put in power an ultranationalist, anti-Russian government. It seemed to threaten, not only vocally, ethnic Russians and other native Russian-speakers in Eastern Ukraine as well as the historical and still vital Russian naval base at Sevastopol, in Crimea, and that province's own ethnic Russian majority. Given those circumstances, which were imposed on him, Putin seemed to have had little choice. Nor would have any imaginable Kremlin leader.

A vital episode amid the February 2014 crisis has been forgotten—or deleted. The foreign ministers of three EU countries (France, Germany, and Poland) brokered a compromise agreement between the Ukrainian president and party leaders of the street protesters. Yanukovych agreed to an early presidential election and to form with opposition leaders an interim coalition government. That is, a democratic, peaceful resolution of the crisis. In a phone talk, President Obama told Putin he would support the agreement. Instead, it perished within hours when rejected by ultranationalist forces in Maidan's streets and occupied buildings. Neither Obama nor the European ministers made any effort to save the agreement. Instead, they fully embraced the new government that had come to power through a violent street coup.

The rest, as the cliché goes, is history. But if Ukraine is indicative, who actually destabilized its flawed, even corrupt, but legal constitutional democracy in 2014? Putin or the Western leaders who imposed an untenable choice on Ukraine and then abandoned their own negotiated agreement?

Will Russia Leave the West?

September 13

SOME FATEFUL QUESTIONS ARE RARELY, IF ever, discussed publicly. One is this: As the established post-1991 "liberal world order" disintegrates and a new one struggles to emerge, where will Russia, the world's largest territorial country, end up politically? The outcome will be fateful, for better or worse.

Geographically, of course, Russia cannot leave the West. Its expanses include vast Far Eastern territories and peoples and a long border with China, but also major European cities such as St. Petersburg and Moscow. For that reason alone, Russia has long been, to varying degrees at various times, both a European and non-European country. Geography, it is said, is destiny, but history is more complex.

The deep divide among Russia's political and intellectual elites between Slavophiles, who saw Russia's true destiny apart from the West, and Westernizers, who saw it with the West, originally debated passionately in the 19th century, has never ended. Arguably, it was only exacerbated by the country's subsequent political history.

It was apparent in the Soviet Communist Party in the 1920s, when rival factions debated and fought over the nature and future of the 1917 Revolution. The long Stalin era, from 1929 to 1953, imposed aspects of Western modernization on the country, such as literacy, industrialization, and urbanization, but also strong elements of what some historians called "Oriental Despotism." These conflicting aspects of the West and the East underlay the struggle, most significantly inside the Communist Party but not only, between anti-Stalinist reformers and neo-Stalinist conservatives during subsequent decades.

Even during the 40-year "Iron Curtain" Cold War, Soviet Russia, for all its elements of isolation, remained linked to the West. The official Communist ideology, however formal, was inherently Western and internationalist. The European nations entrapped in the Soviet Bloc (East Germany, Czechoslovakia, Hungary, Poland, and others) retained their Western currents, as did the Soviet Baltic republics. Those currents flowed from their own Communist parties into the Soviet Russian political establishment. Not surprisingly, many of Mikhail Gorbachev's close advisers who influenced his *perestroika* program for a Westernizing reformation of the Soviet system had themselves been strongly influenced by ideological trends and developments in Soviet Bloc European countries. (A number of them had lived in Prague, for example.)

When the Soviet Union ended in 1991, due largely to Gorbachev's democratizing reforms, it was widely assumed—in Washington, Europe, and by pro-Western factions in Moscow—that Russia was now or would soon be, after a short "transition," an integral part of the US-led West. And yet today, just more than 25 years later, Russia is reviled in Washington and parts of Europe as the "No. 1 threat to the West." Even though this widespread perception is without factual basis, we must ask, what went wrong?

The Western notion that all Soviet anti-Communist "reformers" were pro-Western was mistaken. If we take into account provincial political and intellectual elites, the majority were, and remain, modern-day Slavophiles—a circumstance I was surprised to discover while living in Russia in the 1970s and 1980s—and who now manifest themselves in various forms of "Euro-Asianism" and Russian nationalism. Their influence, abetted by the growing role of the Russian Orthodox Church, whose "ideology" lacks the Western elements of "Communism," has increased very significantly since 1991.

More important were two shocks for Russia that followed the end of the Soviet Union and of the preceding Cold War. First came the social, economic, and demographic catastrophe of the 1990s, associated with Western-promoted democracy and capitalism. Here it is necessary to note again that

Putin is regularly misquoted as having said the end of the Soviet Union caused "the greatest catastrophe of the 20th century." He said instead, "one of the greatest catastrophes," and for the majority of Russians it was a catastrophe.

The second shock was the onset of the new Cold War, for which Washington and much of Europe blame Russia for every mishap, from the Ukrainian crisis of 2014 to the election of President Trump. Many political and intellectual Russians, probably most, do not believe these allegations. They conclude instead that the West seeks only to exclude, isolate, and weaken Russia, no matter Russia's actual intentions. (Here it's also worth noting that while in Soviet times I encountered very little authentic anti-Americanism in Russia, today it is much more widespread among both older and younger generations.)

In addition, educated Russians, with far more access to information than is commonly understood in the West, see Western, particularly American, policies and actions that they interpret as intended to isolate Russia: the expansion of NATO to the country's borders; economic sanctions, along with warnings, as by Senator Jeanne Shaheen, that any "business" with Russia is undesirable; Russophobic demonizing of Putin and thus Russia itself; violations of diplomatic treaties and norms, as occurred recently at the Russian Consulate in San Francisco, suggesting that Washington may no longer want any diplomatic relations with Moscow—or, considering efforts to ban Russia's media outlets *RT* and *Sputnik*, even information relations. As a result, the conclusion of the late, but still influential, Russian philosopher Aleksandr Zinoviev is increasingly quoted as retrospective wisdom about the preceding Cold War: Western foes "were shooting at Communism, but they were aiming at Russia."

Also not surprisingly, Russia is pushing back against, even retreating from, the West. The surge of Slavophile-like ideological movements is one soft expression of this backlash. A more tangible example is Moscow's growing economic self-sufficiency from the West and reorientation toward non-Western partners, from China and Iran to the BRICS countries more generally. There are other manifestations, including, of course, military ones. Meanwhile, the fastest-growing segments of Russia's populace are its millions of Islamic citizens and immigrants from Central Asia. Eventually, demography will influence politics, if it is not already doing so.

All of these Eastern-bound developments may or may not eventually take Russia politically out of the West. If so, this will be clearer after Putin is no longer the country's leader. One indication is that none of his potential successors now visible are, in the Russian context, as "pro-Western" as Putin has been since he came to power in 2000.

What would it mean if Russia leaves—or is driven from—the West politically? Most likely a Russia—with its vast territories, immense natural resources, world-class sciences, formidable military and nuclear power, and UN Security Council veto—allied solidly with all the other emerging powers that are not part of the US-NATO Western "world order" and even opposed to it. And, of course, it would drive Russia increasingly afar from the West's liberalizing influences, back toward its more authoritarian traditions.

The Silence of the Doves

September 20 / September 27

A PERILOUS PARADOX: WHY, UNLIKE DURING THE 40-year Cold War, is there no significant American mainstream opposition to the new and more dangerous Cold War? In particular, from the 1960s through the 1980s, there were many anti–Cold War, or pro-détente, voices in the American political-media-corporate establishment—in the White House, Congress, State Department, political parties, influential print and broadcast outlets, universities and think tanks, major US corporations, even in elections.

That is, debates about Washington policy toward Moscow were the norm during the preceding Cold War, at the very top and at grassroots levels. as befits a democracy. As to the former, I can provide personal testimony. In November 1989, the first President George Bush convened at Camp David virtually his entire national-security team to attend a debate between myself—I was then at Princeton and, as now, a pro-détente advocate—and Harvard professor Richard Pipes, a renowned "hardliner," on the pressing issue of whether the détente under way with the Soviet Union under Gorbachev should be expanded or reversed.

And yet, today, despite escalating perils in US-Russian relations from the

Baltic region and Ukraine to Syria, despite the circumstance that Russia's ruling elites are no longer Communists but professed capitalists, there is virtually none of that. Even the well-organized grassroots anti-nuke movement that once animated pro-détente politics in elections has all but vanished. In the vernacular of the preceding Cold war, political struggles between American "hawks" and "doves" no longer exist. Everywhere, hawks prevail and doves are silent, even in corporations with major Russian investments.

I cannot explain this exceedingly dangerous paradox, only point out some partial factors:

The longtime demonization of Russian President Putin has been an inhibiting factor since the early 2000s. The vilification of President Trump has intensified it. Mainstream Americans skeptical about Washington's Russia policies worry about being labeled "pro-Putin" and/or "pro-Trump." That anyone need worry about such slurs is deplorable, but they do.

There is also the neo-McCarthyism that has grown considerably since Trump's election. As official investigations into alleged "collusion with Russia" become more promiscuous and well-funded campaigns to ferret out "Russian disinformation" in US media unfold, a self-censoring chill has descended on policy discussions. No one wants to be suspected of "collusion with the Kremlin" or of conveying "Russian propaganda." Nor is this merely self-censorship. Major media outlets regularly exclude critics of Washington's Russia policy from their news reports, opinion pages, and TV and radio broadcasts.

On the other hand, some have argued that the persistence and prevalence of Cold War politics is best explained by a nativist American social tradition that "needs an enemy," and more often than not Russia has been assigned this role. Having grown up in Kentucky and lived in Indiana, Florida, New York, and New Jersey, I find no evidence for this "blame the people" explanation. Nor do periodic opinion surveys.

The fault lies with America's governing elites. Two recent developments illustrate that conclusion. US political-media elites fully expected that post-Soviet Russia would become, during the "transition" of the 1990s, Washington's junior and compliant partner in world affairs. When Russia took a different course after 2000, Washington elites blamed not their own illusions and ill-conceived policies but Putin. More recently, as the US-led "liberal world order" shows signs of disintegrating, from Europe to the Middle East, with disparate symptoms from Brexit to Trump's election—US elites and "thought leaders," rather than consider profound historical factors and their own prior policies, again resort to blaming "Putin's Russia."

Where are the liberal Democrats and progressives who once opposed Cold War extremes? Many present-day ones are in the forefront of the new manias. Russiagate allegations did not begin with Trump's election but in the summer and fall of 2016 with pro- Democratic media, led by the *New York Times*, seeding the notion of a "Trump-Putin" conspiracy. Hillary Clinton herself, her campaign already funding the Steele "Dossier," branded Trump a "Putin puppet" in their August televised debate. And when President Obama imposed new sanctions on Russia in December 2016, he cited what became known as Russiagate as a reason, still without presenting any proof.

Congress is now driving Russiagate, with Democrats, many of them self-professed liberals, still in the forefront, among them Representatives Adam Schiff, Jackie Speier, Eric Swalwell, and Maxine Waters, along with Senators Mark Warner and Richard Blumenthal. Abandoning journalistic standards of verifiable evidence, reliable sources, and balanced coverage, the *Times*, joined by the *Washington Post*, are publishing even more sweeping allegations as virtual facts. (For their practices, see the many critical articles by the award-winning journalist Robert Parry at consortiumnews.com.) That print news is amplified almost nightly on pro-liberal MSNBC and CNN. Smaller liberal and progressive outlets are playing the same role.

Not surprisingly, celebrities are also trumpeting Russiagate's most reckless charge that in 2016 America "came under attack by the Russian government." In a recent video produced by Hollywood liberals, Morgan Freeman intoned, "We are at war."

Don't blame trendy celebrities. According to the eminent liberal Democratic intellectual Robert Reich, Russia committed an "unprecedented attack on our democracy," the professor apparently having forgotten or discounted Pearl Harbor and 9/11. And in a major foreign-policy speech on September 21, the "maverick" Bernie Sanders told the Democratic Party, "We now know that the Russian government was engaged in a massive effort to undermine one of our greatest strengths: The integrity of our elections, and our faith in our own democracy." In reality, we do not "know" that.

We do know what many liberal Democrats and progressives once did, but no longer do. They evince no skepticism about intelligence and media Russiagate allegations, despite contrary evidence. They do not protest the growing criminalization of customary "contacts" with Russia—financial, diplomatic, even conjugal, while still promoting the truly "fake news" anti-Trump "Dossier."

Most liberals and progressive express no interest in the role of Obama's Intel chiefs in Russiagate. And even less interest in evidence that Trump's campaign was in fact surveilled by the FBI, as the president later claimed. Instead, Democrats, including liberals, have turned the intelligence agencies into an iconic source of testimony (and leaks). Indeed, Obama's director of national intelligence, James Clapper, whose ethnic slurs about Russians as inherently subverting did not perturb liberals either, is on the advisory board of Hollywood's "Committee to Investigate Russia," which scripted Morgan Freeman.

Above all, liberals once would have been shocked into protest by a recent *Times* article characterizing Special Counsel Robert Mueller's investigative methods as "aggressive tactics," "shock-and-awe tactics to intimidate witnesses and potential targets." Methods, as one source put it, "to strike terror in the hearts of people in Washington." But there is no liberal outrage, no ACLU actions, only articles applauding Mueller for his "scrupulousness" and egging him on, as by Ryan Lizza in the *New Yorker*. Not even when the *Times* suggests that Mueller, unable to find evidence of electoral "collusion," might be "on a fishing expedition" reminiscent of past abuses.

Liberal Democrats even seem indifferent to the slouching toward forms of media censorship. Some of it is soft, such as excluding contrarian voices. But there are adumbrations of harder censorship—official and unofficial campaigns to purge "Russian disinformation and propaganda" from American media, even if expressed by Americans as their own opinion. Thus we have Obama's former UN ambassador, Samantha Power, demanding that we "enhance our vigilance" and her longing for media "gatekeepers" and "umpires." This too betrays not only a disregard for the First Amendment but also contempt for American voters, who presumably, zombie-like, have no critical minds of their own. The normally loquacious ACLU, PEN, and other civil-liberties guardians remain silent.

Privately, some liberal Democrats justify their new illiberalism by insisting it is necessary for the "Resistance" against Trump. But history has long shown that ends-justify-means reasoning does not end well for liberals—or anyone else. Or maybe mainstream "doves" are silent because there no longer are any. This too is, of course, without precedent and exceedingly dangerous.

Has NATO Expansion Made
Anyone Safer?

October 18

TWENTY YEARS AGO, IN 1997, PRESIDENT Bill Clinton made the decision to expand NATO eastward. In order to placate post-Soviet Russia, then weak but heralded in Washington as America's "strategic friend and partner," the Russian-NATO Founding Act was also adopted. It promised that expansion would not entail any "permanent stationing of substantial combat forces." Today they are encamped on Russia's borders and growing. Have twenty years of NATO's expansion actually created the international security it promised?

The expansion of the US-led military alliance, which began in Germany with 13 member states and now stretches to Russia with 29, is the largest and fastest growth of a "sphere of influence" (American) in modern peacetime history. Throughout the process, with hypocrisy that does not go unnoticed in Moscow, Russia has been repeatedly denounced for seeking any sphere of security of its own, even on its own borders.

NATO expansion included two broken promises that the Kremlin has not forgotten. In 1990, the Bush administration and other Western powers assured Soviet leader Gorbachev that, in return for Russia agreeing to a united Germany in NATO, the alliance would "not expand one inch to the east." (Though denied by a number of participants and pro-NATO commentators, the assurance has been confirmed by other participants and by archive researchers.)

The other broken promise is unfolding today as NATO builds up its permanent land, sea, and air power near Russian territory, along with missile-defense installations. NATO "enlargement," as its promoters benignly termed it, continues. Montenegro became a member in 2017 and the "door remains open," Western officials say repeatedly, to the former Soviet republics of Georgia and Ukraine.

NATO is more than the world's largest military alliance. With lavishly funded offices, representatives, think tanks, and other advocates not only in Brussels but in many Western capitals, it is also a powerful political-ideological-lobbying institution—perhaps the world's most powerful corporation, taking into account its multitude of bureaucratic employees in Brussels and elsewhere.

NATO is also very big business. New members must purchase Western-made weapons, primarily US ones. The alliance has, that is, diverse corporate interests that it vigorously promotes. In the United States alone, scarcely a week passes without promotional "news" and commentary produced by NATO-affiliated institutes and authors or based on NATO sources. (The Atlantic Council is an especially prolific source of these media products.)

Asking whether "enlarged" NATO has actually resulted in more insecurity than security requires considering the consequences of several wars it led or in which some of its member states participated since 1997:

• The Serbian war in 1999 resulted in NATO's occupation and annexation of Kosovo, a precedent cited by subsequent annexationists, including Russia when it took back Crimea from Ukraine in 2014.

• The 2003 Iraq War was a catastrophe for all involved and a powerful factor behind expanding organized terrorism, including the Islamic State, and not only in the Middle East. The same was true of the war against Libya in 2011, no lessons of Iraq having been learned.

• NATO promises that Georgia might one day become a member state was an underlying cause of the Georgian-Russian war of 2008, in effect a US-Russian proxy war. The result was the near ruination of Georgia, where NATO remains active today.

• Similarly persistent NATO overtures to Ukraine underlay the crisis in that country in 2014. It resulted in Russia's annexation of Crimea, the still ongoing Ukrainian civil war in Donbass, and another US-Russian proxy war. Meanwhile, US-backed Kiev remains in deep economic and political crisis, and Ukraine fraught with the possibility of a direct US-Russian military conflict.

• There is also, of course, Afghanistan, initially a NATO war effort, but now the longest (and possibly most un-winnable) war in American history.

Any rational calculation of the outcomes of these NATO wars adds up to far more military and political insecurity than security—at most a pseudo-security of simmering crises.

NATO expansion has also bred political-ideological insecurities. The alliance's incessant, ubiquitous media saturation and lobbying in Western capitals, particularly in the United States, has been a major driving force behind the new Cold War and its rampant Russophobia. One result has been the near-end of American diplomacy toward Russia and the almost total militarization of US-Russian relations. This alone is a profound source of insecurity—including the possibility of war with Russia.

During these same 20 years, the enormous resources devoted to NATO expansion have scarcely contributed anything to resolving real international crises, among them economic problems in Europe that have helped inspire its own secessionist movements; international terrorism in the Middle East and the refugee crisis; the danger of nuclear proliferation, which NATO has abetted by spurring a new nuclear arms race with Russia; and others.

Nor has NATO's vast expansion resolved its own internal crises. They include growing military cooperation between NATO member Turkey and Russia; and undemocratic developments in other member states such as Hungary and Poland. And this leaves aside the far-reaching implications of the emerging anti-NATO alliance centering around Russia, China, and Iran—itself a result of NATO's 20-year expansion.

Now consider arguments made by NATO- expansion promoters over the years:

• They say the small Baltic and other Eastern European countries previously victimized by Soviet Russia still felt threatened by Russia and therefore had to be brought into the alliance. This makes no empirical sense. In the 1990s, Russia was in shambles and weak, a threat only to itself. And if any perceived or future threat existed, there were alternatives: acting on Gorbachev's proposed "Common European Home"—a security agreement including all of Europe and Russia; bilateral security guarantees to those once-victimized nations, along with diplomacy on their own part to resolve lingering conflicts with Russia, particularly the disadvantaged status of their ethnic Russian citizens. This argument makes no historical sense either. The tiny Baltic states nearest to Russia were among the last to be granted NATO membership.

• It is also said that every qualified nation has a "right" to NATO membership. This too is illogical. NATO is not a non-selective college fraternity or the AARP. It is a security organization whose sole criterion for "enlargement" should be whether or not new eastern members enhance the security of its current members. From the outset, it was clear, as many Western critics pointed out, it would not.

• Now, it is belatedly argued, Russia has become a threat under Vladimir Putin. But much of what is decried as "Putin's aggression" abroad has been the Kremlin's predictable responses to US and NATO expansionist policies. There is a related negative consequence. Moscow's perception that it is increasingly encircled by an "aggressive" US-led NATO has had lamentable, and also predictable, influence on Russia's internal politics. As NATO expanded, space for democracy in Russia diminished.

For the sake of international security, NATO expansion must end. But is there a way to undo the 20-year folly? Member states taken in since the late 1990s cannot, of course, be expelled. NATO expansion could, however, be demilitarized, its forces withdrawn back to Germany, from which they crept to Russia's borders.

This may have been feasible in the late 1990s or early 2000s, as promised in 1997. Now it may seem to be a utopian idea, but one without which the world is in ever graver danger—a world with less and less real security.

More Double Standards

October 25

MOSCOW AND WASHINGTON HAVE CONFLICTING NARRATIVES—EXPRESSED regularly in their mass media and periodic diplomacy—regarding the history, causes, and nature of the new Cold War. Not surprisingly, both narratives are often self-serving and unbalanced. But the near-consensual US version features an array of double standards that ought to be of grave concern.

I have previously commented on some of these double standards. Moscow is condemned for wanting a sphere of security, or absence of Western military bases, near its borders, while the US-led NATO military alliance has expanded from Germany to countries directly on Russia's borders. (Imagine a Russian-Chinese "sphere" in Canada or Mexico.) NATO's military build-up around Russia is frequently justified by "Putin's lies and deceits." But Kremlin complaints about American "lies and deceit" can hardly be challenged, including the 1990 promise that NATO would "not expand one inch to the east" and the Obama administration's pledge in 2011 that a UN Security Council resolution permitting use of force against Libya would not seek to remove its leader Gaddafi, who was tracked down and assassinated. And then there is professed alarm over Moscow's very few military bases abroad while Washington has some 800.

Now we have more American double standards. When Russian air power and the Syrian army "liberated" the Syrian city of Aleppo from terrorists last year, the US political-media establishment denounced the operation as "Russian war crimes." No such characterizations appeared in coverage of the subsequent US-led "liberation" of the Iraqi city Mosul or Syria's Raqqa, where destruction and civilian casualties may have been considerably greater than in Aleppo. Indeed, on October 19, *Washington Post* columnist David Ignatius was awed by "the overwhelming, pitilessly effective military power of the United States" displayed in Raqqa.

Moscow's nonviolent "annexation" of Crimea in 2014—the Kremlin and most Russian citizens regarded it as "reunification"—continues to inspire anti-Russian sanctions by Washington. American media explain that Crimea was the first forcible modern-day realignment of borders and territory. This narrative omits the Balkan wars in the 1990s and the fate of what was once Yugoslavia, and particularly the US-led NATO annexation of the Serbian province of Kosovo, after a long bombing campaign, in 1999. It also omits secession movements since Crimea—Brexit and the recent Catalonia and Kurdish referenda.

As an outgrowth of their Russiagate coverage, US media now allege that the Kremlin, using its foreign broadcast outlets and social media everywhere, has promoted white-supremacist, neo-Nazi movements in the West, particularly in the United States. Some of this commentary gives the impression that the Kremlin actually created racial conflict in America or is primarily responsible for "exacerbating" it. Meanwhile, the US establishment has virtually nothing to say about the truly ominous growth of extreme-right-wing, even neo-Nazi, movements in US-backed Ukraine.

We will return to this phenomenon later, but briefly stated: with the tacit support, indifference, or impotence of the Kiev government, these movements, some well-armed, are rehabilitating and memorializing Ukrainian Jew-killers during the World War II German occupation—rewriting history in their favor, erecting memorials and renaming public places in their honor, occasionally directly threatening Ukrainian Jews.

Though well-reported in foreign and alternative media, these signs of a rebirth of fascism in a large European country—one supported politically, financially, and militarily by Washington—are rarely, if ever, covered by American mainstream media, notably the *New York Times* and the *Washington*

Post. Where is the balance between these unreported realities and daily allegations of some murky "Russian" divisive posts in American social media?

Finally, also almost daily, American media report that the Kremlin "meddled" in the US 2016 presidential election, warning, "They will be back!" There is as yet no actual evidence in these hyperbolic media accounts, nor any historical balance. Leave aside that Washington and its representatives have "meddled" in nearly every Russian election since the early 1990s. Leave aside even the Clinton administration's large-scale, on-site involvement in Russian President Yeltsin's reelection in 1996. Do note, however, the recent scholarly finding—reported in the *Post* on September 7, 2016—that from 1946 to 2000 (prior to Putin), the United States and Russia interfered in 117 foreign elections.

When pointed out, our new Cold Warriors denounce criticism of these US double standards as "moral equivalence" and pro-Kremlin "whataboutism." But facts being facts, their self-apologetics are really an extreme expression of "American exceptionalism."

The Unheralded Putin —
Official Anti-Stalinist No. 1

November 8

IN NOVEMBER 1961, AT THE FIRST SOVIET Communist Party Congress that publicly condemned Stalin's crimes, the leader, Nikita Khrushchev, unexpectedly called for a national memorial to the tens of millions of victims of the despot's nearly 25-year reign. During the following decades, a fierce political struggle raged between anti-Stalinists and pro-Stalinists, sometimes publicly but often hidden inside the ruling Communist Party, over whether the victims should be memorialized or deleted from history through repression and censorship.

This year, on October 30, anti-Stalinists finally won the struggle when President Putin personally inaugurated a large memorial sculpture, in the center of Moscow, named "Wall of Sorrow" depicting the victims' fate. Though nominally dedicated to all victims of Soviet repression, the monument was clearly—in word, deed, and design—focused on the Stalin years from 1929 to 1953.

I have spent decades studying the Stalin era, during which I came to know many surviving victims of the mass terror and personally observed aspects of the struggle over their place in Soviet politics and history. (I recount these experiences in my book *The Victims Return: Survivors of the Gulag After Stalin.*) As a result, I and my wife of many years, Katrina vanden Heuvel, felt a compelling need to be present at the ceremony on October 30. Having been assured access to the semi-closed event, attended perhaps by some 300 officials, representatives of anti-Stalinist memorial organizations, aged survivors, relatives of victims, and the mostly Russian press)—we flew to Moscow.

It was a special occasion featuring three speakers: Putin, the patriarch of the Russian Orthodox Church, and a representative of a leading memorial organization, Vladimir Lukin. (I have known Lukin since 1976, when he was a semi-dissident outcast in Moscow. Many years later he was Russian ambassador to Washington.) The formal ceremony began just after 5 pm and lasted, after choir hymns, about 45 minutes. At first, I felt the long-anticipated event was marred by the dark, cold, rainy weather, until I heard someone quietly remark, "The heavens are weeping for the victims."

In the context of other anti-Stalinist speeches by Soviet and post-Soviet leaders over the years, Putin's remarks seemed heartfelt, moving, even profound. Without mentioning their names, he alluded to the crucial roles played in the anti-Stalinist struggle by Khrushchev and Mikhail Gorbachev, whose glasnost policies made public the full dimensions of Stalin's mass terror.

One of Putin's remarks seemed especially important. After allowing that many events in Russian history were the subject of legitimate debate, he said Stalin's long terror was not. Other controversial episodes may have their historical pluses and minuses, but the Stalinist terror and its consequences were too criminal and ramifying for any pluses. This, he seemed to emphasize, was the essential lesson for Russia's present and future.

Russia's media being diverse these days, they reacted in three conflicting ways to the memorial monument and Putin's role, at least in Moscow. One was with full approval. Another, expressed in a protest by a number of Soviet-era dissidents, most now living abroad, objected to a memorial to historical victims as "cynical" while there are still victims of repression in Russia. The third view, asserted by ultranationalists, opposed any official condemnation of Stalin's "repression" as detrimental because it weakened the nation's will to "repress" US and NATO encroachment on Russia's borders and the West's "fifth column" inside Putin's own political establishment.

Nonetheless, official state sponsorship of the memorial monument was a historic development—not only a much belated tribute to Stalin's victims and millions of surviving relatives but acknowledgment of the (Soviet) Russian state's prolonged act of criminality. Putin's personal role in the ceremony made this all the more emphatic.

And yet, American media coverage of the October 30 event was characteristic of its general reporting on Russia today—either selectively silent or slanted to diminish the significance of the event, whether out of historical ignorance or a need to vilify everything Putin does and says. The title of the *New York Times* report, on October 30, was representative: "Critics Scoff as Kremlin Erects Monument to the Repressed." Not atypically, the article also contained an untrue assertion, reporting that the Kremlin "has never opened the archives from the [Stalin] period." As all historians of the Soviet period, and any informed Moscow journalist, know, those archives have opened ever wider since the 1990s. This is true of the Soviet Communist Party archive, which holds most of Stalin's personal documents, where I work during periodic visits to Moscow.

But the media malpractice is larger. The persistent demonizing of Putin portrays him as a kind of crypto-Stalin who has promoted the rehabilitation of the despot's reputation in Russia. This is also untrue. Putin's rare, barely semi-positive public references to Stalin over the years relate mostly to the Soviet victory over Nazi Germany, from which, however great Stalin's crimes, he cannot truthfully be separated. For better or worse, Stalin was the wartime Soviet leader.

Nor was October 30 the first time Putin had appeared at a public memorialization of Stalin's victims. He had done so previously, and is still the only Soviet or post-Soviet leader ever to do so. Above all, as I know from my sources, Putin personally made possible politically and financially, against high-level opposition, the creation not only of the new memorial monument but, a few years earlier, a large State Museum of the History of the Gulag, also in Moscow.

It is true that Stalin's reputation in Russia today is on the rise. But, as I explained earlier, this is due to circumstances that Putin does not control, certainly not fully. Pro-Stalin forces in the Russian political-media-historical establishment have used their considerable resources to recast the murderous tyrant in the image of a stern but benign leader who protected "the people" against foreign enemies, traitors, venal politicians, and corrupt bureaucrats.

In addition, when Russia is confronted with Cold War threats from abroad, as it perceives itself to be today, Stalin reemerges as the leader who drove the Nazi war machine from Russia back to Berlin and destroyed it along the way. Not surprisingly, in the recent survey of popular attitudes toward historical figures I cited before, Stalin topped the most-admired list. That is, his reputation has fallen and risen due to larger social and international circumstances. Thus, during the very hard economic times of the Yeltsin 1990s, Stalin's reputation, after plunging under Gorbachev, began to rise again.

It is often reported that Putin's relative silence about controversial subjects in modern Russian history is a kind of sinister cover-up or censorship. Again, this misinterpretation fails to understand two important factors. Like any state, Russia needs a usable, substantially consensual history for stability and progress. Achieving elite or popular consensus about the profound traumas of the Tsarist, Soviet, and post-Soviet pasts remains exceedingly difficult, if not impossible.

Putin's approach, with rare exceptions, has been twofold. First, he has said little judgmental about controversial periods and events while encouraging historians, political intellectuals, and others to argue publicly over their disagreements, though "civilly." Second, and related, he has avoided the Soviet practice of imposing historical orthodoxy though heavy-handed censorship and other forms of suppression. Hence Putin's refusal to stage state events during this 100th anniversary year of the 1917 Revolution—not, as is widely reported, because he "fears a new revolution." He left the public celebrations to the large Russian Communist Party, for which 1917 remains sacred.

American media also regularly assert that Russia has never grappled publicly with, "confronted," its dark Stalinist past. In fact, from 1956 to his overthrow in 1964, Khrushchev permitted waves of revelations and judgments about the crimes of the Stalin era. They were mostly stopped under his immediate successors, but under Gorbachev there was, as was commonly said at the time, a kind of "Nuremberg Trial of the Stalin Era" in virtually all forms of Soviet media. It has continued ever since, though to a lesser degree, with less intensity, and facing greater pro-Stalin opposition. Again, Americans might consider that in Moscow there are two state-sponsored national memorials to Stalin's millions of victims—the Gulag Museum and the new monument. In Washington, there are none specifically dedicated to the millions of American slaves.

Nonetheless, the new memorial to Stalin's victims, however historic, will not end the bitter controversy and political struggle over his reputation, which began with his death 64 years ago. The dispute will continue, not primarily because of one or another Kremlin leader, but because millions of relatives of Stalin's victims and their victimizers still confront each other and will do so for perhaps at least another generation. Because the Stalin era was marked both by the mountain of crimes and the mountain of national achievements I discussed earlier, which even the best-informed and most well-intended historians still struggle to reconcile or balance. And because the nearly 30-year Stalinist experience still influences Russia in ways no less than does a Kremlin leader, even Vladimir Putin, however good his own intentions.

Russiagate Zealots vs. National Security

November 15

A MERICA IS NOW IN UNPRECEDENTED DANGER due to two related crises. A new and more perilous Cold War fraught with the possibility of hot war between the two nuclear superpowers on several fronts, especially in Syria. And the worst crisis of the American presidency in modern times, which threatens to paralyze the president's ability to deal diplomatically with Moscow. (As a reminder, Watergate never accused President Nixon of "collusion with the Kremlin" or his election having been abetted by a Russian "attack on American democracy.")

What Trump did in Vietnam last week was therefore vitally important and courageous, though uniformly misrepresented by the American mainstream media. Despite unrelenting Democratic threats to impeach him for "collusion with the Kremlin," and perhaps even opposition by high-level members of his own administration, Trump met several times, informally and briefly, with Russian President Putin. Presumably dissuaded or prevented by top advisers from having a formal lengthy meeting, Trump was nonetheless prepared. He and Putin issued a joint statement urging cooperation in Syria, where the prospects of a US-Russian war had been mounting. And both leaders later said they had serious talks about cooperating on the crises in North Korea and Ukraine.

What Trump told the US press corps after his meetings with Putin was even more remarkable—and defiantly bold. He reiterated his longstanding position that "having a relationship with Russia would be a great thing—not a good thing—it would be a great thing." He is right: it would be an essential thing for the sake of US national security on many vital issues and in many areas of the world, and should be a priority for both political parties.

Trump then turned to Russiagate, saying that Putin had again denied any personal involvement and that the Russian leader seemed sincere. Trump quickly added that three of President Obama's top intelligence directors— the CIA's John Brennan, Office of National Intelligence's James Clapper, and the FBI's James Comey—were "political hacks," clearly implying that their comments about Russiagate have been and remain less than sincere. He also suggested, correctly, that Russia had been too "heavily sanctioned" by Washington to be the national-security partner America needs.

The immediate reaction of liberal and progressive Russiagaters was lamentably predictable, as was that of their Cold War allies Brennan, Clapper, and Senator John McCain, who never saw the prospect of war with Russia he didn't want to fight. Racing to their eager media outlets, they denounced Trump's necessary diplomacy with Putin as "unconscionable."

Columnist Charles Blow, who from his regular perch at the *New York Times* and on CNN influences many Democrats, followed suit, accusing the president of "a betrayal of American trust and interests that is almost treasonous." He quickly deleted "almost," declaring Trump's presidency to be "a Russian project" and Trump himself "Putin's dupe." In full retro mode, Blow characterized the US president as Putin's "new comrade," apparently unaware that both leaders are known to be anti-Communists.[36]

It's hard not to conclude that promoters of Russiagate have no concern for America's actual national-security interests and indeed, in this regard, are actively undermining those interests. To the extent that Russiagate's crippling of Trump as a foreign-policy president is becoming a major part of the Democratic Party's electoral platform, can the party really be trusted to lead the nation?

Trump's diplomatic initiatives with Putin in Vietnam also demonstrate that a fateful struggle over Russia policy is under way at high levels of the US political-media establishment. Whatever else we may think of the president—I did not vote for him and I oppose many of his other policies—Trump has demonstrated consistency and determination on one existential issue: Putin's Russia is not America's enemy but a national-security partner our nation vitally needs. The president made this clear again following the scurrilous attacks on his negotiations with Putin: "When will all the haters and fools out there realize that having a good relationship with Russia is a good thing, not a bad thing."

Another indication that Trump is prepared to fight for his Russia policy was also noteworthy. He sent his own CIA director to speak with William Binney, a leading member of Veteran Intelligence Professionals for Sanity, which recently published a study concluding that the theft of emails from the Democratic National Committee during the 2016 presidential campaign was not a remote hack by Russia—the foundational allegation of Russiagate—but an inside job. Russiagate zealots quickly dismissed Binney as a "crackpot conspiracy theorist," but he is hardly that.

A retired longtime NSA official, Binney and his colleagues produced a serious alternative explanation of what happened at the DNC. Highly technical aspects of the VIPS report have been seriously contested, including by members of the organization itself, but it cannot be lightly dismissed. It is no more "crackpot conspiracy theory" than was the January 2017 Intelligence Community Assessment that alleged, without the slightest evidence, as we saw, that Putin personally ordered what became known as the "attack on American democracy."

Trump also pointed out, as have others, that the ICA report was not the produce of "17 intelligence agencies" but of a few hand-picked "analysts." He seems to have been suggesting, as I have, that an Intelgate, instead of Russiagate, should first be investigated. This too enraged Democrats, who now defer to US intel chiefs as iconic truth-tellers. They apparently have no memory of the 1976 Senate Church Committee report on gross abuses by US intelligence agencies over the years, including foreign assassinations and violations of Americans' privacy at home, or even their malpractices during the run-up to the not-so-remote Iraq War.

We are clearly at a fateful crossroads in US-Russian relations and in the history of the American presidency. The crux should be American national security in the fullest domestic and international respects, not whether we are Trump supporters or members of the "Resistance." Reckless denunciations make both crises worse. The only way out is nonpartisan respect for verified facts, logic, and rational civil discourse, which Russiagate seems to have all but vaporized, even in once-exalted places.

Russia Is Not the "No. 1 Threat"

November 27

IN THE 1990S, THE CLINTON ADMINISTRATION embraced post-Soviet Russia as America's "strategic partner and friend." Twenty years later, twenty-six since the end of the Soviet Union, the US policy establishment, from liberals to conservatives, insists that "Putin's Russia" is the No. 1 threat to American national security. The primary explanation for how this bipartisan axiom came about, as I have long argued, is to be found in Washington, not Moscow. Whatever the full explanation, it is myopic and itself a threat to US national security.

Threats can be real, uninformed misperceptions, or manufactured by vested interests. In today's real world, Russia is not even among the top five, which are these:

1. Russiagate. Since the late 1940s, when both the United States and the Soviet Union acquired atomic and then nuclear weapons, the first existential duty of an American president has been to avoid the possibility of war with Russia, a conflagration that could result in the end of modern civilization. Every American president has been politically empowered to discharge that duty, even during the most perilous crises, until now.

The still unverified but ever-more-persistent allegations that President Trump has somehow been compromised by the Kremlin and may even be its agent are the number-one threat to America because they hinder, if not cripple, his ability to carry out that existential duty. Recently, for example, his negotiations with Russian President Putin to replace US-Russian conflicts in Syria with cooperation were treated as "treasonous"—not by a successor publication of the John Birch Society but in the pages of the *New York Times* and by other leading media.

Still more, Russiagate alleges that "we were attacked by Russia" during the 2016 presidential election, an act likened to a "political Pearl Harbor." What could be more reckless than to insist we are already at war with the other nuclear superpower? Lest there is any doubt about the gravity of the national-security threat represented by Russiagate, imagine President John F. Kennedy so burdened with such allegations during the 1962 Cuban Missile Crisis. It is unlikely he could have negotiated its peaceful resolution as he did.

2. The demonization of Putin. This too, as I have documented, is unprecedented. No Soviet or post-Soviet leader was ever so wildly, baselessly vilified as Putin has increasingly been for more than a decade. Demonizing Putin has become so maniacal that leading "opinion-makers" seem to think he is a Communist. Joy Reid of MSNBC actually said so, but more telling is the breathless warning on March 30 by *Washington Post* columnist Dana Milbank about "the red menace of Vladimir Putin's Russia."

Mainstream media consumers may be excused for thinking that somehow the Soviet Communist "menace" has been reborn in Moscow, and as an even more fearsome threat. Trump's own CIA Director at the time, Mike Pompeo, evidently believes this uninformed nonsense, or wishes us to do so. Warning that "we still face a threat from the Russians," he explains: "They're Russians, they're Soviets.... pick a name."[37]

Demonizing Putin and "Putin's Russia" as a ramifying threat. It is hard to imagine the plausibility of Russiagate without such a master villain in the Kremlin. And it all but excludes, in effect delegitimizes, the national-security partner most needed by Washington—whoever sits in the Kremlin—in the nuclear age.

3. ISIS and other international terrorist organizations in pursuit of radioactive material to lace with their explosives. This threat would be number one if the US political-media establishment had not conjured up the preceding ones.

Little more needs be said about the looming danger. Imagine even small quantities of radioactive material aboard the planes of 9/11, mixed with the bombs of Paris, Boston, and many other cities, spewed in the air by the fiery explosions and borne by the wind—and wonder if those areas would be inhabitable today. Now consider the value and willingness of Moscow, so often a target of terrorism, as a security partner in this regard given its experiences, sprawling presence between East and West, and exceptional intelligence capabilities. Unlike Russiagate allegations, the threat of terrorism has been amply verified.

4. The proliferation of states with nuclear weapons. In 1949, there were two. Today there are nine. In a new era of transnational ethnic and religious hatreds and wars, such fanaticisms could easily overwhelm the taboo against using forbidden weapons. Iran and North Korea are not the only states capable of acquiring nuclear weapons and the means to deliver them. (Every time the United States militarily attacks a non-nuclear state, others feel the imperative to acquire them as a deterrent.) US-Russian cooperation is essential for preventing more proliferation of all weapons of mass destruction, but threats No. 1 and 2 are preventing Trump from achieving this, even if he wants to do so.

5. Climate change—the science is sound—along with global income inequality, which breeds misery, resentments, fanaticism, and thus terrorism around the world. (According to a report by Scott Shane and others in the *New York Times* on November 7, "The richest 1 percent of the world's population now owns more than half of global wealth, and the top 10 percent owns about 90 percent.") These growing threats rank below the others only because of what a US-Russian bilateral partnership could achieve now. These two require a much larger international alliance and considerably more time.

Why are neither Russia nor China on this list? Russia—because it represents no threat to the United States at all (apart from a nuclear accident or miscalculation) except those Washington and NATO have themselves created. China—because its historical moment as a very great power has come. It may be an economic and regional rival to the United States, but an actual threat (at least thus far) only if Washington also makes it one. The expanding alliance between Russia and China, itself significantly a result of unwise Washington policy-making, is a separate subject.

Why Russians Think America Is Attacking Them

December 20

For 18 months, much of the US establishment has told us, preposterously and without real evidence, that "Russia attacked America" during the 2016 president election. On the other hand, many Russians—in the policy elite, the educated middle class, and ordinary citizens—believe "America has been at war with Russia" for 25 years, and for understandable reasons.

US commentators attribute these views to "Kremlin propaganda." It is true that Russians, like Americans, are strongly influenced by the mass media, especially television. It is also true that Russian television news reporting and commentary are no less politicized than their US counterparts.

But elite and educated Russians are generally better informed and more independent-minded about our political life than most of us are about theirs. They have much more regular access to American news and opinions—from cable and satellite TV, US-funded Russian-language broadcasts and Internet sites, and from Russian sites, such as inosmi.ru, that translate scores of US media articles daily. (Recent prohibiting steps taken by the Department of Justice against *RT* and *Sputnik* can only further diminish American information about Russia.)

Above all, Russians are strongly influenced by what they call "living history." They remember the history of US policy toward post-Soviet Russia since the early 1990s, especially episodes they perceived as having been warlike or acts of "betrayal and deceit"—promises and assurances made to Moscow by Washington and subsequently violated, such as the following:

Presidents Reagan and George H.W. Bush negotiated with the last Soviet Russian leader, Mikhail Gorbachev, what they said was the end of the Cold War on the shared, expressed premise that it was ending "with no losers, only winners." (For this crucial mutual understanding, see two books by Jack F. Matlock Jr., both presidents' ambassador to Moscow: *Reagan and Gorbachev: How the Cold War Ended* and *Superpower Illusions: How Myths and False Ideologies Led America Astray–And How to Return to Reality.*) But readers will recall that in 1992, during his reelection campaign against Bill Clinton, Bush suddenly declared, "We won the Cold War." This anticipated the triumphalism of the Clinton administration and the implication that post-Soviet Russia should be treated as a defeated adversary, as Germany and Japan were after World War II. For many knowledgeable Russians, including Gorbachev himself, this was the first American betrayal.

For the next eight years, in the 1990s, the Clinton administration based its Russia policy on that triumphalist premise, with wanton disregard for how it was perceived in Russia or what it might portend. The catastrophic "shock therapy" economics imposed on Russia by President Boris Yeltsin was primarily his responsibility, but that draconian policy was emphatically insisted on and (meagerly) funded by Washington. The result was the near ruination of Russia—the worst economic depression in peacetime, the disintegration of the highly professionalized Soviet middle classes, mass poverty, plunging life expectancy, the fostering of an oligarchic financial elite, the plundering of Russia's wealth, and more.

All the while, as we have seen, the Clinton administration lauded Yeltsin as its "democrat" and clung to him, as did most leading US political figures, media, and many other influential Americans. Re-making post-Soviet Russia became an American project, as countless American "advisers" encamped to

Moscow and other cities. So many that Russians sometimes said their country had been "occupied." (I treated this subject at the time in my book *Failed Crusade: America and the Tragedy of Post-Soviet Russia.*)

In 1999, Clinton made clear that the crusade was also a military one. He began the still-ongoing eastward expansion of NATO, now directly on Russia's borders. That so many Russians see NATO's unrelenting creep from Berlin to within artillery range of St. Petersburg as "war on Russia" hardly needs explanation. Moreover, herein lies the second "betrayal and deceit" that has not been forgotten.

As readers already know, in 1990, in return for Gorbachev's agreement that a reunited Germany would be a NATO member, all of the major powers involved, particularly the first Bush administration, promised that NATO "would not expand one inch to the east." Many US participants later denied that such a promise had been made, or claimed that Gorbachev misunderstood. But documents just published by the National Security Archive in Washington, on December 17, prove that the assurance was given on many occasions by many Western leaders, including the Americans. The only answer they can now give is that "Gorbachev should have gotten it in writing," implying that American promises to Russia are nothing more than deceit in pursuit of domination.

In 1999, Clinton made clear that NATO expansion was not the non-combat policy Russia had been told it would be. For three months, US-led NATO war planes bombed tiny Serbia, Russia's traditional Slav ally, in effect annexing its province of Kosovo. Visiting Moscow at the time, I heard widely expressed shock, dismay, anger, and perceptions of yet another betrayal, especially by young Russians, whose views of America were rapidly changing from ones of a benign well-wisher to a warlike enemy. Meanwhile, also under Clinton, Washington began its still-ongoing campaign to diminish Moscow's energy sales to Europe, thereby also belying US wishes for Russia's economic recovery.

George W. Bush's administration continued Clinton's winner-take-all approach to post-Soviet Russia. More than any NATO member, Putin's government assisted the United States in its war against the Taliban in Afghanistan after the events of 9/11, saving American lives. In return, Putin expected a genuine US-Russian partnership in place of the pseudo-one Yeltsin had received.

Instead, by 2002, Bush had resumed intrusive "democracy promotion"—interference, or, in today's Russiagate parlance, "meddling"—in Russian politics and NATO expansion eastward. No less fatefully, Bush unilaterally withdrew from the Anti-Ballistic Missile Treaty, the cornerstone of Russian nuclear security. That led to the ongoing process of ringing Russia with anti-missile installations, now formally a NATO project.

In 2008, President Bush tried to fast-track Georgia and Ukraine—both former Soviet republics and Moscow's "red lines" into NATO. Though vetoed by Germany and France, a NATO summit that same year promised both eventual membership. Hardly unrelated, in August Georgian President Mikheil Saakashvili, a Washington protégé, launched a sudden military assault on the Russian protectorate of South Ossetia, inside Georgia, killing a number of Russian citizens. Seeing Saakashvili as an American proxy, the Kremlin intervened.

President Obama came to office promising a "new era of American diplomacy," but his approach to Russia was no different and arguably even more militarized and intrusive than that of his predecessors. During the White House's short-lived "reset" of relations with the Kremlin, then occupied by President Dmitri Medvedev, Obama's vice president, Joseph Biden, told a Moscow public audience, and then Putin himself, that Putin should not return to the presidency. (In effect, Obama and Biden were "colluding" with their imagined partner Medvedev against Putin.)

Other "meddling" was also under way. The Obama administration, notably Secretary of State Hillary Clinton, stepped up intrusive "democracy promotion" by publicly criticizing Russia's parliamentary and presidential elections. Though welcomed by Putin's street opponents, many Russians saw her remarks as characteristic American arrogance.

By 2011, the Obama administration, presumably having lost interest in its own "reset," now betrayed its own partner, President Medvedev, by breaking its promise not to use a UN Security Council resolution in order to depose Libyan leader Gaddafi. Readers will recall that he was tracked by US-NATO war planes and murdered—sodomized with a bayonet—in the streets, a gruesome end Mrs. Clinton later laughingly rejoiced over. All the while, Obama, like his predecessors, pushed NATO expansion ever closer to Russia, eventually to its borders.

Given this history, the fateful events in Kiev in 2014 seem almost inevitable. For anti-Russian NATO expansionists in Washington, Ukraine remained "the biggest prize" in their march from Berlin to Russia, as Carl Gershman, head of the official US regime-change institution, the National Endowment for Democracy, candidly proclaimed in the *Washington Post* on September 26, 2013.

The ensuing crisis led to yet another broken US commitment. In February

2014, readers will also recall, Obama assured Putin that he supported a nego-tiated truce between Ukrainian President Yanukovych and the Maidan street protesters. Within hours, the protesters headed toward Yanukovych's official residence, and he fled, yielding to the US-backed anti-Russian regime now in power.

Then or later, Obama did not, for whatever reasons, ultimately prefer real diplomacy with Russia. He repeatedly refused, or stepped back from, Moscow's offers of cooperation against ISIS in Syria, until finally Putin, after months of pleading, acted on his own in September 2015. Typically, Obama left office by imposing more sanctions, essentially economic warfare, on Russia—this time for the unproven allegations of Russiagate. Indeed, his sanctions included an unprecedented and reckless threat of covert cyber attacks on Russia.

It is through this 25-year history of "American aggression" that many Russians perceive the meaning of Russiagate. For them, a US presidential candidate, and then president, Donald Trump, suddenly appeared proposing to end the long US war against Russia for the sake of "cooperation with Russia."

Russiagate charges—Russians had seen multitudes of American "contacts" with their officials, oligarchs, politicians, wheeler-dealers, ordinary women and men, even orphans ever since the Soviet Union ended—are seen as fic-tions designed to prevent Trump from ending the long "war against Russia." When influential American media denounce as "treasonous" Trump's diplo-macy with Putin regarding Syria and terrorism, for example, Russians see confirmation of their perceptions.

Americans themselves should decide whether these perceptions of US policy are correct or not. Perceptions are at the core of politics, and even if Russians misperceive American intentions, has Washington given them cause to do so? Put another way, is Putin really the "aggressor" depicted by the US political-media establishment or a leader responding to a decades-long "American war against Russia?"

There is one anomaly: Putin, almost alone among high Russian officials, rarely—if ever—speaks of an "American war against Russia." In the context of bellicose statements issued almost daily by the US Congress and main-stream media, might we call this statesmanship?

Part IV

War With Russia?
2018

Four Years of Maidan Myths

January 3

THE UKRAINIAN CRISIS, WHICH UNFOLDED IN late 2013 and early 2014, again requires our attention. It has become a seminal political event of the early 21st century, leading to Russia's annexation of Crimea and to the ongoing US-Russian proxy war in Donbass. It militarized and rooted the epicenter of the new Cold War on Russia's borders, indeed inside a civilization shared for centuries by Russia and large parts of Ukraine. It implanted a toxic political element in American, Russian, Ukrainian, and European politics, possibly in ways we do not yet fully understand. And it has left Ukraine in near-economic ruin, with thousands dead, millions displaced, and others still struggling to regain their previous quality of life.

The events of 2014 also led to NATO's ongoing buildup on Russia's western border, in the Baltic region, yet another new Cold War front fraught with the possibility of hot war. Making things only worse, in late 2017, the Trump administration announced it would supply the Kiev government with more, and more sophisticated, weapons, a step that even the Obama administration, which played a large detrimental role in the 2014 crisis, declined to take.

There are, as we already saw, two conflicting narratives of the Ukrainian crisis. One, promoted by Washington and the US-backed government in Kiev, blames only "aggression" by the Kremlin and specifically by Russian President Putin. The other, promoted by Moscow and rebel forces in eastern Ukraine, which it supports, blames "aggression" by Washington and the European Union. There are enough bad intent, misconceptions, and misperceptions to go around, but on balance Moscow's narrative, almost entirely deleted from US mass media, is closer to the historical realities of 2013–2014.

One myth has been particularly tenacious in Western accounts: what occurred on Kiev's Maidan Square in February 2014 was a "democratic revolution." Whether or not it eventually turns out to have been a "revolution" can be left to future historians, but it hardly seems like one now. Most of the oligarchic powers that afflicted Ukraine before 2014 remain in place four years later, along with their corrupt practices. As for "democratic," removing a legally elected president by threatening his life, as happened to Viktor Yanukovych in February 2014, did not qualify. Nor did the preemptory way the new government was formed, the constitution changed, and pro-Yanukovych parties banned. Yanukovych's overthrow involved people in the streets, but it was a coup.

How much of it was spontaneous and how much directed, or inspired, by high-level actors in the West remains unclear, but a related myth again needs to be dispelled. The rush to seize Yanukovych's residence was triggered by snipers who killed some 80 or more protesters and policemen on Maidan. It was long said that the snipers were sent by Yanukovych, but it has now been virtually proven that the shooters were instead from Right Sector, a neo-Nazi group that was among the protesters on the square.[38]

The anti-democratic origins of today's Kiev regime continue to afflict it. Its president, Petro Poroshenko, is intensely unpopular at home, as are his leading would-be successors. The government remains pervasively corrupt. Its Western-financed economy continues to flounder. And for the most part, Kiev still refuses to implement its obligations under the 2015 Minsk II peace accords, above all granting the rebel Donbass territories enough home rule to keep them in a unified Ukrainian state.

Meanwhile, Poroshenko's government remains semi-hostage to armed ultranationalist battalions, whose ideology and symbols include proudly neo-fascist ones—forces that hate Russia and Western "civilizational" values, to which Maidan was said to aspire, almost equally. The Donbass rebel "republics" have their own ugly traits, but they fight only in defense of their own territory against Kiev's armies and are not sponsored by the US government.

Making things worse, the Trump administration now promises to supply Kiev with more weapons. The official pretext is plainly contrived: to deter Putin from "further aggression against Ukraine," for which he has shown no desire or intention whatsoever. Nor does it make any geopolitical or strategic sense. Neighboring Russia can easily upgrade its weapons to the rebel provinces.

There is also the danger that Kiev's wobbly regime will interpret the American arms as a signal from Washington to launch a new offensive against Donbass in order to regain support at home, but which is likely to end again in military disaster for Kiev. If so, it could bring neo-fascists, who may acquire some of the American weapons, closer to power and the new US-Russian Cold War closer to direct war between the nuclear superpowers. (US trainers will need to be sent with the weapons, adding to the some 300 already there. If any are killed by Russian-backed rebel forces, even unintentionally, what will be Washington's reaction?)

Why would Trump, who wants to "cooperate with Russia," take such a reckless step, long urged by Washington's hawks but resisted even by President Obama? Assuming it was Trump's decision, no doubt to disprove Russiagate allegations that he is a lackey of the Kremlin—accusations he hears and reads daily not only from damning commentary on MSNBC and CNN, but from the once-distinguished academic Paul Krugman, who told his *New York Times* readers on November 17, 2017: "There's really no question about Trump/Putin collusion, and Trump in fact continues to act like Putin's puppet."

Even though there is every "question" and as yet no "in fact" at all, Trump is understandably desperate to end the unprecedented allegations that he is a "treasonous" president—to demonstrate there was "no collusion, no collusion, no collusion." We have here yet another example of how Russiagate has become the No. 1 threat to American national security, certainly in regard to nuclear Russia.

If the media insists on condemning Trump based on dubious narratives and foreign connections, they might focus instead on former vice president Joseph Biden. President Obama put him in charge of the administration's "Ukrainian project," in effect making him pro-consul overseeing the increasingly colonized Kiev. Biden, who is clearly already seeking the 2020 Democratic presidential nomination, bears a heavy personal responsibility for the four-year-old Ukrainian crisis, though he shows no sign of any rethinking or remorse.

In an article in *Foreign Affairs*, Biden and his coauthor, Michael Carpenter, string together a medley of highly questionable, if not outright false, narratives regarding "How to Stand Up to the Kremlin," many involving the years he was vice president. Along the way, Biden repeatedly berates Putin for meddling in Western elections. This is the same Joe Biden who told

Putin not to return to the Russian presidency during Obama's purported "reset" with then President Dmitri Medvedev, and who, in February 2014, told Ukraine's democratically elected President Yanukovych to abdicate and flee the country.

Russia "Betrayed" Not "News That's Fit to Print"

January 10

U S MAINSTREAM MEDIA MALPRACTICE IN COVERING Russia has a long history. There have been three major episodes.

The first was when American newspapers, particularly the *New York Times*, misled readers into thinking the Communists could not possibly win the Russian Civil War of 1918–1920, as detailed in a once famous study by Walter Lippmann and Charles Merz and published as a supplement to the *New Republic*, August 4, 1920. (Once canonical, the study was for years assigned reading at journalism schools, but no longer, it seems.)

The second episode was in the 1990s, when virtually the entire mainstream America print and broadcast media covered the US-backed "reforms" of Russian President Boris Yeltsin, which plundered the state and brought misery to its people, as a benevolent "transition to democracy and capitalism" and to "the kind of Russia we want."[39]

The third and current episode of journalistic malpractice grew out of the second and spread quickly through the media in the early 2000s with the demonization of Vladimir Putin, Yeltsin's successor. It is now amply evident in mainstream coverage of the new Cold War, Russiagate allegations that "Russia attacked American democracy" in 2016, and by much else. Today's rendition may be the worst; certainly it is the most dangerous.

Media malpractice has various elements—among them, selective use of facts, some unverified; questionable narratives or reporting based on those "facts"; editorial commentary passed off as "analysis": carefully selected "expert sources," often anonymous; and amplifications by chosen opinion-page contributors. Throughout is the systematic practice of excluding developments (and opinion) that do not conform to the *Times'* venerable front-page motto, "All the News That's Fit to Print." When it comes to Russia, the *Times* often decides politically what is fit and what is not.

And thus the most recent but exceedingly important example of malpractice. In 1990, as readers know, Soviet Russian leader Mikhail Gorbachev agreed not only to the reunification of Germany, whose division was the epicenter of that Cold War, but also, at the urging of the Western powers, particularly the United States, that the new Germany would be a member of NATO. (Already embattled at home, Gorbachev was further weakened by this decision, which probably contributed to the attempted coup against him in August 1991.) Gorbachev made the decision based on assurances by his Western "partners" that in return NATO would never be expanded "one inch eastward" toward Russia. Today, having nearly doubled its member countries, the world's largest military alliance sits on Russia's western borders.

At the time, it was known that President George H.W. Bush had especially persuaded Gorbachev through Secretary of State James Baker's "not one inch" promise and other equally emphatic guarantees. Ever since Bush's successor, President Bill Clinton, began the still ongoing process of NATO expansion, its promoters and apologists have repeatedly insisted there was no such promise to Gorbachev, that it had all been "myth" or "misunderstanding."

Now, however, the National Security Archive at George Washington University has established the historical truth by publishing, on December 12, 2017, not only a detailed account of what Gorbachev was promised in 1990–1991 but the relevant documents themselves. The truth, and the promises broken, are much more expansive than previously known: all of the Western powers involved—the US, the UK, France, Germany itself—made the same promise to Gorbachev on multiple occasions and in various emphatic ways. If we ask when the West, particularly Washington, lost Moscow as a potential strategic partner after the end of the Soviet Union, this is where an explanation begins.

And yet, nearly a month after publication of the National Security Archive documents, neither the *Times* nor the *Washington Post*, which profess to be the nation's most important and indispensable political newspapers, has printed one word about this revelation. (The two papers are widely important to other media, not only due to their national syndication but because broadcast media such as CNN, MSNBC, NPR, and PBS take most of their own Russia-related "reporting" cues from the *Times* and the *Post*.)

How to explain the failure of the *Times* and *Post* to report or otherwise comment on the National Security Archive's publication? It can hardly be their lack of space or disinterest in Russia, which they featured regularly in one kind of unflattering story or another—and almost daily in the form of "Russiagate." Given their immense news-gathering capabilities, could both papers have missed the story? Impossible, especially considering that three lesser publications—the *National Interest*, on December 12; *Bloomberg*, on December 13; and the *American Conservative*, on December 22—reported on its significance at length.

Or perhaps the *Times* and *Post* consider the history of NATO expansion to be no longer newsworthy, even though it has been the driving, escalatory factor behind the new US-Russian Cold War; already contributed to two US-Russian proxy hot wars (in Georgia in 2008 and in Ukraine since 2014) as well as to NATO's provocative buildup on Russia's borders in the Baltic region; provoked Russia into reactions now cited as "grave threats"; nearly vaporized politically both the once robust pro-American lobby in Moscow politics and previously widespread pro-American sentiments among Russian citizens; and implanted in the Russian policy elite a conviction that the broken promise to Gorbachev represented characteristic American "betrayal and deceit."

Both Russian presidents since 2000—Putin and President Obama's "reset" partner Dmitri Medvedev—have said as much, more than once. Putin put it bluntly: "They duped us, in the full sense of this word." Russians can cite other instances of "deceit," as I have already specified. But it is the broken promise to Gorbachev regarding NATO expansion that lingers as America's original sin, partly because it was the first of many such perceived duplicities, but mainly because it has resulted in a Russia semi-encircled by US-led Western military power.

Given all this, we must ask again: Why did neither the *Times* nor the *Post* report the archive revelations? Most likely because the evidence fundamentally undermines their essential overarching narrative that "Putin's Russia" is solely responsible for the new Cold War and all of its attendant conflicts and dangers, and therefore no rethinking of US policy toward post-Soviet Russia since 1991 is advisable or permissible, certainly not by President Donald Trump.

Therein lie the national-security dangers of media malpractice. And this example, while of special importance, is far from the only one in recent years. In this regard, the *Times* and *Post* seem contemptuous not only of their own professed journalistic standards but of their professed adage that democracy requires fully informed citizens. It also sheds ironic light on the Post's new front-page mantra, "Democracy Dies in Darkness."

US Establishment Finally Declares "Second Cold War'"

January 24

FOR MORE THAN A DECADE, I have been warning about an unfolding new Cold War with Russia. Despite compelling evidence, leading US policy-makers, media commentators, and scholars have adamantly denied its existence, even such a possibility. They have cited post-Soviet Russia's purported weakness; the absence of "ideological conflict"; the non-global nature of any conflicts; the benign nature of Washington policy; etc.

These new Cold War deniers were either uninformed, myopic, or unwilling to acknowledge their own complicity in the squandered opportunity for a real post-Soviet peace, even an American-Russian strategic partnership. But the deniers' most prestigious and influential foreign policy organization, the Council on Foreign Relations (CFR), has now issued a report fully acknowledging, indeed eagerly declaring, that "The United States is currently in a second Cold War with Russia."

The importance of the CFR is not easily exaggerated. As its activities, history, self-proclamations, and *Wikipedia* entry make clear, it is not an ordinary "think tank." Founded nearly a century ago, headquartered lavishly in New York City with a branch in Washington, almost 5,000 selected members, and considerable annual revenue, its aura, influential journal *Foreign Affairs*, and elite membership have long made the CFR America's most important non-governmental foreign-policy organization—certainly for politicians, business executives, media leaders, academics, and others involved with US foreign policy. Almost all of them, including presidential candidates, aspire to CFR membership or its imprimatur in one way or another. (Hence Joseph Biden's recent article in *Foreign Affairs*.)

For decades, the CFR's primary role has been—through its journal, website, special events, and multiple weekly membership sessions—to define the legitimate parameters of discussion about US foreign policy and related issues. Regarding Russia, even the Soviet Union, the CFR, as a professed bipartisan, independent, centrist organization, generally adhered to this role, and not badly. (I became a member in the 1970s and resigned in protest this year.)

The CFR featured varying, even conflicting, expertise and opinions about the 40-year Cold War and thereby fostered intellectual and policy debate. This more ecumenical, pluralist orientation largely ended, however, more than a decade ago. Opinions incompatible with Washington's growing "group think" about Russia were increasingly excluded, with very few exceptions. The CFR—much like Congress and the mainstream media—became a bastion of the new Cold War, though without acknowledging it.

Now it has done so. The CFR's new report, "Containing Russia," by two "bipartisan" veterans of the genre, both longtime CFR fellows, Robert D. Blackwill and Philip H. Gordon, could have been published during the hyperventilated early stage of the preceding Cold War, before it was tempered by the 1962 Cuban Missile Crisis, as reflected in the retrograde word "Containing."[40]

The best that can be said about the report is its banality—some 50 pages and 72 endnotes offering little more than a superficial, though devout, digest of recent mainstream media malpractices. We find here, for example, the usual unbalanced narratives of contemporary events, questionable "facts," elliptical history (when any at all), opinion and ideology passing as analysis, and not a little Russophobia.

Not surprisingly, the still unproven allegations of Russiagate are the pretext and pivot of the CFR report. (Its authors even inflate the scandal's already inflammatory rhetoric: "Moscow's ultimate objective was regime change in the United States.") Thus the first sentence of the introduction by CFR president Richard Haass: "Russia's interference in the 2016 US presidential election constituted an attack on American democracy," echoing the tacky Hollywood celebrity video produced a few months ago. The authors also repeat hyperbolic assertions equating "the attack" with Pearl Harbor and 9/11.

From this, the report goes on to refer, directly and allusively, to the alleged Kremlin-Trump "collusion," and then to project the "threat" represented by Russian President Putin, who is presented as having no legitimate Russian national interests, only "paranoia," to "worldwide" status. Again, every piece of alternative or conflicting reporting, analysis, and sourcing is omitted, as is any mention of retracted and "corrected" mainstream media articles and broadcasts. Nowhere is there any serious concern about the graver dangers inherent in this "second Cold War." In this perilous context, the CFR "recommendations" are of the back-to-the-future kind—back to the initial, unbridled, pre-1962 Cuban Missile Crisis threats, confrontations, and escalations.

Considering how this shabby—some may say shameful—report should reflect on the CFR's reputation, what was the motivation behind its publication? Recalling that it comes on the heels of similar new Cold War exhortations—Biden's article mentioned earlier, Senator Ben Cardin's similar "report" not long ago, leading newspaper editorials demanding a stronger reaction to "Russia's war on the West," and the Trump administration's own myopic doctrinal declaration last week that Russia and China are now a greater threat than is international terrorism—the CFR report's purpose seems to be threefold. To mobilize the bipartisan US policy establishment behind a radical escalation of the new Cold War. (Tellingly, it also criticizes former President Obama for not having done enough to counter Moscow's "growing geopolitical challenge".) To preclude any critical mainstream discussion of past or current US policy in order to blame only Russia. And thereby to prevent the possibility of any kind of détente, as proposed by President Trump.

The CFR report may slam the door, already nearly shut, on such discussions and policies. If so, where is any hope, any way out of this unprecedentedly perilous state of US-Russian relations? Recent opinion surveys suggest that a majority of Americans have no appetite for such reckless policies. Conceivably, they could vote to change Washington's approach to Russia. But for this they would need such candidates and time. Currently, there are neither. As during the 40-year Cold War, the CFR Report seeks to mobilize European allies behind escalating the "second Cold War." In several European countries and parties, there also appears to be little appetite for this. Americans may have to look to Europe for alternative leadership, while hoping that meanwhile Moscow does not overreact.

For now, however, the only hope is that Russiagate allegations do not prevent Trump from becoming the pro-détente president "cooperating with

Russia" he wanted to be. Even if he tries, would the Council on Foreign Relations' like-minded praetorians in Washington—who now present that traditional aspiration as evidence of criminality—permit it?

Russiagate or Intelgate?

February 7

I FIRST RAISED THE QUESTION OF "INTELGATE," perhaps coining the word, nearly a year ago. The recently released Russiagate memo, overseen by Republican Congressman Devin Nunes and declassified by President Trump, raises the question anew.

Having for years researched Soviet-era archive materials (once highly classified) in Moscow, I understand the difficulties involved in summarizing secret documents, in particular ones generated by secretive intelligence agencies. They must be put in the larger political context of the time, which can be fully understood only by using open and other sources as well. And they may be subsequently contradicted by classified materials not yet available.

Nonetheless, the "Republican memo," as it has become known while we await its Democratic counterpart, indicates that some kind of operation against presidential candidate and then President Trump, an "investigation," was under way among top officials of US intelligence agencies for a long time.

The memo focuses on questionable methods used by Obama's FBI and Justice Department to obtain a secret warrant permitting them to surveil Carter Page, a peripheral and short-tenured Trump foreign-policy adviser, and on the role played in this by the anti-Trump "dossier" complied by Christopher Steele, a former British intelligence officer whose career specialization was Russia. But the memo's implications are larger.

Steele's dossier, which alleged that Trump had been compromised by the Kremlin in various ways for several years even preceding his presidential candidacy, was the foundational document of the Russiagate narrative, at least from the time its installments began to be leaked to the American media in the summer of 2016. It has played a central role ever since, possibly even in the US Intelligence Community Assessment (ICA) of January 2017 (when *BuzzFeed* published the dossier), the same month that FBI Director James Comey "briefed" President-elect Trump on "salacious" parts of the dossier—apparently in an effort to intimidate him. Directly or indirectly, the dossier led to the special investigation headed by Robert Mueller.

Even though both the dossier and subsequent ICA report have been substantially challenged for their lack of verifiable evidence, they remain the basic sources for proponents of the Russiagate narrative of "Trump-Putin collision." The memo and dossier are now being subjected to closer (if partisan) scrutiny, much of it focused on the Clinton campaign having financed Steele's work through his employer Fusion GPS.

But two crucial and ramifying question are not being explored. Exactly when, and by whom, was this Intel operation against Trump begun? And exactly where did Steele get the "information" that he was filing in periodic installments and that grew into the dossier?

In order to defend itself against the Republican memo's charge that it used Steele's unverified dossier to open its investigation into Trump's associates, the FBI claims it was prompted instead by a May 2016 report of remarks made earlier by another lowly Trump adviser, George Papadopoulos, to an Australian diplomat in a London bar. Even leaving aside the ludicrous nature of this episode, the public record shows it is not true.

In testimony to the House Intelligence Committee in May 2017, John Brennan, formerly Obama's head of the CIA, strongly suggested that he and his agency were the first, as the *Washington Post* put it at the time, "in triggering an FBI probe." Both the *Post* and the *New York Times* interpreted his remarks in this way.[41,42] Equally certain, Brennan, as widely reported, played a central role in promoting the Russiagate narrative thereafter, briefing members of Congress privately and giving President Obama himself a top-secret envelope in early August 2016 that almost certainly contained Steele's dossier.

Early on, Brennan presumably would have shared his "suspicions" and initiatives with James Clapper, then Obama's Director of National Intelligence. FBI Director James Comey, distracted by his mangling of the Clinton private-server affair during the presidential campaign, may have joined them actively somewhat later. But when he did so publicly, in his March 2017 testimony to the House Intelligence Committee, it was as J. Edgar Hoover reincarnate—as the nation's number-one expert on Russia and its profound threat to America. (As I pointed out previously, his testimony regarding Russia was remarkably uninformed.)

The question therefore becomes: when did Brennan begin his "investigation" of Trump? His House testimony leaves this somewhat unclear, but according to a subsequent *Guardian* article, by late 2015 or early 2016 Brennan was receiving, possibly soliciting, reports from foreign intelligence agencies about "suspicious 'interactions' between figures connected to Trump and known or suspected Russian agents."[43]

If these reports and Brennan's own testimony are to be believed, he, not the FBI, was the instigator—the godfather—of Russiagate. Certainly, his subsequent frequent and vociferous public retelling of Russiagate allegations against Trump suggest that he played a (probably the) instigating role. And, it seems, a role in the Steele dossier as well.

Equally important, where did Steele get his information? According to Steele and his many stenographers—they include his American employers, Democratic Party Russiagaters, the mainstream media, and many other, even progressive, publications—the information came from his "deep connections in Russia," specifically from retired and current Russian intelligence officials in or near the Kremlin. From the moment the dossier began to be leaked to the American media, this seemed highly implausible (as reporters who took his bait should have known) for several reasons.

Steele had not returned to Russia after leaving his post there in the early 1990s. Since then, the main Russian intelligence agency, the FSB, has undergone many personnel and other changes, especially since 2000, and particularly in or near Putin's Kremlin. Did Steele really have such "connections" so many years later?

Even if he did, would these purported Russian insiders really have collaborated with a "former" British intelligence agent under what is so often said to be the ever-vigilant eye of the ruthless "former KGB agent" Vladimir Putin, thereby risking their positions, income, perhaps freedom, as well as the well-being of their families?

It was said originally that his Russian sources were highly paid by Steele. Arguably, this might have warranted the risk. But on January 2, 2018, Steele's employer and head of Fusion GPS, Glenn Simpson, wrote in the *Times* that "Steele's sources in Russia…were not paid." If the Putin Kremlin's purpose was to put Trump in the White House, why would these "Kremlin-connected" sources have contributed to Steele's anti-Trump project without financial or political gain—only with considerable risk? (There is the also the matter of factual mistakes in the dossier that Kremlin "insiders" were unlikely to have made, but this is the subject for a separate analysis.)

We now know that Steele actually had at least three other "sources" for the dossier, ones not previously mentioned by him or his employer. There was information from foreign intelligence agencies provided by Brennan to Steele or to the FBI, which we also now know was collaborating with Steele. There was the contents of a "second Trump-Russia dossier" prepared by people personally close to Hillary Clinton and who shared their "findings" with Steele.[44] And in fact, Steele himself repeatedly cites as a source a Russian emigre associate of Trump—that is, apparently an American, not Russian, citizen.

Most intriguing, there was "research" provided by Nellie Ohr, wife of a top Department of Justice official, Bruce Ohr, who, according to the Republican memo, "was employed by Fusion GPS to assist in the cultivation of opposition research on Trump. Ohr later provided the FBI with all of his wife's opposition research." Most likely, it too found its way into Steele's dossier. (Mrs. Ohr was a trained Russian studies scholar with a PhD from Stanford and a onetime assistant professor at Vassar, and thus, it must have seemed, an ideal collaborator for Steele.)

There is also the core allegation made both by Steele and the ICA report that Putin personally "ordered" and "directed" the Russiagate operation on behalf of Trump, but neither gives a persuasive or consistent motive, especially considering that if exposed—even Steele claims some top-level Kremlin officials feared the purported plot might "backfire"—it would benefit electorally only Hillary Clinton. Nor do their many media stenographers give us a coherent motive.

Some say the operation was "payback" for Clinton having encouraged protests against Putin in Moscow in 2011-2012. No, say others, it was a longer-standing Kremlin preference for Trump going back eight or more years, though this is contradicted in the Steele dossier where some Kremlin officials are said not to favor Trump. Still others say it was payback not against Clinton but for what Putin saw as the US-led doping scandal that battered the Russian Olympic team. Now it's just Putin's general desire to sow "chaos and disorder" in the West. None of these motives make sense given, as I have pointed out, Putin's initial and still ongoing hope to rebuild Russia partly through modernizing economic partnerships with a stable and prospering West, including the United States.

We are left, then, with a ramifying question: how much of the "intelligence information" in Steele's dossier actually came from Russian insiders, if any? (This uncertainty alone should stop Fox News' Sean Hannity and

others from declaring that the Kremlin used Steele—and Hillary Clinton—
to pump its "propaganda and disinformation" into America. These pro-
Trump counter-allegations also fuel the new Cold War.)

We are left with even more ramifying questions. Was Russiagate produced by leaders of Obama's intelligence community, not just the FBI? If
so, it is the most perilous political scandal in modern American history, and
the most detrimental to American democracy. It would indeed, as zealous
promoters of Russiagate assert, make Watergate pale in significance. (To
understand more, we need to know more, including whether Trump associates other than Carter Page and Paul Manafort were surveilled by any of the
intelligence agencies involved. And whether they were surveilled in order to
monitor Trump himself, on the assumption they would be in close proximity
to him, as the president suggested in a tweet.)

If Russiagate involved collusion among US intelligence agencies, as now
seems likely, why was it undertaken? There are various possibilities. Out of
loathing for Trump? Out of institutional opposition to his promise of better
relations—"cooperation"—with Russia? Or out of personal ambition? Did
Brennan, for example, aspire to remain head of the CIA, or to a higher position, in a Hillary Clinton administration?

What was President Obama's role in any of this? Or to resort to the
Watergate question: what did he know and when did he know it? And what
did he do? The same questions would need to be asked about his White
House aides and other appointees involved. Whatever the full answers,
there is no doubt that Obama acted on the Russiagate allegations. He cited
them for the sanctions he imposed on Russia in December 2016, which led
directly to the case of General Michael Flynn; to the worsening of the new
US-Russian Cold War; and thus to the perilous relationship inherited by
President Trump.

With all of this in mind, and assuming Trump knew most of it, did he really have any choice in firing FBI Director Comey, for which he is now being
investigated by Mueller? We might also ask again, given Comey's role during
Hillary Clinton's presidential campaign (for which she and her team loudly
condemned him), whether as president she too would have had to fire him.

Listening almost daily to the legion of former US intelligence officers
condemn Trump in the media, we may wonder if they are increasingly fearful
it will become known that Russiagate was mostly Intelgate. For that we may
need a new bipartisan Senate Church Committee of the mid-1970s. Once
famously, it investigated and exposed misdeeds by US intelligence agencies
and led to reforms that are no longer the preventive measures against abuses

of power they were intended to be. (Ideally, everyone involved would be granted amnesty for prior misdeeds, ending all talk of "jail time," on the condition they now testify truthfully.)

Such a full, inclusive investigation of Intelgate would require the support of leading Democratic members of Congress. This no longer seems possible.

What Russiagate Reveals About America's Elites

February 21

RUSSIAGATE'S NEARLY TWO YEARS OF ALLEGATIONS and investigations were instigated by top US political, media, and intelligence elites. They have revealed profoundly disturbing characteristics of people who play a very large role in governing our country. Six of these barely concealed truths are especially alarming.

1. Russiagate's promoters evidently have little regard for the future of the American presidency. At the center of their allegations is the claim that the current president, Donald Trump, achieved the office in 2016 due to a conspiracy ("collusion") with the Kremlin; or to some dark secret the Kremlin uses to control him; or due to "Russian interference" in the election; or all three. This means, they say outright or imply daily, that the president is some kind of Kremlin agent or "puppet" and thus "treasonous."

Such allegations are unprecedented in American history. They have already deformed Trump's presidency, but no consideration is given to how they may affect the institution in the future. Unless actual proof is provided in the specific case of Trump—thus far there is none—they are likely to leave a stain of suspicion on, or inspire similar allegations against, future presidents. If the Kremlin is believed to have made Trump president or corrupted him, why not future presidents as well?

That is, Russiagate zealots seek to delegitimize Trump's presidency but risk leaving a long-term cloud over the institution itself. And not only the presidency. They now clamor that the Kremlin is targeting the 2018 congressional elections, thereby projecting the same dark cloud over the next Congress, even if embittered losers do not explicitly blame Putin's Kremlin.

2. Russiagate promoters clearly also have no regard for America's national security. By declaring that Russia's "meddling" in the 2016 US presidential election was "an attack on American democracy" and "an act of war" comparable to Pearl Harbor and 9/11, they are practicing the dictionary meaning of "war-mongering." Can this mean anything less than that the United States must respond with "an act of war" against Russia? It is noteworthy that Russiagaters rarely, if ever, mention the potentially apocalyptic consequences of war between the two nuclear superpowers, an abiding concern once shared by all enlightened elites.

Closely related, Russiagate accusations against Trump, whom they characterize as a "mentally unstable president," risk provoking him to stumbling into just such a war in order to demonstrate he is not the "Kremlin's puppet." By casting doubt on Trump's loyalty to America, they also limit his capacity, possessed by all American presidents since the onset of the atomic age, to avert or resolve nuclear crises through diplomatic instead of military means, as President Kennedy did in the Cuban Missile Crisis.

In short, American elites themselves have made Russiagate the number-one threat to US national security, not Russia.

3. Having found no factual evidence of such a plot, Russiagate promoters have shifted their focus from the Kremlin's alleged hacking of DNC emails to a social-media "attack on our democracy." In so doing, they reveal their contempt for American voters, for the American people.

A foundational principle of theories of representative democracy is that voters make rational and legitimate decisions. But Russiagate advocates strongly imply—even state outright—that American voters are easily duped by "Russian disinformation," zombie-like responding to signals as how to act and vote. The allegation is reminiscent of, for people old enough to remember, the classic Cold War film *Invasion of the Body Snatchers*. But let the following representatives of America's elite media speak for themselves:

• According to *Washington Post* columnist Kathleen Parker, Russia's social-media intrusions "manipulated American thought.... The minds of social media users are likely becoming more, not less, malleable." This, she goes on, is especially true of "older, nonwhite, less-educated people." *New York Times* columnist Charles Blow adds that this was true of "black folks."[45,46]

• *Times* reporter Scott Shane is straightforward, writing about "Americans duped by the Russian trolls." Evan Osnos of the *New Yorker* spells it out without nuance: "At the heart of the Russian fraud is an essential, embarrassing insight into American life: large numbers of Americans are ill-equipped to assess the credibility of the things they read."[47,48]

• Another *Post* columnist, Dana Milbank, even rehabilitates a Leninist concept. "Putin," he tells readers, "has played Americans across the political spectrum for suckers." In particular, he turned Trump's millions of voters "into the useful idiots of the 21st century." To be clear, according to Milbank's demeaning of US citizens generally, "Putin made fools of Americans."[49]

These denigrators of the American people are, of course, lead writers for some of our most elite publications. Their apparent contempt for "ordinary" citizens is not unlike a centuries-old trait of the radical Russian intelligentsia. That tradition has long viewed the Russian *narod* (people) with similar contempt, while maintaining that the rarified intelligentsia therefore must lead them, and not always in democratic ways.

4. Russiagate was initiated by political actors, but elite media gave it traction, inflated it, and promoted it to what it is today. These most "respectable" media include the *New York Times*, the *Washington Post*, the *New York Review of Books*, the *New Yorker*, and, of course, CNN and MSNBC, among others. They proclaim themselves to be factual, unbiased, balanced, and an essential component of American democracy—a "fourth branch of government."

Maybe a "branch," but far from fact-based and unbiased in its reporting and commentary on Russiagate. The media's combined loathing for Trump and "Putin's Russia" has produced, as we have seen repeatedly, one of the worst episodes of malpractice in the history of American journalism. This requires a special detailed study, though no leading media critics or elite journalism schools seem interested.

Nor are elite media outlets above slurring the reputations of anyone who dissents from contemptuous aspects of Russiagate, even members of their own elite. Recently, for example, the *Times* traduced a Facebook vice president whose study suggested that "that swaying the election was not the main goal" of Russian use of Facebook. Similarly, a brand name of liberal-progressive MSNBC, John Heilemann, suggested on air, referring to questions about Russiagate posed by Congressman Devin Nunes, "that we actually have a Russian agent running the House Intel Committee on the Republican side." The Democratic senator being interviewed, Chris Murphy, was less than categorical in brushing aside the "question."[50,51]

Not to be overlooked, elite media have done little, if anything, to protest the creeping Big Brother-like censorship programs now being assiduously promoted by other elites in government and private institutions in order to ferret out and ban "Russian disinformation," something any American might be "guilty" of entirely on his or her own. Instead, leading media have abetted and legitimized these undemocratic undertakings by citing them as sources.

5. Then there is the Democratic Party's role in promoting Russiagate. Preparing for congressional elections in 2018, this constituent component of the American two-party system seems less a vehicle of positive domestic and foreign-policy alternatives than a party promoting conspiracy theories, Cold War, and neo-McCarthyism. A number of local candidates say these electoral approaches are less their own initiatives than cues, or directives, coming from high party levels—that is, from Democratic elites.

6. Finally, but no less revealing, American elites have long professed to be people of civic courage and honor. Russiagate has produced, however, very few "profiles in courage"—people who use their privileged positions of political or media influence to protest the abuses itemized above. Hence another revelation, if it is really that: America's elites are composed overwhelmingly not of "rugged individualists" but of conformists—whether due to ambition, fear, or ignorance hardly matters.

Russiagate Amnesia or Denialism

February 28

M ANY RUSSIANS, I HAVE ALREADY EXPLAINED, have an awareness of "living history"—memories of past events that continue to influence current ones. Russiagate suggests that Americans have significantly less historical awareness—or that its promoters willfully ignore past American events and practices.

A fundamental Russiagate tenet is that the Kremlin sought, primarily through social media, "to create or exacerbate divisions in American society and politics" in 2016. Even if true, there is no evidence that this purported campaign had any meaningful impact on how Americans voted in the presidential election. But even it somehow did, the social and political "divisions" were hardly comparable to those in our not so distant past.,

Those past divisions included Jim Crow segregation and the black civil-rights struggle; the social-political barricade in American life—even in families—generated by the Vietnam War; and the religious-political division over abortion rights during several electoral cycles. There were also "divisions" associated with Watergate, which drove a president from office, and with the House impeachment of President Clinton. To assert that the considerably lesser "divisions" in the country in 2016 were any less American in origin or needed to be exacerbated by Russia is a kind of amnesia or denialism uninformed by history.

Closely related is the claim that "Russian propaganda and disinformation" played in 2016 an unprecedented, oversized role in America, and continue to do so. But I recall, at least since my schoolboy days in Kentucky, that this was an everyday allegation back then as well, including during the civil-rights struggle. A primary source of those dire warnings was none other than then FBI director, J. Edgar Hoover, whose writings were often assigned in schools as cautionary readings.

Hoover's essential theme was, of course, that Americans posing as loyal citizens were actually agents of Soviet (Russian) Communist "propaganda and disinformation." That allegation was also widely used by many others, mainly for political purposes, and perhaps widely believed. When blacklisting reached Hollywood in the 1950s, films were "investigated" for latent "Communist propaganda," and purportedly found. This was a search for, so to speak, "Russian trolls" in the movies, not so unlike those said to be found today in social media.

On similar ahistorical grounds, Russiagaters go on to allege that Russia "meddled" in the 2016 US presidential election and thus committed "an act of war against America." Whatever "meddle" means—the word is both capacious and imprecise—governments have meddled in the elections of other states for centuries in one form or another. Israel has, of course, meddled in US elections for decades. More to the point, according to a study reported by the *New York Times*, on February 17, 2018, the US government ran 81 "overt and covert election influence operations" in foreign countries from 1946 to 2000. (Soviet and post-Soviet Russia ran 36 such operations during the same period.)

As readers already know, official and unofficial American institutions have been deeply involved in—meddled in—Russian political life ever since the end of the Soviet Union in 1991. The instance that should dispel any amnesia is, of course, the financial, on-site, hands-on American effort to help reelect a badly failing President Yeltsin in 1996. (There is some doubt as to whether he really was reelected). Nor was this, as we saw, covert, having been apparent at the time and US mass media later boasting about it. Two wrongs may not make a right, but less amnesia would put the lesser Russiagate allegations of "meddling," none of the truly significant ones yet having been proven, in perspective.

One way or another, to some degree or another, at least two US intelligence agencies, the CIA and FBI, have played unsavory roles in Russiagate. And yet, many mainstream American media outlets and leading Democrats are exalting them as paragons of verified, nonpartisan information, including their recurring leaks to media. This is puzzling and probably best explained by willful amnesia or denial since not a few of these same media and politicians had previously been highly skeptical, even sharply critical, of both agencies.

Leave aside well-documented CIA assassinations and FBI persecution of civil-rights leaders, including Martin Luther King, Jr. Recall instead only the quality of CIA information that led President Kennedy to the Bay of Pigs disaster, President Lyndon B. Johnson and Congress ever deeper into the Vietnam War, and the nation to the catastrophic war in Iraq, whose consequences still linger. And yet information provided by the CIA regarding Russiagate is to be accepted uncritically? Is its past role, and that of the FBI, forgotten or forgiven?

Unable to provide proof linking the Kremlin or President Trump to the alleged original sin—the hacking and dissemination of DNC emails—media investigators and special counsel Robert Mueller himself have settled for seeking and prosecuting past financial misdeeds on the part of Trump "associates," notably Paul Manafort. (Manafort's laundered millions having originated mostly in Ukraine, not Russia, why is this not actually Ukrainegate? Or Russiagate without Russia?)

Here too precedents are forgotten or deleted. The "shock therapy" urged on Moscow by Washington in the 1990s led to the creation of a small group of Russian billionaire oligarchs and the "globalization" of their wealth, lavishly between the United States and Russia. Predictable scandals ensued. Two resulted in high-profile US convictions for money laundering and other financial improprieties, not unlike the charges against Manafort.

One involved the Bank of New York, the other a Harvard University institute. Both featured Americans and "Kremlin-linked" officials of the

Yeltsin government, which the Clinton administration, to say the least, strongly supported. One scandal dwarfed the charges against Manafort financially, billions of dollars having been involved, and both did so politically. In the end, however, the Manafort and other Russiagate financial cases, like their predecessors, are likely to turn out to be mostly the everyday corruption of the 1 percent and its servitors. This too seems to have been forgotten or, considering the fully bipartisan nature of the American corruption, deleted.

A final example of amnesia is particularly remarkable and known to readers. Even though the new or "second" Cold War with Russia has been unfolding for nearly 20 years, the head of America's most prestigious think tank and foreign-affairs organization, the Council on Foreign Relations, discovered it only recently and "unexpectedly." Is such myopia on the part of one of the most acclaimed US foreign-policy experts amnesia—he did not remember what the preceding Cold War looked and sounded like—or denial of the role he and his fellow experts played in bringing about the "second" one?

Whatever the explanation, all of these "unprecedented" aspects of Russiagate are part of a new, more dangerous Cold War. We should worry that Marx's famous adage—history repeats itself, first as tragedy, then as farce—may in this case turn out to be, first as tragedy, then as something worse.

How Washington Provoked—and Perhaps Lost—a New Nuclear-Arms Race

March 7

PRESIDENT PUTIN'S SPEECH TO BOTH HOUSES of the Russian parliament on March 1, somewhat akin to the US president's annual State of the Union address, was composed of two distinct parts. The first approximately two-thirds was pitched to the upcoming Russian presidential election, on March 18, and to domestic concerns of Russian voters not unlike those of American voters: stability, jobs, inflation, health care, education, taxes, infrastructures, etc.

The latter part of the speech was, however, devoted solely to recent achievements in Russia's strategic, or nuclear, weapons. These remarks, though also of electoral value, were addressed directly to Washington. Putin's overarching point was that Russia has thwarted Washington's two-decade-long effort to gain nuclear superiority over—and thus a survivable first-strike capability against—Russia. His conclusion was that one era in Russian-American strategic relations has ended and a new one begun. This part of Putin's speech makes it among the most important he has delivered during his 18 years in power.

The historical background, to which Putin refers repeatedly for his own purposes, is important. Ever since the United States and Soviet Union, the two nuclear superpowers, acquired the ability to deliver transcontinental warheads against the other, three alternative approaches to this existential reality have informed debates and policy-making: nuclear-weapons abolition, which is a necessary goal but not an achievable one in the foreseeable future; a quest for nuclear superiority, making a devastating first-strike immune from an equally catastrophic retaliation and thus "survivable" and thinkable; and mutual security based on "Mutual Assured Destruction" (MAD), which required that both sides have roughly equal nuclear capabilities and neither strive for first-strike superiority.

During the preceding Cold War, by the late 1960s and early 1970s, both Washington and Moscow officially embraced the mutual security approach. MAD, however fearful its apocalyptic reasoning, was accepted as the safest— only rational—orientation, along with the need to maintain rough strategic parity. Hence the succession of US-Soviet nuclear arms treaties, including reductions in arsenals. Nuclear technology continued to develop, making weapons ever more destructive, but MAD and the parity principle contained the technology and kept the nuclear peace despite some near misses.

This approach reached its most hopeful apogee in the late 1980s when President Reagan and the last Soviet leader, Mikhail Gorbachev, expanded their understanding of "mutual security." They agreed that any strategic "build up" by one side would be perceived as a threat by the other, which would then undertake its own reactive buildup. They agreed to end this perilous dialectic that had driven the nuclear-arms race for decades. And in

1987, they abolished for the first (and still only) time an entire category of nuclear weapons, those borne by intermediate-range missiles.

That exceedingly hopeful opportunity, the legacy of Reagan and Gorbachev, was lost almost immediately after the Soviet Union ended in 1991—squandered in Washington, not in Moscow. Beginning in the 1990s, successive US administrations—under Bill Clinton, George W. Bush, and Barack Obama—sought de facto nuclear superiority over post-Soviet Russia. Animated by rampant post–Cold War (misconceived) triumphalism and by a perception that Russia was now too weak, demoralized, or supplicant to compete, they did so in three ways: by expanding NATO to Russia's borders; by funding ever more destructive, "precise," and "usable" nuclear weapons; and, in 2002, by unilaterally withdrawing from the 1972 Anti-Ballistic Missile Treaty.

The ABM treaty, by prohibiting wide deployment of anti–missile defense installments (each side got one exception at home), had long guaranteed mutual security based on the underlying principles of MAD and parity. Bush's abolition of the treaty in effect nullified those principles and signified Washington's quest for nuclear superiority over Russia.

Today, there are scores of deployed US missile-defense installments, now officially a NATO project, around the world, particularly on land and at sea targeted at Russia. From the beginning, Washington maintained, as it does today, that "Our missile defense has never been about Russia," only about Iran and other "rogue states." No sensible observer has ever believed this fairy tale, certainly not Moscow.

All of Russia's new nuclear weapons itemized by Putin on March 1, long in development, have been designed to evade and render useless Washington's global missile-defense program developed over decades at great financial, political, and real security costs. The US political-media establishment has mostly dismissed Putin's claims as a "bluff," "aggressive," and "saber-rattling." But these traits have never characterized his major policy statements, nor do they this one.

If even only a quarter of Putin's claims for Russia's new strategic weapons is true, it means that while Washington heedlessly raced for nuclear superiority and a first-strike capability, Moscow quietly, determinedly raced to create counter-systems, and—again assuming Putin's claims are substantially true—Russia won. From Moscow's perspective, which in this existential instance should also be ours, Russia has regained the strategic parity it lost after the end of the Soviet Union and with it the "mutual security" of MAD.

Read carefully, Putin's speech also raises vital political questions. At one point, he remarkably says "we ourselves are to blame" for the dire strategic condition in which Russia found itself in the early 2000s. Presumably he is referring to his own "illusions" about the West, particularly about Washington, to which he has previously alluded. Presumably he is also referring to his fruitless appeals to "our Western partners" for policies of mutual security instead of NATO expansion and unilateral missile-defense deployments, "illusionary" appeals for which he has sometimes been criticized by actual anti-Western forces in Russia's political-security establishment. As Putin ruefully admits, his "Western partners" did not "listen." This is compelling evidence that Putin himself changed in response to US-NATO policies during his years in power, but also that he is capable of change again, given Western initiatives.

In the speech, Putin does not comment directly on past nuclear-arms races, but he makes clear that another, more dangerous, one looms, depending on how Washington reacts to Moscow's new weapons. Washington can accept the parity—the deterrent—Russia has restored and return to full-scale nuclear arms negotiations. Or it can try again to surpass Moscow's parity.

If Washington chooses the latter course, Putin says, Moscow is fully able and ready to compete, again and again, though he makes clear he would prefer instead to commit his remaining years of leadership, legacy, and national resources to Russia's modernization and prosperity, which he spells out (yet again) in the first two-thirds of his speech. Putin insists, that is, Russia's new weapons are not for any kind of aggression but solely for its legitimate military defense and, politically, to bring Washington back to détente-like policies and particularly to nuclear arms negotiations. The Kremlin, he adds, is "ready."

Even having made a compelling and obviously proud presentation of what Russia has unexpectedly achieved, does Putin really believe Washington will "listen now"? He may still have some "illusions," but we should have none. Recent years have provided ample evidence that US policy-makers and, equally important, influential media commentators do not bother to read what Putin says, at least not more than snatches from click-bait wire-service reports. Still worse, Putin and "Putin's Russia" have been so demonized it is hard to imagine many leading American political figures or editorial commentators responding positively to what is plainly his hope for a new beginning in US-Russian relations.

If nothing else, strategic parity always also meant political parity—recognizing that Soviet Russia, like the United States, had legitimate national interests abroad. Years of American vilifying Putin and post-Soviet Russia are essentially an assertion that neither has any such legitimacy. Now, making matters worse, there is the Russiagate allegation of a Kremlin "attack" on the United States. Even if President Trump understands, or is made to understand, the new—possibly historic—overture represented by Putin's speech, would the "Kremlin puppet" charges against him permit him to seize this opportunity? Do the promoters of Russiagate even care?

History has taught that technology sometimes outruns political capacity to control it. Several of Russia's new nuclear weapons were unforeseen. (If US intelligence was not fully aware of their development prior to Putin's speech, what were those agencies doing instead?) It is no longer possible to dismiss Russia, again declared to be America's number-one threat, as anything less than a nuclear superpower at least fully equal to the United States.

If Washington does not "listen now," if instead it again strives for superiority, we may reasonably ask: We survived the preceding Cold War, but can we survive this one? Put differently, is what Putin displayed but also offered on March 1, 2018, our last chance? In any event, he was right: "This is a turning point for the entire world."

Russia Endorses Putin, the US and UK Condemn Him (Again)

March 22

US POLITICAL AND MEDIA ELITES ARE characterizing Putin's overwhelming victory in Russia's presidential election on March 18 as a "fraud" and "sham" that "does not matter." Both assertions are untrue. They are made mostly by professed authorities whose opinions about Russia are based not on actual knowledge but on political and ideological biases.

Russian presidential and parliamentary elections are, of course, far from fully free and fair. The Kremlin has overwhelming "administrative resources," including unlimited funds, control of the national television networks and many newspapers, and influence over who is, and is not, on the ballot.

But the March 18 election was not greatly constricted or fraudulent. Putin's rivals, including outspoken anti-Putin ones, were permitted to debate on national television (though without Putin himself), and to conduct their campaigns throughout the country relatively freely with whatever resources they had, including in the significantly freer print media and on the nearly uncontrolled Internet. Voters knew the candidates and what they represented. According to many on-site observers, there was relatively little fraud. A frequent complaint that Putin's campaign helped "get out the vote" by busing its voters to polling places is no doubt true, but also not uncommon in the United States.

In short, there is no reason to doubt the magnitude or authentic nature of Putin's victory. The Kremlin hoped for a 70 percent turnout of eligible voters with a 70 percent vote for Putin. The turnout was somewhat less, 67 percent (but larger than the just under 58 percent in the 2016 US presidential election), while Putin's victory margin, 77 percent, exceeded the Kremlin's goal.

As for its authenticity and explanation, we have the reporting even of a Moscow correspondent of the *New York Times*, which competes with the *Washington Post* for being the most unrelentingly anti-Putin newspaper. On March 18, he wrote: "Russian voters gave…Putin their resounding approval" and a "popular mandate" for his next six-year term. "There is no question that Mr. Putin is wildly popular among Russians." The *Times* correspondent concluded: "There was no need for extensive rigging…because of Mr. Putin's genuine popularity."

So widely and deeply "resounding" was Putin's victory that he got 70 percent of the vote even in Moscow, where opposition candidates usually run relatively well, in sharp contrast to his less than 50 percent in 2012. Moreover, there is ample polling and anecdotal evidence that contrary to Western impressions, Putin is exceedingly popular among the youngest voters, many of whom regard him even more favorably than do middle-age and older generations. This means that the "Putin generation," as it is called, is likely to play an important political role even after he leaves the scene.

More generally, nationalistic, anti-Western candidates gained approximately 20 percent of the vote, with "liberal," pro-Western ones so favored by US political-media elites less than 5 percent. Assuming that few "liberals" voted for Putin but many anti-liberals did, this too speaks volumes about current and future Russian politics—and about highly selective, if not deluded,

US media coverage. (It is often reported correctly that Alexei Navalny, the anti-corruption crusader and radical Putin opponent, was excluded from the ballot. But it is also true that preelection polls showed him with about 2 percent popular support, hardly enough to have affected the outcome.)

US commentary also attributes Putin's popularity to his "aggressive, anti-Western foreign policies." This assumes that most Russians favor policies hostile, even aggressive, toward the West, and that Putin relies on such attitudes for his power. These assumptions are also untrue or at least significantly so. Until the US-Russian proxy war in Georgia in 2008 and even prior to the Ukrainian crisis in 2014, Putin pursued cooperation with both Europe and the United States, during which his popularity ratings remained well above 60 percent. The annexation of Crimea in 2014 boosted his popular support to more than 80 percent.

The explanation is not complicated. Most Russians still credit Putin with having "saved Russia"—and their own families—from the catastrophic economic and social shock-therapy "reforms" of the Yeltsin 1990s. This "living history" remains the basis of Putin's enduring popularity, despite more recent economic hard times. And when Russians perceive their country as being under attack by foreign powers—as most Russians interpret US-NATO policies in recent years, particularly in Ukraine—they rally around a "strong leader," a reaction also not unknown in the United States.

Slurring the integrity and values of Russian voters is just that—a slur, and one on the rise in the United States, due partly to "Russiagate," though not only. Thus when Senator John McCain and others declare that Putin's victory was a "sham" and "every Russian citizen…was denied the right to vote in a free and fair election," as reported by the *Times* on March 20, they are publicly denigrating and insulting those citizens—again without the slightest factual knowledge of what they are denouncing.

The election results should give Washington's militant cold warriors serious second thoughts. Regime changers who hope US economic sanctions will turn Russia's oligarchs and even its people against Putin and depose him should by now understand that these policies are counter-productive. The Russian people rallied around Putin. And the size of his electoral victory gives him even more authority over financial oligarchs who fear the people because so many citizens still loathe them as the plunderers of the country in the 1990s. Exceedingly rich oligarchs, even those with their assets and families parked offshore and private jets on standby, understand this persistent reality and look to Putin to protect them now and in the future. The election returns confirm that he can continue to do so, if he chooses.

The election should also discredit the growing number of American commentators who equate Putin's Russia with Stalin's "totalitarianism." Proponents of this preposterous equation again reveal themselves as knowing (or caring) little about Russia's political realities today and nothing about Stalin's long terroristic rule, which destroyed millions of Soviet families.

In reality, to emphasize again, the Russian political system today is a mix of authoritarian and democratic elements, what political scientists call "soft authoritarianism." The real discussion should be the relative weight of the two components and what this may bode for Russia's future and for US-Russian relations. One thing is certain and borne out by history: Russian democratic reformers stand very little chance in conditions of Cold War and no chance at all if the new Cold War results in actual war.

Coincidentally or not, the reported assassination attempt against Sergei Skripal and his daughter in the UK has given Putin demonizers another opportunity to denigrate his reputation, no matter what Russian voters think. There are some parallels with Russiagate in the United States. Both scandals are said by high officials to have been "an act of war." Both are said to have been ordered by Putin personally. And in both cases, there are as yet no verified facts, only allegations.

As for the appalling act committed in the Skripal case, not only are there no facts, there is no common sense. Putin had no possible motive, certainly not on the eve of the Russian presidential election, with the World Cup competition in Russia upcoming, and with the toxicity of Russiagate already poisoning relations with the West. Nor did Putin ever say, as he is widely mistranslated, that "traitors" should be killed. They will, he said instead, eventually "shrivel up" (*zagnutsia*) and wither away from the self-inflicted guilt and shame of their act of betrayal. Moreover, quite a few better- known Russian intelligence defectors have lived safely in the West, sometimes publishing accounts of their feats.

Contrary to many media accounts, nor was Skripal a "Russian spy." He was a British spy, having covertly gone to work for UK intelligence in the 1990s, been arrested and convicted in 2004, and made part of an exchange of captured Russian and Western spies in 2010, which resulted in Skripal's residence in the UK. If Putin wanted him dead, why not kill him in Russia or why let him leave for the West? And if some high-placed state assassin wanted Skripal dead, why try to kill him with a lethal nerve agent that might be traceable and could harm many other people? Why not a gun, a knife, or a car "accident"?

Though the nerve agent loosely termed "Novichok" was developed in the

Soviet Union decades ago, the Organization for the Prohibition of Chemical Weapons certified in 2017 that Russia had fully destroyed all of its stockpiles and facilities for making such weapons.[52] Still more, the formula for "Novichok" was published years ago and could have been replicated by any number of competent states or individuals. And if the nerve agent was so quickly "lethal," why are the Skripals and others said to have been affected still alive and out of hospital?

There is also this crucial consideration. When Russia and the United States recruit spies in the other country, or send them there, they assure them, in so many words, "If you are caught, we will try to get you out, to bring you home." For decades, this has resulted in the kind of spy swaps of which Skripal was part in 2010. If either side seriously harms an exchanged spy, the efficacy of such exchanges and the sanctity of such intelligence agency promises are undermined, if not made invalid. As a former intelligence official, Putin above all would have understood this and thus still less have had any motive.

Which is to say, Putin's electoral victory was mostly authentic; the official version of what happened to the Skripals may not be.

Russophobia

April 4

A NALYZING WHY THE NEW COLD WAR is more dangerous than was its 40-year predecessor, I seem to have minimized the role of Russophobia. I understood its strength among some nationalities of the former Tsarist and Soviet empires now in the West, but Russophobia had not been a large causal factor, unlike anti-Communism, in the preceding Cold War. I've long been influenced by the compassionate words of George Kennan, the architect of containment, published in *Foreign Affairs* in 1951 about the Russian people:

"Give them time; let them be Russians; let them work out their internal problems in their own manner...towards dignity and enlightenment in government."

But recent Russophobic statements by former chief US intelligence officials and other influential American opinion-makers have caused me to reconsider this factor. Here are some examples:

• Former Director of National Intelligence James Clapper spoke on NBC national television about "the Russians, who typically, are almost genetically driven to co-opt, penetrate, gain favor." And former CIA Director John Brennan warned that Russians "try to suborn individuals and they try to get individuals, including US citizens, to act on their behalf either wittingly or unwittingly." Former FBI director James Comey added, "They're coming after America."[53,54,55] How would we react if these intelligence chiefs had said the same about another ethnic people? Or if Senator John McCain repeatedly characterized another nation as "a gas station masquerading as a country?"

• Russia's presidential election, a kind of referendum on Putin's 18 years as leader, gave him, as we saw, a resounding, nearly 77 percent endorsement. The election was widely dismissed by leading US media outlets as "a sham," which denigrates, of course, the integrity of Russian voters. Indeed, a leading Putin demonizer earlier characterized Russian public opinion as a "mob's opinion."[56]

• A *Rolling Stone* writer goes further, explaining that "Russia experts" think "much of what passes for civil society in modern Russia is, in fact, controlled by Putin."[57] Civil society means, of course, non-state groups and associations, that is, society itself.

• A *Washington Post* editorial headline on April 3, 2018, asks: "Is It a Crime to Worship God? According to Russia, Yes." This about a country where the Orthodox Church is flourishing and Jews are freer than they have ever been in Russian history.

• On March 7, 2018, the *Post's* international columnist, David Ignatius, downplayed the personal causality of the Kremlin leader because "President Vladimir Putin embodies this Russian paranoid ethic."

• Even a *Post* sports columnist is so afflicted that, referring to Olympic doping allegations, he characterizes Russian 2018 medal winners as representatives of "a shamed nation."[58]

• A *New York Times* columnist quotes approvingly a *Post* columnist, an expert on Russia, for asserting that "Putin's Russia" is "an anti-Western power with a different, darker vision of global politics...[a] norm-violating power."[59]

- The title of an article by CNN's Russia expert begins: "Russia's Snark."[60]
- Another prominent media commentator advises, "Treat Russia Like the Terrorist It Is." Yet another terms Russia "Gangster's Paradise."[61,62]
- A leading policy expert on Russia and former US official has decided that the West doesn't have a Putin problem: "In fact, it has a Russia problem."[63]
- Deploring Russia, the Harvard policy intellectual Graham Allison has a regret: "The brute fact is that we cannot kill this bastard without committing suicide."[64]
- According to a longtime *Fox News* Russia expert, Ralph Peters, now a guest on CNN, Putin behaves as he does "because they are Russians."[65]
- A *Post* book editor tells readers that Russians tolerate "tyrants like Stalin and Putin" because "it probably seems normal."[66]
- A prominent Russia expert and NPR commentator wonders "whether Russia can ever be normal."[67]
- And impossible to overlook, there are the ubiquitous cartoons depicting Russia as a menacing rapacious bear and alternatively as an octopus whose grasping tentacles ensnare the globe.

How to explain this rampant Russophobia? Three important but little noted books provide useful history and analyses: David S. Foglesong's *The American Mission and the "Evil Empire"*; Andrei P. Tsygankov's *Russophobia*; and, most recently, Guy Mettan's *Creating Russophobia*, which equates it with "Russo-madness."

They examine various factors: ethnic peoples, now independent states with large diasporas, and with historical grievances against both the Tsarist and Soviet empires; historical developments and immigration beginning in the 19th century; today's US military-industrial complex's budgetary need for an "enemy" after the end of the Soviet Union; other present-day anti-Russian lobbies in the United States and the absence of any pro-Russian ones.

All need to be considered, but three circumstances are certain. American attitudes toward Russia are not historically or genetically predetermined, as evidenced by the "Gorbymania" that swept the United States in the late 1980s when Soviet President Gorbachev and US President Reagan tried to end the previous Cold War. The unprecedented demonization of the current Kremlin leader, Putin, has expanded to Russia more generally. And Russophobia is much more widespread and deeper among American political and media elites than among ordinary citizens. It was, after all, elites, not the American people, who gave us the new Cold War.

Russiagate and the Risk of Nuclear War

April 18

T HE 1962 CUBAN MISSILE CRISIS REMAINS A LANDMARK event in the preceding Cold War. It was the closest the United States and (then-Soviet) Russia ever came to intentional nuclear war. Its lessons have been taught ever since. No such confrontation between the two nuclear superpowers should ever be permitted again. If it happens, only diplomacy of the kind practiced by President Kennedy during the Cuban crisis, including secret negotiations, can save both countries, and the world, from catastrophe.

Accordingly, in the decades following that sobering event, Washington and Moscow enacted forms of cooperation to limit their conflicts and prevent a recapitulation of the Cuban episode—mutual codes of Cold War conduct; a myriad of public and secret communications; nuclear-arms agreements; periodic summit meetings; and other regularized processes that kept the nuclear peace.

The new Cold War has vaporized, however, most of those restraining conventions, especially since the conflict over Ukraine in 2014 and even more since Russiagate began to unfold in 2016. During the first two weeks of this April, thus arose in Syria the real possibility of a new Cuban-like crisis and of war with Russia.

The danger developed less in the context of Syrian developments than that of Russiagate. For more than a year, President Trump had been hectored—mainly by Democrats and much of the media—to "get tougher" with Russia and its President Vladimir Putin in order to demonstrate he was not beholden to the Kremlin.

To his credit, Trump remained publicly committed to his campaign promise to "cooperate with Russia," but while also "getting tougher." He sent weapons to Ukraine, imposed mounting economic sanctions on Moscow, and expelled large numbers of Russian diplomats, even shutting a Russian consulate in the United States, as President Obama had unwisely done. But Russiagate advocates continuously moved the goal posts of "tougher" until the end zone, war, loomed on the horizon.

As it did during the fraught days from April 7, when reports appeared that Syrian President Assad had used chemical weapons against his own people in

Douma, to the launching of US missiles against Syria on the night of April 13-14.

This might well have resulted in war with Russia because of two little-noticed red lines drawn by the Kremlin. In his speech on March 1, Putin stated that Russia's new missiles were available to protect Moscow's "allies," which clearly included Damascus. And shortly later, when perhaps scores of Russian troops were killed in Syria by US-backed anti-Assad forces, Moscow's military and civilian leadership vowed "retaliation" if this happened again. They meant Russian counter-strikes specifically against American forces in Syria and any US launchers of the weapons used. (Russian troops are embedded with many Syrian units and thus potential collateral damage.)

And yet, an evidently reluctant Trump launched more than a hundred missiles at Syria on August 13-14. Just how reluctant he was to risk a Cuban-like crisis, to risk any chance of war with Russia, is clear from what actually happened. Rejecting more expansive and devastating options, Trump chose one that gave Russia (and thus Syria) advance warning. It killed no Russians (or perhaps anyone else) and struck no essential political or military targets in Damascus, only purported chemical-weapons facilities. The Kremlin's red lines were carefully and widely skirted.

Nonetheless, the events of April were ominous and may well forebode worse to come. The very limited, carefully crafted attack on Syria was clearly not undertaken primarily for military but political reasons related to Russiagate allegations against Trump. Just how political is indicated by the fact that no conclusive evidence had yet been produced that Assad was responsible for the alleged chemical attack and that the missiles were launched as chemical weapons investigators were en route to Douma.

We might fault Trump for being insufficiently strong—politically or psychologically—to resist warfare demands that he prove his "innocence," but the primary responsibility lies with Russiagate promoters who seek obsessively to impeach the president: politicians and journalists for whom a porn actress, Stormy Daniels, seems to be a higher priority than averting nuclear war with Russia. They are mostly Democrats and pro-Democratic media, but also Republicans like Senator Lindsey Graham, who declared, "If…we back off because Putin threatens to retaliate, that is a disaster for us throughout the world." (No, senator, that is a Cuban missile crisis that was not resolved peacefully and a catastrophe for the entire world.)

More generally, as I have repeatedly warned, for the first time since the onset of the nuclear age, there is not in the White House an American president fully empowered—"legitimate" enough, Russiagaters charge—to negotiate with a Kremlin leader in such dire circumstances, as Trump has discovered every time he has tried. Or, in an existential crisis, to avert nuclear war the way President Kennedy did in 1962.

Given the escalating Cold war dynamics evidenced in recent months, not only in Syria, this generalization may be tested sooner rather than later. It doesn't help, of course, that Trump has surrounded himself with appointees who apparently do not share his opinion that it is imperative "to cooperate with Russia," but instead "adults" who seem to personify the worst aspects of Cold War zealotry and lack elementary knowledge of US-Russian relations over the years.

As President Reagan liked to say, it takes two to tango. In Moscow's policy elite, there are influential people who believe "America has been at war against Russia"—political, economic, and military—for more than a decade. Their views are often mirror images of those of Lindsey Graham and other US establishment zealots.

In this decision-making context, Putin still appears to be, in words and deeds, the moderate, calling Western leaders "our partners and colleagues," asking for understanding and negotiations, being far less "aggressive" than he could be. Our legions of Putin demonizers will say this is a false analysis, but it too should not be tested.

Criminalizing Russia

April 25

FOR MORE THAN A DECADE, THE US political-media establishment has increasingly demonized, delegitimized, and now criminalized the Russian state and its leadership. This began with the personal vilification of President Putin and has grown into a general indictment of Russia as a nation. As President Obama's former intelligence chiefs John Brennan and

James Clapper and other US authorities have told us, any Russian "linked to the Kremlin," Moscow officialdom generally, "oligarchs," or certain traits is inherently suspicious.

"Crimes" said to be committed by today's Kremlin, from America and the UK to Syria, have expanded the indictment beyond charges once leveled against Soviet Russia. The newly minted world affairs pundit Joe Scarborough, who believes the United States alone "spent the past 100 years inventing the modern age," devotes a column warning *Washington Post* readers multiple times that "our democracy is under attack by the Russians."[68,69]

There are many weightier and more far-reaching allegations. Canada's foreign minister, echoing Washington, indicts Russia for its "malign behavior in all of its manifestations...whether it is cyberwarfare, whether it's disinformation, assassination attempts, whatever it happens to be."[70]

On April 20, the Democratic National Committee, still mourning its defeat in 2016, went farther. It is seeking a formal indictment of "whatever it happens to be" by suing the Russian government for conspiring with the Trump campaign to deprive Hillary Clinton of her rightful victory in the 2016 presidential election. Central figures in this "act of unprecedented treachery" are stated to be "people believed to be affiliated with Russia."[71]

It follows, of course, that a criminal Russia—frequently termed a "mafia state," also incorrectly—can have no legitimate national interests anywhere, not on its own borders or even at home. And with such a state, it also follows, there should be no civil relations, including diplomacy, only warfare ones. Thus when a group of US senators visited Moscow in early July, another *Post* columnist, Dana Milbank, who seemed not to know or care there were precedents for the timing, indicted them for "visiting your foe on the Fourth of July" and equated it with "meeting with wounded Taliban fighters on Veterans Day."[72]

Lost, forgotten, or negated in this mania is why Russia was generally understood to matter so greatly to US national security during the 40-year Cold War that the result was myriad forms of growing and prolonged cooperation, even official episodes of détente. The reasons also apply to Russia today.

Even middle-school children presumably know the most existential reason. Like the United States, Russia possesses enormous arsenals of weapons of mass destruction, including nuclear ones. A conventional US-Russian war—as both sides are now flirting with in Syria and may soon do so in Ukraine or the Baltic region—could slip into nuclear war. As I reported earlier, at a recent meeting of Washington's highly respected Center for the National Interest, several well-informed experts thought that on a scale of 1 to 10, the chances of war with Russia today are 5 to 7.[73]

Today's Cold War includes another existential danger in the form of international terrorists in pursuit of radioactive materials to make their attacks immeasurably more devastating and the consequences more enduring. Ask real experts the chances of that happening in a major city, and of the importance of the Kremlin's full cooperation in preventing it.

Almost equally important is the reason called "geopolitical." Even after the Soviet Union, Russia remains the largest territorial country in the world. It possesses a disproportionate share of the planet's natural resources, from energy, iron ore, nickel, timber, diamonds, and gold to fresh water. It is also one of the world's leading exporters of weapons. Still more, Russia is located squarely between East and West, whose civilizations are in conflict, and part of both. Months ago, I raised the possibility that Russia might "leave the West," driven out by the new Cold War or by choice. That possibility is now said by a top Kremlin aide and ideologist to be inescapable.

Herein lies more myopia constantly perpetuated by the American media: sanctioned, criminal Russia is "isolated from the international community." This is an Anglo-American conceit. Multi-dimensional relations between "Putin's Russia" and non-Western countries such as China, Iran, India, and other BRIC nations are thriving. And it is there that most of the world's territory, people, resources, and growing markets are located. For them, Russia is not criminal but an eagerly sought partner.

Given all the warfare talk emanating from the US political-media establishment, consider also Russia's renewed military capabilities or, as strategists like to say, "capacity to project power." There is no reason to doubt Putin's March 1 inventorying of Moscow's new weapons systems. The Kremlin demonstrated its formidable military capabilities by destroying ISIS's entrenched grip on Syria following Russia's intervention in September 2015, even though most US pundits and other professed experts falsely claim this was Washington's achievement.

When there is military parity between Washington and Moscow, as during the preceding Cold War and now again, it is imperative to cooperate, not to ostracize. Otherwise, as President Reagan said when he decided to meet the Kremlin halfway in the late 1980s, there will be no winners,

There are also Moscow's under-rated capabilities for conflict resolution, not only its vote on the UN Security Council. Various recent examples could be cited, but remember Russia's essential role in the nuclear-weapons agreement with Iran; its behind-the-scenes part today in attempts to resolve the conflict with North Korea; its potential as a deciding partner in bringing peace to Syria; and the role it is likely to play when the United States finally decides to leave Afghanistan. If not criminalized, Russia can be a vital peacemaker, and there is ample reason to think that the Kremlin is ready to do so again.

Long ago, when I first developed my own "contacts" and "ties" with "Communist" Russian society and, yes, with Kremlin and many other officials, I often said and wrote, "The road to American national security runs through Moscow." The same is no less true today. This necessity may now seem futile, as US political-media elites mindlessly criminalize Russia.

On the other hand, President Trump's ambassador to Russia, Jon Huntsman, stated publicly on April 24: "My president has said repeatedly that he wants a better relationship with Russia…with Putin…. You can call it a desire for détente."[74] If so, it is imperative to support the president's initiative, even if only this one.

America's Collusion With Neo-Nazis

May 2

WE MUST RETURN YET AGAIN TO Ukraine because of what the orthodox US political-media narrative continues to omit—the still growing role of neo-Nazi forces in territories governed by US-backed Kiev. Even Americans who follow international news may not know the following:

• That the snipers who killed scores of protestors and policemen on Kiev's Maidan Square in February 2014—triggering a professed "democratic revolution" that overthrew the elected president, Viktor Yanukovych, and brought to power a virulent anti-Russian, pro-American regime—were sent not by Yanukovych, as is still widely reported, but almost certainly by the neo-fascist organization Right Sector and its co-conspirators.[75]

• That the pogrom-like burning to death of ethnic Russians and Russian-speaking Ukrainians in Odessa shortly later in 2014 reawakened memories of Nazi extermination squads in Ukraine during World War II has been all but deleted from the American mainstream narrative even though it remains a painful and revelatory episode for many Ukrainians.

• That the Azov Battalion of some 3,000 well-armed fighters, which has played a major combat role in the Ukrainian civil war and now is an official component of Kiev's armed forces, is avowedly "partially" pro-Nazi, as evidenced by its regalia, slogans, and programmatic statements, and well-documented as such by several international monitoring organizations. Congressional legislation recently banned Azov from receiving U.S. military aid, but it is likely to obtain some of the new weapons recently sent to Kiev by the Trump administration due to Ukraine's rampant network of corruption and to sympathizers in Kiev's security ministries.

• That storm troop-like assaults on gays, Roma, women feminists, elderly ethnic Russians, and other "impure" citizens are widespread throughout Kiev-ruled Ukraine, along with torchlight marches reminiscent of those that inflamed Germany in the late 1920s and 1930s. That a sacred Holocaust gravesite in Ukraine has been desecrated and looted.[76] And that police and legal authorities do virtually nothing to prevent these neo-fascist acts or to prosecute them. On the contrary, Kiev has officially encouraged this violence by systematically rehabilitating and even memorializing leading Ukrainian collaborators with Nazi German extermination pogroms during World War II. Kiev is renaming streets in their honor, building monuments to them, rewriting history to glorify them, and more.

• Or that Israel's official annual report on anti-Semitism around the world in 2017 concluded that such incidents had doubled in Ukraine and the number "surpassed the tally for all the incidents reported throughout the entire region combined." By the region, the report meant the total in all of Eastern Europe and all former territories of the Soviet Union.[77]

The significance of neo-Nazism in Ukraine and tacit US support or tolerance of it should have caused widespread outrage, but Americans cannot be faulted for not knowing these facts. They are very rarely reported and still less discussed in mainstream newspapers or on television. To learn about them, Americans would have to turn to alternative media and their independent non-mainstream writers.

Lev Golinkin is one such important American writer. He is best known for his book *A Backpack, A Bear, and Eight Crates of Vodka*, a deeply moving and highly instructive memoir of his life as a young boy brought to America by his immigrant parents from Eastern Ukraine, a place now torn by tragic civil and proxy war. But Golinkin has also been an unrelenting and meticulous reporter of neo-fascism in "our" Ukraine and defender of others who try to chronicle and oppose its growing crimes, including Ukrainian Jews.

For the record, this did not begin under President Trump but under President George W. Bush, when then President Viktor Yushchenko's "Orange Revolution" began rehabilitating Ukraine's wartime killers of Jews. It grew under President Obama, who, along with Vice President Biden, were deeply complicit in the 2014 Maidan coup and what followed. Then too the American mainstream media scarcely noticed.

Even avid followers of US news probably missed this, for example. When the co-founder of a neo-Nazi party and now repackaged speaker of the Ukrainian parliament, Andrei Parubiy, visited Washington in 2016, 2017, and 2018, he was widely feted. He spoke at leading think tanks, met with Senator John McCain, Rep. Paul Ryan, and Senator Chuck Schumer, as well as with the editorial boards of the *Washington Post* and the *Wall Street Journal*.[78] Imagine the message this official embrace sent back to Ukraine—and elsewhere.

Fascist or neo-Nazi revivalism is under way today in many countries, from Europe to the United States, but the Ukrainian case is of special importance and a particular danger. A large, growing, well-armed fascist movement has reappeared in a large European country that is the political epicenter of the new Cold War—a movement that not so much denies the Holocaust as glorifies it.

Could such forces come to power in Kiev? Its American deniers and minimizers say never, because it has too little public support (though perhaps more than Ukrainian President Poroshenko). The same was said of Lenin's party and Hitler's until Russia and Germany descended into chaos and lawlessness. Ominously, a recent Amnesty International article reports that Kiev is losing control over these radical groups and over the state's monopoly on the use of force.[79]

For four years, the U.S. political-media establishment, including prominent American Jews and their organizations, has at best ignored or tolerated Ukrainian neo-Nazism and at worst abetted it by unqualified support for Kiev. Typically, the *New York Times* may report at length on corruption in Ukraine, but not on the very frequent manifestations of neo-fascism. And when George Will laments the resurgence of anti-Semitism today, he cites the British Labor Party but not Ukraine.

When Ukrainian fascism is occasionally acknowledged, a well-placed band of pro-Kiev partisans quickly asserts—maybe, but the real fascist is America's number one enemy, Russian President Putin. Whatever Putin's failings, this allegation is either cynical or totally uninformed. Nothing in his statements over 18 years in power are akin to fascism. Nor could there be, as I explained earlier.

We are left, then, not with Putin's responsibility for the resurgence of fascism in a major European country allied with Washington, but with America's shame—and possibly an indelible stain on its reputation—for tolerating Ukraine's neo-Nazis, even if only through silence.

At least until recently. On April 23, a courageous first-term congressman from California, Ro Khanna, organized a public letter to the State Department, co-signed by 56 other members of the House, calling on the U.S. government to speak out and take steps against the resurgence of official anti-Semitism and Holocaust denialism both in Ukraine and Poland. "Ro," as he is known to many in Washington, is a rare profile in courage, as are his co-signers. Thus far, little has resulted from their wise and moral act.

In a righteous representative democracy, every member of Congress would sign the appeal and every leading newspaper lend editorial support. Not surprisingly, the mainstream media has yet even to report on Rep. Khanna's newsworthy initiative. Also not surprisingly, he has been slurred—and promptly defended by Lev Golinkin.

The previous 40-year experience taught that Cold War can corrupt American democracy—politically, economically, morally. There are many examples of how the new edition has already degraded America's media, politicians, even scholars. But the test today is how our elites react to neo-fascism in U.S.-supported Ukraine. Protesting it is not a Jewish issue. It is an American one.

"Informant" Echoes of Dark Pasts

May 23

THE REVELATION THAT A LONGTIME CIA-FBI "informant," professor emeritus Stefan Halper, had been dispatched to "interact" with several members of Donald Trump's campaign in 2016 raises new and old issues.[80] For me, some of them revive Soviet-era memories.

A year ago, I asked if Russiagate was largely "Intelgate," pointing to compelling evidence. The revelation about Halper, essentially an Intel undercover operative, is further indication that US intelligence agencies were deeply involved in the origins and promotion of allegations of "collusion" between Trump and the Kremlin. (We do not know if other informers were deployed covertly to "investigate" the Trump campaign, what the two agencies did with Halper's information, or whether he was connected in any way to UK intelligence officer Christopher Steele and his dossier.)

The issue is not President Trump, support him or not, but two others: our own civil liberties which can be threatened by "informants" and the indifference of US organizations and media that no longer profess or defend these liberties as inalienable principles of American democracy.

Notably, the venerable ACLU has not loudly protested Intelgate or related transgressions in this regard, if at all. Why should it when the standard-setting *New York Times*, in two articles and an editorial, unconditionally defended Halper's clandestine mission. The *Times* did so by claiming that Russiagate is based on "facts" that "aren't disputed"—that "there was a sophisticated, multiyear conspiracy by Russian government officials and agents, working under direct orders from President Vladimir Putin, to interfere in the 2016 presidential election in support of Donald Trump."[81,82]

In actual fact, aspects of this narrative have been strongly questioned by a number of qualified critics, though their questioning is never printed in the *Times*. Even if there was such a "multiyear conspiracy," for example, how does the *Times* know it was carried out under Putin's "direct orders"?

It is merely an assumption based on two seriously challenged documents, as we have already seen: the January 2017 Intelligence Community Assessment and Steele's dossier. But they are enough for the *Times* to charge that Halper's targets had "suspicious contacts linked to Russia" and for its columnist Paul Krugman again, tweeting on May 19, to call them "treason." (These "Russian contacts" are so vague they could apply to many New York City taxi drivers.)

Indicative of the *Times'* coverage of Russia and Russiagate, the paper then proceeds to factual misrepresentations about three of Halper's targets. General Michael Flynn did nothing wrong or unusual in talking with the Russian ambassador to Washington in December 2016. Other presidents-elect, we have also seen, established similar "back channels" to Moscow. Carter Page was not "recruited by Russian spies." They tried to do so, but he helped the FBI expose and arrest them. And Paul Manafort had not, during the time in question, "lobbied for pro-Russian interests in Ukraine," as I and others have also pointed out more than once.

The *Times* ends by asserting what it must know to be untrue—that no information collected by Halper or Steele had been made public prior to the November 2016 election. Widely read articles alluding to that information were published as early as July 2016 by Franklin Foer and then by Michael Isikoff and David Corn.[83,84,85] The *Times* itself ran a number of insinuating "Trump-Putin" stories and editorials as well as accusatory opinion pieces by former Intel chiefs like the CIA's Michael Morell and the NSA's Michael Hayden—all prior to the election.[86,87] The allegations were so well-known that in their August debate Hillary Clinton accused Trump of being Putin's "puppet."

Of course, the *Times* was not alone among media outlets that once deplored civil-liberties abuses but justified the Halper operation. The *Washington Post* also unconditionally did so, as in a May 21 column by Eugene Robinson denouncing critics of those Russiagate practices for "smearing veteran professionals" of the agencies. Had they not dispatched Halper, Robinson exclaimed, it "would have been an appalling dereliction of duty." Proponents of civil liberties might consider Robinson's statement "appalling."

As usual, MSNBC and CNN were in accord with the *Times* and the *Post*. On May 17, for instance, CNN's Don Lemon summoned former Director of National Intelligence James Clapper himself to vouch for Halper's "informant" mission: "That's a good thing because the Russians pose a threat to the very basis of our political system." Lemon did not question Clapper about civil liberties or anything else. Nor did he book anyone who might have done so. The new cult of Intel is mainstream orthodoxy.

Not a word about constitutional civil liberties in any of this media coverage. Surely the "informant" and "contacts" themes—the Clinton-sponsored Center for American Progress recently posted 70-plus purportedly suspicious "contacts" between Trump's people and Russia—reminded some editors, writers, or producers about those practices during the McCarthy era. (If not, they should read the classic book *Naming Names*, by former *Nation* editor and publisher Victor Navasky.)

My own reminders come from, so to speak, the other side. I lived in Soviet Russia periodically from 1976 to 1982 (the year those authorities banned me from the country) among open and semi-closeted Communist Party dissidents. Those were the years of Brezhnev's "vegetarian" surveillance state. Russian friends called it "vegetarian" because the era of Stalin's mass arbitrary arrests, torture, and executions had long passed. KGB suppression now relied significantly on "softer" tactics, among them clandestine informers and accusations of "contacts with the CIA and American imperialism."

I was instructed by Moscow friends how to detect informers or, in any case, to be ever mindful "informants" might be present even at intimate gatherings of "friends." As an American living among targeted people, I tried to take every precaution to avoid being a damning "contact." In the end, though, I was cited by the KGB in cases against at least two prominent dissidents, one jailed and the other hounded. (Both later became leading human-rights figures under Gorbachev and Yeltsin: one as head of the organization Memorial, the other as founder of Moscow's Museum of the History of the Gulag.)

Surveillance was, of course, very different and far more consequential in the repressive pre-Gorbachev Soviet Union than in America today. But a number of episodes on both sides involved professors who were intelligence operatives. In the Russiagate saga, there is already Halper and the still-shadowy Professor Joseph Mifsud, who befriended the very minor, very inexperienced, and apparently clueless Trump "aide" George Papadopoulos. (Originally said to be a Russian intelligence "asset," there is some evidence that Mifsud may have worked for British intelligence. In any event, he has vanished.)

This should not surprise us. Not all US or Russian intelligence officers are assassins, recruiters, or even spies. Some are highly qualified scholars who hold positions in colleges, academies, and universities, as has long been the case both in Russia and in the United States. As a result, I myself had over the years—I will confess—knowing personal "contacts" with several Soviet and post-Soviet Russian "intelligence officers."

Two held the rank of general and were affiliated with higher-educational institutions (one as a professor), which is where I first met them. Another intelligence general I met privately headed the former KGB (now FSB)

archives. The others, more junior, were working on their doctoral disserta-
tions, a step toward promotion, in the same Stalin-era archive where I was
doing research for a book.

We took many lunch and smoking breaks together. Most of our discussions
focused on archival "secrets" of the Stalin Terror of the 1930s. Sometimes
talk did wander to current concerns—for example, whether Kentucky bour-
bon, which they had not sampled but I eventually provided, was superior to
Russian vodka. No other "collusion" ever resulted.

Why This Cold War is More Dangerous Than the One We Survived

June 6

A FORMAL MEETING BETWEEN PRESIDENTS TRUMP AND Putin is being seriously discussed in Washington and Moscow. Ritualized but substantive
"summits," as they were termed, were frequently used during the 40-year
US-Soviet Cold War to reduce conflicts and increase cooperation between
the two superpowers. They were most important when tensions were highest. Some were very successful, some less so, others were deemed failures.

Given today's extraordinary political circumstances, we may wonder if
anything positive would come from a Trump-Putin summit. But it is necessary, even imperative, that Washington and Moscow try because this Cold
War is more dangerous than was its predecessor. By now, the reasons should
be clear, but it is time to recall and update them. There are at least ten:

1. The political epicenter of the new Cold War is not in far-away Berlin,
as it was from the late 1940s on, but directly on Russia's borders, from the
Baltic states and Ukraine to another former Soviet republic, Georgia. Each
of these new Cold War fronts is fraught with the possibility of hot war.
US-Russian military relations are especially tense today in the Baltic region,

where a large-scale NATO buildup is under way, and in Ukraine, where a US-Russian proxy war is intensifying.

The "Soviet Bloc" that once served as a buffer between NATO and Russia no longer exists. And many imaginable incidents on the West's new Eastern Front, intentional or unintentional, could easily trigger actual war between the United States and Russia. What brought about this situation on Russia's borders— unprecedented at least since the Nazi German invasion in 1941— was, of course, Washington's exceedingly unwise decision, in the late 1990s, to expand NATO eastward. Done in the name of "security," it has made all the states involved only more insecure.

2. Proxy wars were a feature of the old Cold War, but usually small ones in what was called the "Third World," in Africa, for example. They rarely involved many, if any, Soviet or American personnel, mostly only money and weapons. Today's US-Russian proxy wars are different, located in the center of geopolitics and accompanied by too many American and Russian trainers, minders, and possibly fighters. Two have already erupted: in Georgia in 2008, where Russian forces fought a Georgian army financed, trained, and minded by American funds and personnel; and in Syria, where in February scores of Russians were killed by US-backed anti-Assad forces. Moscow did not retaliate, but it has pledged to do so if there is "a next time," as there very well might be.

If so, this would in effect be war directly between Russia and America. The risk of a direct conflict also continues to grow in Ukraine. The country's US-backed but politically failing President Petro Poroshenko seems periodically tempted to launch another all-out military assault on rebel-controlled Donbass, which is backed by Moscow. If he does so, and the assault does not quickly fail as previous ones did, Russia will certainly intervene in eastern Ukraine with a truly tangible "invasion."

Washington will then have to make a fateful war-or-peace decision. Having already reneged on its commitments to the Minsk Accords, the best hope for ending the four-year Ukrainian crisis peacefully, Kiev seems to have an unrelenting impulse to be a tail wagging the dog of US-Russian war. Its capacity for provocations and disinformation seem second to none, as evidenced again recently by the faked "assassination and resurrection" of journalist Arkady Babchenko.

3. Years-long Western, especially American, demonization of the Kremlin leader, Putin, is also unprecedented. Too obvious to spell out again here, no Soviet Communist leader, at least since Stalin, was ever subjected to such prolonged, baseless, crudely derogatory personal vilification. Whereas Soviet leaders were regarded as acceptable negotiating partners for American presidents, including at major summits, Putin has been made to seem to be an illegitimate national leader—at best "a KGB thug" or murderous "mafia boss."

4. Still more, demonizing Putin has generated widespread Russophobic vilification of Russia itself, or what the *New York Times* and other main-stream-media outlets have taken to calling "Vladimir Putin's Russia." Yesterday's enemy was Soviet Communism. Today it is increasingly Russia, thereby also delegitimizing Russia as a great power with legitimate national interests. "The Parity Principle," as I termed it during the preceding Cold War—the principle that both sides had legitimate interests at home and abroad, which was the basis for diplomacy and negotiations, and symbolized by leadership summits—no longer exists, at least on the American side.

Nor does the acknowledgment that both sides were to blame to some extent for the previous Cold War. Among influential American observers who even recognize the new Cold War, "Putin's Russia" alone is to blame. When there is no recognized parity and shared responsibility, there is ever-shrinking space for diplomacy, but more and more for increasingly militarized relations, as we are witnessing today.

5. Meanwhile, most of the Cold War safeguards—cooperative mechanisms and mutually observed rules of conduct that evolved over decades in order to prevent superpower hot war—have been vaporized or badly frayed since the Ukrainian crisis in 2014, as the UN General Secretary António Guterres, almost alone, has recognized: "The Cold War is back—with a vengeance but with a difference. The mechanisms and the safeguards to manage the risks of escalation that existed in the past no longer seem to be present."[88] Trump's recent missile strike on Syria carefully avoided killing any Russians, but Moscow has vowed to retaliate against the US if there is a "next time," as there may be.

Even the decades-long process of arms control may, an expert warns, be coming to an "end."[89] It would mean an unfettered new nuclear-arms race as well as the termination of an ongoing diplomatic process that buffered US-Soviet relations during very bad political times.

In short, if there actually are any new Cold War rules of conduct, they are yet to be formulated and mutually accepted. Nor does this semi-anarchy take into account the new warfare technology of cyber-attacks. What are its implications for the secure functioning of existential Russian and American nuclear command-and-control and early-warning systems that guard against an accidental launching of missiles still on high alert?

6. Russiagate allegations that the American president has been compromised by—or is even an agent of—the Kremlin are also without precedent.

These allegations, as we have seen, have already had profoundly dangerous consequences. They include the nonsensical, mantra-like declaration that "Russia attacked America" during the 2016 presidential election; crippling assaults on President Trump every time he speaks with Putin in person or by phone; and making both Trump and Putin so toxic that most American politicians, journalists, and intellectuals who understand the present-day dangers are reluctant to speak out against US contributions to the new Cold War.

7. Mainstream media outlets have, we know, played a woeful role in all of this. Unlike in the past, when pro-détente advocates had roughly equal access to influential media, today's new Cold War media continue to enforce their orthodox narrative that Russia is solely to blame. They offer not diversity of opinion and reporting but "confirmation bias." Alternative voices (with, yes, "alternative" or opposing facts) rarely appear any longer in the most influential newspapers or on national television or radio.

One alarming result is that "disinformation" generated by or pleasing to Washington and its allies has consequences before it can be corrected. The Ukrainian fake Babchenko assassination (allegedly ordered by Putin, of course) was quickly exposed, but not the official version of the Skripal assassination attempt in the UK, which led to the largest US expulsion of Russian diplomats in history before London's initial account could be thoroughly examined. This too—Cold War without debate—is unprecedented, precluding the frequent rethinking and revising of US policy that characterized the preceding 40-year Cold War.

8. Equally lamentable, and very much unlike during the 40-year Cold War, there still is virtually no significant opposition in the American mainstream to the US role in the new Cold War—not in the media, not in Congress, not in the two major political parties, not in think tanks, not in the universities, not at grassroots levels. This continues to be unprecedented, dangerous, and contrary to real democracy.

Consider again the still thunderous silence of scores of large US corporations that have been doing profitable business in post-Soviet Russia for years, from fast-food chains and automobile manufacturers to pharmaceutical and energy giants. Contrast their behavior to that of CEOs of PepsiCo, Control Data, IBM, and other major American corporations seeking entry to the Soviet market in the 1970s and 1980s, when they publicly supported and even funded pro-détente organizations and politicians. How to explain the continuing silence of their counterparts today, who are usually so profit-motivated? Are they also fearful of being labeled "pro-Putin" or possibly "pro-Trump"?

9. And then there remains the widespread escalatory myth that today's Russia, unlike the Soviet Union, is too weak—its economy too small and fragile, its leader too "isolated in international affairs"—to wage a sustained Cold War, and that eventually Putin, who is "punching above his weight," as the cliché has it, will capitulate. This too is a dangerous delusion—one that cannot be attributed to President Trump. It was, we saw earlier, President Obama who, in 2014, as approvingly reported by the *New York Times*, set out to make Putin's Russia "a pariah state."

Washington and some of its allies certainly tried to isolate Russia. How else to interpret fully the political scandals and media campaigns that erupted on the eve of the Sochi Olympics and again on the eve of the World Cup championship in Russia? Or the tantrum-like, mostly ineffective, even counter-productive cascade of economic sanctions on Moscow?

But Russia is hardly isolated in world affairs, not even in Europe, where five or more governments are tilting away from the anti-Russian line of Washington, London, and Brussels. Despite sanctions, Russia's energy industry and agricultural exports are flourishing. Moreover, geopolitically, Moscow has many military and related advantages in regions where the new Cold War has unfolded. And no state with Russia's modern nuclear and other weapons is "punching above its weight." Contrary to Washington's expectations, the great majority of Russians have rallied behind Putin because they believe their country is under attack by the US-led West. Anyone with a rudimentary knowledge of Russia's history understands it is highly unlikely to capitulate under any circumstances.

10. Finally (at least as of now), there is the growing warlike "hysteria" fueled both in Washington and Moscow. It is driven by various factors, but television talk "news" broadcasts, as common in Russia as in the United States, play a major role. Only an extensive quantitative study could discern which plays a more lamentable role in promoting this frenzy—MSNBC and CNN or their Russian counterparts. The Russian dark witticism seems apt: "Both are worst" (*Oba khuzhe*). Again, some of this American broadcast extremism existed during the preceding Cold War, but almost always balanced, even offset, by informed, wiser opinions, which are now largely excluded.

Is my analysis of the graver dangers inherent in the new Cold War itself extremist or alarmist? Some usually reticent specialists would seem to agree with my general assessment. As I reported earlier, experts gathered by a centrist Washington think tank thought that on a scale of 1 to 10, there is a 5 to 7 chance of actual war with Russia. There are other such opinions. A former head of British M16 is reported as saying that "for the first time in living memory, there's a realistic chance of a superpower conflict." And a respected retired Russian general tells the same Washington think tank that any military confrontation "will end up with the use of nuclear weapons between the United States and Russia."[90,91]

A single Trump-Putin summit cannot eliminate these new Cold War dangers. But US-Soviet summits traditionally served three corollary purposes. They created a kind of security partnership—not a conspiracy—that involved each leader's limited political capital at home, which the other should recognize and not heedlessly jeopardize. They sent a clear message to the two leaders' respective national-security bureaucracies, which often did not favor détente-like cooperation, that the "boss" was determined and they must end their foot-dragging, even sabotage. And summits, with their exalted rituals and intense coverage, usually improved the media-political environment needed to enhance cooperation amid Cold War conflicts.

If a Trump-Putin summit achieves even some of those purposes, it might pull us back from the precipice.

Summitgate vs. "Peace"

July 11

WE NEED TO REMEMBER THAT US-RUSSIAN (Soviet and post-Soviet) summits are a long tradition going back to FDR's wartime meeting with Stalin in Tehran in 1943. Every American president since FDR met with a Kremlin leader in a summit-style format at least once. Several did so multiple times. The purpose was always to resolve conflicts and enhance cooperation in relations between the two powers. Some summits succeeded, some did not, but all were thought to be an essential aspect of White House-Kremlin relations. (At least one seems to have been sabotaged. The third Eisenhower-Khrushchev meeting, scheduled for Paris in 1960, was aborted by the Soviet shoot-down of a US U-2 spy plane sent, some think, by "deep state" foes of détente.)

As a rule, American presidents have departed for summits with bipartisan support and well-wishes. President Trump's upcoming meeting with Russian President Putin, in Helsinki on July 16, is very different in two respects. US-Russian relations have rarely, if ever, been more dangerous. And never before has a president's departure—in Trump's case, first for a NATO summit and then the one with Putin—been accompanied by allegations that he is disloyal to the United States and thus, as an "expert" told *CNN*'s Anderson Cooper on June 27, someone "we cannot trust." Such defamations were once hurled at presidents only by fringe elements in American politics.

Now, however, in a kind of manufactured Summitgate scandal, we are being told this daily by mainstream publications, broadcasts, and "think tanks." According to a representative of the Center for American Progress, "Trump is going to sell out America and its allies."[92] The *New York Times* and the *Washington Post* also feature "experts"—chosen accordingly—who "worry" and "fear" that Trump and Putin "will get along."[93,94] The *Times* of London, a transatlantic bastion of Russophobic Cold War advocacy, captures this bizarre mainstream perspective in a single headline: "Fears Grow Over Prospect of Trump 'Peace Deal' with Putin."[95]

Peace, it turns out, is to be feared. A Washington establishment against "peace" with Russia is, of course, what still-unproven Russiagate allegations have wrought. A New York magazine writer summed them up by warning that the Trump-Putin summit could be "less a negotiation between two heads of state than a meeting between a Russian-intelligence asset and his handler."[96]

The charge is hardly original, having been made for months on MSNBC by the questionably credentialed "intelligence expert" Malcolm Nance and, it seems, the selectively informed Rachel Maddow. Many other "experts" are doing the same. Considering today's perilous geopolitical situation, it is hard not to conclude again that much of the American political establishment, particularly the Democratic Party, would prefer trying to impeach Trump to averting war with Russia, the other nuclear superpower. For this too, there is no precedent in American history.

Not surprisingly, Trump's dreaded visit to the NATO summit has only inflated the uncritical cult of that organization, which has been in search of a purpose and ever more funding since the end of the Soviet Union in 1991. The *Times* declares that NATO is "the core of an American-led liberal world order," an assertion that might startle some non-military institutions involved in the "liberal world order" and even some liberals. No less puzzling is the ritualistic characterization of NATO, in the same July 9 *Times* editorial, as "the most successful military alliance in history." It has never—thankfully—gone to war as an alliance, only a few "willing" member (and would-be member) states under US leadership.

Even then, what counts as NATO's "great victories"? The police action in the Balkans in the 1990s? The disasters in the aftermath of Iraq and Libya? The longest, still-ongoing US war in history, in Afghanistan? NATO's only real mission since the 1990s has been expanding to Russia's borders, and that has resulted in less, not more, security for all concerned, as is evident today.

The only "Russian threats" since the end of the Soviet Union are ones provoked by US-led NATO itself, from Georgia and Ukraine to the Baltic states. Who has actually benefited? Only NATO's vast corporate bureaucracy, its some 4,000 employees housed in its new $1.2 billion headquarters in Brussels, and US and other weapons manufacturers who profit from each new member state. But none of this can be discussed in the American mainstream because Trump uttered a few words questioning NATO's role and funding, even though the subject has been on the agenda of Washington think tanks since the 1990s.

Also not surprising, and unlike on the eve of previous summits, mainstream media have found little place for serious discussion of today's dangerous conflicts between Washington and Moscow—those regarding nuclear weapons treaties, cyber-warfare, Syria, Ukraine, Eastern Europe, military confrontation in the Black Sea region, even Afghanistan. It's easy to imagine how Trump and Putin could agree on conflict-reduction and cooperation in most of these realms. But considering the way the *Post, Times,* and Maddow traduced a group of US senators who recently visited Moscow, it's much harder to see how the defamed Trump could implement any "peace deals."

Nor is the unreasonably demonized Putin without constraints at home, though none like those that may cripple Trump. The Kremlin's long-delayed decision to raise the pension age for men from age 60 to 65 and for women from 55 to 60 has caused Putin's popular ratings, though still high, to drop sharply. Popular protests are under way and spreading across the country.

On another level, segments of Russia's military-security establishment still believe Putin has never fully shed his admitted early "illusions" about negotiating with an always treacherous Washington. Like their American counterparts, they do not trust Trump, whom they too view as unreliable and capricious.

Russian "hard-liners" have made their concerns known publicly, and

Putin must take them into account.[97] As has been a function of summits over the decades, he is seeking in Trump a reliable national-security partner. Given the constraints on Trump and his proclivities, Putin is taking a risk, and he knows it.

Even if nothing more specific is achieved, everyone who cares about American and international security should hope that the Trump-Putin summit at least results in a restoration of the diplomatic process, longstanding "contacts" between Washington and Moscow," now greatly diminished, if not destroyed, by the new Cold War and by Russiagate allegations. Cold War without diplomacy is a recipe for actual war.

Trump as Cold War Heretic

July 18

O N JULY 16, PRESIDENT TRUMP HELD a summit meeting with Russian President Putin in Helsinki. Given fraught US-Russian confrontations from Ukraine and the Baltic and Black Sea regions to Syria, Trump had a vital national-security duty to meet with the Kremlin leader in this august way.

As with previous summits, details will come later, but the two leaders seem to have reached several important agreements. They revived a US-Russian diplomatic process tattered by recent events, apparently including negotiations to reduce and regulate nuclear weapons and thus avert a new arms race. They suggested a joint effort to prevent Iran, Russia's Middle East partner, from threatening "Israeli security," as Putin put it, on that nation's borders. They also agreed on the need for a mutual effort to relieve the "humanitarian crisis" in Syria. And there was talk of promoting US-Russian "business ties," a nebulous aspiration considering Western economic sanctions on Russia. (This may have been a signal by Trump that he would not object, as President Obama had, if the European Union diminished or terminated its sanctions.)

Historically, in once "normal" Cold War times, these summit achieve-ments would have been supported, even applauded, across the American political spectrum. Predictably, they were not, eliciting only a torrent of denunciation. Idioms varied, from the *Washington Post* to MSNBC and CNN, but the once-stately *New York Times*, as is now its custom, set the tone. Its front-page headline on July 17 blared: "Trump, At Putin's Side, Questions U.S. Intelligence on 2016 Election." Another headline below explained, "Disdain for U.S. Institutions, and Praise for an Adversary."

The *Times'* "reporting" itself was fulsomely prosecutorial, scarcely men-tioning what Trump and Putin had agreed on. Its columnists competed to indict the American president. An early entry, on July 16, before any-thing was actually known about the summit results, came from Charles Blow, whose headline thundered: "Trump, Treasonous Traitor." The title of Michelle Goldberg's entry, on July 17, was less alliterative: "Trump Shows the World He's Putin's Lackey."

As I predicted in the weeks prior to the summit, the same toxic message bellowed through the realm of mainstream print and cable "news": Trump had betrayed and shamed America before the entire world. As has been the case for years regarding "the Russia threat," almost no dissenting voices were included in the "discussions," apart from a few equally unqualified Trump representatives.

The media coverage, not Trump himself at the summit, was shameful. Media were reporting "news" of the kind they wanted, amplifying leading political figures, also across the spectrum. Senator John McCain, as usual on the subject of Russia, led the vigilante posse: "No prior president has ever abased himself more abjectly before a tyrant." He added for personal emphasis: "One of the most disgraceful performances by an American pres-ident in memory." Republican Senator Bob Corker, chair of the Foreign Relations Committee echoed McCain: "A sad day for our country and every-one knows it." Democratic Senator Charles Schumer agreed, demanding that the Senate "hold the president accountable for ... Helsinki."[98,99]

Most unusual, given the traditional non-political public role of Intel chiefs was former CIA director John Brennan. He quickly appeared as Trump's prosecutor and judge, declaring that the president's behavior in Helsinki "exceeds the threshold" for impeachment and, still more, "was nothing short of treasonous."[100]

Only one major political figure stood apart from and above this political-media kangaroo court, Senator Rand Paul of Kentucky. Defending the president's meeting with Putin on behalf of US national security, Senator Paul emerged as the only visible statesman in Congress.[101] (In the past, the US Senate was often led by distinguished statesmen, but now by the likes of McCain, Lindsay Graham, and other members who rarely see a war, cold or hot, they are not eager to fight.)

Yet unproven Russiagate allegations, of course, underlay this "Trump Derangement Syndrome," as it has been termed. Hence the charges that in Helsinki Trump allied with Putin "against US intelligence agencies." (Commentators wanted, it seemed, for Trump to have publicly water-boarded Putin into a confession of having hacked the DNC's emails.) Despite all we now know about the role of the CIA and other intelligence operatives in the past and in Russiagate, the pursuers of Trump, particularly liberal Democrats and their media, wish to judge him by the rectitude of "agencies" whose sharpest critics they once were. "Derangement," indeed.

So much so that an astonishing and exceedingly wise comment by Trump, before and again at the summit, was barely noticed or derided. Trump's remark relates directly to the most fateful question in US-Russian relations: Why has the relationship since the end of the Soviet Union in 1991 evolved into a new and more dangerous Cold War?

For 15 years, the virtually unanimous American bipartisan establishment answer has been that Putin, or "Putin's Russia," is solely to blame. Washington's decision to expand NATO to Russia's border, bomb Moscow's traditional ally Serbia, withdraw unilaterally from the Anti-Ballistic Missile Treaty, carry out military regime change in Iraq and Libya, instigate the 2014 Ukrainian crisis and back the coup against the country's legitimate president, and considerably more—none of these US policies, only "Putin's aggression," led to the new Cold War.

This explanation has long been a rigid orthodoxy tolerating no dissent, excluding, even slurring, well-informed proponents of alternative explanations. The result has been years without real public debate, without any rethinking, and thus no revising of the triumphalist, winner-take-all "post–Cold War" approach first adopted by President Bill Clinton in the 1990s and continued in spirit and most practices ever since, from President George W. Bush to President Obama. This unassailable orthodoxy has now led to a new Cold War fraught with possibilities of actual war with Russia.

Suddenly, whether due to common sense or wise advice, President Trump broke with this years-long, untrue, and increasingly dangerous orthodoxy.

In a tweet on July 15, he wrote, "Our relationship with Russia has NEVER been worse thanks to many years of U.S. foolishness and stupidity." Asked in Helsinki about the new Cold War, he formulated his explanation more diplomatically: "I hold both countries responsible. I think that the United States has been foolish. I think we've all been foolish. We should have had this dialogue a long time ago."[102]

Everything in those remarks by President Trump is factually and analytically true, profoundly so. But they are also outright heresy and perhaps the real reason his meeting with Putin is being so denounced by political and media elites that have made their careers on orthodox dogmas at the expense of American and international security.

Heretics are scorned or worse, but sometimes in history they prevail. However strongly Americans may disapprove of President Trump's other words and deeds, everyone, anywhere across our political spectrum, who wishes to avoid war with Russia—again, conceivably nuclear war—must support and encourage his heresy until it is no longer heresy, until the full debate over reckless US policy since the 1990s finally ensues, and until that approach changes, as should have happened, as Trump said, "a long time ago." It is not too late, but it may be the last chance.

Sanction Mania

August 15

THE BIPARTISAN SENATE CAMPAIGN TO IMPOSE new, "crushing" sanctions on Russia needs to be seen in historical context. Broadly understood, sanctions have been part of US policy toward Russia for much of the past 100 years.

During the Russian civil war of 1918–1920, President Woodrow Wilson sent American troops to fight against the emerging Soviet government. Though the "Reds" were the established government of Soviet Russia by

1921, Washington continued to deny the USSR diplomatic recognition until President Franklin D. Roosevelt established formal relations in 1933. During much of the 40-year Cold War, the United States imposed various sanctions on its superpower rival, mainly related to technological and military exports, along with periodic expulsions of diplomats and "spies" on both sides.

Congress's major political contribution was the 1975 Jackson–Vanik Amendment. The legislation denied Moscow customary trading status with the United States, primarily because of Kremlin restrictions on Jewish emigration from the Soviet Union. Indicative of how mindlessly habitual US sanctions had become, Jackson–Vanik was nullified only in late 2012, long after the end of the Soviet Union and after any restrictions on Jews leaving (or returning to) Russia. Even more indicative, it was immediately replaced, in December 2012, by the Magnitsky Act, which purported to sanction individual Russian officials and "oligarchs" for "human-rights abuses." The Magnitsky Act remains law, supplemented by additional sanctions leveled against Russia as a result of the 2014 Ukrainian crisis and Moscow's annexation of Crimea.

Looking back over this long history, there is no evidence that any US sanctions ever significantly altered Moscow's "behavior" in ways that were intended. Or that they adversely affected Russia's ruling political or financial elites. Any pain inflicted fell on ordinary citizens, who nonetheless rallied "patriotically" around the Kremlin leadership, most recently around President Putin. Historically, sanctions were not problem-solving measures advancing American national security but more akin to temper tantrums or road rage, making things worse, than to real policy-making.

Why, then, Washington's new bout of sanction mania against Moscow, especially considering the very harsh official Russian reaction expressed by Prime Minister Dmitri Medvedev—Obama's onetime "reset" partner and generally considered the most pro-Western figure in Russia's political hierarchy? Medvedev called the Senate's proposed measures "a declaration of economic war" and promised that the Kremlin would retaliate.

One explanation is an astonishing assumption recently stated by Michael McFaul, the media-ubiquitous former US ambassador to Moscow and a longtime Russia scholar: "To advance almost all of our core national security and economic interests, the US does not need Russia."[103] Such a statement by a former or current policy-maker and intellectual may be unprecedented in modern times—and is manifestly wrong.

US "core" interests "need" Russia's cooperation in many vital ways. They include avoiding nuclear war; preventing a new and more dangerous arms race; guarding against the proliferation of weapons and materials of mass destruction; coping with international terrorists; achieving lasting peace in Syria and elsewhere in the Middle East; fostering prosperity and stability in Europe, of which Russia is a part; promoting better relations with the Islamic world, of which Russia is also a part; and avoiding a generation-long confrontation with a formidable new alliance that already includes Russia, China, Iran, and other non-NATO countries. If McFaul's assumption is widespread in Washington, as it seems to be, we are living in truly unwise and perilous times.

A second assumption is no less myopic and dangerous: the Kremlin is weak and lacks countermeasures to adopt against the new sanctions being advocated in Washington. Consider, however, the following real possibilities:

Moscow could sell off its billions of dollars of US Treasury securities and begin trading with friendly nations in non-dollar currencies, both of which it has already begun to do. It could restrict, otherwise undermine, or even shut down many large US corporations long doing profitable business in Russia, among them Citibank, Cisco Systems, Apple, Microsoft, PepsiCo, McDonald's, Johnson & Johnson, Procter & Gamble, Ford Motor Co., and even Boeing. It could end titanium exports to the United States, which are vital to American civilian and military aircraft manufacturers, including Boeing. And terminate the sale of rocket engines essential for NASA space travel and US satellite operations. The world's largest territorial country, Russia could charge US airlines higher tariffs for their regular use of its air space or ban them altogether, making them uncompetitive against other national carriers. Politically, the Kremlin could end its own sanctions on Iran and North Korea, alleviating Washington's pressure on those governments. And it could end the Russian supply transit to US troops fighting in Afghanistan used since the early 1990s.

None of this seems to have been considered by Washington's sanction zealots. Nor have four other circumstances:

Sanctions against Russia's "oligarchs" actually help Putin, whom the US political-media establishment so despises and constantly indicts. For years, he has been trying to persuade many of the richest oligarchs to repatriate their offshore wealth to Russia. Few did so. Now, fearful of having their assets abroad frozen or seized by US measures, more and more are complying.

Second, new sanctions limiting Moscow's ability to borrow and finance investment at home will retard the country's still meager growth rate. But the Kremlin coped after the 2014 sanctions and will do so again by turning away even more from the West and toward China and other non-Western partners, and by developing its own capacity to produce sanctioned imports. (Russian agricultural production, for example, has surged in recent years, becoming a major export industry.)

Third, already unhappy with existing economic sanctions against Russia, European multinational corporations—and thus Europe itself—may tilt even farther away from their capricious "transatlantic partner" in Washington, who is diminishing their vast market in the East.

And fourth, waging "economic war" is one impulsive step from breaking off all diplomatic relations with Russia. This too is actually being discussed by Washington zealots. Such a rupture would turn the clock back many decades, now in an era when there is no "globalization," or international security, without Russia.

What reason do Washington's fanatical Cold Warriors, most of them in the Senate, give for imposing new sanctions? Their professed reasons are various and nonsensical. Some say Russia must be sanctioned for Ukraine, but those events happened four years ago and have already been "punished." Others say for "Russia's aggression in Syria," but it was Putin's military intervention that destroyed the Islamic State's terrorist occupation of much of the country and ended its threat to take Damascus, an intervention that greatly benefited America and its allies, including Europe and Israel. Still others insist the Kremlin must be sanctioned for its "nerve agent" attack on Sergei Skripal and his daughter in the UK. But the British government's case against the Kremlin is less than cogent, as a reader of articles in *Johnson's Russia List* will understand.

Ultimately, the new bout of sanction mania is in response to Russia's alleged "attack on American democracy" during the 2016 presidential election. In reality, there was no "attack"—no Pearl Harbor, no 9/11, no Russian parachuters descending on Washington—only the kind of "meddling" and "interference" in the other's domestic politics that both countries have practiced, almost ritualistically, for nearly a hundred years. Whatever "meddling" Russian actors did in 2016 may well have been jaywalking compared to the Clinton administration's highly intrusive political and financial intervention on behalf of Russian President Yeltsin's reelection campaign in 1996.

We are left with the actual and perverse reason behind the new anti-Russian sanctions campaign: to thwart and punish President Trump for his policy of "cooperation with Russia." And Putin for having met and cooperated with Trump at their July Helsinki summit. This bizarre reality is more than a whisper. According to a *New York Times* "news analysis," as well as other published reports, a "bipartisan group of senators, dismayed that Mr. Trump had not publicly confronted Mr. Putin over Russia's election meddling, released draft legislation" of new sanctions against Moscow. "Passage of such a bill would impose some of the most damaging sanctions yet."[104]

Leave aside that it is not Russian "meddling" which is delegitimizing our elections but instead these fact-free allegations themselves. Remember instead that for doing what every American president since Eisenhower has done—meet with the sitting Kremlin leader in order to avoid stumbling into a war between the nuclear superpowers—in effect both Trump and Putin are being condemned by the Washington establishment, including by members of Trump's own intelligence agencies.

Who, as a result, will avert the prospect of war with Russia, a new Cuban missile–like crisis, conceivably in the Baltic region, Ukraine, or Syria? Not any leading representative of the Democratic Party. Not the current Russophobic "bipartisan" Senate. Not the most influential media outlets that amplify the warmongering folly almost daily. In this most existential regard, there is for now, like it or not, only President Donald Trump.

What the Brennan Affair Reveals

August 22

J OHN BRENNAN, FORMER PRESIDENT OBAMA'S CIA director, is back in the news. When President Trump met with Russian President Putin in Helsinki, he was scathingly criticized by much of the US political-media establishment. Brennan, however, went much farther, characterizing Trump's press conference with Putin as "nothing short of treasonous." Trump revoked Brennan's security clearance, the continuing access to classified information usually accorded to former security officials. In the political-media furor that followed, Brennan was widely heroized as an avatar of civil liberties and free speech and Trump denounced as their enemy.

Leaving aside the missed occasion to discuss the "revolving door" involving former US security officials using their permanent clearances to enhance their lucrative positions outside government, what the subsequent political-media furor obscures is truly important and ominous.

Brennan's allegation was unprecedented. No US top-level intelligence official had ever before accused an American president of treason, still more in collusion with the Kremlin. (Impeachment charges against Presidents Nixon and Clinton, I have already noted, did not involve Russia.) Brennan clarified his charge: "Treasonous, which is to betray one's trust and to aid and abet the enemy." Coming from Brennan, a man presumed to be in possession of dark secrets, as he strongly hinted, his accusation was fraught with alarming implications.[105,106]

Brennan made clear he hoped for Trump's impeachment, but in another time, and in many other countries, his allegation would suggest Trump should be removed from the presidency urgently by any means, even a coup. No one, it seems, noted this extraordinary implication with its tacit threat to American democracy. (On July 19, 2016, the *Los Angeles Times* saw fit to print an article, by James Kirchik, suggesting that the military might have to remove Trump if he were to be elected, thereby having the very dubious distinction of predating Brennan.)

Why did Brennan, a calculating man, risk making a charge that might reasonably be interpreted as sedition? The most plausible explanation is that he sought to deflect growing attention to his role as the godfather of the entire Russiagate narrative, as I suggested back in February. If so, we need to know Brennan's unvarnished views on Russia.

They were set out, alarmingly, in a *New York Times* article on August 17. Brennan's views are those of Joseph McCarthy and J. Edgar Hoover in their prime. Western "politicians, political parties, media outlets, think tanks and influencers are readily manipulated, wittingly and unwittingly, or even bought outright, by Russian operatives...not only to collect sensitive information but also to distribute propaganda and disinformation... I was well aware of Russia's ability to work surreptitiously within the United States, cultivating relationships with individuals who wield actual or potential power...These Russian agents are well trained in the art of deception. They troll political, business and cultural waters in search of gullible or unprincipled individuals who become pliant in the hands of their Russian puppet masters. Too often, those puppets are found."

All this, Brennan assures readers, is based on his "deep insight." All the rest of us, it seems, are constantly vulnerable to "Russian puppet masters" under our beds, at work, in our relationships, on our computers. Clearly, there must be no "cooperation" with the Kremlin's grand "Puppet Master," as Trump said he wanted early on. (People who wonder what and when President Obama knew about the unfolding Russiagate saga need to ask why he would keep a person like Brennan so close for so long.)

And yet, scores of former intelligence and military officials rallied around this unvarnished John Brennan, even though some said they did not entirely share his opinions. This too is revealing. They did so, it seems clear enough, out of their professional corporate identity, which Brennan represented and Trump was degrading by challenging the intelligence agencies' Russiagate allegations against him.

It's a misnomer to term these people representatives of a hidden "deep state." In recent years, they have been amply visible on television and newspaper op-ed pages. Instead, they see and present themselves as members of a fully empowered and essential branch of government. This too has gone largely undiscussed while nightingales of that branch—such as David Ignatius and Joe Scarborough in the pages of the the *Washington Post*—have been in full voice.[107,108]

The result is to further criminalize any advocacy of "cooperating with Russia," or détente, as Trump sought to do in Helsinki with Putin. A Russophobic hysteria is sweeping through the American political-media establishment, from Brennan and—pending actual evidence against her—those who engineered the arrest of the young Russian woman Maria Butina (imagine how this endangers young Americans networking in Russia) to senators preparing new "crippling sanctions" against Moscow and editors and producers at the *Times*, *Post*, CNN, MSNBC, and other media outlets. As the dangers of actual war with Russia grow, the capacity of US policy-makers, above all the president, are increasingly diminished. To be fair, Brennan may be only a symptom of this American crisis, some say the worst since the Civil War.

There was a time when many Democrats, certainly liberal Democrats, could be counted on to resist this kind of hysteria and spreading neo-McCarthyism. (Brennan's defenders accuse Trump of McCarthyism, but Brennan's charge of treason without any evidence was quintessential McCarthy.) After all, civil liberties, including freedom of speech, are directly involved—and not only Brennan's and Trump's.

But Democratic members of Congress and pro-Democratic media are in the forefront of the new anti-Russian hysteria, with few exceptions. A generally liberal historian tells CNN viewers that "Brennan is an American hero. His tenure at the CIA was impeccable. We owe him so much." In the same vein, two *Post* reporters write of the FBI's "once venerated reputation."[109,110]

Is this the historical amnesia I pointed out earlier? Is it professional incompetence? A quick Google search would reveal Brennan's less than "impeccable" record, FBI misdeeds under and after Hoover, as well as the Senate's 1976 Church Committee report of CIA and other intelligence agencies' very serious abuses of their power. Or have liberals' hatred of Trump nullified their own principles? The critical-minded Russian adage would say, "All three explanations are worst."

"Vital" US Moles in the Kremlin

August 29

FOR NEARLY TWO YEARS, MOSTLY VACUOUS, malignant Russiagate allegations have drowned out truly significant news directly affecting America's place in the world. In recent days, for example. French President Emmanuel Macron declared: "Europe can no longer rely on the United States to provide its security." He called instead for a broader kind of security "and particularly doing it in cooperation with Russia."[111] About the same time, German Chancellor Angela Merkel and Russian President Putin met to expand and solidify a crucial energy partnership by agreeing to complete the Nord Stream 2 pipeline from Russia, despite US attempts to abort it. Earlier, on August 22, the Afghan Taliban announced it would attend its first ever major peace conference—in Moscow, without US participation.

Thus does the world turn, and not to the wishes of Washington. Such news would normally elicit extensive reporting and analysis in the American mainstream media. But amid all this, on August 25, the ever-eager *New York Times* published yet another front-page Russiagate story—one that if true would be sensational. Hardly anyone seemed to notice.

According to the *Times*' regular Intel leakers, US intelligence agencies, presumably the CIA, has had multiple "informants close to…Putin and in the Kremlin who provided crucial details" about Russiagate for two years.

Now, however, "the vital Kremlin informants have largely gone silent." The *Times* laced the story with the usual misdeeds attributed to Putin and equally untrustworthy commentators, as well as the mistranslated Putin statement incorrectly having him say all "traitors" should be killed. But the article's sensation is that the US government had moles in Putin's office.

Skeptical or credulous readers will react to the *Times* story as they might. Actually, a lesser version of it first appeared, which I noted earlier, in the *Washington Post*, an equally hospitable Intel platform, on December 15, 2017. I found it implausible for much the same reasons I had previously found implausible the Steele dossier, also purportedly based on "Kremlin sources." But the *Times*' expanded version of the mole story raises new questions.

If US intelligence really had such a priceless asset in Putin's office— the *Post* story implied only one, the *Times* writes of more than one—imagine what they could reveal about Enemy No. 1 Putin's perhaps daily intentions abroad and at home. Why, then, would any American Intel official disclose this information to any media at the risk of being charged with a treasonous capital offense? And now more than once? Or, since "the Kremlin" closely monitors US media, at risk of having the no less treasonous Russian informants identified and severely punished? Presumably, this why the *Times*' leakers insist that the "silent" moles are still alive, though how they know we are not told. All of this is even more implausible, and the *Times* article asks no critical questions.

Why leak the mole story again, and now? Stripped of extraneous financial improprieties, failures to register as foreign lobbyists, tacky lifestyles, and sex having nothing to do with Russia, the gravamen of the Russiagate narrative remains what it has always been: Putin ordered Russian operatives to "meddle" in the US 2016 presidential election in order to put Donald Trump in the White House, and Putin is now plotting to "attack" the November congressional elections in order to get a Congress he wants. The more Robert Mueller and his supporting media investigate, the less actual evidence turns up. And when it seemingly does, it has to be massaged or misrepresented, lest it seem to be Russiagate without Russia.

Nor are "meddling" and "interfering" in the other's domestic policy new in Russian-American relations. Tsar Aleksandr II intervened militarily on the side of the Union in the American Civil War. President Woodrow Wilson sent troops to fight the Reds in the Russian Civil War. The Communist International, founded in Moscow in 1919, and its successor organizations financed American activists, electoral candidates, ideological schools, and pro-Soviet bookstores for decades in the United States. With the support of the Clinton administration, American electoral advisers encamped in Moscow to help rig Russian President Boris Yeltsin's reelection in 1996.

And that's the more conspicuous "meddling" apart from the decades-long "propaganda and disinformation" churned out by both sides, often via forbidden short-wave broadcasts to Soviet listeners. Unless some conclusive evidence appears, Russian social media and other meddling in the 2016 presidential election was little more than old habits in modern-day forms. (Not incidentally, the *Times* story suggests that US Intel had been hacking the Kremlin, or trying to do so, for many years. This too should not shock us.)

The real novelty of Russiagate is the allegation that a Kremlin leader, Putin, personally gave orders to affect the outcome of an American presidential election. In this regard, Russiagaters have produced even less evidence, only suppositions without facts or much logic. With the Russiagate narrative being frayed by time and fruitless investigations, the "mole in the Kremlin" may have seemed a ploy needed to keep the conspiracy theory moving forward toward Trump's removal from office by whatever means. Hence the temptation to play the mole card again now as yet more investigations generate smoke but no smoking gun.

The pretext of the *Times* story is that Putin is preparing an attack on the November 2018 elections, but the once "vital," now silent, moles are not providing the "crucial details." Even if the story is entirely bogus, consider the damage it is doing. Russiagate allegations have already delegitimized a presidential election and a presidency in the minds of many Americans. The *Times'* expanded version may do the same to congressional elections and the next Congress. If so, there is an "attack on American democracy"—not by Putin or Trump, as we saw previously, but by whoever godfathered and repeatedly inflated Russiagate.

As I have argued earlier, such evidence that exists seems to point to John Brennan and James Clapper, President Obama's head of the CIA and of National Intelligence respectively, even though attention has been focused on the FBI. If nothing else, the *Times's* new "mole" story reminds us of how central "intelligence" actors have been in this saga.

Arguably, Russiagate has brought us to the worst American political crisis since the Civil War and the most dangerous relations with Russia in history. Until Brennan, Clapper, their closest collaborators, and others deeply involved are required to testify under oath about the real origins of Russiagate, these crises will continue to grow.

Afterword

"The Owl of Minerva spreads its wings only with the falling of dusk."
—Hegel

War With Russia?, LIKE A BIOGRAPHY of a living person, is a book with-out an end. The title is a warning—akin to what the late Gore Vidal termed "a journalistic alert-system"[112]—not a prediction. Hence the question mark. I cannot foresee the future. The book's overarching theme is informed by past and current facts, not by any political agenda, ideological commit-ment, or magical prescience.

To restate that theme: The new US-Russian Cold War is more dangerous than was its 40-year predecessor, which the world survived. The chances are even greater, as I hope readers already understand, that this one could result, inadvertently or intentionally, in actual war between the two nuclear super-powers. Herein lies another ominous indication. During the preceding Cold War, the possibility of nuclear catastrophe was in the forefront of American mainstream political and media discussion, and of policy-making. During the new one, it rarely seems to be even a concern.

As I finish War With Russia?, the facts and mounting crises they document grow worse, especially in the US political-media establishment where, as readers also understand, I think the new Cold War originated and has been repeatedly escalated. Consider finally a few examples from the latter months of 2018, some of them not unlike political and media developments during the run-up to the US war in Iraq or, historians have told us, when the great powers "sleepwalked" into World War I:

• Russiagate's core allegations, none of them yet proven, had become a central part of the new Cold War. If nothing else, they severely constrained President Trump's capacity to conduct crisis-negotiations with Moscow while they further vilified Russian President Putin for having, it was widely asserted, personally ordered "an attack on America" during the 2016 presidential campaign. Hollywood liberals, it will be recalled, quickly omitted the question mark, declaring, "We are at war." In October 2018, the would-be titular head of the Democratic Party, Hillary Clinton, added her voice to this reckless allegation, flatly stating that the United States was "attacked by a foreign power" and equating it with "the September 11, 2001, terrorist attacks."[113]

Clinton may have been prompted by another outburst of *New York Times* and *Washington Post* malpractice. On September 20 and 23 respectively, those exceptionally influential papers devoted thousands of words, illustrated with sinister prosecutorial graphics, to special retellings of the Russiagate narrative they had assiduously promoted for nearly two years, along with the narrative's serial fallacies, selective and questionable history, and factual errors. (In the front of its issue, the *Times* reporters explained that "the goal of the project ... was to bring people back to a story they might have abandoned.")

Again, for example, the now-infamous Paul Manafort was said to have been "pro-Kremlin" during the period at issue when in fact he was pro-European Union. Again, the disgraced General Michael Flynn was accused of "troubling" contacts when he did nothing wrong or unprecedented in having conversations with a Kremlin representative on behalf of President-elect Trump. Again, the two papers criminalized the idea that "the United States and Russia should look for areas of mutual interest," once the premise of détente. And again, the *Times*, while assuring readers its "Special Report" was "what we now know with certainty," buried the nullifying acknowledgment deep in its some 10,000 words: "No public evidence has emerged showing that [Trump's] campaign conspired with Russia." (The white-collar criminal indictments and guilty pleas cited were so unrelated they again added up to Russiagate without Russia.)

Astonishingly, neither paper gave any credence to an emphatic statement by Bob Woodward—normally considered the most authoritative chronicler of Washington's political secrets—that after two years of research he had found "no evidence of collusion" between Trump and Russia. Endorsing the *Post* version, a prominent historian even assured his readers that the widely discredited anti-Trump Steele dossier—the source of so many allegations—was "increasingly plausible."[114,115]

Nor were the *Times*, *Post*, and other print media alone in these practices, which continued to slur dissenting opinions. CNN's leading purveyor of Russiagate allegations tweeted that an American third-party presidential candidate had been "repeating Russian talking points on its interference in the 2016 election and on US foreign policy."[116] Another prominent CNN figure was, so to speak, more geopolitical, warning, "Only a fool takes Vladimir Putin at his word in Syria," thereby ruling out US-Russian cooperation in that war-torn country.[117] Much the same continued almost nightly on MSNBC.

For most mainstream media outlets, Russiagate had become, it seemed, a kind of cult journalism that no counter-evidence or analysis could dent—though I try in this book—and thus itself increasingly a major contributing factor to the new Cold War. Still more, what began two years earlier as complaints about Russian "meddling" in the US presidential election became by October 2018, for the *New Yorker*[118] and other publications, including the *Times* and the *Post*, an accusation that the Kremlin had actually put Donald Trump in the White House. For this seditious charge, there was also no convincing evidence—nor any precedent in American history.

• At a higher level, by fall 2018, current and former US officials were making nearly unprecedented threats against Moscow. The ambassador to NATO threatened to "take out" any Russian missiles she thought violated a 1987 treaty, a step that would certainly risk nuclear war.[119] The Secretary of the Interior threatened a "naval blockade" of Russia.[120] In yet another Russophobic outburst, the soon-to-retire ambassador to the UN, Nikki Haley, declared that "lying, cheating and rogue behavior" are a "norm of Russian culture."[121]

These may have been outlandish statements by untutored political appointees, though they inescapably again raised the question: who was making Russia policy in Washington—President Trump with his avowed policy of "cooperation" or someone else?

But how to explain, other than as unbridled extremism, comments by a former US ambassador to Moscow, himself a longtime professor of Russian politics and favored mainstream commentator? According to him, Russia had become a "rogue state," its policies "criminal actions," and the "world's worst threat." It had to be countered by "preemptive sanctions that would go into effect automatically"—"every day," if deemed necessary.[122] Considering "crushing" sanctions then being prepared by a bipartisan group of US senators "to punish" Moscow[123], this would be nothing less than a declaration of permanent war against Russia: economic war, but war nonetheless.

• Meanwhile, other new Cold War fronts were becoming more fraught with hot war, none more so than Syria. On September 15, 2018, Syrian

missiles accidentally shot down an allied Russian surveillance aircraft, killing all fifteen crew members. The cause was combat subterfuge by Israeli warplanes in the area. The reaction in Moscow was indicative—and potentially
ominous.

At first, Putin, who had developed good relations with Israel's political
leadership, said the incident was an accident caused by the fog of war. His
own Defense Ministry, however, loudly protested that Israel was responsible.
Putin quickly retreated to a more hardline position, and in the end vowed to
send to Syria Russia's highly effective S-300 surface-to-air defense system, a
prize long sought by both Syria and Iran.

Clearly, Putin was not the ever "aggressive Kremlin autocrat" unrelentingly portrayed by US mainstream media. Still a moderate in the Russian
context, he again made a major decision by balancing conflicting groups
and interests. In this instance, he accommodated longstanding hardliners
("hawks") in his own security establishment.

The result was yet another Cold War tripwire. With the S-300s installed
in Syria, Putin could in effect impose a "no-fly-zone" over large areas of the
country, which had been ravaged by war due, in no small part, to the combat presence of several foreign powers. (Russia and Iran were there legally;
the United States and Israel were not.) If so, it meant a new "red line" that
Washington and its ally Israel would have to decide whether or not to cross.
Considering the mania in Washington and in the mainstream media, it was
hard to be confident restraint would prevail.

All this unfolded around the third anniversary of Russia's military intervention in Syria in September 2015. At that time, Washington pundits
denounced Putin's "adventure" and were sure it would fail. Three years later,
"Putin's Kremlin" had destroyed the vicious Islamic State's grip on significant
parts of Syria, for which it still got no credit in Washington; all but restored
President Assad's control over most of the country; and made itself the ultimate arbiter of Syria's future. In keeping with his Russia policy, President
Trump probably was inclined to join Moscow's peace process, though it was
unlikely the mostly Democratic Russiagate party would permit him to do so.
(For perspective, recall that, in 2016, presidential candidate Hillary Clinton
called for a US no-fly zone over Syria to defy Russia.)

• As I finish this book, another Cold War front also became more fraught.
The US-Russian proxy war in Ukraine acquired a new dimension. In addition to the civil war in Donbass, Moscow and Kiev began challenging the
other's ships in the Sea of Azov, near the vital Ukrainian port of Mariupol.
Trump was being pressured to supply Kiev with naval and other weapons to

wage this evolving maritime war, yet another potential tripwire. Here too the president should instead have put his administration's weight behind the long-stalled Minsk peace accords. But that approach also seemed ruled out by Russiagate, which by October 2018 included yet another *Times* columnist, Frank Bruni, branding all such initiatives by Trump "pimping for Putin."[124]

After five years of extremism exemplified by these more recent examples of risking war with Russia, there remained, for the first time in decades of Cold War history, no countervailing forces in Washington—no pro-détente wing of the Democratic or Republican Party, no influential anti-Cold War opposition anywhere, no real public debate. There was only Trump, with all the loathing he inspired, and even he had not reminded the nation or his own party that the presidents who initiated major episodes of détente in the 20th century were also Republicans—Eisenhower, Nixon, Reagan. This too seemed to be an inadmissible "alternative fact."

And so the eternal question, not only for Russians: what is to be done? There was a ray of light, though scarcely more. In August 2018, Gallup asked Americans what kind of policy toward Russia they favored. Even amid the torrent of vilifying Russiagate allegations and Russophobia, 58 percent wanted "to improve relations with Russia" as opposed to 36 percent preferring "strong diplomatic and economic steps against Russia."[125]

This reminds us that the new Cold War, from NATO's eastward expansion and the Ukrainian crisis to Russiagate, has been an elite project. Why, after the end of the Soviet Union in 1991, US elites ultimately chose Cold War rather than partnership with Russia is a question beyond the limits of this book and perhaps my ability to answer. As for the role of US intelligence elites, what I have termed Intelgate, efforts are still under way to disclose it fully, and being thwarted.[126]

A full explanation of the Cold War choice would include the political-media establishment's needs—ideological, foreign-policy, budgetary, among others—for an "enemy."[127] Or, Cold War having prevailed for more than half of US-Russian relations during the century since 1917, maybe it was habitual. Substantial "meddling" in the 2016 election by Ukraine and Israel, to illustrate the point, did not become a political scandal.[128] In any event, once this approach to post-Soviet Russia began, promoting it was not hard. The legendary humorist Will Rogers quipped back in the 1930s, "Russia is a country that no matter what you say about it, it's true." Back then, before the 40-year Cold War and nuclear weapons, the quip was funny, but no longer.

Whatever the full explanation, many of the consequences I have analyzed along the way continue to unfold, not a few unintended and unfavorable to America's real national interests. Russia's turn away from the West, its "pivot to China," is now widely acknowledged and embraced by many Moscow policy thinkers.[129] Even European allies occasionally stand with Moscow against Washington.[130] The US-backed Kiev government still covers up who was really behind the 2014 Maidan "snipers' massacre" that brought it to power.[131] Mindless US sanctions have helped Putin to repatriate oligarchic assets abroad, an estimated $90 billion already in 2018.[132] Mainstream media persist in distorting Putin's foreign polices into something "that even the Soviet Union never dared to try."[133] And when an anonymous White House "insider" exposed in the *Times* "the president's amorality," the only actual policy he or she singled out was Russia policy.[134]

I have focused enough on the surreal demonizing of Putin—the *Post* even managed to characterize popular support for his substantial contribution to improving life in Moscow as "a deal with the devil"—but it is important to note that this "derangement" is far from world-wide.[135] Even a *Post* correspondent conceded that "the Putin brand has captivated anti-establishment and anti-American politicians all over the world."[136] A worldly British journalist confirmed that as a result "many countries in the world now look for a reinsurance policy with Russia."[137] And an American journalist living in Moscow reported that "ceaseless demonization of Putin personally has in fact sanctified him, turned him into the Patron Saint of Russia."[138]

Again, in light of all this, what can be done? Sentimentally, and with some historical precedents, we of democratic beliefs traditionally look to "the people," to voters, to bring about change. But foreign policy has long been the special prerogative of elites. In order to change Cold War policy fundamentally, leaders are needed. When the times beckon, they may emerge out of established, even deeply conservative, elites, as did unexpectedly Ronald Reagan and Mikhail Gorbachev in the mid-1980s. But given the looming danger of war with Russia, is there time? Is any leader visible on the American political landscape who will say to his or her elite and party, as Gorbachev did, "If not now, when? If not us, who?"

We also know that such leaders, though embedded in and insulated by their elites, hear and read other, non-conformist voices, other thinking. The once-venerated American journalist Walter Lippmann observed, "When all think alike, no one is thinking." This book is my modest attempt to inspire more thinking.

Endnotes

1. *Wall Street Journal*, May 11, 2018
2. Quoted in *Wall Street Journal*, October 14, 2014
3. Quoted in *New York Times*, March 5, 2014
4. *Washington Post*, March 14, 2014
5. *New York Times*, March 15, 2014
6. Fred Hiatt, July 15, 2013
7. *Times Literary Supplement*, June 22, 2018, p. 2
8. Keith Gessen, *New York Times*, June 18, 2018
9. Michael Wines, *New York Times*, February 20, 2000; and BBC News, June 16, 2001
10. *New York Times*, December 15, 2004
11. Bret Stephens, *Wall Street Journal*, November 28, 2006
12. Joel Goldberg, Fox Cable News, March 9, 2018
13. Robert Kagan, *wsj.com*, September 7, 2018
14. Blaine Harden, *New York Times*, September 24, 2017
15. Quoted by Carol Morello, et al., *Washington Post*, July 20, 2018
16. Anne Applebaum, *Washington Post*, July 8, 2018
17. Robert Legvold reviewing Chris Miller, *Putinomics*, in *Foreign Affairs*, May/June 2018, p. 201
18. Martin Gilman interviewed by Mark Whitehouse, *bloomberg.com*, July 9, 2018
19. *Times* editorial, July 17, 2018
20. Quoted by John McCormack and Jenna Lifts, *The Weekly Standard*, July 30, 2018, p. 16

21. David Leonhardt, September 19, 2018
22. Nadezhda Azhgikhina, *TheNation.com*, April 10, 2018
23. Marlene Laruelle, *Johnson's Russia List*, September 10, 2018
24. Kremlin.ru, May 7, 2018
25. See, for example, the Moscow *Times* report in *Johnson's Russia List*, September 7, 2018.
26. See, e.g., Susan B. Glasser, *politico.com*, December 22, 2017
27. Frank-Walter Steinmeier, quoted in *AFP*, June 18, 2016
28. For the former quote, see Patrick Armstrong and Steve Shabad, *Johnson's Russia List*, July 31, August 1, August 4, 2014.
29. For the latter, youtube.com/watch?v=TS17WJW8qE
30. Carlos Lozada, *Washington Post*, June 17, 2018
31. Joe Scarborough, *Washington Post*, August 13, 2018
32. Kremlin.ru, May 25, 2018
33. Kremlin.ru, March 8, 2018
34. Quoted by Andrew Kuchins, *Johnson's Russia List*, December 8, 2017
35. Timothy Heritage, *Reuters.com*, September 30, 2009
36. *New York Times*, November 12, 2017
37. *Washington Free Beacon*, July 26, 2017
38. Ivan Katchanovski, orientalreview.org/2015/09/11
39. For this episode, see my *Failed Crusade: America and the Tragedy of Post-Communist Russia*, exp. pb edition, 2001
40. cfr.org/report/contain-russia
41. *washingtonpost.com*, May 23, 2017
42. *nytimes.com*, May 24, 2017
43. the guardian.com/uk-news/2017/apr/13/british-spies-first-to-spot-trump-team-links-russia
44. theguardian.com/us-news/2018/jan/30/trump-russia-collusion-fbi-cody-shearer-memo
45. *washingtonpost.com*, February 13, 2018
46. *nytimes.com*, February 18, 2018
47. *nytimes.com*, February 18, 2018;
48. newyorker.com/news/news-desk/reading-the-mueller-indictment-a-russian-american-fraud
49. *Washington Post*, February 21, 2018
50. *nytimes.com*, February 19, 2018;
51. thedailybeast.com/msnbc-analyst-john-heilermann-suggests-devin-nunes-compromised-by-russia

52. opcw.org/news/article/opcw-marks-completion-of-destruction-of-russian-chemical-weapons-stockpile/
53. nbcnews.com, May 28, 2017
54. *reuters.com*, May 23, 2017
55. quoted in *New York Times*, June 9, 2017
56. Masha Gessen, *New York*, July 25-August 7, 2016, p. 45
57. Tim Dickinson, April 3, 2018
58. Jerry Brewer, February 24, 2018
59. Ross Douthat quoting Anne Applebaum, *New York Times*, March 23, 2014
60. Jill Dougherty, cnn.com, March 29, 2018
61. Eli Lake, *bloomberg.com*, March 9, 2018
62. Mark Galeotti, *guardian.com*, March 23, 2018
63. Thomas Graham, *Financial Times*, June 1, 2015
64. national interest.org/feature/america-russia-back-basics-21901
65. hoover.org/research/vladimir-putin-and-russian-soul
66. Michael Farquhar, *washingtonpost.com*, September 26, 2014
67. Gregory Feifer, *foreignpolicy.com*, June 22, 2015
68. *Washington Post*, January 5, 2018
69. *Washington Post*, August 13, 2018
70. *washingtonpost.com*, April 23, 2018
71. *washingtonpost.com*, April 20, 2018
72. *Washington Post*, July 8, 2018
73. nationalinterest.org/feature/stumbling-war-russia-25089
74. *bloomberg.com*, April 24, 2018
75. gordonhahn.com/2016/03/09
76. Shmuel Herzfeld, Haaretz.com, September 16, 2018
77. jta.org, January 28, 2018
78. alternet.org/grayzone-project/john-mccain-and-paul-ryan-hold-good-meeting-veteran-ukrainian-nazi-demagogue-andriy
79. amnesty.org/en/latest/news/2018/03/ukraine
80. *theintercept.com*, May 18, 2018
81. *New York Times*, May 16, 2018
82. *New York Times*, May 21, 2018
83. slate.com/articles./news-and-politics/cover-story/2016/07
84. yahoo.com/news/u-s-intel-officials-probe-ties-between-trump-adviserand-kremlin-175046002
85. motherjones.com/politics/2016/10
86. *New York Times*, August 5, 2016

87. *New York Times*, August 10, 2016
88. un.org, April 13, 2018
89. Eugene Rumer, carnegieendowment.org, April 17,2018
90. Quoted by Gerald F. Seib, *wsj.com*, April 16, 2018
91. nationalinterest.org, April 4, 2018
92. Max Bergmann quoted by C.J. Hopkins, counterpunch.com, July 10, 2018
93. Mark Landler, *New York Times*, June 29, 2018
94. Ann Gearan, *Washington Post*, June 30, 2018
95. *Times* of London, June 28, 2018
96. Jonathan Chait, *New York*, July 9-22, 2018
97. Lyle Goldstein, nationalinterest.org, July 14 2018
98. Quoted in *New York Times*, July 17, 2018
99. Quoted in thehill.com, July 26, 2018
100. Quoted in *New York Times*, July 17, 2018
101. See Burgess Everett and Elana Schhor, *politico.com*, July 16, 2018
102. Quoted in *New York Times*, July 17, 2018
103. Tweet, August 10, 2018
104. Neil MacFarquhar, *nytimes.com*, August 12, 2018
105. Quoted by Felicia Sonmez and Carol Morello, *washingtonpost.com*, August 19, 2018
106. Cited by Mattathias Schwartz, *New York Times Magazine*, June 27, 2018
107. *washingtonpost.com*, July 26, 2018
108. *washingtonpost.com*, August 12, 2018
109. Douglas Brinkley with Don Lemon, August 17, 2018
110. Matt Zapotosky and Devlin Barrett, *washingtonpost.com*, August 14, 2018
111. TASS, August 27, 2018
112. Victor Navasky and Katrina vanden Heuvel, eds., *The Best of The Nation*, New York, 2000, p. xvii
113. Reported by Felicia Sonmez, *washingtonpost.com*, October 2, 2018
114. Woodward, realclearpolitics, September 14, 2018
115. Kai Bird, *The Washington Post*, September 30. 2018
116. Jim Sciutto, Tweet, May 1, 2018
117. Nic Robertson, CNN.com, September 18, 2018
118. Jane Mayer, October 1, 2018, pp. 18-26
119. Kay Bailey Hutchison quoted by businessinsider.com, October 2
120. southfront.org, September 30
121. Michael Schwirtz, *nytimes.com*, September 17
122. Michael McFaul, *washingtonpost.com*, September 28, 2018
123. *Washington Post* editorial, September 9

124. *New York Times*, October 7
125. news.gallup.com/poll/241124
126. On September 22, 2018, the *Times* reported that Deputy Attorney General Rod Rosenstein had proposed secretly recording President Trump. Rosenstein denied the report, but the *Times* did not retract its story. On the same day, the *Times* also reported that intelligence agencies had dissuaded the president from declassifying documents directly related to Intelgate.
127. Two leading geopolitical thinkers have presented at least partial explanations. See John Mearsheimer, *Foreign Affairs*, September/October 2014; and Anatol Lieven, *Survival*, Vol. 60, issue 5, 2018
128. See, e.g., Kenneth P. Vogel and David Stern, *politico.com*, January 11, 2017; and Aaron Mate, *TheNation.com*, December 5, 2017
129. Sergei Karaganov, *Johnson's Russia List*, September 24, 2018
130. Andrew Rettman, euobserver.com, September 26, 2018
131. Ivan Katchanovski, *Johnson's Russia List*, September 17, 2018
132. Tyler Durden, ibid., September 24, 2018
133. Jackson Diehl, *Washington Post*, March 19, 2018
134. *New York Times* opinion page, September 6, 2018
135. Anton Troianovski, *Washington Post*, September 9, 2018
136. Anton Troianovski, *washingtonpost.com*, July 12, 2018
137. Patrick Cockburn, *Johnson's Russia List*, September 24, 2018
138. Jeffrey Tayler, *theatlantic.com*, March 18, 2018

Index

About the Author

Stephen F. Cohen is Professor Emeritus of Politics at Princeton University, where for many years he was also director of the Russian Studies Program, and Professor Emeritus of Russian Studies and History at New York University. He grew up in Owensboro, Kentucky, received his undergraduate and master's degrees at Indiana University, and his Ph.D. at Columbia University.

Cohen's other books include *Bukharin and the Bolshevik Revolution: A Political Biography*; *Rethinking the Soviet Experience: Politics and History Since 1917*; *Sovieticus: American Perceptions and Soviet Realities*; (with Katrina vanden Heuvel) *Voices of Glasnost: Interviews With Gorbachev's Reformers*; *Failed Crusade: America and the Tragedy of Post-Communist Russia*; *Soviet Fates and Lost Alternatives: From Stalinism to the New Cold War*; and *The Victims Return: Survivors of the Gulag After Stalin*.

For his scholarly work, Cohen has received several honors, including two Guggenheim fellowships and a National Book Award nomination.

Over the years, he has also been a frequent contributor to newspapers, magazines, television, and radio. His "Sovieticus" column for *The Nation* won a 1985 Newspaper Guild Page One Award and for another *Nation* article the 1989 Olive Branch Award. For many years, Cohen was a consultant and on-air commentator on Russian affairs for CBS News. With the producer Rosemary Reed, he was also project adviser and correspondent for three PBS documentary films about Russia: *Conversations With Gorbachev*; *Russia Betrayed?*; and *Widow of the Revolution*.

Cohen has visited and lived in Soviet and post-Soviet Russia regularly for more than forty years.

He lives in New York City with his wife, Katrina vanden Heuvel, who is editor and publisher of *The Nation*. They have a daughter, Nicola (Nika). Cohen also has two other children, Andrew and Alexandra.